AF132843

# Returning to Paradise?

*A Memoir of a Young Afro-Caribbean Man's re-migration from the UK, to Teach at the University of the West Indies (UWI), and Raise his Family, in 1980s Barbados – Part 1: up to 1984*

'This beach ain't always been no paradise'[1]

'Fool me once, fool me twice
Are you death or paradise?'[2]

David R. Bradshaw

Ex Libris Press

Published in 2024 by Ex Libris Press
Bradford on Avon
Wiltshire
BA15 1ED

Origination by Ex Libris Press
www-ex-librisbooks.co.uk

Typeset in 10/13 point Minion Pro

Cover design by Patrick Towning
Cherry Design - Email address: pattowning@gmail.com

Printed by CPI Ltd.
Chippenham, Wiltshire

ISBN 9781912020034

© 2024 David R. Bradshaw

The right of David R. Bradshaw to be identified as the author of this work has been asserted by him in accordance with the Copyright, Designs and Patents Act 1988.

All rights reserved. No part of this book may be reproduced, stored in a retrieval system, or transmitted, in any form at any time or by any means (mechanical, electronic, photocopying, recording, or otherwise) without the prior, written, permission of both the copyright owner and the above publisher of this book, nor be otherwise circulated in any form or binding or cover other than that in which it is published and without a similar condition being imposed on the subsequent purchaser.

All photographs, unless otherwise indicated, are from the author's personal collection. Every effort has been made to seek permission for use of all copyright items in this book. In the event that any item has been overlooked, the publisher will be glad to rectify this on reprint.

A CIP catalogue record of this book is available from the British Library.

*For my Children – ALL of them*

# Contents

| | |
|---|---|
| Foreword | 7 |
| 1 Arrival in my native Caribbean, as an immigrant – August 1979 | 11 |
| First days at 'the Office', and at 'the House', in Barbados | 18 |
| 3 Meeting my new colleagues in the UWI Law Faculty | 33 |
| 4 Settling into Domestic Life at home in Barbados | 44 |
| 5 Preparation for Entry into the classroom at Cave Hill Campus | 57 |
| 6 Commencing actual teaching at UWI | 67 |
| 7 A first Caribbean Christmas - December 1979 | 79 |
| 8 A New Year (and academic term) in Barbados – January to Easter 1980 | 96 |
| 9 Some Dear Friends from West Germany holiday with us in Barbados - May 1980 | 103 |
| 10 My First Summer Term at UWI – May to July 1980 | 113 |
| 11 The End of my First Academic Year at UWI and Summer Holidays 1980 | 120 |
| 12 A Not-expected (and Non-UWI) Assignment – Summer to Autumn, 1980 | 136 |
| 13 The Start of my Second Academic Year at UWI (1980-81) – including my first trip to another UWI Campus outside Barbados | 141 |
| 14 A First trip to South America | 148 |
| 15 A New Sibling for Noel and Kim | 161 |
| 16 Claire-Louise Comes Home – and some 'Fall-Out' therefrom | 171 |
| 17 Claire-Louise's First Trip outside Barbados – February 1981 | 182 |
| 18 Comparative Law Trip to Venezuela – Eastertide 1981 | 196 |
| 19 The Third Term of my Second Year at UWI – Summer 1981 | 208 |
| 20 A Family Holiday in England (and Continental Europe) – Midsummer 1981 | 215 |
| 21 The First Term of my Third Academic Year at UWI – Autumn 1981 | 240 |
| 22 The Earlier Part of the Second Term of my Third Academic Year at UWI – Spring 1982 | 248 |
| 23 The Later Part of the Second Term, and the Third Term, of my Third Academic Year at UWI – Spring and Summer 1982 | 264 |
| 24 The First Arrival of Vere and Mikki in England; and the Birth of the Fourth Child of Philomena and myself – September 1982 | 274 |
| 25 My First Term on Sabbatical Leave at a Belgian University – Autumn 1982 | 283 |
| 26 Christmas with Philomena and Our Children in Swindon; and my Second Term on Sabbatical Leave in Belgium – December 1982 to Spring 1983 | 293 |
| 27 Spring and Summer 1983 in Swindon with Philomena and Our Children (and a Side Trip to Barbados) | 305 |

28 Vere's Return to England; and my Setting Up Home in Belgium with
   my Matrimonial Family – from Late Summer 1983 ................. 318
29 Starting a New Family Life, and New Academic Year, in Belgium
   – Autumn and Early Winter 1983 ................................ 332
30 What should have been my Second Term at the VUB 1983-84
   – Spring 1984 .................................................. 342
31 The post-Easter period to Summer in Antwerp, 1984 – and Preparing to '
   Start Over', Yet Again! ........................................ 351

Notes .............................................................. 367

# FOREWORD

This book is the fourth in a series of memoirs. The sequence has taken the reader from my earliest childhood in my native Caribbean island of Montserrat up to the age of eight years old (*Growing up BAREFOOT under Montserrat's sleeping Volcano*), to my school days in Swindon, Wiltshire, England until the age of 18 (*Swimming without mangoes*), and then on to my university student days, earliest marriage and parenthood, as well my initiation as a university Law lecturer (*Fledging and Learning to Fly* ). This latest volume deals with what happens when I return to my native West Indies, with my wife, Philomena, and our then two children – one only six weeks old – to try to advance my career as a legal academic and help my dear wife, **Philomena**, raise our family in a tropical *milieu* (which some might regard as 'Paradise')!

The time between each volume of the series and its sequel has grown progressively longer, alas. From only three years between the first (in 2010) and second (in 2013), to four between the second and third (in 2017). Publishing the present fourth volume in 2024 has, therefore, taken me much longer than the gestation period of an elephant – which is what I wrote about in the *Acknowledgements* section of the third volume. Indeed, the seven years that it has taken for me to complete this 'Part 1', only, of my family's life in Barbados (and elsewhere) whilst I was employed by the University of the West Indies (UWI) up to 1984 (and beyond) is longer than the combined period that it took to gestate, and give birth to, ALL my children – to whom this book is dedicated.

I, thus, thank my God – as well as **Philomena** and those children – for helping to sustain me throughout the seven years and, thereby, enable me to complete this book to its publication. Regarding that long 'gestation period', in addition to my Creator and my family, I would like to thank, first of all, several members of the University Library of Cambridge University ('the UL'), where I, normally, do my writing during the working week. Those persons include – but are not limited to – **Julian Fuller** who cheerily (more often than not!) opens the heavy doors of the UL at 9am, most mornings - to allow me to 'get in' and 'get on' – and who always has time for a quick exchange of greetings/pleasantries as I enter or leave the UL; **Tim Nicholas**, for all his practical help, and stories about his travels to the Spanish island of Gran Canaria; and **Onesimus Ngundu**, of the 'Bradshaw Room' in the UL, who never fails to warmly greet me as one 'Brother' to another whenever we see each other; and **Sarah Chapman** in the Music Department of the UL, not least for our exchanges of chocolate/Easter eggs to each other!

Outside of the UL, but within Cambridge University, I would like to thank **Lizz Edwards-Waller** of the Squire Law Library, in particular, for all her invaluable help with my computer issues relating to the manuscript of this book – as well as her colleagues

**Kate Faulkner** (for showing me how to turn on the computer in the first place!), **Jane Whelehan** and the other Library staff at the Squire for any assistance that they rendered to me in this connection.

Outside of Cambridge University altogether, I must also thank, profusely, my squash partner – or opponent, rather – **Dave Ellwood**, for taking on the challenging job of being Editor of my rather poorly-written first draft of the manuscript (MS) of this book. He has done an excellent job – for a neophyte in that role – by pointing out, especially, my former many over-long sentences scattered throughout the MS. This book would be all the poorer without Dave's interventions. So, thank you Dave! And – despite the fact that you hate sentences beginning with that aforesaid three-letter word – I look forward to our future 'battles' 'on court' (regarding our very energetic racquet sport) as well as 'in the editing suite' (for improving my rough MS of Part 2 of this 'Barbados family saga').

Even after making the edits based on Dave's hard work, however, I still wished to have some feedback on the edited MS - from someone whom I trusted, in Barbados itself. The ideal candidate turned out to be my good friend - and current employee of UWI at Cave Hill Campus, Barbados, in the Main Library there – **Natalie Bannister**. Natalie proved to be a most efficient, and speedy, 'second editor' for me – and I was able to adopt most of her suggested further changes to the edited MS. Alas, owing to certain issues beyond her control, she had to reluctantly withdraw, from continuing with her wonderful work for me, at the end of her reading the first one-third of the revised draft.

Accordingly, a substitute for Natalie needed to be found – who was also Barbadian (or 'Bajan') - for the remaining two-thirds. None other than the long-standing family friend of – and spiritual adviser to – my family came forward to fill the breach. That person was the nationally well-known priest in Barbados, **Monsignor Vincent Blackett** – formerly known as **Father Harcourt Blackett** – who kindly took on the task in question, despite his many other obligations as the Founder of the **Friends of Jesus Missionary Society** (**FJCMS**), of which I am a Trustee. So, thank you – yet again – Dear Father Harry, for ALL your much-appreciated help, and feedback, to me in this matter.

I also wish to thank my former fellow commuter from Cambridge to London, and back, on weekdays – from the time when I worked at BBC World Service in the 1990s and beyond – **Patrick Towning**. Like my Editor, Dave, Patrick was taking on a role that he had never done before – namely, be the creator of the front cover for a new book. As an experienced and professional graphic artist - in London, Leeds and elsewhere - however, he took on the challenge in question in order to help his old commuter buddy out. In so doing, he has succeeded spectacularly, in my humble opinion.

I hereby also thank my possible 'distant cousin' – now living and working in Barbados again – **Frances Okosi**. That is for all her much-appreciate support to me in this project – and, not least, for taking the photo of, and supplying it to me *gratis*, the beach scene that brightens up the front cover of this book. Like me, Frances has African blood in her veins – and probably more than the 43.8% Nigerian that the DNA test reveals I have in my own. That DNA test was kindly bought for me, one Fathers' Day a few years ago, by my CHILDREN - to whom this book is dedicated and who might well be regarded as the 'recurring theme' which pervades this book.

'Saving the BEST plaudits for last, I would like to PROFUSELY thank **Mr Roger Jones** for, once more, being the person who was the CATALYST to this book coming into existence! For, not only did he physically 'put it together' as its 'typesetter', he is also its publisher (in effect). Moreover, and above all, the MS - which, as stated, has taken me some seven years to write, would still only be on my computer waiting for some publisher to come along, but for Roger. For, he it was, who in our exchange of Christmas emails in December last, casually wrote to me as follows:

'Hello David. Good to hear from you [holidaying in Barbados with your family]. Pleased all going well and that you are plugging away on the fourth volume of your memoir[s]. Of course, I would be pleased to turn it into a book for you. Just get in touch when you're ready'. After a meet-up in Jersey at Easter - with our respective wives, Philomena and Hazel, in tow - the rest is history, as they say!

*David R. Bradshaw*
*University Library (UL), Cambridge, UK - July 2024*

*Chapter 1*

# Arrival in my native Caribbean, as an Immigrant – August 1979

There I was, at London's 'Heathrow Airport', waiting to emigrate. This was to be the second time in 20 years that I was leaving a country, in which I had been resident for most (if not all) of my life up to that time of departure, for a new one. However, I was not alone on that later occasion. I had a wife with me – namely, Philomena, my spouse of only three years. In addition, we had our two small children with us – our eldest son, 'Noel', of some 22 months old, and his much younger brother, 'Kristian Kim', of only six weeks of age (and whom we were already starting to refer to only by his second name). But where were we heading to? A popular song of that time began with words along the lines of: 'Hey, I'm going to Barbados'.[3] And that well-known West Indian island was, indeed, to be our very destination.

This book is a sequel to *Fledging and Learning to Fly*.[4] That earlier memoir ended at London's Heathrow Airport in the summer of 1979. It chronicled how I had left school in 'Swindon, Wiltshire' (following schooldays dealt with in my even earlier memoir entitled *Swimming without mangoes*)[5] and had gone on to work in banking in England's capital city, before taking up the study of Law and eventually graduating from 'Cambridge University' prior to qualifying as a 'Barrister-at-Law'. It also recounted how I had married, Philomena, my childhood sweetheart in the mid-1970s, and how we had been blessed with our first son whilst still living in Cambridge, before going on to live in Leeds where I had taken up my first post as a Law lecturer in that city's oldest university. The finale of that memoir dealt with the birth of our second son in Yorkshire and then our making the major decision, and undertaking the mobilisation required, to relocate the whole family to the island of Barbados in the West Indies – the region of my birth and early childhood (dealt with in my first published memoir, entitled *Growing up BAREFOOT under Montserrat sleeping Volcano*).[6] This new work, therefore, takes up the tale and deals with 'what happened next'.

Having said goodbye, that day in August 1979, to my wife's paternal uncle, Michael, his wife, Gill, and their two young sons, Marc and Jonathan, at the boarding gate of Heathrow's Terminal 3, the thought struck me that my little family and I were then all on our own. Henceforth, Philomena and our own two sons had only me to depend on - if we were all to 'sink or swim' in our new life. As we eventually boarded our flight, however, I was full of confidence for the four of us. After all, my little family and I were then proceeding under the apparently safe hands of the University of the West Indies – my new employers. That educational establishment – which referred to itself as 'UWI' for short – was paying for each of us to fly out to Barbados and part of my contract was that it would also be providing us with 'suitable housing' during my initial three-year term as a Law lecturer with itself. We, therefore, had a roof over our heads to look forward to, as well as a regular income for some time to come. That was so even though Philomena – as a qualified school teacher – had no plans, or indeed any wish, to go back to the profession she had given up in Cambridge, a few months before Noel's birth in that city in September 1977. She loved being a 'mum' looking after, and indeed being the first teacher of, her two young sons far too much! Moreover, my UWI salary seemed, on paper, to be quite sufficient for us all to live on comfortably – even though the university would be docking my pay by about 10% to cover its costs of providing my family with our accommodation.

The other reason why I was fairly confident about the 'step into the dark' which my little family was about to take arose from the fact that Barbados was not entirely unknown to either Philomena or myself. That is because the two of us had spent the first part of our honeymoon on that Caribbean island in late July, and early August, 1976 – just over three years before our current flight there – and we had loved nearly everything about the place that we had encountered there. The weather had been wonderful – but so, on the whole, did we find the local people there, and the general high standard of life which they seemed to enjoy. For us, then newly-weds, there seemed little not to like about the territory and we wanted to be part of the healthy, and mainly outdoor, lifestyle which we had earlier witnessed there. What could possibly go wrong with our decision?

Certainly, the flight itself, to our new homeland, went smoothly enough. For a start, unlike our only previous trip to Barbados from England, Philomena and I actually got to sit together on the plane. We were not separated by an aisle, as had been the case on our post-nuptial flight on 'Caribbean Airways' – which, incidentally, had taken the 'scenic route' to our honeymoon island, via 'Luxembourg' as well as somewhere in the 'Azores' for refuelling stops. On this more recent occasion, however, we were cocooned in the luxury of 'British Airways', which kindly gave us what it called the 'bassinet position' in the plane. That location was right in front of the wall, in the centre of the aircraft, from which a screen descended for the showing of the in-flight films. Below that covering, a table could be extracted from the wall and, upon that platform, we were able to place baby Kim's 'carrycot'. He was therefore able to sleep several times in that portable bed, on the temporary counter, whenever he needed to – right in front of his parents' protective eyes. That blessing freed up Philomena and myself not only to interact with Noel, but also to eat our in-flight meals, whenever they came, or simply watch a movie whilst our elder son also slept. We made a first stop at the Caribbean island of 'Antigua', to allow some passengers to disembark and to take on a small number of new ones, but within eight to nine hours or so of leaving London we had landed safely in Barbados. That contrasted markedly with the extra five hours or so which was needed to get our aircraft to the same destination, from our London starting point, to allow us to begin our honeymoon on that island in 1976.

If our journey this time proved to be smooth and enjoyable, however, things seemed to go wrong almost from the moment of our landing at the airport in Barbados! First of all, the name of the place had changed since our honeymoon visit. Then it had been 'Seawell' – a nice, short name that I liked a lot. Now, it was something much longer - namely, 'Sir Grantley Adams International Airport' (after the island's first premier). If memory serves me correctly, the terminus building was still the old one which Philomena and I had encountered in 1976. They were, however, already building a much more modern one a few hundred yards away - but still somewhat adjacent to the old Seawell buildings. If, however, a little familiarity with the island already had to be set aside upon our arrival, that was nothing compared to what happened next. The lady from UWI who met us - holding a board marked 'BRADSHAW', as we exited the arrivals area of the airport - had some alarming news for my family. She said : 'Welcome to Barbados! I'm afraid I have to tell you that your house is not yet ready. It requires quite a bit of work to be done on it – which will take about another four or five days!'.

Such 'unglad tidings' did not herald the best of starts to our new life. There we were, with Kim in his 'Maclaren Baby Buggy', Noel tired out after the long flight, and Philomena and myself full of expectation as to what our new home would be like, suddenly having to come to terms with such an unexpected blow. However, the UWI lady – who was short, but extremely friendly, and who went on to tell us that her name was 'Mrs Velma Abrahams' – was smiling as she told us the next piece of news. She declared to us the following words: 'To make up for the unavailability of your home, UWI has booked you into "The Paradise Beach Hotel" – all expenses paid - until your house becomes ready!'. Philomena and I looked at each other and began to smile too. For we both remembered that the particular hotel just mentioned by Mrs Abrahams was one of the best ones on the island, and that it possessed a lovely beach upon which we had enjoyed spending one of our honeymoon days in 1976. During that earlier time in Barbados, we had hired a small motor bike and had done a tour of the island, day by day and a little at a time. Paradise Beach had been one of the more upmarket places we had stopped at during that tour, and we may have even savoured a drink or two at the hotel itself. By contrast with Mrs Abrahams' initial news, therefore, things were definitely starting to look more positive for my little family.

If memory serves me correctly, the four of us had travelled out to Barbados on a Saturday morning. We had arrived on the island that same day – but in the afternoon. That was because, even though our flight had taken eight to nine hours, Barbados was some five hours behind the time in London. Accordingly, once we had duly checked into our large family room at the hotel, there was little to be done but enjoy its amenities over our arrival weekend in question. There was nothing much that I could reasonably do with UWI, or its Law Faculty, until the coming Monday. Thus, to fully enjoy the best what the Paradise Beach Hotel had to offer, was the objective which Philomena and myself set ourselves to achieve for our family - from the start of our time there.

By the time we had settled into our room, however, it was already too late and dark for Philomena and I to take our sons into the Caribbean Sea - which lapped the beach with gentle waves, right next to the hotel. More likely, we simply opted to have our first dinner in the restaurant overlooking the shore that first evening – prior to returning to our room to put our sons, and then ourselves, to bed. I remembered well, however, that Mrs Abrahams had told us that UWI was funding our stay on an 'all expenses paid' basis. Accordingly, once we had helped Noel to choose something suitable for himself from the children's menu, both Philomena and myself 'went to town' and ordered what was perhaps the most expensive thing on the hotel's written offerings for adults. Lobster! It was a dish which we both loved, but which we had rarely been able to afford during our relatively recent engaged or married life together. We also chose our favourite Caribbean drink – an alcoholic concoction called 'rum punch'. Philomena had breastfed baby Kim prior to our dinner, so he was probably fast asleep again whilst the other three members of our family dined. Sitting there that first night, therefore, with my deluxe seafood dinner and cocktail, and seeing how already settled and happy my family around me was, I genuinely felt that I was literally in the place that our hotel, and its nearby beach, were named after - 'Paradise'.

That feeling of contentment was to continue into the next day, as our family had our breakfast in the same beachside restaurant. All the more so, since I could then see, by the morning's light, the blue-green of the calm Caribbean Sea lightly breaking on the shore only yards away but then continuing away from us as far as the horizon. Personally, I could not wait to take Philomena into it again, for the first time in three years – and to introduce my two little sons to one of the best features of their father's West Indian heritage. Before that, however, the three eldest members of our party had to fill themselves up with breakfast. The hotel's menu for that first meal of the day included freshly-squeezed orange juice, honey-smoked bacon, fried eggs, muffins, maple syrup and other delicacies which owed more to a North American origin (as were most of the guests in the restaurant), it seemed to me,) than from local provenance. On that first morning, I was quite happy to 'put on hold' trying to seek out a true Caribbean breakfast – including my specially ordering what is my favourite item thereof called 'fried plantain' which is derived from a staple that my elder son might have regarded as just an overly large banana. During our meal, I marvelled at the view to the nearby beach and beyond – as well as at the efficient and friendly staff dressed in their white shirts and black trousers or skirts, who busied themselves with taking and serving orders from fellow guests. I was also intrigued, as much as my elder son seemed to be, with the good number of 'blackbirds' – somewhat smaller in build than the common 'singing' variety I knew so well back in England - which kept making flying sorties to and from our restaurant's tables to try to steal bits of toast and other breakfast debris. Usually, they were chased off by one waiter or another, but it was good to witness a plucky one or two succeeding in their daring foraging, from time to time.

*Fig 1: One of our family's first breakfasts at the Paradise Beach Hotel, Barbados in August 1979. The photo shows Philomena and Noel at our table - with an open view to the Caribbean Sea. (Kim is hidden in his carrycot, on the far side of the table, possibly fast asleep after his first 'feed' of the day from his mum)*

After breakfast, it was time to enter the Caribbean Sea with our sons for their first time. What an absolute delight! I could not have felt more fulfilled with my life at that moment. All my hard studying of the Law for going on 10 years (from the time I had first studied the subject at night school after just leaving school in 1971),[7] in order to win the lectureship position which was responsible for me being in that particular place at that moment, had been worthwhile. That was because it meant that, by that first dip, I was giving to my two children a large part of their father's patrimony – namely, an introduction to, and a first-familiarity with, the Caribbean Sea! Indeed, that great expanse of salt water was the western part of the Atlantic Ocean, in which I had first learned to swim about a quarter of a century before and which had been such a major part of the earliest schooldays in my native neighbouring island - as chronicled in my first book of memoirs entitled *Growing up BAREFOOT* under Montserrat's sleeping Volcano.[8] At that moment, it was my own children's turn to encounter that Sea for the first time. Would they take to its salty waters? Would they sink or swim? To ensure that they would certainly float, Philomena and I had, before leaving England, bought the boys some devices called 'water wings' or 'arm bands'. These were plastic tubes which fitted over the upper arms of each child and which could then be inflated by Philomena, or myself, blowing air into each band. Miraculously, perhaps, once properly inflated, the devices kept Noel and Kim so well afloat in the sea that there was nothing either could do to get a wet face or head. They both appeared to love the experience from their first immersion with the bands – perhaps, helped, most of all, by the fact that the water was warm, on first contact, not unlike the unchlorinated equivalent that they encountered every day at their bathtime! Accordingly, all four of us were soon bobbing about happily in the sea, as the morning sun became ever hotter and the beach filled up with hotel guests, as well as local Barbadian, or 'Bajan', people coming to the venue for their Sunday 'sea bath'. There was no doubt about it, in my own head – Philomena and myself had made the right decision to bring our little family to Barbados in order to start a new life there. It seemed, to me at least, that the more we four experienced life on the island – and admittedly it was only our first morning – the more we all appeared to like it!

There was even a special surprise to come later that Sunday – in the evening. It occurred somewhat after we had finished that first swim. We had gone back to our room to shower and wash the sand off the boys in the bath, then had enjoyed some light snacks for lunch in our beachside restaurant and, after that, had taken the first Caribbean 'siesta' of our stay. When we had all woken up from that, it would have still been too hot outside at that time to go back into the sea. Once the early evening had begun to return, however – perhaps a little after 4pm – Philomena and I would have taken the boys back into the water with us. Or, at least, we would have combined doing that with a longish walk along Paradise Beach with Kim in his 'pushchair'. After another freshening-up operation of the four of us in our bathroom, we would then have dressed for dinner – followed by a call at the hotel's bar whilst we waited for the first 'sitting' to begin. There, I saw a short, but rather stout, man in a suit who seemed somewhat familiar. As our family arrived next to him at the bar, I realised that it was none other than a well-known comedian from English television shows who went by the professional name of 'Les Dawson'. That was to be my very first brush with a celebrity figure – other than my encounters with famous personalities in the legal world from whence I had come back in England, such as 'Lord Denning', the judge, or 'Professor Horton Rogers', the academic and leading legal textbook author.

Mr Dawson seemed to be keen to speak to us. Since I knew who he was and that he did not know me, I put out my hand for him to shake whilst also saying something like: 'Pleased to meet you, Les. Fancy seeing you here! I'm David Bradshaw and this is my wife, Phil, and our children, Noel and Kim'. He warmly shook my hand and then Philomena's before proceeding to lead the conversation, starting with the question: 'What brings you to Barbados?'. That told me immediately that he had discerned - possibly from my non-Bajan accent as well as from the evidence of our 'mixed-race' family unit that I had just introduced him to - that we were not local. I, therefore, explained to him how it came about that we were staying temporarily at the hotel, and that we had in fact newly emigrated to the island from England. Philomena and I must have continued talking with him for about a half-an-hour. What struck me was how serious his demeanour was, compared to his TV 'comic' personality. He was holding a drink and had been standing alone at the bar when my little family had come along. He was quick to smile in the right places, but meeting him left me with a feeling that he possessed an underlying melancholy. However, before I had been able to have too much of an opportunity to compare him with what I knew of the sad figure of 'Tony Hancock' - who, famously, had fallen into that category of the 'tragic-comedian' before his eventual suicide - one of the waitresses came to tell our family that our dinner table was ready. My wife and I accordingly said 'so long' to Mr Dawson, with me being fully confident that we would see him again during our stay. Alas, for the remainder of our sojourn at the hotel, that was never to be the case. It is interesting to report, however, that despite my first impressions of Mr Dawson, he did not, after all, go the way of the self-destructive Mr Hancock but, rather, died of a heart attack at a Manchester hospital in England some 14 years later.[9]

## Chapter 2

# First days at 'the Office', and at 'the House', in Barbados

After the excitement, and rest, of my family's first two nights at Paradise Beach, a Monday morning had dawned in our new country. I needed to go to work! Not literally, of course, but I certainly felt obliged to visit the Law Faculty of my new employers, UWI, to let the head of that department know that I (and my family) had safely arrived in Barbados and that I was reporting for duty. For although it was still August, and in the middle of the 'long vacation' which university academics were fortunate to enjoy at that time – both in England and at UWI - I needed to start preparing for my forthcoming classes which would begin in early October. That was only about six weeks, or so, away – and I still did not know, for sure, what subjects I would be teaching!

I had specifically applied to UWI for an advertised post of lecturer in 'Comparative Law' – even whilst my family still lived in Cambridge and I was studying to become a Barrister at 'Lincoln's Inn' in London. My third book of memoirs, *Fledging and Learning to Fly*,[10] recounts how it came about that, owing to UWI's delay in processing my application (and for the economic security of my family), I had felt obliged to accept a competing Law lectureship offered to me at Leeds University - prior to hearing from UWI, after starting work at Leeds, that my application to that Caribbean establishment had been successful! In that third book, I also told of how my dilemma had been solved by the Deans of the two Law faculties in question – by their agreeing among themselves, that I could stay on in Leeds, for one academic year only, and then immediately take up my longer-term position at UWI. However, given that someone must have had to step in for me at UWI, to teach Comparative Law during 1978-79, I was rather worried (as I walked, the mere half a mile or so, up the hill from the Paradise Beach Hotel to the 'Cave Hill Campus' of the university) that my substitute 'Comparatist' had been a great success in his temporary role and that I would be faced with impossibly large shoes to fill. Or, indeed, that he or she might have been so successful, during their stint, that my new Dean may have decided to confirm that substitute in the Comparative Law post, and then relegate me to some new subject which might have been unfamiliar to me!

The new Dean turned out to be 'Professor Telford Georges'. He was a shortish, middle-aged, man of a darkish complexion. He had a very smiley, and friendly face, framed by a pair of black-rimmed spectacles which made him look extremely wise. Indeed, he must have been something of a sage - for I knew, from my previous reading about him, that he had held senior positions as a judge in various territories of the English-speaking Caribbean. Moreover, he may still have also been 'sitting on the bench' in some of those countries, on a part-time basis, and thus combining such role with that of being Dean of UWI's Law Faculty . One of the first things he said to me, after we had made our first polite introductions and he had welcomed me to the Faculty,[11] was: 'We are going to work you hard this coming academic year!'. I was somewhat alarmed by those words. Accordingly, I quickly asked whether he meant that he was going to require me not to teach Comparative Law and to deliver, instead, some other course (which might have been unfamiliar to me). To my great relief, he answered: 'Comparative Law is yours!'. He expanded on that by saying: 'Whilst you stayed in Leeds for the past academic year, we employed a young American lawyer, on a one-year contract, to teach Comparative Law. His name is Bruce Zagaris, but his contract has ended and he has returned to the States'.

Left – Fig 2: A photo of Professor Telford Georges, as shown on the cover of a biography about him written by my future colleague at UWI, Cave Hill Campus – the future 'Professor Albert Fiadjoe' (in collaboration with two other co-authors, 'Professor Gilbert Kodilinye' and 'Ms Joyce Cole Georges'). The book is entitled 'Telford Georges: A Legal Odyssey' and the photo on its cover shows Professor Georges dressed as a judge but looking very much as the Author remembers him in their first ever meeting in August 1979

Professor Georges then went on to explain to me what he meant by saying he would have to 'work me hard' over the coming academic year. He said that one of the members of the permanent Faculty – a 'Mr Tony Bland' – had just succeeded in winning a one-year sabbatical (which he would be spending at his former university in 'Birmingham', England). Moreover, that Tony's main subject, which he lectured and tutored in as 'Course Director' at UWI, was 'Private International Law' – a discipline also better-known, by many, as 'The Conflict of Laws'. Professor Georges added that he knew, from my application, that I had studied Tony's subject at Cambridge, and that, therefore, he wanted me to take over the lecturing and tutoring of it during Tony's sabbatical year. In other words, he was telling me that I would have to lecture, and be Course Director of, *two* mainstream subjects during the coming year – subjects which were two of the four optional (out of, perhaps, a total list of 10) courses which Final Year Law students at UWI had to pass examinations in, in order to be able to graduate with their Bachelor of Laws, or 'LL.B', degrees.

I was not fazed by the surprise new obligation imposed on me by Professor Georges. For, I felt full of energy, and drive, at that time. Moreover, and after the wonderful 'induction' into my new life in Barbados which I had just undergone at the Paradise Beach Hotel over the past few days, I wanted to have much more of the same, for myself and my immediate family, and was more than ready to work my socks off to ensure that. However, I also realised that I would have to start fairly soon on the task of preparing my lectures. For although I had 'lecture notes' from my student days for both subjects, I had not taught either of them at Leeds University and, thus, had no written exposition of my own, setting out each subject systematically, for the novice undergraduate.

Whilst I was still in Professor Georges' office, he told me that he also wanted me to tutor, for three hours a week, a subject which I had indeed taught at Leeds, under his counterpart Dean there, Professor Horton Rogers. That last teaching mandate was the easiest burden which he placed on my shoulders that morning, since that would mean my largely repeating the exercises that I was, by then, quite experienced in – namely, teaching in my own office (as opposed to doing so in a large lecture theatre) small groups in a subject called the 'Law of Torts'. That was a lighter burden to me, since I found tutoring to be a lot easier than lecturing. The former presupposed that the student had already been to a lecture on the area of the tutorial topic in question, and had followed that up by some personal reading and research thereon. Thus, in my view at the time, the tutorial should be a kind of discussion group, with all participants having some prior knowledge of the subject matter in question and, thus (theoretically, at least) be able to contribute to the discussion. The lecture, on the other hand and as I understood things, assumes no knowledge on the undergraduate's part and is usually a one-way process with the lecturer setting out the principles involved and the student taking down, in his or her notebook (in those late 1970s, pre-laptop-computer days) selected items from those principles which he or she might wish to recall later. Moreover, whilst the tutorial at UWI (as I would soon find out) may have contained up to 10 students in the tutor's own relatively small room or office, a lecture in the same subject might contain five to 10 times that number and be given in a large auditorium or 'theatre'.

Before parting from my new Dean's company, he told me that he wanted to show me my new office and asked me to follow him. He then took me past several ladies who were positioned by typewriters outside his office, which was located in a self-contained section of the Faculty and which was air-conditioned. As we passed, he introduced the Faculty's secretaries to me, including 'Pearl', 'Wilma' and 'Audrey'. Immediately outside the door to this secretarial unit, and to its left, were about 10 steps, which Professor Georges led me down. At the bottom of these was an office, which he told me would be mine for the coming academic year. He led me inside. It was certainly smaller than my last office at Leeds. Moreover, it had a concrete floor –with no carpet! Those 'design flaws' hit me at once. Just as quickly, however, I noticed the view that was to be seen behind the desk in the room – namely, a vista to the port of Bridgetown and the blue Caribbean Sea beyond. 'Surely', I thought to myself, 'despite the smallness of this office and the absence of a carpet, I am going to be happy here'. It seemed to me that all I needed to do, to start to feel at home, was to put my books, when they arrived from England in the near future, on the bookshelves already located on one wall of the room. On the three empty walls, I could also hang a few personal photographs from England (such as my group snap from my *Call to the Bar* at Lincoln's Inn, and that more recently taken with the members of my last Law Faculty at Leeds University).

As I walked back from my meeting with Professor Georges, in order to go over to the main administration building at Cave Hill Campus to see Mrs Velma Abrahams to find out how things were coming along with the house which my family had been promised, my head was buzzing. I now knew precisely what I would be teaching in Barbados. Three subjects – only one of which I had had any experience of actually lecturing or tutoring! That one legal area, with which I was *au fait* as a teacher, was 'Torts' – and, for that, I had only been a tutor so far. The other two subjects, for which I was to be responsible for lecturing as well as tutoring, I had *no* acquaintance of *teaching* at all – having only been a mere student of both. I, therefore, already felt the pressure to get cracking on making up the relevant lecture notes – and the sooner the better! Philomena and our children, I thought to myself, would just have to get used to me being absent from them during the immediate days ahead – even whilst we were still temporarily installed at the Paradise Beach Hotel. My wife would, however, want to know what was happening in relation to our more permanent home on the island, and that, hopefully, was what I was about to find out from Mrs Abrahams.

It was good for me to see our UWI 'meeter and greeter' again – on that second occasion, located in her own office at the campus. During that latter meeting, whereas she insisted on me addressing her as 'Velma', she also preserved her professional air by always referring to me as 'Mr Bradshaw'. She told me that the house allotted to my family would be ready in about two days' time and that she herself would be driving us to it from our hotel, since the property was situated in another part, or 'parish', of the island. After my family's recent happy experience at our beachside hotel, the most crucial question I had for her was: 'How far will our house be from the beach?'. 'Only a few minutes' walk away' was her answer – which, of course, delighted me! I knew, then, that all would be well with Philomena about our housing situation, since she – even more than me, arguably - loved the beach. All the more so if it happened to be next to the Caribbean Sea - as she would be having to spend a great deal of her time there, playing with and looking after our two small sons. Velma asked me whether I would like to take my family the following morning to see the house – even before the necessary works being done on it had been completed. I jumped at her kind offer. For I knew that Philomena, even more than me, would be concerned about the size of, and amenities to be found inside, our allotted university accommodation – and I, for one, wanted to check out that 'nearby' beach. Velma and I, accordingly, agreed to meet at a post-breakfast hour the next morning, at the reception of our hotel, so that she could take my family on a visit to our prospective new home.

Before leaving each other's company for that day, Velma introduced me to her own boss – the chief administrator at the campus, who went by the name of 'Mrs Austin Alleyne'. It had been Mrs Alleyne who had corresponded with me about the air tickets for my family's emigration from Leeds to Barbados. That had included the complicated issue of our needing four tickets to travel, but only three of us being in existence at the time! Such was the case, owing to our new baby having only been born on 6th July 1979, and Mrs Alleyne and I having been in correspondence about my family's emigration from at least three or four months before that happy event. The chief administrator had also helped me with the issue of my not having sufficient funds to pay for the tickets in advance and then having to claim a reimbursement only after we had arrived on the island. Rather, at her suggestion, it was arranged for UWI to pay for our tickets to the British Airways office in Barbados - and all we had to do then was to go into the counterpart office in Leeds, with a certain reference number, to actually collect the tickets. It may well have been what Philomena and I had been preparing to do, by planning to have a (pre-ticket-collection) picnic lunch in Leeds city centre, when, near the airline's office there, her 'waters broke'! That dramatic event had forced us to abandon our plans, in order to get her to the city's maternity hospital for the birth of Kim, only about two hours later![12] When I finally met Mrs Alleyne in her office, at Velma's introduction, I therefore warmly and enthusiastically thanked her (as Velma's manager) for all her previous help to me and my family whilst we had been in Leeds. She turned out to be a tall, brown-skinned, lady with a very erect bearing. Whilst she struck me as not being given to over-excitement, she nevertheless cordially accepted my expressed gratitude and, on her part, welcomed me to the island and to the staff of the university.

The next morning, Velma kept her appointment with my family and myself. As we had done a few days before at the airport, we all squeezed into her smallish blue car – with Philomena in the back, holding Kim in her arms, and Noel sitting beside her. Shortly after starting out, Velma gave my wife and myself a refresher course in Barbados' geography in order to help us with our bearings. She reminded us that our hotel, and UWI's Cave Hill Campus, were just on the border with the neighbouring parish of 'St James', to the north of the parish of 'St Michael' (where we all then were) and which latter district also contained the island's capital – 'Bridgetown'. She then revealed that our house was situated in a third parish, which was another coastal one situated on the other side of Bridgetown - namely, the only one (of the 11 in the island) without a saint's name and which was called 'Christ Church'. Velma added that it was in that most southerly parish that the island's only airport was situated and also the one in which she herself lived.

Fig 3: Map of Barbados – showing its 11 parishes, including 'St Michael' ('M'), 'St James' ('S') and 'Christ Church' ('Ch Ch') in the west and south of the island, as well as places encountered by the Author, or his entire nuclear family, during the earliest days of his/its emigration to the island, including the Airport (in Ch Ch, indicated by the aeroplane symbol), the 'Cave Hill' and 'Black Rock' areas (close to 'UWI' in M), and the 'Oistins' area (close to 'Hygiea' and 'Maxwell Beach' in Ch Ch)

Philomena and myself were not to be disappointed when we finally reached the house. It seemed a very large building to me – painted, on the outside, in a confectionary pink hue! The house had no road number, but Velma told us that we had to refer to it by its name – namely, the odd-sounding (to my mind, at least) 'Hygeia'! It was situated in the middle of a circular and paved driveway, which allowed Velma (after opening the large gates to gain entrance) to steer her car and its passengers all the way around the house, before we saw an old lady in the grounds and stopped. Having spoken to the lady, Velma introduced Philomena and myself to her. She turned out to be a retired midwife who went by the name of 'Mrs Payne'. Velma explained, in front of us all, that Mrs Payne would be living in the property too, but in a small part of it which was self-contained. That was the reason, Velma went on to explain, why there was a delay in handing Hygeia over to us immediately – namely, in order to make Mrs Payne's self-contained part of the house completely separated from my family's part, but still with enough amenities in the former section to render Mrs Payne comfortable in her living arrangements.

Owing to my perceiving Mrs Payne as being perfectly friendly and extremely respectful to my family and myself – she already seemed very fond of baby Kim and almost as equally taken with his older brother – I, for one, was quite happy with the intended arrangements which Velma had just described. Mrs Payne, though 80 years old, or more, seemed to me to be extremely 'with it' – both physically and mentally. She was short and of a very light-brown complexion. 'Clearly, a mixed-race lady', I thought to myself, 'who might therefore be empathetic to a mixed-race family, literally, living right "on top of her" '!. Emboldened by that thought, I then said to Velma, in the older lady's hearing: 'Perhaps, in due time, Mrs Payne might be willing to do some babysitting, for Philomena and me!'. They both smiled at my suggestion.

Mrs Payne had a slight American accent which was mixed with her Bajan one, it seemed to me. My hearing was already starting to differentiate between the Bajan accent, which one might hear from the locals on the beach, and that spoken by the 'White' or brown-skinned professional classes – like Mrs Alleyne at the university, for example. Mrs Payne's definitely belonged to the latter group – but her ethnicity seemed to be combined with something more. Velma confirmed my perception by telling us that Hygeia was owned by an American, who still lived in the United States – and that Mrs Payne was a very good friend of that person. That was the reason, Velma added, why it was a condition of his leasing Hygeia to UWI (for sub-letting to one of its staff's families) that Mrs Payne had to be allowed to live out her final days in a small part of the property. Clearly, I thought to myself, the friendship between the Yankee landlord and Mrs Payne had left its mark on our soon-to-be neighbour – accent-wise!

Having met, and spoken with, Mrs Payne for a good while, Velma then excused herself and my family in order to show us the inside of our, considerably larger, part of Hygeia. We entered through a small door on the very opposite side of the house from Mrs Payne's side. That led to the kitchen. It was large – with a high ceiling. We were confronted not only with an enormous American-style fridge and a cooker with an oven, but also with a sizeable table upon which the three oldest members of my family should soon be able to eat our meals (seated on its accompanying chairs). It was the adjoining room, however, which really knocked me out. For that space was the main living room of the house, and it was huge! Upon entering it, I started to appreciate its enormous size as well as its very high ceiling. Then, the thought struck me that one might be able to have a good game of five-a-side football in there – and, certainly, a badminton one, at least! The latter speculation was likely to have been the more realistic one, for there would have been no problem at all fitting a full-size court for that racquet sport into the expanse – with room enough for some spectators all around it. In fact, only about eight identical, small, blue-coloured, armchairs were dispersed around the perimeter of the large oblong chamber in question. If anything, therefore, the room was somewhat oversized, as a general living area, for a family of two adults and two small children. I pushed that negative thought out of my mind, however, since I could already imagine that the four of us would be spending most of our time outside the house – given the climate of Barbados and its usual good weather - so that an unnecessarily cavernous home should never be a problem for us.

Beyond the living room from the kitchen, one had to climb a short stairway comprising about six steps. These led to the bedroom area of the main part of the house – below which, Mrs Payne's own self-contained section was situated. Velma showed us the master bedroom first, which was located at the far left from the top of the stairs. It turned out to be a large and airy room, with what might be termed, by hotels of a certain quality, a 'queen-size' bed, positioned in the centre of the room. What impressed me more, however, was not the substantial expanse of the bed but, rather, what was above it – namely, a huge mosquito net! Accordingly, the more I saw of the room, the more it felt to me like one which might be found in a very comfortable hotel. Indeed, not even our room at the Paradise Beach contained such a net for the sleeping comfort of those slumbering on its main bed. That positive impression of our new home's main sleeping chamber was buttressed by my spotting on the wall, near a second (exterior) door which led to an outside balcony, an air conditioning unit! That amenity meant that Philomena and myself should have the device by which to keep cool on any particularly hot night which we might encounter during our future life in Hygeia – and which apparatus should probably also be able to keep any lurking mosquitoes at bay. Added to the comforts of our future bedroom, however, was one more thing which Philomena and myself had never been privileged enough to enjoy during our past married life together at either our flat (and then cottage) in Cambridge, or at our subsequent house in Leeds – namely, an en suite bathroom! What luxury, it seemed to me, we were coming to enjoy as part of our new life in Barbados.

Having shown Philomena and myself the inside of our future bedroom, Velma then took us through the exterior door and onto our balcony outside. The view from there looked south-eastwards, she told us, towards a small fishing village about a mile or two away, called 'Oistins'. That information reminded me that we were somewhere near the sea – but, to my disappointment, the Caribbean's waters were not discernible from the balcony itself. What was very near, however, was a very modern house next door and I wondered who lived there and whether my family would, in time, come to know and make friends with our new neighbours, as we had done with 'Jill and Dale Hutchison' whilst living in the married students' quarters at my old college in Cambridge. Or, again, as we had equally managed to do with 'Mr and Mrs Bradbeer' whilst living, afterwards, in our little cottage in the village of 'Coton' near that university city, or with 'Bob and Edith' during the last academic year at Leeds. Velma also showed Philomena and myself that the balcony in question was not only immediately outside our own future bedroom, but that it also ran along past the outside of the middle bedroom, as well as to the third one further along. What fun, I imagined, our little family might be able to have in the future, playing games of 'hide and seek', in and out of the three bedrooms, and using the balcony to 'secretly' get from one to another without ever using the main door to any of them.

Velma then showed us into the middle bedroom. This also contained a double bed – but had no en suite amenity. It was certainly large enough to accommodate Kim's cot as well – which we had shipped to Barbados, as part of our possessions, before leaving Leeds the previous month. Accordingly, when Velma next showed us the third and final bedroom, situated immediately at the top of the stairs from the living room and which we found to be similarly furnished and containing the same amenities as the middle one, Philomena and I quickly made a decision about where we would locate our sons' sleeping quarters. That would be in the middle bedroom next to us – so that the boys would both be together and near to us at the same time. We would then be able to hear Kim quickly if he woke up crying in the night, and they would be company for each other as they gradually developed together.

There was also one other amenity located in the 'general bedroom quarters' upstairs – namely, a further room, which was smaller than any of the bedrooms, but still of an adequate size and which contained a shower and toilet, but no bath. That extra 'washroom' was located to the right of the third bedroom – the one immediately at the top of the stairs – and would be perfect, if Philomena and myself earmarked that third bedroom as our family's 'guest room'. And such a spare bedchamber would surely be needed soon, since we were now resident in 'exotic Barbados', and, therefore, my wife and I fully expected to have many a relative or friend from England, or wider afield, on a regular basis, eagerly wanting to visit us to share some of our newly-gained Caribbean sunshine, among other things.

Having enjoyed Velma's guided tour of our new house, there was just one more 'amenity' that I really was dying to see, very much indeed – not only for myself but also for the other members of my family. That, of course, was the beach 'nearby'! Thus, with Velma as a willing accomplice, Philomena and I set off walking down 'Maxwell Coast Road' – the thoroughfare which, our UWI guide told us, was now part of our new address – with Noel holding his mother's hand and me carrying Kim in my arms. Within 10 minutes or less, we had arrived at the entrance to the beach – on a bend in the road. From there, we could see a large high-rise hotel named 'The Welcome Inn' on our left, and a much smaller establishment, or bar, called 'The Tourist Trap', on our right.

Continuing straight on for about 100 yards, Velma told us that we had reached what our family could henceforth regard as its very own 'Maxwell Beach'! What a delight that was for me. That was because the sandy shore before us seemed to be as long, and wide, as our present temporary base at Paradise Beach, but it was also a great deal more quiet. For one thing, there seemed to be no commercial activities going on - either on the beach itself, or in the sea - such as the water skiing, 'parasailing', or riding on a 'jet-ski', which tourists seemed to spend a great deal of their time (and money) on, near our hotel. Rather, 'our' future beach was barely populated at all and the few persons that we did see there were either calmly walking along the sands or, perhaps, having a quick dip in the adjoining Caribbean Sea. To my mind, therefore, Maxwell Beach would be the perfect 'family spot' for Philomena to spend many a day to come whilst looking after our two small sons – much better, perhaps, than our current touristic, commercialised, and far more busy, resort base (which I also liked, of course, but only on a temporary basis). Moreover, I could already foresee a future routine for me which would be connected with our new beach – namely, a daily 'jogging' regime, whereby I would get up about 6 o'clock each morning to then run down to the beach, have a swim for about 20 minutes or so, before gently trotting back, showering and then getting dressed prior to leaving home to do my 'lecturing' at Cave Hil

*Fig 4: The Author with Noel, at Maxwell Beach, soon after first moving into 'Hygeia' – the family's new home in Barbados. In the background, to the left, can be seen the bay leading to 'Oistins', as well as 'Atlantic Shores' behind that*

*Fig 5: Philomena, holding Kim, and beside Noel – at Maxwell Beach (in the shallows), soon after first moving to the family's new home nearby*

What an introduction, therefore, for me and my family to our new life in Barbados! Things were turning out to be even better than I had even dared to imagine. Certainly, they were many times better than when Philomena and I had first moved to Leeds with just Noel, about one year before. On that occasion, the accommodation office at the university employing me there had originally provided us with keys to a house in a very run-down part of that city, which we had the choice of renting but which (in my opinion) was totally uninhabitable and should have been condemned. Although Philomena and I had quickly rejected that initial allocation to us and had ended up with a nice semi-detached house in a middle-class area of that major Yorkshire city, near the world famous cricket venue of 'Headingley',[13] to now have our own detached Hygeia and its comfortable amenities, and to be no more than 10 minutes' walk away from our 'own' family-friendly beach, right beside the Caribbean Sea, was to have 'arrived', as far as I was concerned. And yet….

Having walked back to Hygeia, after our 'recce' with Maxwell Beach – which, on that first occasion, did not include our 'trying out' the sea there with a quick family dip – Philomena and I said a quick 'see you again soon' to Mrs Payne. With our sons and Velma, we then left her supervising the works being performed by a few local young men on her part of the house. Velma's driving us in her car, around the paved inner perimeter of the garden once more in order to get to the exit, made me realise one potential disadvantage of the house. That had to do with its location – on the landward side of the Caribbean Sea! For, although the exit from the house was on Maxwell Coast Road, the front of it (to which access could be gained from its large living room), had a raised outside veranda which ran the length of that room (but only about 10 feet wide), and that patio overlooked one of Barbados' major roads! The principal thoroughfare in question was named 'Highway 7' – the main road from Bridgetown to Sir Grantley Adams International Airport – and which major route, at the point where it passed our house, was also more locally called 'Maxwell Main Road'. Indeed, as Philomena and myself would soon find out, buses, taxis and general car traffic would at most times of the day, and even regularly during evenings and nights, be passing by our future veranda and master bedroom. Would my family and I be able to enjoy our new location in peace – when not at Maxwell Beach, of course?

Leaving Hygeia behind after that first visit, Velma soon delivered us back to our hotel with a promise to be in touch again as soon as she got word of the completion of the works being done on our future home. That next contact from her occurred as soon as two days later. I can recall, however, that there was one day - whilst still at Paradise Beach awaiting Velma's further update - when Philomena and I decided to take the boys to Bridgetown by bus. It was time, we jointly agreed, for us all to see the island's capital city together. The trip may well also have been partly to carry out an errand on my part, since I may have had to look into getting my work permit – previously arranged by UWI before my arrival – stamped into my passport. Whether for pure leisure purposes or not, however, I remember walking in the city pushing Kim in his carrycot, placed on wheels and with Philomena holding Noel's hand. We were by 'The Careenage' – an area of Bridgetown beside a wide watercourse, which is really a river before it goes into the Caribbean Sea and which is full of boats and small ships, including the tourist vessel named 'The Jolly Roger'. Suddenly, and

Fig 6: Noel and Kim in Bridgetown, near 'The Careenage', in August 1979

unexpectedly, Philomena began to cry!

It had become clear, from our bus journey to the city, that Barbados was not really suited for (or used to) parents taking their babies in carrycots on public buses. It was also equally clear, as I tried to push Kim in his own baby carriage around the city, that the small pavements of the capital were also not fit for such a purpose – especially with the mass of shoppers trying to make their own respective progress all around us. But surely, I had thought to myself, something else must be upsetting my wife. I, thus, asked her to tell me what was troubling her, which merely brought forth an even greater volume of tears. My frustration with her at that unexpected development certainly did not help the episode – but, little by little, it became clear to me that Philomena was simply coming to terms with the enormity of what she had done by emigrating with me and the children to Barbados! She was now 5000 miles or so from home – and, approximately, half a world away from her own mother and brothers (regarding whom, we had made no plans, as yet, to see again for, perhaps, several years to come). Moreover, I knew very little, then, of the syndrome known as 'post-natal depression', and that, too, might have been taking its toll on her that particular day. After all, baby Kim was still only about six to seven weeks old at that time. Unfortunately, being ignorant (and, possibly, wrong-footed, since Philomena had never shown any similar 'breakdown' during our elder son's earliest childhood days) I merely shook her firmly by the shoulders and said something along the lines of: 'Pull yourself together! If you had felt any misgivings about emigrating with me and the children to this island, you should have said so before we left England. Not now, after we are already here and have just arranged our new home and what I am soon to be teaching at the university, etc'. Bless her! That is, especially, because shortly afterwards, she was back to her usual calm self again, as we walked together with our sons to catch our bus back to the borderlands with St James parish and our hotel. By the time we had returned to Paradise Beach, had our family dip in the Caribbean Sea in the late afternoon, and then she and I had enjoyed our lobster dinner and rum punches (again!), Philomena was back to being fully 'on board' with the 'family enterprise'. It had been a hot afternoon in Bridgetown – the main cause, perhaps, of a completely unexpected episode with my wife, which I prayed would never be repeated during the rest of our days in Barbados.

As soon as that very evening, perhaps, we received a message from Velma to say that our house was then ready for our moving in and that she would, therefore, be coming to drive us to Hygeia the next morning after breakfast. Accordingly, within two or three days of our last meeting with her, when she had introduced us to our new home and Mrs Payne, we again travelled with her to the parish of Christ Church, and the Maxwell district therein, in order to get installed in our new abode. Once Velma had left our little family to return to her UWI office, the reality of our new life really dawned on me. Living-wise, we were now on our own – apart from Mrs Payne, of course, who I was already pretty sure would be willing to help us to with advice and tips to enable us get by. One of those bits of guidance, which Philomena and I needed to ask her for, almost immediately, was: "Where was the nearest supermarket?". That was because it was necessary for us to buy some basic provisions for the house – not least, some baby food items for our younger son, as well as some milk to make tea for Philomena. Mrs Payne was to tell us that the nearest such superstore was at Oistins village, some two miles or so away. Moreover, given the absence of pavements (or 'sidewalks', as she called them) between Maxwell and Oistins on Highway 7, she strictly advised us not to attempt to walk there. Rather, she recommended that we should take a bus. Philomena and I could see, however, after our jitney excursion to Bridgetown with Kim's carrycot just a day or so before, that such public transport could not be a long-term solution for us. We would just have to buy a car as soon as possible!

Fortunately, before she had left our little family at Hygeia that first morning of our new life there, Velma had made me a wonderful offer in order to tide me over for the short term. She had said that she lived in the 'Atlantic Shores' area of our new parish, on the other side of Oistins, and, therefore, had to drive right past my new home each morning, and back again each evening, to get to and from her work place at Cave Hill Campus. Accordingly, she offered to take me with her, and bring me home again, each workday until I was in a position to make alternative transport arrangements. I could hardly believe her kindness – which seemed perfectly genuine and well beyond the call of her duties – but I jumped at her offer. From the following morning, therefore, I began to travel with Velma each day, to and from, the UWI campus – making sure that I was always ready to return home with her at her usual 'knocking-off' time, even though I may have wanted to stay on in my office to finish off some lecture or other which I may have been preparing. Before, the first of those 'school run' trips began however, through a tip from Mrs Payne, we found a small 'mini-mart' – which was clearly mainly intended for island-visitors, with 'tourist prices' to match, therefore – across the road, on Highway 7, and a few hundred yards along in the Oistins direction, in which to buy-in some staple provisions for our new home. Later that day, after our first visit to Maxwell Beach for our first family dips there, Philomena and I decided to brave the bus and take a ride with our sons – but without Kim's Baby Buggy or carrycot – to Oistins, for a bigger shop for items to fill our larder at Hygeia. We clearly had to limit ourselves to the amount we bought, since that was conditioned by the volume and weight we could both carry on the return bus home, in conjunction with our having to convey our sons as well. Something would have to be done, and done quickly, about acquiring a vehicle if my family's new life, based at Hygeia, was to become an enjoyable 'going concern'!

Thus, one of the first things that I set about doing on my first full day of 'work' in my new office at the Cave Hill Law Faculty, starting from my new Barbados home, was to write to 'Mr Victor Cooke' – UWI's Finance Officer at the campus. During the initial 'commute' journey with Velma to the university that morning, I had asked her about whether our employer ever granted car loans to new members of staff. She had told me that she knew that it did, indeed, do so from time to time - but that such grants lay in the gift of Mr Cooke, to whom I would have to go to see in order to put in my application.

She also cautioned me that he could be quite a moody person and that I should not expect a smooth, or quick, outcome.

Velma turned out to be right. I found him to be a shortish, light-skinned and thick-set man, who wore spectacles and sported a pencil-moustache. He did not strike me as a being a jolly man in any sense. Nevertheless, he listened politely to the story of my family's plight – concerning where we were situated on the main airport road from Bridgetown, some miles from the nearest supermarket, and having to try to move around with our two small boys (one still a babe in arms). And though he made responses to the effect that the car loan process normally took 'at least one month or more' to be granted, he also said that he would see what he could do - as an exception - to speed things up in my own case. As I departed from Mr Cooke's office that morning, I wondered whether he would be as good as his word. Or whether, perhaps, Velma's gloomy prediction (based on her past experiences), of 'no smooth, nor quick' positive result, from my UWI car loan application, would prove the more correct.

*Fig 7: Photo of Mr Victor Cooke, the Finance Officer at UWI, Cave Hill Campus when the Author and his family first arrived in Barbados in August 1979 – and in whose hands lay the fate of the Author being able to get a car loan from UWI to enable them to purchase their own private means of transportation around the island*

*Chapter 3*

# Meeting my new colleagues in the UWI Law Faculty

After my meeting with Mr Cooke, all I could do about the acquisition of a car for my family was to wait. In the interim, I first went back to my office – situated up a small hillock from the main administration buildings which housed the said UWI Finance Officer, Velma and their colleagues. After greeting the ladies in the 'Secretariat' of the Law Faculty, I went on towards my own new university accommodation. To the right of it, I saw that my neighbour's door was opened. That caused me to wonder whether such was the way that lecturers worked in my new university – with their entrances kept open, in order, perhaps, to help one's office to keep cool (despite the fact that each such room also contained an air conditioning unit). I popped my head around my neighbour's portal and saw that it was occupied by a young man of approximately the same age as myself. He, too, was brown-skinned – but slightly Hispanic-looking and sporting a moustache as well as a headful of black, wavy hair. He looked friendly and I introduced myself to him as his new colleague next door. He put out his hand and said, with what sounded to me somewhat like a Welsh accent but which (I would come to learn) was the distinctive 'Trinidadian' lilt: 'Hi! I'm Michael. Michael Castagne'. I took his hand in mine, warmly shook it and replied: 'Pleased to meet you, Michael!'.

Thus began a first meeting, which seemed, to me, to have the potential to lead to a friendship which could be long-lasting. The two of us seemed to 'hit it off' immediately. We began our acquaintanceship by exchanging information about what each of us were respectively lecturing on during the coming academic year. His main subject, if memory serves me correctly, was 'Public International Law' – which was a little related to one of my own courses (namely, the 'Private' aspects of such Law, otherwise known as The Conflict of Laws). He told me, however, that he was particularly interested in the protection of 'Human Rights' and particularly impressed me by revealing that he was the 'Secretary', or leader, of a local branch of 'Amnesty International' in either Barbados or his native 'Trinidad'. During that first conversation, we soon also established that we were both practising Catholics, but it may well have been as much as a few weeks later that he first invited me to one of the 'Prayer Meetings' that he went to after work, after revealing to me, at the same time, that he regularly attended the same.

If I had acquired not only a new neighbour but also a potential good friend in Michael from the first, the same could not be said about my colleague on the other side

*Fig 8: 'Michael Castagne', on the left of this photo, in 1985 – some six years after the Author first met him, as his next-door neighbour at the Cave Hill Campus of UWI, Barbados. By that time, Michael had emigrated to Trinidad, married his wife, 'Andrea', and they had been blessed with their first child, 'Christopher' – who also appear in this photo*

of my office – the left side, as I looked at my door. It was a lady. I met her either that first full day at work for me, or within a day or two after. She turned out to be a middle-aged, dark-skinned, woman who told me that she was originally from 'Guyana' – the former 'British Guiana' – on the mainland of South America. During that first encounter, she revealed that, like me, she had only just arrived in Barbados from England and that the main subject that she would be teaching was 'Company Law'. From that initial meeting, she let me know that she had suffered some sort of bad experience in Britain – whether in the teaching world, or in general life, I can no longer recall – and was now adamant that she 'never wanted to return there!'. It may have just been a question of the inclement weather which she had experienced over sustained periods in London, for example, but, given her somewhat 'negative' outlook on life, I was somewhat weary of her from the first. Her name too, put me off a little – for she told me it was 'Mrs Lurline Stanford-Johnson', but, yet, she never spoke (to me, at least) of having an extant husband, nor of having any offspring from him (or from anyone else!).

If my first meeting with Mrs Stanford-Johnson had left me underwhelmed, however, that with her other immediate neighbour (to the left of her office) had caused a reaction from me of a wholly different kind! For that third new colleague turned out to be someone I already knew from my days as a student at Cambridge University – where he had also been a Law 'postgrad' at the time. I had last seen him, his wife and their two small children, in late 1978 – when my own family had left that East of England university city to go to live in the more northern one of Leeds, in Yorkshire. At that time, he had not told me of any similar ambition to mine of wanting to teach Law at UWI (or at any other university, for that matter). Rather, I had understood that he wanted to qualify as a Barrister, after graduating with his LL.B degree at 'Jesus College, Cambridge', and then return home to practise Law in his native Bahamas. Either that, or go into the diplomatic service in his motherland, since he had already gained a 'Doctorate in Philosophy', or 'Ph.D', from some North American university in 'International Relations', or the like. His name was 'Peter' – 'Dr Peter Maynard'. A brown-skinned man, of over six feet in height, he and I were to have a warm (if somewhat awkward) embrace, outside our offices, at the realisation that, henceforth, we were to be near-neighbours, as well as colleagues, at the UWI Law Faculty for the coming 1979-80 academic year. I could also anticipate that, as we had done back in Cambridge two to three school years before, our two families would probably end up spending a lot of our spare time together in the near future – particularly as Peter told me that his own had just been housed by our new university in Christ Church parish too!

Fig 9: Photo of Dr Peter Maynard, some years after the Author had first met him at the Law Faculty of UWI, Cave Hill Campus in August 1979 – looking much the same as the Author remembers him from that bygone era. Another lawyer who has managed to 'age well', therefore

Peter's presence on the teaching staff of UWI's Law Faculty, thus, was a major surprise for me. All the more so, since I already 'knew' most of the other members of that staff – if only by name! That is because, for some years prior to travelling out to Barbados with my family (and even before applying for my post at Cave Hill in the spring to summer period of 1978), I had obtained a 'Faculty Handbook' from the university campus in Barbados and had, merely by perusing it from time to time, inadvertently learned, by heart, the names of the long-established members of that Law-teaching department. I had accomplished that feat notwithstanding the fact that I had never set out to learn those names. Rather, I had been far more interested in noting what qualifications such members had each acquired - and from which universities - in order to judge whether I, myself, stood any chance of joining their number when I came to apply for any vacant post in the Faculty. But learn the names, as well as the qualifications and so forth, of each such long-established member I certainly did – almost unconsciously. The member, however, whose background I was most impressed with, and whom I badly wanted to meet (and get on with), was one of the Faculty's most senior academics. His name was 'Professor Ralph Carnegie'. I had noted from the Handbook that Professor Carnegie had not only obtained his M.A degree from 'Oxford University', but that he had also spent a few years (prior to coming to UWI) as a teaching fellow of 'Jesus College' in that oldest English university. I rather hoped, therefore, that his 'Oxbridge' connection, and my own, would lead to a future good friendship between the two of us and, perhaps, even encourage a link to form among our respective families.

It is likely that I did not meet the professor – or 'Ralph' as he insisted that I refer to him from the first – until a few days, or even weeks, after my first full day at my new office. When the meeting came to pass, however, I was not to be disappointed. He turned out to be a very fair-skinned (and thick-set) man, with a slightly over-large (and balding) head. To some extent, he seemed to me to resemble my late father somewhat! But what endeared him to me most, from that initial encounter, was his pronounced, but educated, Jamaican accent - as well as his quickness to break into a laugh regarding something I may have said during our conversation. He was to tell me that he was the Course Director in the 'Law of Contract' subject (as well as that for 'Constitutional Law') in UWI's LL.B degree programme. Moreover, he particularly welcomed me to the Faculty as one of the teachers of Torts Law – since, together with his own 'Contracts', the two legal areas formed the general 'Law of Obligations'.

*Fig. 10: Photo of Professor A. Ralph Carnegie – taken, most likely, a few years after he and the Author first met at the UWI Law Faculty in later 1979*

Professor Carnegie, however, was not the only one in the Handbook with an Oxford degree. For, I had also noted, in that guide, that there was someone in the Faculty named 'Marston Gibson' – who was stated there to be somewhat like me, in the sense of possessing a first degree in Law (from UWI, in his case), but also a postgraduate one (a 'Bachelor of Civil Laws', or 'B.C.L', where he was concerned) as well as being licensed to practise Law as a Barrister (or 'Attorney-at-Law', as the profession was called in the

English-speaking Caribbean territories). I was also to meet Marston in my first weeks at the Cave Hill Campus and he turned out to be, like Michael and myself, a young man in his twenties. He was, however, much darker than Michael or myself and also, it seemed to me, more quick-witted and fast-talking. I was soon to learn, perhaps from Marston's own mouth, that (just like Ralph Carnegie) he was a 'Rhodes Scholar'. Like Ralph, too, Oxford did not seem to have deprived Marston of his local Caribbean island accent – though, in the latter's case, his speech pattern was distinctly Bajan!

*Fig 11: Photo of Marston Gibson – taken much later than when the Author had first met him, as a young man, at the UWI Law Faculty, and when he had already attained, arguably, the highest legal position in Barbados*

There were also a couple more senior members of staff noted in the Faculty Handbook, and whom I also keen to meet. One of those was one 'Dr N.J.O Liverpool'. In my recollection, Dr Liverpool held the office of 'Head of the Teaching Department' at the Faculty during the period in which I first arrived. That meant that he was in charge of deciding which members of the Faculty taught which subject – and presumably, therefore, he would have collaborated with Professor Georges, prior to my arrival, for the latter to have been able to give me my full quota of subjects during our, already

*Fig 12: Photo of Dr N. J. O. ('Nick') Liverpool, taken perhaps many years after the Author had first met him at the UWI Law Faculty in 1979 and well before he had attained the very highest office in his native island of 'Dominica'. If so, the years were kind to him, as, to the Author, the photo shows him looking as young as he did at their first Cave Hill Campus meeting*

recounted, first meeting. I knew, from the Handbook, that Dr Liverpool had also studied in England – and, indeed, had obtained his doctorate (his Ph.D) at the University of Hull in Yorkshire. When I did eventually meet him, although he asked me to call him 'Nick' immediately, I did not warm to him as I had done with Professor Carnegie. He was very dark and balding – but still a youngish-to-middle-aged man. I also formed the impression that Nick had not taken to me very much either, although I could not quite fathom why at the time. I was to discover quite soon afterwards, however, that, perhaps, his coolness to me was because I had not been born of the fairer sex!

Another senior member mentioned in the Handbook was one 'Professor P.K. Menon'. According to that volume, he possessed a large number of degrees - from various universities in India, USA and Canada – and, from his surname, I rather guessed that he was likely to be a native from the Indian sub-continent. My speculation proved to be correct, when we finally met in those first few days of mine at Cave Hill. And despite his rather long list of qualifications, he turned out to be one of the most modest and mild-mannered persons that I have ever met – certainly, in my university career thus far, as either student or teacher. His modesty caused me to like him immediately - for I was attracted to his lack of pretentiousness and his reserve, when, it seemed to me, he had every reason to be the opposite. My anticipation, therefore, was that I would be able to get on well at the Faculty with 'P.K.' – as he asked me to call him. However, given his middle-aged status, and seniority at UWI, I could not really envisage the two of us being future 'drinking buddies' or similar.

*Fig 13: Photo of Professor P.K. Menon, showing him looking even younger than the Author remembers him appearing on their first meeting in 1979. The Author is extremely grateful to his successor Course Director of the Comparative Law LL.B course at UWI Cave Hill Campus – 'Dr Asya Ostroukh', Senior Lecturer in Law – for not only sending him the photo in April 2024, but also for taking 'the photo of the original' herself*

After meeting P.K, there was yet one more person, also with an Indian surname, mentioned in the Handbook whom I very much wanted to meet. That was one 'Dr R.L Chaudhary' – and who, the volume revealed, had obtained his Ph.D from London University in England. When I did eventually encounter him for the first time, during those first few weeks of mine at the Faculty, in my perception he turned out to be just as keen to meet me. He was friendly and outgoing to me from the start. Indeed, it may well have been him who had instigated our first contact by knocking on my

*Fig 14: Photo of Dr R.L. Chaudhary, better known to his UWI colleagues as 'Roop' – sent to the Author by his daughter, Corinna Chaudhary, in March 2024 and who stated that she believed it was 'taken for the university in the late 1980s'*

door, as he was passing, and introducing himself to me! For, his own office was a few levels below, and to the right of, my own and he had to pass mine, *en route*, to reach his. He asked me to call him 'Roop' and he quickly wanted to know all about where I had come from before arriving in Barbados, whether I had a family with me, and other personal matters. On his own side, he volunteered that he was, indeed, a native of India but that he had lived and studied for many years in London. He also told me that he, too, was married – to a West German woman – and that he and his wife had a single child, namely a daughter who was at secondary school on the island. I rather got the impression that Roop very much wanted to be friends, and when I told him that my own wife was a native of England and that we had two young sons with us who were English-born, that seemed to seal our positive connection for the future.

I have already mentioned my meeting with my immediate neighbour at the Faculty, Mrs Stanford Johnson. She was not referred to in the Handbook since, like me, she was a new recruit. However, there were three other women on our teaching staff who were so mentioned, whose names, therefore, I knew by heart, and whom I, accordingly, also very much wanted to meet. The first of those was one 'Margaret DeMerieux'. I was attracted to her French-sounding surname and by the fact that the Handbook told me that she possessed a post-graduate Law degree – a 'Master of Laws', or 'LL.M' - from an English university. That was Manchester – which, to my mind, would have been an unexciting, north of England, city to a Caribbean person, as much as Leeds (from whence I had just arrived) had been to me. However, when I did finally meet 'Miss DeMerieux', or 'Margaret' - as she allowed me to refer to her from our first encounter - in one of my initial days at the Faculty, she turned out to be anything but 'unexciting'! Rather, she was - to my eyes, at least – something of a very colourful character. For, like Michael, my other next-door-neighbour, she was a Trinidadian national. Unlike my nearest male colleague, however, she had lived and studied in England for many years – and was already in her early middle-age by the time of our meeting. Margaret seemed to be a happy-go-lucky person, and, from the brown, school-girl type, pinafore dress she wore, she did not seem very trendy – or even mindful of what other people may have thought of her fashion sense. From the first, she seemed somewhat interested in me – and almost playful. For example, although she wanted me to call her by her first name, and told me that she had a brother by the name of 'David', she seemed to prefer to teasingly refer to me as 'Bradshaw'! I took such verbal sparring in good heart and this seemed to help propagate our already budding future friendship even more.

*Fig 15: Photo of a portrait of Margaret DeMerieux, evidently painted some years after the Author first met her in 1979, but revealing that she had hardly aged at all since that initial encounter (in his opinion). He is extremely grateful to his successor Course Director of the Comparative Law LL.B course at UWI Cave Hill Campus – Dr Asya Ostroukh, Senior Lecturer in Law – for not only sending him the photo in April 2024, but also for taking the photo herself*

The second female Faculty member, mentioned in the Handbook, was one 'Norma Forde'. When I finally managed to acquaint myself with her, I perceived her as being very different from Margaret. That was so, not only in her light-brown complexion compared to Margaret's own dark one but also in the way she came across to me as one very serious woman. For that first encounter with her, it had been necessary for me to make my way out of the Law Faculty building and across a field to an annex building about two hundred yards away. There I found 'Miss Forde' – who, for some reason, seemed to prefer to have her office apart from the rest of her colleagues inhabiting the main building. Like Margaret, she was an early middle-aged spinster. Unlike the former, however, Norma turned out to be not only Bajan but also someone who seemed to take a great deal of care about her appearance. She even had her shortish-length hair coloured a bright hue, which was somewhere between orange and red! Her coiffure was also decorated with a band of cloth made of a colourful material – most likely, in order to coordinate with that of her dress. I had felt obliged to go across the field to meet with Norma not only for curiosity's sake, but also because she was the Course Director of, and lecturer in, the Law of Torts course - which subject Professor Georges had tasked me with tutoring over the coming academic year. I was, therefore, able to ask her for past worksheets, which she had given out to her students the year before - so that I could start using them in order to get familiar with local West Indian legal cases in our subject.

For, I would not have previously encountered such cases in my exclusive training, and teaching, to date, in the Law of England. Norma, was, indeed, able to help me with the requested reading matter – but she did so with typical Bajan efficiency and formality. It was clear to me, from that first encounter, that Norma's physical 'apartness', regarding the location of her office, would probably also apply to her attitude to social closeness with her Faculty colleagues.

*Fig 16: Photo of Miss Norma Monica Forde, looking much like the Author remembers her from their first meeting in later 1979, in 'her special annex' of the UWI Law Faculty – but* sans *the headband that he recalls she often wore at that time*

Of the 'three Handbook ladies', the last which I was to meet was one 'Dorcas White'. I had already discovered, most likely from Margaret DeMerieux, that Dorcas was a 'Miss' too. I am fairly sure, however, that I already knew that Dorcas was, like me, a native of Montserrat! Perhaps, I had first been told about her during my honeymoon trip with Philomena to the land of my birth in August 1976. If so, that revelation would most likely have been made by the then Editor of the 'Montserrat Mirror' - my native island's then weekly newspaper - whom my new wife and I had met during our post-wedding holiday.[14] He would have known that Dorcas had been a journalist in Montserrat too, prior to her taking up the study of the Law, and who had remained at the UWI Law Faculty after graduating there – a place which I may well have mentioned to him that I was seriously thinking of applying to, in order to teach there myself sometime in the near future. At any rate, I very much wanted to meet Dorcas – but would have to wait for that opportunity until a week or so before the start of lectures, in the new academic year ahead, beginning October 1979. That was because Dorcas was a lecturer based at one of the other three campuses which taught Law to first year undergraduates on the LL.B degree programme run by my new university – namely, UWI's campus at 'Mona' in 'Jamaica'. (The other two were at: UWI's campus at 'St Augustine' in 'Trinidad and Tobago'; and the campus of the 'University of Guyana' ('UG') situated in 'Georgetown', the capital of that latter country. Such 'undergrads' were then obliged to transfer to

UWI's Cave Hill Campus in Barbados, for their Second and Final Years, in order to complete their degree). Dorcas, being on the UWI staff at Mona Campus, meant that she would have to travel to Barbados, from Jamaica, for my very first 'Faculty Board' meeting of the UWI Law Faculty taking place at Cave Hill Campus in late September of that forthcoming first academic year of mine.

I made an extra effort to seek Dorcas out, prior to the start of the meeting in question. Alas, though I perceived her to be friendly enough to me, she was certainly not as warm or effusive as I had hoped she would be. Nevertheless, I had to admit to myself that she was an attractive, brown-skinned, early middle-aged woman. Her most distinctive feature to me, however, was the colourful 'turban' which she wore on her head. From the first, I noted that she seemed to like to score points verbally. She may even have joked with me about my not being a 'real' Caribbean person any longer, since I had lived outside the region for so long. I had noted in the Handbook that, unlike Margaret DeMerieux for example, she did not appear to have ever studied outside the Caribbean herself, nor even to have undertaken any postgraduate studies to Masters degree level, for instance. Perhaps, I thought to myself, I would find, in my fellow Montserratian, not so much an ally and helper (in my, hoped-for, future progression in my chosen career at UWI) but, rather, someone who was antipathetic to me for being an outsider. That negative thought was to be reinforced that same evening of our first meeting, at a party held by Professor Georges, at his house in a rural part of St James parish, for members of the Law Faculty and their partners, among others. At the function, I had introduced Dorcas to Philomena – our two children having been left in the babysitting care of Mrs Payne back at Hygeia, perhaps for the first time. I quickly perceived, during that introduction, that Dorcas was not impressed! That was not so much because of the actual person, or personality, of my wife, it seemed to me, but rather because of the principle of my

*Fig 17: Photo of Miss Dorcas White, the Author's fellow-Montserratian Lecturer on the UWI Law Faculty, taken perhaps much later than when he first met her at Cave Hill Campus in 1979 - but showing her looking just as young (and, arguably, just as mischievous) as at that initial encounter. Always one for fashionable headgear, she has graduated from wearing a turban (that the Author always knew her sporting, whilst he was at UWI) to a grander chapeau by the later time of the photo being snapped*

having chosen to marry an English person rather than one of my own kind – someone, perhaps, like herself. I could, of course, have been totally wrong in my perception – but I consoled myself with the thought that only time would tell whether the only two Montserratians on the UWI Law Faculty would ever become close colleagues, or even friends!

Even without my compatriot, Dorcas, however – who, in any case, lived in distant Jamaica and who I would only see in Barbados once every term when she travelled over for Faculty Board meetings – I could see that I had the potential to gain some good professional, and social, friendships among my new colleagues at UWI. Certainly, there was one very dynamic, and young, member of staff among our number who seemed to go out of his way to make me feel at home in the Faculty. For, within a week or so of my arrival at Cave Hill, he invited me and my family to a barbecue with his own clan. When I told him that I not only had a wife with me in Barbados, but also two small boys – one a baby in arms - his reply was his typical: 'No problem. I have a wife and young family too!'. That colleague of mine was a young man of about my age, but of a distinct Chinese appearance who went by the name of 'Mr Chuck'! Despite his Oriental looks, however, he had an accent like that of Professor Carnegie – for the former, too, was also a native of Jamaica. Moreover, like my favourite professor, thus far, in the Faculty, my other new Jamaican colleague was also a Rhodes Scholar who had studied Law at Oxford. His first name was 'Delroy' – which was, perhaps, a giveaway regarding which Caribbean island he had his origins in. From our first meeting, I could see that he was something of a 'wheeler-dealer' in knowing just how to engage (in a positive way) with whomsoever he was involved. I rather suspected that he would not always remain in the teaching of the Law, but, rather, might someday go far in the world of politics.

*Fig 18: Delroy Chuck, a few years after the Author had first met him at the UWI Law Faculty in 1979 - and after he had returned to his native Jamaica and, perhaps inevitably, about to enter the world of politics*

*Chapter 4*

# Settling into Domestic Life at home in Barbados

After consulting Philomena at home, I was extremely happy to accept Delroy Chuck's invitation and to return the friendly overtures which he was clearly displaying towards me. Thus, about one week after we had landed in Barbados, we found ourselves at 'Barclay's Park', on the east coast of the island, enjoying the hospitality of my young Jamaican colleague and that of his wife and family. Surprisingly to me, owing to Delroy's unreconstructed Jamaican accent, his spouse turned out to be a Barbadian wife (with her own local accent). They had two small children, as I recall, just like Philomena and myself, but with at least one of theirs being a girl. At the gathering, Delroy seemed to have invited many other people from his wife's side of the family – including her father. That older man, I was to discover during the barbecue, was a 'Williams' – one of, perhaps, seven brothers who were all professional people on the island, several working in the Law, including one of their clan who was already a senior judge and who would soon become the 'Chief Justice of Barbados'. Delroy had clearly married into a prominent Bajan family, and I smiled to myself as I recalled my first impression of him as being something of a 'politician'!

Perhaps it was because of my connection with Delroy's wider 'in-law family' that my then, still outstanding, car loan application with the university was beneficially affected, as far as its related legalities were concerned. That was because the lawyer whom UWI employed in Bridgetown (to draw up the contract with the lecturer in question, who was to repay the required loan by regular deductions from his or her monthly salary), was none other than one 'Mr Colin Williams, Attorney-at-Law' – the brother of Delroy's father-in-law! I well remember regularly contacting Mr Cooke, at his Campus Finance Office, by phone most weekdays, to see how my loan application was then proceeding. On one of those occasions, out of exasperation perhaps, he responded by saying that the application still had to be drawn up by UWI's lawyer 'in town'. When I asked him who that lawyer was, and he told me that it was Mr Colin Williams, I was able to retort that I had already met Mr Williams - at a recent family barbecue hosted by my colleague in the Law Faculty, Delroy Chuck. I added that I knew the Bridgetown Attorney was a sort of 'uncle-in-law' to Mr Chuck and was sure that Mr Williams would wish to help me speed things up, if at all possible. As a result of that discussion, Mr Cooke asked me to leave matters with him, and he would try to set up an appointment for me to visit Mr

Williams, in Bridgetown, as soon as possible. Within a day or two, I received a call from Mr Cooke asking me to go to see the Bridgetown lawyer, at his office, the next morning (the address and time for which he also gave me).

I was happy to see Mr Williams the next day, and to have some small talk with him about his extended family prior to signing the necessary paperwork for UWI – that is to say, for Mr Cooke - to be willing to release the necessary funds to me for my new car. In fact, what happened was not that Mr Cooke actually put a bundle of Barbados dollars into my hands and say: 'Now go and get your car'. Rather, he authorised me to go out and look for a car, from among the several dealers in Bridgetown, up to a certain maximum amount – and then, when I had found the model I wanted, to ask the dealer to contact him at UWI for the release of the funds from the university to the dealer, directly. That latest communication with Mr Cooke, thus, ushered in an exciting time for Philomena and myself as *émigrés* to Barbados. For it meant that we could choose a brand-new car for ourselves – for the first time in our lives – from among a number of different brands of automobile which were to be found on the island, including 'Ford', various Japanese *marques* such as 'Toyota' and 'Suzuki' and, perhaps, even the more up-market 'Mercedes'! When we began our search in earnest, however, and started to phone around a variety of dealers to find out whether they had any new cars for sale in stock (and, if so, which models), Philomena and I were to be in for quite a shock. Nearly all of them told us that they had a waiting list for new cars – and because such vehicles only came by ship to Barbados, about once every three or four months, our waiting time might be as long as that or even greater!

Philomena and I soon agreed that we certainly could not wait as long as another quarter of a year for a car. Even after our first few weeks without one, we had found it almost impossible to get around - as a family unit. I was still dependent on Velma to take me to work at UWI, and bring me home again, each day and even doing a social thing like attending Delroy's family barbecue had necessitated Delroy himself having to come to pick us up in his own vehicle at Hygeia and delivering us back again after the outing. Accordingly, something had to be done to remedy the situation – even taking a step which might, with hindsight, prove to be rather unwise. That is where 'Simpson Motors of Bridgetown' came into the picture. For that dealers, exceptionally, did have some new cars in stock – namely, a number of 'Skoda' models made in the 'Czechoslovakia' (as it then was). Back in England (and even in 'West Germany', where the 'Best Man' at our wedding, 'Berndt Schuhmacher', and his family lived), people made fun of that 'Czech' vehicle brand, since it was, in Western European eyes, regarded as being one of the worst make of cars in the world! Owing to Philomena and myself being so desperate for our own family's transportation means, however, the two of us bit the bullet and agreed to acquire, a readily available, one for our family!

I knew that Berndt would 'laugh his head off' when he found out which brand of vehicle I was voluntarily choosing for my family's car. In order to stave off some of his future ribbing, therefore, I went for the 'top of the range' Skoda model which Simpsons had on offer – something called the '120 LS'. The 'LS' part might have been short for the German (and perhaps Czech) word '*luxus*', which means 'luxury'. Certainly, the car looked (and even smelt) nice enough. It was brand new, after all – with four doors, front seats which had headrests, and fitted out with interior upholstery which was velvety and black. The exterior of the vehicle was even painted in a nice shade of lime-green! That had been the only colour, of the 120 LS model, immediately available at the time – but it suited Philomena and myself, since the first car we had ever bought, second-hand, back in our Cambridge days, had also been a green one. However, the fact that that first vehicle of ours, which we had named 'Noddy',[15] had often broken down on us, whilst we had owned it, should have been something of a warning sign to the two of us.

In fact, Simpson Motors also represented a brand of car manufacturer from Japan named 'Suzuki'. And, it so happened, that the dealer also had a few new models of a brand of Suzuki vehicle called the 'Carry'. That model, however, seemed to me to be little more than a box on wheels – with windows on its four sides. Moreover, although there were more colours available in that make, such as 'Cambridge blue' or the more ubiquitous white, I just could not see myself driving my family around the island in such a vehicle, which rather reminded me of a van or even a little bus. I was confirmed in my rejection of that, only other, choice of new vehicle available to me from Simpson Motors at the time, when - a day or two after choosing our Skoda - I saw my near-neighbour at the Faculty, Peter Maynard, drive into its car park in his new, light-blue, little bus! The fact that he was a tall man, seemingly having to hunch himself up in order to fit behind the driving wheel of his van, made the scene all the more amusing to me.

The day came for me to actually pick up my family's new 'limousine' from Simpsons. Perhaps, it had been Velma who had shuttled me to those dealers – for one last time in her own car. As I write this, it has suddenly come back to me that Velma's car was a Skoda too – but an older model and much different in shape from the one I was about to pick up. Gingerly, I drove my 120LS out of the showroom area of the dealers, situated on the northern edge of the city, and into the very busy late afternoon 'rush hour' traffic. It had been the first time I had ever driven a car on the island – although I had rented a small motor bike, to get Philomena and myself around, during our honeymoon three years before.[16] I was struck immediately with the feeling that the roads in Barbados were really very narrow – much too slender, practically, for two-way traffic, which included some wide public buses which often passed me by, heading in the opposite direction. I was determined, however, to get the car and myself safely past 'Government House', then down 'Pine Road, Belleville', around the expansive 'Garrison Savannah' racecourse, and, finally, on to the coast road called Highway 7. It would only be a matter of another two miles, or so, along that road, away from the Bridgetown direction, that a special lady would see her new present. For, the date was 5th September 1979 – Philomena's 27th birthday!

And, boy, did we have a happy birthday outing in our new car – once I had brought it safely home to Hygeia. I was so very proud, and delighted, to take my wife and our children 'out' for the first time – 'as one unit' - in our very own car. I could see that Philomena was joyful too – and it was, perhaps, the first time since we had arrived on the island that she could imagine our little family ever being successful in 'making a go of it' in our new life in that new country of ours. Not that we went very far that evening. Rather, we simply drove about a mile or two away, in the direction of Bridgetown, then turned left from Highway 7 and into a crescent-shaped beachside road named 'St Lawrence Gap'. That road, in fact, was the very one where my wife and I had spent the Barbados leg of our honeymoon trip some three years before. We had stayed in a small hotel, located right on the beach, called 'Sandhurst' - as I recounted in *Fledging and Learning to Fly*.[17] I suppose that we went back to that location for Philomena's birthday celebration because both of us wanted to feel a sense of nostalgia that particular evening. Not that we actually ventured inside the 'Sandhurst Hotel' itself. Rather, we simply stayed a few 'doors' away, at a beachside bar which sold basic meals – such as fried 'flying fish' and rice - as well as the rum punches that we both liked, in addition to something suitably 'soft' for our eldest son, Noel. Moreover, with our younger son, Kim, already pre-fed with breast milk and settled before we set out from home in our new car, I was a contented man as I sat at our table surrounded by my 'birthday girl' and our two little sons – just a few yards from the calm Caribbean Sea. On that occasion, as I looked at the happy face of my wife, I surely would have said something to her along the lines of: 'I never would have believed, during our honeymoon, as we swam on this very beach, that just a few years later we would be back here again – living, long-term, in this country, with our two lovely young sons, our new car and possessing our large, comfortable, home just a mile or so from this place. Let us both never fail to praise the Lord for the good fortune that He has bestowed on us'.

And give thanks to the Almighty, Philomena and I certainly did - and often - in those early days of ours living at Hygeia, in Maxwell. That is because we were able to do so quite easily thanks to another piece of good fortune or, perhaps, another example of 'Divine Providence'. For, within a day or two of our first moving into Hygeia, we had asked Mrs Payne if she happened to know whether there was a Roman Catholic church nearby where we could attend Mass on a Sunday. To our great surprise, she told us that, although she herself was not a Catholic, she well-knew that there was indeed one, just two blocks (or 'gaps') away along Highway 7 in the Bridgetown direction! That would have meant just a short walk there for us – of no more than about 10 minutes, or the same sort of time as it would take us to walk to Maxwell Beach. I merely needed, then, to find out what time the Mass was held on a Sunday. Furthermore, on the day before our attending our first one whilst living in Hygeia, when I made the recce myself, on foot (since we still had no car in those very first days), I discovered that the church was called 'St Dominic's' and that the family service there began at 10am on the Sabbath.

In addition, I found the church to be a very modern-looking one, built 'in the round' and, thus, somewhat like a mini version of Liverpool's RC Cathedral back in England (which latter celebrated edifice had only been completed, just over 10 years before, in

1967). Unlike that Merseyside Cathedral situated in Philomena's native city, however, St Dominic's was built somewhat like a theatre - in that you entered it at street level and, then, you had to look down a gentle slope in order to see the 'stage', or altar, below. During that first visit, I also discovered that the parish priest of 'our' new church was also somewhat 'modern'. That was because he turned out to be a young man, of not more than about 30 years old. The astonishing thing for me, however, in that Caribbean setting, was that he was a blond, White man! More curious still was the fact that he spoke to me with an immediately recognisable American accent. He was quick to tell me that his name was 'Father Daniel Gennerelli', but that he preferred to be called 'Father Dan'. He was also keen to find out my own name, as well as my background. He seemed very pleased to discover that I was new to the island, had a wife from England as well as two young sons, and that I was a Law lecturer at UWI. I might have guessed, from his interest in me on that very first occasion, that he was already thinking ahead about how I, and my wife perhaps, might be 'of service' in the general life of his parish!

In those earliest days 'before the car' – or 'BC', perhaps – something else memorable happened to us. It occurred during the second weekend of our time at Hygeia. That unforgettable episode was the arrival of a hurricane. Reportedly, no such major storm had passed so close to Barbados for decades - let alone actually hit the island. Within 10 days or so of our moving into Hygeia, however, one such tropical tempest was announced, heading westwards across the Atlantic from Africa. During the 'Hurricane Season' each year, from about June to November, Barbados is a potential target for such violent cyclonic events since it is the first island, among those in the Caribbean, which is due west from that continent. In that particular instance, however, the most amazing thing of all, to me, was the moniker that was given to the superstorm – namely, 'Hurricane David'! I was to joke, afterwards, that, when my mother, back in England, eventually heard about the terrifying storm menacing Barbados, she was to remark to her friends: 'Fancy my son going all that way with his family, only to be injured, or worse, by his namesake hurricane!'.

The other main woman in my life, Philomena, had also been extremely worried about the coming tropical cyclone – owing to the announcements made during Barbados radio and television broadcasts, for at least several days before the estimated time of arrival of the 'eye of the storm' (or its centre). Given my contrary personality, however, I was positively looking forward to its appearance. For, even as a young boy growing up in Montserrat in the 1950s and early '60s,[18] my appetite for hurricanes had been whetted by my great-grandmother, 'Joanna', who used to tell me about the awful ones which she had 'survived' on that island in bygone years – ones which had, indeed, even killed some of her fellow countrymen and women! None, however, had come to Montserrat whilst I had lived there, and I really wanted to experience one - at least once in my life. Hurricane David seemed to me, therefore, specially sent by God for me to have my own personal wish come true – even though I also realised that it would pose a grave danger to human life, and property, if it actually impacted on the island. I tempered my potentially 'destructive thoughts' with the more soothing ones arising from the fact that, the day before it was actually due to arrive, local broadcasters on radio and television were saying that the eye would not pass over Barbados after all, but, rather, only at a distance out to sea – and, thus, the island would only receive a lesser sideswipe from the hurricane and not the full force of damage which it otherwise might have sustained.

And so, it came to pass. Philomena insisted on our two children sleeping with us both, in our master bedroom, on the night when Hurricane David came a-calling. For herself, she might really have preferred to have tried to sleep under our bed. For the sake of showing a brave face to Noel, however, she stayed within the covers on top of it, with our elder son between the two of us, for his safety. We also brought Baby Kim beneath the sheets too, rather than leave him alone in his cot - for there had seemed little chance that Philomena would sleep at all that night and, thereby, risk lying on top of him. I, too, heard the wind start up around the expected 'calling hour', as well as the storm's heavy rains 'power-washing' the external walls of Hygeia. I had felt secure in our large stone house, however - but I did spare a thought or two for the not-so-lucky neighbours in the gaps nearby, who lived in much smaller, wooden homes, with galvanised roofs. Some of those buildings, I had imagined, would surely have been damaged - even if islanders, generally, were being spared the full force of David. However, owing to the fact that I had felt safely cocooned in our sturdy home, I missed most of the worst aspects of the storm in our neighbourhood – by, against my own desire, simply falling asleep!

After waking up early the next morning, after I had got out of bed, I noted that Philomena and the boys were all still fast asleep. The storm had passed and all was eerily quiet outside. When I looked out of the exterior door to our room, which led to the balcony, what a view met my eyes! Coconut fronds, and branches of other trees, were to be seen everywhere – not only in the garden of the modern house next door but also in the middle of Highway 7, among other places. Unsurprisingly, there was very little traffic to be seen on that main road, and what few vehicles did brave an appearance proceeded along the thoroughfare very gingerly and at very low speeds. As silently as possible, I got dressed quickly and went downstairs, out of our kitchen door, and around the side of the house to Mrs Payne's 'front door'. There were a few branches broken off the 'shaddock' (or grapefruit-like) tree which grew above the laundry-outhouse in our garden, but I would have ignored those during my errand. I just had to make sure that our old lady, nearest neighbour, had, like my own nuclear family, survived the storm in one piece. To my relief, I found her to be perfectly fine. Indeed, I even discovered that she was a little like me - in wondering what all the doom and gloom had been about beforehand. She proceeded to tell me that she had lived a long time on the island, and had witnessed several such tempests. She added that she thought that what David had brought in its wake,[19] during the night just passed, was 'nothing special'. In fact, she concluded our brief conversation by telling me that she had a young relative staying with her to make sure that she would be alright during the storm – a great-niece called 'Sandra'.

Consequently, I was soon able to leave Mrs Payne, with confidence about her ongoing safety, and return to my own family in our part of the house. There, I gently woke Philomena and told her that I had been to visit our elderly neighbour and had found her safe and sound. I then asked her to take a look, from our balcony, to see some of the damage which I had previously witnessed. She was, evidently, rather shaken by what she saw outside. Moreover, she might even have immediately said a silent prayer of thanks to the Almighty that the effects of the hurricane had not been worse for us and our little boys (still sleeping in our bed), and that all four of us, and our home, had all come through it unscathed. Not too long afterwards, our telephone rang. It was Velma Abrahams. She had called to tell me that Cave Hill Campus, like most schools and other educational establishments on the island, was closed for the day because of the hurricane. Accordingly, she was letting me know that she would not be stopping by to give me a lift to work in her car, as usual – it being a weekday. I thanked her for her contact and news, and immediately made plans with Philomena to go out, after breakfast on my unexpected 'holiday', to view some of the damage caused by David. We needed to get some shopping for the house in any case, so we decided that we, and our boys, would take the bus to the 'Supercentre' supermarket in Oistins.

After our two sons had woken up and we had fed them as well as ourselves, we took them out to the bus stop, across the road from our house on Highway 7, and waited for a public conveyance, which plied that route, to come along. There was still very little traffic on the road, even though it was already mid-morning by then. A 'Barbados Transport' bus, painted in the usual blue and yellow livery of the island's flag, did eventually come along, from the Bridgetown direction, heading to Oistins. As we drove slowly along - after our family had boarded - I could hardly believe my eyes. For not only was the Caribbean Sea still raging in the aftermath of the storm on our right-hand side, but it was also splashing over the sea wall and into the road that we were passing along. Moreover, it was no longer its usual blue colour but, rather, it had become an angry grey-black one and was actually depositing sand, from the beach, into the middle of the highway. Those shore side deposits had slowly accumulated during the previous hours and our bus was forced to make its way to Oistins in an extremely cautious fashion - in order to avoid hitting random piles of former-beach, or other vehicles trying to do the same thing. Rather than being worried by the spectacle, however, I was somewhat elated. For, at long last, I was witnessing, 'live and in full technicolour', something of the power of a hurricane. Furthermore, even though what I was seeing was only the after-effects of David, and it had not even hit the island as forcefully as it might have done, I could then see, for myself, something of the work of one of the most powerful 'forces of nature'. Accordingly, I told Noel to make sure that he took a good look out of the windows of the bus at the raging sea, the branches of trees which had been forcefully broken off and strewn all along our route, the sand building up in the middle of the highway from the beach, and so on. As I went on to explain to him: he had to try to 'take it all in' that morning because hurricanes only usually struck a Caribbean island, such as the one we were then living on, extremely rarely and, therefore, he may never live to see another one. Even though he was still not yet two years old, he seemed to understand what I was trying to impress upon him, and to grasp something of the importance of the events that we were witnessing from the vantage point of our bus. At the very least, he seemed to clearly appreciate why it was that we would not be going swimming in the sea that day or, perhaps, for the next few days ahead.

Within a short time afterwards, however, our family's life, and our spending a large part of it on our local beach, had returned to normality. Hurricane David had passed on - to wreak havoc in some of the more northerly islands of the Caribbean and even reach as far as the southern states of America. It had even caused loss of human life in its wake - so Barbados, and our own family living in it, had indeed been lucky. By the time we had acquired our car on Philomena's birthday a week or so later, the Caribbean Sea had returned to its normal calm and translucent blue. We were therefore ready to explore some of the other coastlines on the island, other than our own at Maxwell, in our family's Skoda. As a result, that was the period in which we first discovered 'Oistins Beach'.

That discovery was made just after our possessions, which had been sent by sea through a firm of international forwarding agents in Leeds, had arrived in Barbados and my new university had arranged for them to be delivered from the port in Bridgetown to our home at Hygeia. It had been exciting to open the many 'tea chests', containing our stuff, and unearthing familiar things again such as our crockery, pots and pans and other household items which we had last seen at our old house in Yorkshire, England. Also delivered to our home were my Law books from my former office at Leeds University as well as my bicycle (with its basket still intact on its front handlebars), which I had used to get to work from our home in Leeds to my former Law Faculty in that city. I could see straight away that, given the 10-mile distance or so from Hygeia to Cave Hill in the neighbouring parish, as well as the awfully narrow and busy Barbados roads, I would never be able to replicate that feat at my new university. Moreover, the item I most wanted to retrieve from our newly arrived possessions had nothing to do with the Law, or my means of transport to my new Faculty to teach that subject. Rather, it was an inflatable boat – the very one which Philomena and myself had taken to Greece and back, on my rucksack, when we had still been students in the summer of 1974!

We had only ever used that yellow-coloured inflatable that one summer. Indeed, despite travelling to, perhaps, 10 or more countries during that particular vacation, we had only used it once or twice – namely, in the warm, blue waters of the Ionian Sea whilst staying on the island of Corfu.[20] In those early September 1979 days, however, I really wanted to repeat the 1974 Greek island experience – but with my two young sons as our rubber boat's passengers, instead of just my then fiancée and myself – in the similarly tepid waters of the Caribbean.

Accordingly, with our newly-arrived inflatable, our family set off to Oistins Beach in our car one fine day during that birthday month of Philomena, Noel and myself.

We had been tipped off by Mrs Payne about how good that beach would be for small children - or by her great-niece, Sandra, who was becoming a regular visitor to our elderly neighbour and whom we were all starting to get to know quite well (as well as Sandra's daughter, 'Abigail', who was about five years old at the time). Whoever it was who gave us the useful advice about the new beach, however, find it we did - and Philomena and I were delighted with that discovery. That is because it was situated in a half-moon shaped bay – a crescent of extremely shallow water, for at least 50 yards or so out to sea, which was gently lapping where it met the fine, golden sand of the beach. As there were no big waves in that little bay, it was, therefore, an extremely safe place to allow our boys to play on the sand near the water's edge – or to allow Noel to venture in and out of the sea by himself, with his armbands on of course, whenever he wished to do so. Baby Kim, too, could easily be taken into the water (in his own armbands also) by his mother or myself and was able to start trying to stand up, by himself, in the shallow water - buoyed up by his water wings as well as by the salinity of the sea beneath him.

*Fig 19: Noel and Kim at Oistins Beach – within a few months of the family first arriving in Barbados in the late summer of 1979. In the background can be seen the calm and shallow Caribbean Sea – which made it a very safe place for the boys to wander into, and out of, the waves easily*

What I most wanted to do, however, was to get my sons afloat - inside the boat itself – and then to gently take them out, little by little, into the deeper waters of the bay. Naturally, I had to inflate the craft first and, unfortunately, I had mislaid the foot pump, way back in 1974, and had never replaced it. It was, thus, extremely hot work trying to get the boat seaworthy, by blowing it up using just my breath, and doing so in the Bajan sunshine. That rather negative and exhausting experience led me, at the end of playing with the inflated boat that first time, to deflate it again only as much as was absolutely necessary to be able to squeeze it back into our car for the journey back home to Hygeia. Before that, however, I set about gently launching my newly-discovered, and re-inflated, craft into the waters of Oistins Bay with my elder son on board and with its two red, plastic oars (with their wooden handles) inserted into the holes, or 'rowlocks', on each of its sides. Noel quickly took to the new toy - and to the rowing action which I showed him how to perform - like a duck to water. I tied a piece of cord to the craft's bow, so that it would not drift away from me with him inside. In addition, when I was perfectly satisfied that my elder son had mastered the skill of keeping the inflatable perfectly stable, and with Philomena's prior agreement, I lifted his baby brother inside the boat too – at the farthest end away from where Noel was sitting. Then I was able to pull them round, gently by the cord, in a circular motion – with Noel interrupting his rowing actions whilst I did so. Both boys seemed to love the sensation of floating on the water in 'their boat' and their enjoyment delighted me also. It had been, I thought, well worth carrying the inflatable thing half-way round Europe some five summers before for its 'test-sailings', and to keep it afterwards, just in order to experience a moment such as the one I was having then.

What a pity, therefore, that the joy of my family's adventures with our very own watercraft was not to become a permanent feature in our lives. For, either because of its age, or because of the damage caused by transporting a half-inflated craft from home to the bay and back each time we used it, it developed a series of punctures very quickly after its first launch at Oistins Beach. So many small holes, indeed, that I soon decided that it had become irreparable and had to be discarded. Such a setback to one of my expectations, however – which had been realised, if only for a short time – did not prevent us from enjoying our newly-discovered bay, and attached beach, for many a month into the future. More than that, Oistins Bay, and its golden sands, were located about half-way to another wonderful place of happiness, and family diversion – which 'other place' we nearly always visited, in our car, after finishing our sea-bathing at the first.

That other special location was at the back of the place where we had first arrived, as a family, just one month or two before – namely, Seawell Airport, or Grantley Adams International (as it was to be re-named at about the time of which I am writing). Our clan called that new area of our special delight 'the Back of the Airport', simply. For, it was situated directly across from the main terminal buildings, and on the far side of its two runways. But to get to 'our' special area took some finding - initially. That was because one could not reach it by proceeding to the terminal building first. Rather, at least one mile beforehand, on the main road from Oistins to the airport – that is to say, on another part of Highway 7 (which began in Bridgetown and proceeded right past our Hygeia home on its way further south and east to Oistins and beyond) – one had to make a turning on the right side of the road. That diversion was sign-posted to the village of 'St Christopher'. By driving down that very small road towards, and then passing through, the named village - with its sparsely numbered, and diminutive, chattel houses (and, sometimes, one or two of their inhabitants to be seen inside or nearby, as well as plenty of the brown-coloured sheep which they often kept and which always looked more like goats to me) - eventually, one would arrive at the Back of the Airport. The distance from the main road to that happy place, where we would park up and exit our car, was perhaps a good mile, or perhaps nearer two. It was, however, a haven of peace there - in total contrast to what one might imagine was going on across the two runways which we could see before us, at the front of the terminal, with its many departing and arriving passengers, their well-wishers, the taxi drivers, porters, immigration staff and the like - all of whom were located less than a quarter of a mile away!

In fact, however, our family did not always find itself alone at that special place for us. For we always parked our Skoda in a small cutting, off the road from St Christopher village, in which stood a building with a name on its roof which stated something like 'Barbados Aero Services'. By the time my little family had been going to our familiar parking area for a while, we would come to see that the building was sometimes used by young men – dressed in the white shirt, and black trousers, of pilots. And although we never became friends, or even acquaintances, with any of those professional-looking people, they all seemed to tolerate our presence and, perhaps, at least some might have been sympathetic to the reason Philomena and I were bringing our small children to that place. Most of the 'pilots' were White, but there was the odd brown man (but never a woman) among their number. Over time, I came to the conclusion that the individuals in question were not part of any flight crew of the big international carriers that came from England or USA, such as British Airways or 'American Airlines', for example. Rather, I surmised that they flew the very small planes which were kept in several hangars nearby – perhaps, in order to provide charter flights to neighbouring Caribbean islands, or even to South America.

What was it, one might well ask, that kept my family returning to the Back of the Airport? The answer is: simply to watch different types of aircraft both taking off and landing. For, having now travelled on board an aeroplane himself - all the way from London to our new island home not more than a few months before - it seemed to me that Noel had become very much intrigued by such craft. His interest was further boosted by the fact that the flight path of, for example, the British Airways' 'Jumbo Jet' - and its counterparts in several American airline companies which flew into Barbados on almost a daily basis - was directly over Oistins Bay. Thus, such huge, noisy, planes would fly, quite low, right over our heads at the beach there. In other words, immediately above where we might have been having our sea baths not more than five minutes or so before the super large craft in question landed at the international airport – which was situated less than five miles to the east of where we then were.

Accordingly, it almost seemed to be my duty to try to develop my elder son's interest in aeroplanes even further, by Philomena and myself taking him, and his little brother, to our special Back of the Airport place in order to get as close to those 'big birds in the sky' as we could – once they had landed, or just before they took to the skies again. It rather enriched our post-swimming routine that Noel's father rather liked 'plane spotting' too - and that his mother really did not mind such large aircraft, whilst baby Kim seemed, over time, to develop a similar fascination with such 'flying machines' which his elder brother almost seemed to be born with!

For myself, I preferred to watch the take-off phase of the larger planes, such as the 'Jumbos'. That is because the procedure gave us all the opportunity to see an elaborate set of operations unfolding before our eyes - at length, and in almost slow motion. That included our being able to witness the passengers walking out of the terminal building across the runway and then going up one, or other, of the two sets of stairways outside the plane before disappearing into its belly. Eventually, we would see each of the two doors, to the interior of the craft, close and each of the stairways then driven away by the truck it was respectively attached to. After that, we would see a very odd-looking, and squat, vehicle go to the front landing wheel of the plane, become attached to it, and thereafter slowly push the plane straight back from its parking bay at the terminal until it reached the first of the two main runways. At that point, the odd-looking 'pusher' vehicle would stop and then detach itself from the aircraft. Once the former vehicle was clear of the plane and on its way back towards the terminal building, we would be able to hear the jet engines of aircraft rev up to a sustained and high volume as it slowly turned 90 degrees left, from facing the terminal, and into the direction of the runway itself. Its front would then be directed, roughly, towards Oistins as the crow flies. Remaining stationary, in such a new location and direction, for about one minute, we all could then see the plane very slowly, and even somewhat ponderously, taxi down the runway for several minutes until it came to the very end of the strip. I say 'end', but, in fact, there was no buffer, as such – for, rather than terminate, the dead-straight runway transformed into a curve which the craft would slowly navigate around until it reached the other strip connected to the other side of the bend. It was at this point that Noel, egged on by myself admittedly, would become very excited. For the plane would stop, just for a moment or two, and put its engines into full throttle. Then, as if releasing its brakes, it would begin to hurtle down the new runway in the direction opposite to that which it had come down the first one. As it did so, Philomena and I would join Noel in chanting, loudly, so as to be able to hear one another over the roar of the plane's engines: 'Faster! Faster! Faster!'. Within, perhaps, 20 to 30 seconds after it had started its acceleration down the take-off runway, and was just passing the point where we were nearest to it, we would be able to see it leave the ground. 'Up in air!' was then our repeated refrain, as the craft would soar away from us into the blue Bajan skies, taking up the wheels of its landing gear as it did so.

Soon, we would do the same thing for every take off which we witnessed from our Back of the Airport place of wonder – usually with me holding our baby son in my arms, and bouncing him gently during the 'Faster! Faster!' and 'Up in the air' phases (which he quickly grew familiar with and seemed to love). Little did I know then that, slowly but surely, I was turning my two young sons into aeroplane-mad little boys – who might one day wish to become airline pilots themselves!

*Fig 20: Philomena (holding Kim) as they, and Noel, watch a 'TriStar' jet (belonging to 'British West Indian Airways', or 'BWIA') take off from the 'Back of the [Grantley Adams International] Airport' within the first year of the family's arrival in 1979*

*Fig 21: Philomena and Kim, as the latter watches a 'Jumbo' jet (belonging to 'Air Canada') land at the 'Back of the [Grantley Adams International] Airport' within the first year of the family's arrival in 1979*

*Chapter 5*

# Preparation for Entry into the classroom at Cave Hill Campus

Once our family had acquired its new car and we had achieved our independence in transportation, I started driving myself in the Skoda to my office at Cave Hill Campus each weekday morning during that September. For, as much as I loved my domestic bliss at home, and going to Oistins Beach and the Back of the Airport with my wife and children (especially at weekends), I was also very much preoccupied by the main reason that I was in Barbados – at least, as far as the University of the West Indies was concerned. That, of course, was to teach the Law to several groups of undergraduates at the Faculty of that name. Accordingly, I was most mindful of the fact that I had to 'get my act together' before my students arrived - at the end of that month, or the beginning of October – or, at least, have my lecture and tutorial notes written, and put into an orderly form.

To help me get both physically and mentally into shape for the challenges ahead at Cave Hill, I took up running again with much enthusiasm. That was something which I had not done since my last cross-country race for my old school in Swindon when I was 18 years old – an event which I wrote about in *Swimming without mangoes*.[21] In those bygone days, however, I used to run five or more miles during a race. Throughout the September 1979 weekdays in question, however, I merely had to 'jog' to the end of one of the roads on which Hygeia was situated, namely Maxwell Coast Road. Even then, I did not extend myself to the entirety of the crescent-shaped thoroughfare, but only as far as where it curved left towards the Welcome Inn Hotel – a distance of not even a quarter of a mile. Half a mile, there and back - if I choose to be generous with the ground distances involved. However, it was not a case of my being lazy, in setting out for my run each weekday morning from home. For I still had more exercise ahead of me, after reaching the curve at the bottom of my coast road – namely, a type of exertion which involved using the amenity at the end of that thoroughfare.

For such other endeavour was the part of the early morning outing which I was most looking forward to. It was to have a swim in the Caribbean Sea at Maxwell Beach - just as the sun was coming up, or just after it had already risen, at about 6am. The gentle run down to the seashore from home, therefore, was just my idea of how to warm my muscles up – prior to whipping off my shorts and then plunging into the salt water in just my swimming trunks. The only other item which I needed as I left home, therefore, was a small towel - with which to dry myself after the swim. That early morning dip, however, would be like no ordinary entry into the sea thus far in my life. For, along with it, I needed to have a structure attached, in order for such activity to be counted as 'exercise' - in my mind, at least. Accordingly, on that first September morning on which I underwent my new 'regime', I swam out to sea, from where I had left my towel on the beach, for a distance of 100 yards, or so. At that point, I turned left and into the direction of the rising sun, before swimming parallel to the beach in the direction of Oistins and with my back to Bridgetown. I was then heading towards an outcrop of rocks, which was man-made and which had been so situated to act as some sort of breakwater to stop the sand on Maxwell Beach from being slowly washed away. At any rate, such promontory was a fair distance away – perhaps as much as 400 yards from the point at which I had turned left after setting out from the beach.

I soon found that by the time I had swum to, or rather near, the outcrop and then swam back to the start of my turn, before returning to the beach to retrieve my towel and dry myself, I had done more than enough morning's exercise to satisfy myself. Consequently, I quickly discovered that the amount of effort involved, and the time it took - in swimming my self-imposed 'work-out' course each day - very much depended on how calm the sea was on any particular occasion. If benign, I would be able to swim the distance in question very easily and, perhaps, be back inside Hygeia, and hungry for my pre-drive-to-Cave Hill breakfast, within half an hour of first leaving home just before sunrise. However, if the sea was choppy, I could find myself already quite exhausted - after only completing the first leg, to reach my turning point near the rocky outcrop. I would, however, always persevere and swim back to my starting point – but, on such occasions, I might be up to 30 minutes later in getting back home compared to the much better timeliness which I achieved on the more usual calm mornings. Despite the variations in daily sea conditions, however, during that first September in Barbados, and in the immediately following months of my initial term at Cave Hill, I religiously followed my jogging and swimming regime. That routine, I felt sure at the time, put me in good stead for my being able to tackle the challenges ahead of firstly, preparing for, then facing, and thereafter continuing with, my first classes of UWI Law students.

There was one other factor which helped me to so organise myself during the period in question. That was the presence, on the Law Faculty scene, of an individual male who was about 10 years older than myself. His name was 'Peter'. Like me, he had just arrived at UWI, from an English university, to teach Law for the first time at Cave Hill and was feeling, perhaps, somewhat like a 'fish out of water' or, at least, very much a 'new boy'. Unlike me, however, he was contracted to be at UWI for one academic year only – as he had merely 'swapped' places with a Senior Lecturer, with tenure, in my new Law Faculty for the 12 months in question. Peter, whose surname was 'Morton', was such a senior teacher at Birmingham University, in England's second largest city, and Tony Bland, whose Conflict of Laws course I would be teaching in Tony's place for one academic year, had gone over to Birmingham to substitute for Peter's role there for that period.

Peter would, thus, be taking over Tony's other main course at Cave Hill – which was the 'Law of Trusts'. When I first met Peter (perhaps in the 'Senior Common Room', or 'SCR', of the campus, which is where we both usually went for lunchtime sandwiches and soft drinks) he was to give me the foregoing short account of why he was then present at UWI. He was to also tell me that he was rather worried about what he had to teach, since he would somehow have to adapt his English legal materials to suit the needs of the West Indian undergraduates whom he would soon be teaching. I informed him that such a situation was also my difficulty - exactly! Thus, it was probably because Peter and myself found ourselves in similar 'boats' at Cave Hill, that we seemed to hit it off – from the first.

*Fig 22: Photo of Peter Morton, (one of a set of three) sent to the Author by 'Yvonne Morton' in March 2024 with the words: '...here are a couple of photos of Peter from our wedding in 1982 [,] so it's close to the time you wanted.'*

Peter was an Englishman. His being a White teacher did not bother me, in the least. Indeed, his race and colour were probably plus points for me, since I had just come from teaching at Leeds University and most of my former colleagues there had also been White English males! Certainly, I felt comfortable around him and he seemed to be the same with me. In many ways, he especially reminded me of a former colleague at Leeds, with whom I had become very close during my earliest days at the oldest university in that city – namely, one 'Michael Passey'. In those days, I used to spend a great deal of time in Michael's room, drinking tea with him and just talking about teaching and life in the Leeds Law Faculty, generally. And history started repeating itself with Peter, once it became clear to me that he appreciated my company after our first few meet-ups in the SCR. For, we always had our tea and chats in 'his' office – which, in fact, belonged to his fellow-Englishman, Tony Bland, and which room Peter would be occupying during Tony's absence in Birmingham. For though Tony's working quarters lacked the clear view to Bridgetown Harbour which my own afforded, it was full of books and sported a carpet on its floor. It was, thus, a much more inviting and comfortable space than my own. Accordingly, during that September, and for weeks afterwards, perhaps not even one working day went by when the two of us lecturers, with English universities experience, did not get together to share 'tea and sympathy' – once we had indulged in the same for the very first time. Moreover, I found such meet-ups to be of great help to me in settling my teaching soul into my new life at Cave Hill Campus.

It was my fellowship with Peter, perhaps, which had been the catalyst in causing me to persist with at least one of the things which I started doing from that September - namely, wear a shirt with a collar and, in addition, a tie! After all, that was what I had done every working day whilst I had been teaching at Leeds University, and it would never have occurred to me to turn up at the Law Faculty there without a 'collar and tie'. To my mind, therefore, to simply continue that process, at my new place of teaching, was simply to act 'normally'. But that was to reckon without the heat of the Barbados sun – especially in the middle of the day – not to mention the teasing nature of my lecturer colleagues in the faculties of Law and other subjects, at the Cave Hill Campus of UWI - particularly those who frequented the SCR, each lunchtime, to eat, drink and/or play cards or dominoes. Those, mainly male, colleagues used to gently tease me, at first, for being so 'over-dressed'. One of those, who always engaged in all three or four said activities in the SCR, was a senior member of the Cave Hill community whose name was 'Professor Woodville Marshall'. He was, perhaps, the Dean of the History Faculty at that time. Moreover, I soon discovered that he was a graduate of Cambridge University also – where he had obtained his Ph.D degree. To encounter him for the first time in the SCR, however, one might have thought that he had just come directly from the rum shop at the bottom of Cave Hill! He often wore a flowery, short-sleeved shirt, grey trousers and – always – a pair of sandals. No one could look more affectedly 'laid back' in my new academic community, it seemed to me. In addition, when I tried to deflect his mild criticism of my own dress sense by telling him that it might have to do with something rubbing off from my time at Cambridge – regarding which background I told him that I understood he had in common with myself, he rejected, out of hand, such sameness in front of his dominoes-playing peers at the table, by declaring: 'I tried to spend as little time as possible in Cambridge whilst "studying" there and usually got away to London on the train as often as I could'.

In Professor Marshall, therefore, I would find no soulmate for my 'Englishness'. In Peter Morton, however, I was able to do so – although he himself never wore a tie in the Bajan heat. He did, however, clothe himself in long-sleeved shirts, just like me. There was also one other thing which marked me out as 'different' in those earliest days – which Peter did not seem to particularly notice, nor comment to me on, but which colleagues, such as Professor Marshall, would no doubt have mocked me for behind my back. That was something that even Peter could not join me in - not even on a halfway house basis. It had to do with my hair. Whilst in England – certainly since the days of my marriage to Philomena – I had been in the habit of having my hair 'relaxed', chemically, to make it easier to comb and look after. In those days, that was quite a common practice among

West Indian males in Britain, particularly those living in London – and it was to London that I would go for the process, about once every three months, even whilst living in Cambridge and then Leeds. The style, which I would usually ask for, was something called a 'jerry-curl'.

When I first arrived in Barbados with my family in August 1979, I naturally wanted to continue the practice of jerry-curling my hair, in order to make it easily, and quickly, manageable - after my early morning swims - before going to work. Not surprisingly, I knew of no local hairdressers who could perform the task when we first arrived at Hygeia. I had spotted the sign for one, however, on Highway 7 - about a quarter of a mile from our home, in the direction of Bridgetown. Accordingly, one early September day, I decided to just walk into that hair studio – which was, in fact, situated in a part of a private home. To my surprise, it was staffed by a White lady, who seemed even more amazed that a Black man was coming to the establishment for her services! She had one or two other White ladies under hair dryers at the time, and they seemed equally astounded. In my naivety about the workings of the Bajan class system at that time, I politely asked the young hairdresser if she could give me a jerry-curl. After a little hesitation, during which she asked me to describe what that entailed, she agreed to perform the service for me. She duly set to work using the necessary white 'relaxer cream', and then put me in hair rollers, to be followed by a session under a dryer myself. When, eventually, she took the rollers out, the result was nothing like my usual hairstyle! Indeed, there was now not one curl in sight on my head. For my hair had become jet black - and straight as ever! It was probably too late to reverse the process, and I did not want to risk losing all my hair by the hairdresser so trying. Consequently, and perhaps unconvincingly, I thanked the lady for her services, paid her, and exited the salon as fast as I could.

Needless to say, I resolved never to go back to that particular hairdresser again – one who had probably never cut, nor treated, a Black man's hair in her life before. Meanwhile, however, I had to live with my new hairstyle – one that would take many months to grow back 'naturally' again. Fortunately, Philomena did not think it was too tragic and nor, it seemed, did my new friend and colleague at the Faculty, Peter. Certainly, he did not show any reluctance to accompany me to the SCR each weekday lunchtime - once I had turned up at the Faculty with the new hairstyle, and notwithstanding my wearing a collar and tie to boot. Looking back now, I realise that I must have 'stood out like a sore thumb' among my peers in the SCR, or even just those in the Law Faculty. I was well used to doing that, however – or being 'a sore thumb' – whether at secondary school in Swindon, England (as the first Afro-Caribbean pupil there, until my younger brothers, 'John' and 'George', also joined it in later academic years), the Leeds University Law Faculty teaching staff (as the only Black member thereof), or otherwise. However, even if I did not mind being 'noticed', I was nevertheless resolved, from my earliest days at UWI, to stand out for the right reason – namely, because I was perceived by the students to be one of the best teachers in the Law Faculty!

And suddenly, all the students arrived! They came from many corners of the

English-speaking Caribbean – and also from Guyana in South America. So, as well as local Barbadians, the largest percentage of undergraduates whom I would be teaching seem to emanate from Jamaica. The next largest group seemed to be from Trinidad and Tobago. Then came the Guyanese - as far as the numbers whom I would be teaching were concerned. There were, however, also some who came from more diminutive states or dependencies and whom persons from the aforementioned three larger territories (all of which either had their own UWI campus, or housed the University of Guyana) often amusingly called 'the small islands'. Thus, I had students visiting my office to enquire about my courses who came from 'St Lucia', 'Grenada' and 'St Kitts', among others. Alas, however, no one came to me from my own native island of Montserrat – and, indeed, I was not to discover any student anywhere at all in my new Faculty from that 'smallest of the small islands', for the whole of that first UWI academic year of mine!

The subject which I most wanted to 'sell' to my would-be students was Comparative Law, not unnaturally. For I had been recruited especially for that particular course, and the fact that I was also to be the lecturer for another Final Year course - The Conflict of Laws - was merely fortuitous (and, as seen, something which I did not even learn that I would be teaching until I had actually arrived at Cave Hill, a month or so before the start of the new academic year). What strategy, however, was I going to use to attract students in their Third (and Final) Year, to Comparative Law? That was an issue for me because any potential takers of that course would have already spent at least one academic year at Cave Hill, and would, thus, not have encountered me at all during their previous three terms (when, of course, I had still been teaching at Leeds University). Moreover, Comparative Law was an 'elective course' – one which a Final Year student studied in order to broaden his or her intellectual horizons and not simply to learn legal rules, such as those to be found in Company Law, for example. The latter subject, an ambitious young student might well think, would be a better course to sign up for since, from the expertise gained from it, he or she should be better able to 'make money', later on when they eventually qualified.

Given that I knew, from the outset of my arrival at Cave Hill, that I would be 'up against stiff competition' in the recruitment of students process - from the likes of Lurline next door and her Company Law course, or even from my old Cambridge University fellow alumnus and Lurline's neighbour on the other side of her office, Dr Peter Maynard and his Public International course - I had felt obliged to 'advertise' myself as best I could. Accordingly, during the first week of the new academic year (when the students were given their 'Freshers' week' and, therefore, had no classes as yet) I put up notices around the Faculty – and, especially, on the doors of the 'Law Library' and that leading to the entrance of the space where the secretaries and the Faculty Administrator worked. Those posters were to announce the fact that I was the new Course Director of Comparative Law – recently arrived from teaching in England at Leeds University, after having previously studied the subject in question at Cambridge University. The notice also stated that I would be in my office – Room 4 – every day for the then current

Freshers' Week, from 9am to 1pm and 2pm to 5pm, in order to meet would-be students of the course and to discuss what it would cover, teaching times and so forth.

I made sure, therefore, that despite my 'tea and sympathy' meetings with Peter Morton, and our regular lunch time trips to the SCR that week, I was always to be found in my room during the advertised times. It was an interesting 'see and be seen' interlude for me. Some students simply walked past my open door and looked in at me, with curiosity, as they passed. I was an easy target, as you had to pass my door in order to go on to other offices on the same floor as mine such as Michael Castagne's next door, or to one of those on a lower deck than my own, including Peter Morton's two levels further below. Slowly but surely, however, one or two plucked up sufficient courage to gingerly cross the threshold into my office. I remember, especially, one of the first of those brave ones being a certain 'Charles Hospedales'. I was as surprised about him, as he seemed to be about me, at that encounter. For, my having just come from Leeds University, he was not at all what I had been expecting as a typical UWI Law student. Rather, he was already a middle-aged man! He was soon to tell me, however, in his lovely lilting accent, that he was from Trinidad - a large island to the south of Barbados - and that he had, relatively recently, 'retired' from being a school teacher there! He also related that, though he had advanced in his previous career to become an headmaster, he had always hankered after becoming a lawyer, throughout his life. He concluded by divulging that now that he had reached his 'senior' age and could afford to stop teaching, he had decided to embark upon his heart's desire concerning the Law. I was delighted to meet him and I did my best to persuade him that Comparative Law was just the course for an 'academic' person like himself. I was also happy to see that, within a day or two of that first meeting, he had indeed registered for my course.

Charles may well have departed my office to start spreading the word that, despite my collar and tie and straightened hair, I had struck him as being a 'regular guy' with a passion for my subject. For, not very long after that first encounter in Room 4, I had another Trinidadian come there to see me, in order to find out more about Comparative Law. On that later occasion, it was a young woman, of a more usual Final Year student age that I had been used to at Leeds and other universities in England. She turned out to be a good friend of Charles, and, like him, seemed to be attracted by the idea that my course would look at aspects of the history of Spanish Law – which Law would have obtained in Trinidad, from the European 'Conquistadores' who had first settled in her native island and had given that territory its Spanish name. Alas, unlike the case of Mr Charles Hospedales' most memorable moniker for me, I have long since forgotten the name of his much younger, female, compatriot who was to join him in my first cohort of Comparative Law students at UWI, 1979-80.

The other Caribbean state, from which I seem to attract my first group of Comparative Law students, was Guyana. As mentioned earlier, that country is not an island but, rather, an independent nation which is part of the South American continent. Nevertheless, the Caribbean Sea lies just outside its north-eastern border and its capital, Georgetown, is, perhaps, less than one hour's flying time south of Trinidad's main metropolis, 'Port of Spain'. Historically, the territory in question once had Roman-Dutch Law constituting part of its body of governing rules and, interestingly, its neighbour, to the south, is 'Suriname' – which was formerly a colony of 'The Netherlands', and was, indeed, once known as 'Dutch Guiana'.[22] And from that South American country, I was again approached about my course, by an 'older man'. He was not as 'senior' as Charles from Trinidad – but that prospective student was somewhat older than most of his peers in the Final Year. His name was 'George' and he was, perhaps, in his mid to late-thirties. I liked him from the first, however, and he seemed to like me too. Indeed, he more or less told me that he would be registering for my course - within minutes of our first conversation - and he went on to then invite me to a 'little drinks party' that he and a few fellow-Guyanese students were holding, in their campus student accommodation, that very evening. It was, of course, in my interest to accept the kind invitation - and I happily did so!

It was at that party that I managed to 'recruit' a few more Guyanese students to join their compatriot, George, in my class. However, my first Comparative Law group was not only to be made up of 'Trinis' and Guyanese nationals. Rather, I also managed, through my 'come and talk to me in Room 4' invitation which I strategically placed around the Faculty, to attract one person from the 'Eastern Caribbean' island of St Lucia – which was not so far from either my native Montserrat or from Barbados. I still remember that student's name, also - which was 'Wilkie Larcher' - and, again, like both Charles and George, he was somewhat older than the average age of the typical Final Year student. Nevertheless, I was delighted to recruit him into the class also, since - like most St Lucians - he spoke a French patois (in addition to Standard English) and knew that his island had once been ruled by pre-Napoleonic French Law.

There were also two surprise members who signed up for my first Comparative Law class. Or, at least, a couple of students who registered for my course who were most intriguing to me, for various reasons. First, they were brother and sister. Second, they were Bajans! As mentioned earlier, most of the members of my first cohort of Comparatists seemed to come from territories which had experienced some sort of 'Foreign Law' influence. By this, I mean: countries which had some legal ancestry apart from England's 'Common Law'. Barbados, however – perhaps, more than most other Caribbean islands - only ever had English settlers. Accordingly, it was good for me to see two students wanting to come to my class not mainly because they wished to learn more about the 'exotic' background of their own nation's Laws. The biggest surprise of all, however, relating to the siblings' wish to join my Comparative Law group, was that they were White! Their names were 'John' and 'Carol Hanschell' and they were, perhaps, the only wholly-Caucasian students in the whole of the Barbados Law Faculty – and I was fortunate enough to have both of them in my class!

By the end of the Freshers' Week , therefore, I had a Comparative Law class of about 10 to 15 students. That was par for the course for me – since, even as a student at

Cambridge, my own class in that subject did not exceed that upper number (despite the fact that we were being taught by the famous 'Professor Tony Jolowicz'[23]). I was content, therefore, that I had a 'going concern', for the academic year ahead, in my pet subject. Moreover, I had managed to successfully liaise with 'Andrew Burgess', my colleague who was in charge of devising the Law Lecturers' respective timetables in the Faculty, and had been given times for my classes which I more or less wanted. Certainly, that was the case for me insofar as those included the final two hours on a Friday morning. That was because it meant that I could give my second lecture, in Comparative Law for that week, in the first hour, and then hold a seminar for the whole class in the second hour – during which we would be able to have coffee and biscuits whilst the student for the week was discussing his or her paper, with the rest of the class listening and preparing to ask him or her questions about it, in a relaxed and informal atmosphere. At the end of the second lesson, it would be lunchtime – and, as I would have no further classes for the week, the weekend could begin for me!

*Fig 23: Photo of Andrew Burgess, evidently taken when he was somewhat older than when the Author first met him in the 1979-80 academic year at UWI, Cave Hill Campus (during which period he was always bespectacled) – and after his, then youthful, black beard had turned Father-Christmas-like and he had, perhaps, progressed to wearing contact lenses*

I had no such qualms about recruiting for my Conflict of Laws classes. I had heard from Professor Georges, when he had asked me to teach the subject for the one academic year of Tony Bland's sabbatical at Birmingham University, that the subject had been very popular under Tony and that he had attracted at least 50 students in the year leading up to his sabbatical. I figured, therefore, that even if I only attracted half as many during my 'substitution' for Tony, I would still be happy enough. For I surmised that Tony could always get the numbers up again, when he returned from his sabbatical, and, whether he did so or not, it would be his course, and not mine, in any event! As I was to find out very soon, however, many of those who came to my lectures in Comparative Law would also attend my 'Conflicts' ones as well – though many that came to the latter did not also want to register for the more 'purely academic' Comparative course. Thus, when Freshers' Week was over and I went to meet both sets of students for my first class in each of the two respective subjects, I was to happily discover that I had more students than I might have expected - for each of them.

*Chapter 6*

# Commencing actual teaching at UWI

The initial Monday of my first teaching session at Cave Hill came around soon enough after the campus' Freshers' Week had ended. My 'baptism of fire' class would be that very morning in the Faculty's 'Seminar Room' - a largish space with the desks set out in the form of a rectangle - with plenty of chairs around its perimeter on three sides. I imagine that it could, perhaps, have seated 50 people at a squeeze. That first morning, however, it needed nowhere near that kind of capacity and I was perfectly content with my 10 to 15 students – older and younger – who had signed up for my course.

They all seemed happy enough to sit near to the front of the room, where I began by standing and facing them - on the side of the room without any chairs and which had a blackboard behind me. There were, however, seats on the diametrically opposite side of the room in question, where they could have 'kept their distance', if they had really wanted to. I opened proceedings by welcoming them to the class and then sent a sheet of paper around to ask them to kindly put their names down on it – including their Christian names, as I told them I wished to make the classes fun and enjoyable for them and, thus, first names terms would be the order of the day in my going forward with them. I also explained how we would next meet for a double class, every Friday, and that each student in the class would (eventually, in their allotted week) be asked to prepare a paper for discussion, during the second hour, on a topic and which I had lectured to them on, a week or so before. I made it clear that it would be worth each student's while to prepare his or her paper as well as possible, since the topic of such paper might well find itself in the examination 'Finals' at the end of the academic year. I could see my students' ears prick up at that last bit of information, and some of them even passed knowing smiles to one or other of their counterparts in the room.

Soon after my opening remarks, I began my very first lecture at Cave Hill - in earnest. I can still remember its basic details, even now. It was to explain to them what Comparative Law was all about. I wrote on the blackboard, behind me, a number of foreign words, including '*Droit comparé*', '*Derecho comparado*', and the longer '*Rechtsvergleichung*'. Many of them seemed pleasantly captivated by my familiarity with those three foreign European languages, that appeared on the board – particularly those from Trinidad where Spanish was the second language taught in schools and where Spanish-speaking 'Venezuela' was only nine miles separated from their native island, at the nearest point. Whether familiar with the words which I wrote on the board or not, I was happy to tell the whole class that each expression was the name of our present subject, respectively, in 'France' (including its overseas Caribbean 'departments' in nearby 'Guadeloupe' and 'Martinique'), 'Spain' (and in Spanish-speaking lands, and former Spanish colonies, such as Venezuela) and in West Germany. Also, that in each language in question, the words meant 'Law compared'. Thus, I was thereby able to make the crucial point that our subject was not an area of domestic Law, such Criminal Law or Contract Law. Or even a body of rules with 'foreign' components, such as is found in the Law between states in 'Public International Law', or in the domestic Law of a country dealing with civil cases containing a foreign element (which, I told the class, was the concern of my other teaching subject of Private International Law or The Conflict of Laws).

By that introduction to their new subject, I had managed to tell my first group of UWI Law students, by reference to some of its foreign names, what Comparative Law was not. I then had the rest of the lecture, however, to 'sell' to them what the subject was positively about. That included my expounding on what 'Law' it was that we were going to 'compare' during our course. It was accordingly my delight to reveal to them that the answer to that particular issue – namely, that it was up to the teacher of the class in question and his students! I told them that I had decided to compare the 'Common Law' legal systems of the world (as represented, particularly, by that of England and the English-speaking territories of the Caribbean), with that of the major countries belonging to the 'Civil Law' tradition (as represented by France and the French Caribbean territories, as well as by Spain and the many countries of nearby 'Latin America'). I was then able to reveal that whilst we would, naturally, look at the historical roots of the two major legal traditions in question, we would also spend time exploring different modern aspects of the systems. Thus, I explained that we would, for example, compare legal training in the two traditions – and see how a student became a lawyer or judge in, say, France in contrast to England or Jamaica. In addition, I disclosed that we would also devote study time examining the different types of lawyers in the two legal traditions. Not the least important of my revelations to the class, that first Monday morning, was my explaining that we would analyse, in the coming weeks, the differing approaches to what judges 'do', or are supposed to do, in the two traditions – and, for example, try to answer the question: can they 'make' Law?

I could see that most of the class had been quite happy with what I had said about my subject thus far. No one seemed, to me, to be in the room under 'false pretences', and perhaps thinking that my subject was another one of those 'get-rich-quick' courses, such as Company Law or 'Tax (or Revenue) Law'. Moreover, I had taken great pains to underline that our 'Law compared' subject was mainly an academic one – but a discipline which was worthwhile pursuing, since, by looking at other legal systems in the world, or aspects of the same, it helped a lawyer, or would-be one, to understand his or her own domestic one (in which they lived and operated) so much the better.

Finally, I was able to reveal to my students that having spent the First Term looking at aspects of the two 'Major Legal Systems' of the world, we would do a bit of micro-Comparative Law, by studying aspects of French Contract Law in some detail. Also, that we would do so by studying real French cases, often decided by the highest civil court in 'Paris', and that we would compare similar factually, and legally, problematical cases in England (or the English-speaking Caribbean territories where I could find something apposite). This would be to enable us to discover how differently such cases might have been decided.

It is quite possible that, by the end of that very first class, one or two of the students who had come to listen to me had made their respective decision that my subject was not for them. However, I cannot recall any significant loss of numbers when we met again on the Friday of that first teaching week. Charles of Trinidad, George of Guyana, John and his sister Carol from Barbados, Wilkie from St Lucia, and the majority of their would-be cohort of Comparatists, were all there for my second lecture in the subject. Indeed, there might even have been one or two new members of the class, in addition. That Friday, therefore, I was more than happy about the way my beloved subject – the one that I had applied to UWI to specifically teach – had 'taken off' under me.

What, however, of my other lecturing subject – The Conflict of Laws? It will be remembered that, though I had studied that subject at Cambridge, I had never taught it before. Moreover, I had not known that I would be asked to teach the subject until I had met Professor Georges upon my first arriving in Barbados in August 1979 – just a month or so before. Accordingly, the situation meant that, of necessity, I had a lot of lecture notes to write for that second course of mine and I decided that, given my other main duty with lecturing in Comparative Law, I would have to write my Conflicts lectures as that latter course went along.

As it happened, I had given a good deal of thought (during those post-August 1979 weeks leading up to first teaching week in October) about how to adapt the standard English text book on the subject - by the authors, 'Professors Cheshire and North', and entitled *Private International Law* - to my new Caribbean environment. I had inherited Tony Bland's worksheets – but not his lecture notes - for the Conflicts course which he had given up to the end of the 1978-79 academic year, before he had departed on sabbatical leave. From those teaching materials, I could see that there were hardly any Caribbean legal cases decided, or least reported, in our particularly exotic subject. Nevertheless, I very much wanted to start my own Conflicts lectures with a 'local' flavour - in an effort to try to capture the imaginations of my would-be students for their quaint new subject, from my very first lecture.

That initial Conflicts lecture happened to take place on a Tuesday – the day after my first, relatively-relaxed, Comparative Law debut one. I was much more nervous for that subsequent one, however, but nevertheless determined to get off to a flying start. My composure was helped, somewhat, by the lecture being assigned to take place in the Faculty's rectangular-shaped Seminar Room. I found the space, nonetheless, to be much more packed, when I walked into for that first Conflicts lecture, than it had been the previous day for my opening one in Comparative Law. Predictably, I was wearing my shirt and tie - and my hair was still as straight as the day I had walked out of my

White Bajan hairdresser's salon some weeks before, after newly arriving on the island. If some of my would-be students – who were not also part of my Comparative Law class – wanted to have an initial reason for comparing me unfavourably with Tony Bland, they did not have to look very far beyond me, standing there in front of them, during my real baptism of fire at UWI! Even so, I was determined to win any 'doubters' over when I entered the room – and was confident enough to believe that I would be able to do so.

Once more, I had to start the course by explaining what my subject was about and why, in particular, it was called by two very different names - namely, Private International Law as well as The Conflict of Laws. In doing so, I was at pains to spell out that our subject was a branch of domestic Law – and dealt with cases which came before our domestic courts which contained a 'foreign' element. I explained that it was, therefore, very different from Public International Law, which, latter similarly-named subject, governed the rules between nation states and where, in theory, there should only be one body, or set, of rules across all the countries of the world. I was then able to go on to explain that though our subject was an area of the domestic Law of each country of the world, each such state might have a different rule from others (including its nearest neighbours), for the case before its courts which contained the foreign element in question. I might well have given the example of a Barbados court being asked to rule on the age of capacity to marry, of a foreign national then currently living (from age 16) in Barbados (say, a Frenchman from nearby Martinique). In doing so, I would have pointed out that Barbados Law would say that this issue is to be determined by the Law of the country in which the man is 'domiciled' (basically, the country which the man regards as his 'home' at the time). However, French (and, thus, Martinique) Law might well, on the other hand, say that such question is to be referred to the Law of the man's nationality. Accordingly, there would be a 'conflict' in the two domestic legal systems in question – and that showed why our subject had its latter alternative name. Which Law is chosen by the Barbados court, to resolve the conflict, could be crucial for the outcome of the case - since the age of capacity might be 16 in Barbados (the Law of the man's domicile), but the later age of 18 in Martinique (the Law of his nationality). On such assumption, I would have gone on to explain to my class, if our man had undergone a marriage ceremony in, say, Venezuela at the age of 17, which Law the Barbados court applied - to determine the validity of his marriage (his nationality Law (18), or his domiciliary Law (16)) - would be crucial for its ruling on whether he was ever validly married.

For the purposes of that first Conflicts lecture, I can certainly remember drawing on my own experience in first coming to Barbados for my honeymoon with Philomena in 1976. Our flight from London had landed for refuelling, for some hours, in 'Santa Maria de Azores' – an island in the Atlantic Ocean belonging to Portugal, but nearly 900 miles west of Lisbon on the European mainland. I asked the class to imagine that I, as a British national and then resident England, had got off the plane in Santa Maria, for a few hours, had then hired a car to look around that island, and had subsequently had a road accident with a German fellow-passenger doing a similar hired-car tour, before our flight had continued on to Barbados. I asked the class to think about what Law a Barbados court should apply to the case if I sued my fellow-passenger in Bridgetown for compensation for my injuries in the crash: Portuguese (the Law of the place of the accident); English (the Law of my, the claimant's, domicile at the time); German (the Law of the defendant's nationality and domicile at the time); or even Barbados domestic Law, without any reference to its (Barbadian) Conflict of Laws rules (that is to say, the wholly domestic Law of the court)?

By the use of such examples, and without giving any immediate answers as I voiced them, I told my first class of would-be Conflicts students that those were the types of questions which would be covered during the course. In so only giving them 'part of the story', I was trying to whet their appetites for the lessons ahead in our subject. Not unnaturally, however, I also gave my students, that first Tuesday morning, the formal explanation of what our subject was about. That is to say, I explained that it always concerned cases 'containing a foreign element' and where one or more of three questions arose. Firstly, does the court have 'jurisdiction' over such a case at all? If so, what Law (whether that of the court's own country, or some other 'foreign' Law) governed the question? And, thirdly, an issue which only came up from time to time, namely the resolution of the question which asked: in what circumstances will a court recognise, and give effect to, a judgment which had been obtained abroad?

Giving that first lecture in Conflicts convinced me that I would have to work very hard, in relation to that particular course, in order to deliver it well during Tony Bland's absence. I knew, as I walked out of the Seminar Room after that first class, that whereas my Comparative Law sessions would be a great deal of 'fun', for both myself and my students – since I was determined to make it so – Conflicts was going to be mainly a lot of strenuous work, for me. Looking back, therefore, I would not be surprised if someone were to tell me now that I had even decided to skip lunch that day with Peter Morton in the SCR, for once, in order to start preparing, immediately, for Lecture 2 in the subject, which I was due to give in just two days' time.

I soon graduated to a more general, and painstaking, regime for the preparation of my classes - which was to lead to unexpected consequences. However, at the time when I began the more disciplined practice in question, I had felt myself to be extremely healthy – owing, no doubt, to my early morning runs down to Maxwell Beach and the half-hour or more swims which followed. Accordingly, as I was also in extremely good spirits, mentally, I thought nothing of the long hours I then began putting into the preparation of my lectures. In drawing up those lessons, I, naturally, concentrated on The Conflict of Laws. I would do most of the reading up, and note making, in my office - far into every weekday evening, apart from Wednesdays and Fridays. Thus, I would begin such regime on Monday afternoon, almost as soon as I had completed my Law of Torts tutorials – of which I had three different groups, for one hour each, starting from 2pm. In fact, at 5pm, when I had finished with the last of the three groups, I would make a bee line for Peter Morton's office and ask if he would like to share some tea with me. He always said 'Yes' to that invitation and immediately countered it by asking me to stay in his room to drink the pick-me-up in question and have a chat with him. I would then quickly go up a few flights of steps to the 'Faculty Kitchen' and make the hot brew for the two of us. I soon began to look forward to such a respite period with Peter, each Monday afternoon – not least because I knew that such tea (and sympathy) break would be the calm before the storm. For the 'tempest' around the corner would be the preparation, and/or polishing up, of a lecture for my 'guest teaching subject', the following morning at 11am.

Reluctantly, therefore, I would take my leave of Peter, by about 5.30pm, and repair to my own office to begin the necessary crafting process. Such 'composing' always took place in that latter venue – although, in theory, I had two realistic alternative ones. First, there was the Law Library – only a matter of about 10 to 20 yards' distance from my room. However, I ruled out that possibility, as being too busy a place for me – a location full of students, often whispering at their quietest, if they even bothered to try obeying the rules about keeping silence within the place. For Conflicts, however, I nearly always had to visit the Library at several points during my preparation evenings - in order to borrow Law reports or textbooks which I would need to help me in devising the forthcoming lecture in that subject. I could always have perused the borrowed tomes within the precincts of the Library itself. However, owing to lecturers in the Faculty having been given unlimited rights to borrow as many books as they needed from that place, I always rather preferred to fully exercise that right.

The other place where I could realistically have gone to prepare my lectures was at my own home in Maxwell. Most likely, that is what the majority of the other lecturers in the Faculty did – with the exceptions, perhaps, of just Peter Morton and myself. I ruled out such domestic preparation also, however, because, for me, as at Leeds University before I came to Barbados, 'Work' and 'Home Life' were never to be mixed. Rather, to my mind at least, 'Home' was a place strictly for its enjoyment with my family. 'Work', on the other hand, was something which I had to discipline myself to do, in a place where such discipline was rendered easier since there were no distractions, such as the 'home comforts' in the shape of my wife and my children.

Thus it was, that I would work away in my office until at least 7.30pm every Monday, Tuesday and Thursday during that First Term of mine at Cave Hill. Sometimes, I would feel obliged to go on even later to, perhaps, 9pm and, certainly, at least until I had read, and understood, the latest legal case or article on the topic for the next day's lecture (so that I could make reference to it, in the class, as necessary). Consequently, when it is remembered that dusk falls in the Caribbean by 6.30pm, if not earlier, it will be realised that I did most of my preparation with darkness outside my windows.

Finally, I would feel that I had done enough on the particular weekday evening in question and I would be able to walk out to the Faculty car park, to be reunited with my hard-won Skoda car. Often, it would be the last one remaining there – or, at least, one of only a handful (since even the small number of students who had use of a car, and who utilised the Law Library at that time of evening, were allowed to use the same space for their vehicles too). How I would greatly enjoy the drive home to my wife and children – still, at least, a 30-minute journey away in the next parish of Christ Church! During that happy journey, I by-passed Bridgetown by going through 'Eagle Hall' and skirting around about half of the circle that was the Garrison Savannah. Within 20 minutes or so, however, I would be driving along Highway 7, in my resident parish, and passing such English sounding 'villages' as 'Worthing' and 'Hastings', with the Caribbean Sea on my right. It mattered not that it was, by then, much too dark to *see* the ocean. It was enough for me, at that late hour, that I could *hear* the waves splashing on the beaches as I passed, and smell the sea air through the open windows of my Skoda. And then would occur the *pièce de résistance* of my long day: Philomena greeting me with a kiss at the kitchen entrance of our home, Hygeia, and then asking me how my day had gone.

Naturally, the other persons whom I also very much wanted to meet and greet, upon first arriving home, were our sons, Noel and Kim. However, they were nearly always already asleep - in bed and cot, respectively - owing to my late arrival home. I would still go upstairs to visit them, however, and give them each a gentle kiss - to avoid waking them. Seeing Philomena and my two little sons again, for the first time in more than 12 hours, always made me feel that the travails of my long day had been worthwhile – if only to enable me to help provide our little family with such security, and togetherness, as we were then enjoying. I would then have a quick shower in order to get rid of the detritus of the day, and afterwards rejoin Philomena downstairs in our combined kitchen/dining room to savour, with her, the supper which she would have lovingly prepared for us that evening.

Alas, after my very first Monday of such a regime, much the same would have to be repeated the following day and then every Monday and Tuesday for the rest of the term in question, and the one following. That is because, I also had to give a Conflict of Laws lecture on Thursdays at 11am. Moreover, since I had arranged my timetable so that I could have the middle day of the week without any classes, Tuesday evening was the best time for such preparation, if I did not wish to do it, instead, during my 'day off' itself. Given that I hardly saw my two little boys on a Monday or Tuesday at all – and, certainly, not in a non-sleeping mode when I could play and interact with them – I had early resolved that Wednesdays would be a 'family day only' for me, and that I would not go to Cave Hill, at all, that day. Fortunately for me, I was able to agree this with my colleague, Andrew Burgess, when we had been negotiating the timetable for my lectures and tutorials for that first academic year of mine at UWI. However, in order to stick to that resolution, I felt obliged to prepare for my Thursday classes by the end of Tuesday evening - which included my Conflicts lecture, as the top priority. When such preparation was over, however, what a wonderful day, on the morrow, I would have to look forward to!

On such Wednesday mornings, I would wake early as normal and do my usual run and swim. By the time that I returned from Maxwell Beach, however, both Noel and Kim would be up and about too. Accordingly, what a delight it was for me to be able to take time with them and help each one – especially our younger child, who was still just a baby, really – to have their respective breakfasts. On those midweek mornings, I had time to interact with our boys and try to make them laugh. No dashing off, perhaps as soon as they were each awake, with a quick kiss and then a wave goodbye, as I got into our car for the journey to work.

Above all, there was no need for me to get involved in the rush hour traffic, speeding past our home in the general direction of Bridgetown - and beyond, where Cave Hill Campus lay. Rather, on Wednesdays, not only would all four of us be leaving in our Skoda after the rush-hour, but also we would most likely be heading in the opposite direction from most of the passing traffic and, thus, away from Bridgetown. That is because our family's favourite place to go, for a day out and picnic, was on the eastern side of the island – more or less opposite to Bridgetown (which was situated at the southerly end of the island's 'West Coast'). That venue of my family's desire also had a counterpart English place name - namely, 'Bath' - which, coincidentally, was also the name of the well-known city, no more than about 30 miles from the English town of Swindon where Philomena and myself had first met at school (as detailed in *Swimming without mangoes*[24]). Bath in Barbados, however, was certainly not a place of any great size. Indeed, in my view, it could hardly be called a 'village' at all though, perhaps, it might have passed for a 'hamlet'. Whichever way the place should have been officially described, however, it was a delightful discovery for us. For one thing, it was situated right by the sea! For another, although it was on the eastern, and therefore, Atlantic Ocean side of the island, there were no waves, to speak of, to be found there. That was the case despite the fact that, just five miles or less, to the north of Bath was the town of 'Bathsheba' – a place on the Atlantic with a plethora of waves that were huge enough to attract the 'surfing crowd' of mainly teenage, White, Barbadians. Our little family, however, wanted no waves at all – for the safety and enjoyment of our two small sons in the water – and that is exactly what the sea at Bath gave us.

There were other delights at the Bajan Bath too. It was a place with only about 10 or so houses at that time. Moreover, there were no shops at all - which one might well expect to find in a village. And even the small number of houses, which existed there, were not occupied on a full-time basis. Rather, Philomena and I, after discussion, came to the conclusion that the homes belonged to some well-off White Bajans, who used them as second, holiday, properties. Additional homes, therefore, which would be used mainly at weekends, or during summer vacations, for example. Certainly, it was our little family's fortune that, whenever we made the journey to Bath on a Wednesday – via such places as Oistins, the front of Grantley Adams International Airport, 'Sam Lord's Castle Hotel' in the parish of 'St Philip', and the front of 'Codrington College' in the neighbouring one of 'St John' – we never saw any family, or individual, occupying any of the houses. Indeed, very often, it was our own family of four that were the only ones in the place though, now and again, we did encounter a small team of government workers sweeping the beach in order to clear it of fallen debris from the Christmas-tree-like 'casuarinas' pines (which shielded the beach from the harsh sun), who were engaged in removing the piles of seaweed which had washed up from the sea.

*Fig 24: Kim, Philomena and Noel sitting at the picnic table nearest to Bath Beach in the St John parish of Barbados within the first year of our family's arrival on that island in 1979. The family's 'Skoda' motor car can be seen in the background of the photo*

For me, the most delightful feature of Bath in Barbados, however, was the warmth of the sea water there. Both Philomena and myself agreed that it seemed to be a few degrees warmer than our other favourite sea-bathing place at Oistins, much nearer to our home in Maxwell. Moreover, because the water was so still and undisturbed by waves or currents, to my wife and myself, there seemed to be no better place on the whole island (as far we knew it) where we could put our baby into the sea (wearing his arm bands, or water wings) and to just let him float about and, thereby, have fun in safety. I used to joke about the uniqueness of the water at that place with Philomena, by saying that it was 'warm like a soup'! Certainly, our children seemed to love the sea, at that location, as much as their parents and we spent hours just soaking and splashing about in it there. In addition, we were left to our own devices and, so, able to work up an appetite, undisturbed by the regular inhabitants of the place or by the few workers we sometimes encountered cleaning the beach. Luckily for us, we were able to take our choice from among the small number of picnic tables which were fixtures on the beach – positioned as if, somehow, a teacher, and his small family, were expected to happen along to that very site on their day out and who might just be in need of a flat eating surface above the sand, with seating, in order to enjoy their repast.

And enjoy our picnic, we certainly always did. Above all, the children would have wanted something refreshing to drink, after their lengthy fun time in the water, and Philomena would already have prepared, at home, something local named 'Kool-Aid'. That consisted of different flavoured powders – usually made from a variety of citrus fruits – which somewhat reminded me of 'sherbet' which I had often bought, from a nearby 'corner shop', on my way to primary school back in Swindon, England in the 1960s. When mixed with water and ice, Philomena could make quite a quantity of the zesty drink, which would be enough to satisfy our family for the whole of our day out – though the ice would surely have all but melted by the time we came out of the sea at Bath for our lunch time picnic.

As far as food was concerned, Philomena would often have prepared some cooked rice the night before – as well as a quantity of fried chicken. Fortunately, Noel liked such a combination of those Caribbean 'staples' just as much as his parents. Kim, in the days of our first trips to Bath, would have had something special from a jar bought at our local Oistins supermarket for babies being weaned, but would no doubt have joined his elder brother and parents in devouring the mangoes which we would have brought with us for our 'afters'. A short post-lunch nap would then have been in order for both boys, whilst their mum and dad relaxed by the water's edge reading one of the local newspapers, or a novel in Philomena's case, until the children awoke with their afternoon 'second wind' and ready for yet more fun. Another short swim by the whole family could then be enjoyed, followed by a shower at the toilet facilities, conveniently located near the beach in question. Then it would be back to the Skoda, for the slow return drive to Christ Church parish and Maxwell – perhaps, via a stop at the 'Anglican' seminary nearby, known as Codrington College, in order to have a short but refreshing walk in its peaceful grounds. As an antidote to the stresses associated with my working life at Cave Hill – especially in the preparation of lectures in my first academic year there – no finer day out, for that purpose, on the island could have been imagined by me.

After my glorious Wednesdays with my family at Bath, it can be anticipated just how heavy of heart I would have dragged myself back to my duties at Cave Hill on Thursday mornings. I really did not look forward, at all, to the Conflicts lecture ahead of me at 11am on such mornings. Nevertheless, I somehow managed to continue - if mechanically - performing my runs, down to Maxwell Beach, and then my swim, in order to try to get myself fired up for my challenges in the day ahead. After the half-hour or so drive around Bridgetown, I usually arrived at the campus sometime around 8.30am. I would shut my office door, so as not to be disturbed by passers-by, and would immediately start revising the lecture notes which I had prepared beforehand, on the Tuesday evening. Fullest concentration was my requirement for that particular period and, thus, I would hate it if a student knocked on my door to interrupt me with some query relating to some future tutorial, for example. That seldom happened, however, and, just before 11am, I would leave my room, with my lecture notes, to walk the short distance to the Seminar Room in order to deliver, to my Conflicts students, the lesson which I had painstakingly prepared for them.

Such tension and stress, week after week leading up to the end of the term in December, must surely have had an adverse effect on my health. Yet, I did not really see it that way. To me, I had little choice but to work 'flat out' in preparing for my classes. The compensation was my Wednesdays off, with just my family to 'entertain' – as well as the ordinary weekends, of course. Not all of my classes, however, were as stressful as the Conflicts course which I was directing in Tony Bland's absence. For example, I had little trouble with my Monday afternoon tutorials, in the Law of Torts, since I had actually taught that very course at Leeds University, immediately prior to arriving at Cave Hill. Consequently, I already had excellent notes from that earlier experience and could usually leave the preparation for such classes until after my Comparative Law lecture on the same Monday morning itself.

Then came my favourite Comparative Law classes. After the tension of preparing for, and then delivering, my Thursday Conflicts lecture, I would have two hours of tutorials, with two different groups, in that very subject, after lunch that day – which I found much more relaxed (for me at least), since the students themselves had to do their own pre-assigned work for such classes and, therefore, they ended up doing most of the talking in them. Once those tutorials were over, however, I was free to prepare for my Comparative Law lecture the next morning – which I would do with more alacrity than I could muster for my Conflicts ones. After all, I already had some excellent notes from my own involvement as a student, or teacher, with bygone classes in that subject at Kingston, Cambridge and Leeds – and it was something of a nice challenge to see how, using more local textbooks about Latin American legal systems, for example, I could adapt my notes to make my lectures even more relevant to students from the English-speaking Caribbean counterpart systems. Thus, if I sometimes had to work late into the evening in my office on a Thursday, in order to finish off the preparation of Friday morning's Comparative Law lecture, that was a relatively enjoyable contrast to how I felt on Tuesday evenings when preparing the Conflicts equivalent for two days ahead. Moreover, on a Thursday evening, I could also look forward to the second hour of the Comparative Law session, when I could sit back and listen to one of my students in that subject giving his or her 'paper' to the rest of the class on some pre-assigned topic, to be then followed by a general discussion among the class on the content of the presentation in question. All the more so, since the discussion would take place in the civilised atmosphere of 'coffee and biscuits' - as supplied by me.

Little by little, therefore, my first teaching term at Cave Hill progressed – with plenty of tension, interspersed with fewer periods of joy, regarding my teaching 'career'. Above all, what I was most aware of were the very long hours I felt obliged to put into the preparation of my classes, each week up to December. Extensive hours, only really relieved by my glorious 'family-time-only' Wednesdays and weekends, in addition to my favourite Comparative Law classes. There was one other 'happy event', however, to look forward to ahead of me that First Term, and which helped to keep me going. That was: the first Caribbean Christmas, of Philomena, the children and myself – as a family – to come!

*Chapter 7*

# A first Caribbean Christmas - December 1979

As is clear from the prequel to this book, which is entitled *Fledging and Learning to Fly*,[25] Philomena and myself, whilst students in the 1970s, loved to travel. That took place throughout the Continent of Europe – predominantly in France, Germany, Italy and Spain. After the birth of our first son in 1977, however, our travelling days had become very curtailed - mainly owing to financial reasons. The position was exacerbated when our baby, Kim, had been born in July of 1979. Nevertheless I had promised Philomena that, even with just one salary only coming to our family, when we emigrated to Barbados just six weeks after our younger son's arrival, we would still try to travel around the Caribbean region, as and when time allowed us to do so. Moreover, with my first academic term at UWI slowly drawing to its closure, I was determined to keep that promise to my wife. In preparation for that, I had written to one of my relatives in my native Montserrat, soon after first arriving in Barbados, to ask whether we could come to spend our first Caribbean Christmas, as a family, with them.

In *Growing up BAREFOOT under Montserrat's sleeping Volcano*,[26] I had recounted how my younger brother, John, and myself had been brought up by our great-grandmother, Joanna, in the 1950s and early 60s in that more northerly, but smaller, Caribbean island referred to in the book's title. Our being raised by an elderly relative had been due to our parents having already emigrated to England - as had our own mother's mother - and, thus, Joanna had been the nearest next of kin, on our mother's side, with whom our mamma could leave her two young sons in the care of. In *Fledging and Learning to Fly*, I described how I had deliberately planned part of my honeymoon trip to include a visit to Montserrat - following my marriage to Philomena in July 1976.[27] That had been done with the intention of not only introducing my new wife to my native island, but also to the woman, still living there, who had raised me from the age of two years (and from just nine months of age, in my brother's case). In addition, that post-wedding trip to Montserrat had also been for the carrying out of a promise that I had made to Joanna, some years before I had even met Philomena, on the night in August 1961 when my brother John and I had left her to emigrate to England to rejoin our parents already living there – and when I had only been eight years old, to John's seven. That promise had been that one day, sometime in the future, I would return to see her again!

Accordingly, in that month of December 1979 - just three years after that honeymoon trip visit - it could be expected that the main person, with whom my family would be wanting to spend our first Caribbean Christmas, must have been Joanna. From my own point of view, that would have been a most ideal scenario. Unfortunately, however, between our post-nuptial visit to Montserrat in 1976 and our proposed Christmas 1979 trip there, Joanna had died![28] That had happened in 1978, whilst I had been studying to become a Barrister in London and within our first son's first few months of life. I had, therefore, not had a realistic opportunity of getting back to Montserrat for her funeral – which, in those days, nearly always took place very quickly after the passing of the loved-relative, in any event.

Which other relative, accordingly, could I possibly have asked to host my family during what would be only my second visit back to Montserrat after leaving there in 1961? The answer is: someone on the paternal side of my family. For, as described in *Growing up BAREFOOT*,[29] my father, 'James Alfred Bradshaw', or just 'Jim' as he was more commonly known, was one of seven siblings, from the same mother and father, who had survived to full age – one of six sons and one daughter parented by my paternal grandfather, 'Joseph Leacock Bradshaw', and his partner 'Mary Susanna Ryan'. As I have also recounted in *BAREFOOT*,[30] although my father had been the very first of those siblings to emigrate to England – in November 1953 – his only sister, Mary, and four of his brothers, had followed his pioneering example soon afterwards. The book also reveals how just one brother, however, had stayed behind in the Caribbean – though he did, in fact, leave his native Montserrat for the Dutch-West Indian island of 'Aruba', in order to work in the oil industry there.[31] Finally, in *BAREFOOT*,[32] I describe how the brother in question eventually returned to Montserrat, after more than 20 years in Aruba, in order to, in effect, retire quietly there. It was to that brother of my father to whom I had written from Barbados, to ask whether Philomena, myself and our two small children could possibly be allowed to come to spend our Christmas holidays with him that coming December 1979 - and who, fortunately, had answered in the affirmative.

That only Caribbean-based sibling of my father was called 'Joseph' – that is to say, the one brother who was named after his own father, and my grandfather, Joseph Leacock. I would, however, always call him 'Uncle Joe', rather than by his longer moniker. I had never actually met him in my life before, since, for the reasons given in more detail in *BAREFOOT*,[33] I had never left the 'Amersham'-'Plymouth'-'Kinsale' triangular area of southern Montserrat until I eventually emigrated to England in 1961, whereas my father and his siblings all came from an area of Central Montserrat called 'Dyers'. Moreover, it was to his native Dyers village that Uncle Joe had retired, when he had returned at the end of his working life in Aruba.

Thus it was that, as soon as my First Term at Cave Hill had ended, Philomena and I set off with our two children to fly to Montserrat for Christmas. It must have been a very exciting time for us all – not least myself, for I was going to be doing, for at least a few weeks at one stretch, something that I most loved doing. That was to spend time with my family, without the worries of my working life in the Law Faculty immediately hanging over me. I was also going to be introducing my first- and second-born sons to their father's native island, and that of their grandfather, Jim, as well as starting to educate them as to their Caribbean 'roots' – factors that, somehow, even then, meant a great deal to me as a matter of 'family history'.

Our boys, Philomena and myself would have said 'au revoir' to Mrs Payne, downstairs from us in Hygeia, given her a suitable present and wished her a Happy Christmas. We would then have packed up our Skoda with two suitcases full of mainly infantile things which we would need for Kim and also, but to a lesser extent, for his older brother, Noel. Above all, however, we took Kim's carrycot and Baby Buggy – for, not only would that be somewhere for him to sleep during the relatively short flights we had to take, but, also, the Buggy part would be an invaluable 'carriage' in which to transport him around Plymouth – the main town of Montserrat and, indeed, its little capital – once we reached my native land. It was still not possible, in that December 1979 era, to fly directly to Montserrat from Barbados. Instead, one needed to get to the former's neighbouring island of Antigua first, and then change onto a smaller aircraft for the short onward 'hop' to our final destination. There was, however, a choice open to Philomena and myself regarding how we would proceed from our new home island in order to get to Antigua. The most exciting way, perhaps, was with the 'island-hopping' airline called 'LIAT' – the initials for which actually stand for 'Leeward Island Air Transport', but which some wag, some years before, alternatively Christened as: 'Leave Island Any Time'. Had we taken LIAT, then, apart from the risk of our journey time being more and more late at each leg, we might have ended up landing at the neighbouring islands of St Lucia, Martinique, Dominica, Guadeloupe and, perhaps, even St Kitts, *en route* - before finally getting to Antigua. Such a prospect would have been too daunting for either Philomena or myself, and we would, therefore, have opted for the more secure British Airways, one-stop only, flight from Barbados to Antigua (after which our aircraft would have proceeded on to London, in just one more leg, without us).

At any rate, we duly arrived in Antigua without any special adventure befalling us. We then had to find our LIAT flight connection for going on to Montserrat. Though just about a 15-minute 'flit' away, that was not necessarily going to be easy. For, as recounted in *Fledging and Learning to Fly*,[34] the last time that my wife and I had tried to make such a connection (during our honeymoon trip in 1976, to visit my great-grandmother, Joanna) our LIAT flight into Antigua from St Lucia had arrived late and, thus, our connecting flight to my native land had left without us! On that later occasion, there were four persons in our party. Might the same thing happen again? Fortunately, the British Airways arrival into Antigua had been in good time, and our onward connection was still waiting on the ground. Accordingly, that meant that we would be getting into Montserrat that very afternoon.

Uncle Joe Bradshaw was there at 'Blackburne Airport', Montserrat waiting for us - after our short hop over from Antigua. Even as we were clearing immigration, and Philomena and I were getting the green shamrock arrival stamp impressed into our respective passports, I spotted him. He had the same general body shape as my late father (who had died in England in April 1979 – just four months before my family's emigration to Barbados). Perhaps he was a little taller, but Uncle Joe was surely as stocky as his younger brother, Jim, had been. There was also something familiar about the curvature of the former's back which resembled that of my late father's. Moreover, there were a number of giveaway familial features, including the light brown skin colouring as well as the balding pate of the head. What little hair remained, at the sides of my uncle's crown, was somewhat wavy – just as was the case with my dad's coiffure. Though Uncle Joe wore dark sunglasses, which made him stand out from the crowd of persons waiting for their respective families - as, perhaps, being more prosperous than most - I found his likeness to my late father to be absolutely remarkable. That was because, in my view, Uncle Joe was much more like Dad than the latter was to their younger sibling - the man I called 'Uncle Tom' back in Swindon - or, say, their other brothers in London such as those whom I called 'Uncle Willy' and 'Uncle Hammy'.

At any rate, our family of four had soon cleared immigration and customs and found Uncle Joe waiting, just beyond, to greet us. He had guessed who we were, in advance of our first words to each other, and, after a relatively formal handshake with me, I happily heard him say that I looked like my mother! I quickly introduced Philomena to him and showed him our two small sons. On his own side, he had someone to introduce to us also. For, standing beside him, was a young boy of about 12 or 13 years old. Uncle Joe told us that the youth was his son, 'Melvin' – who was, accordingly, my first cousin. I, thus, shook Melvin's hand at once – though I had not even known of his existence, prior to our arrival in Montserrat. I wondered, therefore, whether Uncle Joe had a 'surprise' wife waiting for us at his home in Dyers – or, indeed, any more children there, for that matter. I began to mentally rebuke myself, a little, for not having asked my mother, back in England, for more information about my uncle - prior to coming to Montserrat. Would there even be enough room in his house to accommodate the four of us arriving from Barbados – in addition to Uncle Joe, his wife and their children (if any, in addition to Melvin)? As we all climbed into the taxi, which my uncle had kindly arranged for us, I realised that my immediate family and I were in for something of a Caribbean Christmas adventure. Moreover, free of Cave Hill Campus and all its associated tensions of late, I sat back in the hired vehicle and resolved to enjoy the 'unknown ride ahead' as much as was possible.

Very soon our small party of new arrivals, plus Uncle Joe and Melvin, had arrived in Dyers and entering the home of my father's older sibling. It was a larger version of the chattel house belonging to my great-grandmother, Joanna, in which I had been raised by her from the ages of two to eight years old and which I wrote about in *Growing up BAREFOOT*.[35] My uncle, however, seemed to have much more room inside his own home and, in addition, the luxury of being able to give us four visitors a whole bedroom exclusively for ourselves. Certainly, he also had his own bedroom in the more central part of the house and, if memory serves me correctly, there was a third one for Melvin as well. His home also possessed a large kitchen, but the shower was immediately outside the house – which was no significant hardship to myself or Philomena. When time came for our ablutions, we would just have needed to fill up a plastic bowl of water, heated up a little in the kitchen, to enable the three elder members of my party to each have their tepid wash in the shower unit space, or to give Kim a baby bath, from time to time.

If Uncle Joe's lack of bathroom facilities inside his home did not phase me, however, I was more immediately struck by the surroundings outside it. That was because the landscape around his property was one of rolling hills. It was, thus, quite different from the region around Amersham, in the south of the island, where my brother, John, and I had grown up with my great-grandmother, Joanna, and her husband, 'Maas Bab'. In that latter area, there was just one, fairly gentle, slope from our chattel house all the way up to the 'Soufriere Hills' – the dormant volcano situated a mile or two above Joanna and Maas Bab's home – which incline, on the other side of the house, went steadily down to the Caribbean Sea which was about a mile below at Kinsale. In Dyers, however, situated more in the centre of Montserrat and well away from the sea, the scenery was far more undulating - such as I remembered it being in a part of 'Wales' once, during my first ever camping experience with Philomena in the 'Brecon Beacons' hills there, when we were still undergraduate students in the mid-1970s.[36]

*Fig 25: The Author's paternal 'Uncle Joe' – more formally known as 'Mr Joseph Bradshaw' – standing on his land at Dyers, Montserrat. This photo was probably taken by the Author at the time of his family's visit, to his Uncle Joe, for Christmas 1979 – and shows, in the background, the hilly topography of the Dyers area*

I could hardly stop reminding myself that such rise-and-fall land was the place where my own father had grown up as a child himself. The topography was truly beautiful – but I imagined, also, that he and his siblings must have had to work really hard upon it, in helping their parents to cultivate crops on such rolling ground. At least, I had thought to myself - during my imagination of my father performing his agricultural chores in bygone years - my brother, John, and myself, further south during our Amersham early-childhood days, only had fairly smooth land upon which to do our own cotton, and tomato, picking chores when helping out Joanna and Maas Bab.

The other thing which surprised me about Dyers, moreover, was just how 'chilly' it got in the evenings there – much more so than in Barbados at the equivalent time of year. The reason for that, perhaps, was that, unlike Maxwell in Barbados, where we lived close to the sea, Dyers was, most likely, several hundreds of feet 'above sea level'. Accordingly, my little family soon got used to having to wrap-up well at night, both for our going to bed as well as during the evening hours which preceded it.

There was plenty of evidence, scattered about his home, to show that Uncle Joe was, at that time of his life, very much a 'God-fearing man'. Certainly, there was a Bible prominently placed in his living room and I suspected that he had one more, at least, close to his bed in the room which he kept for himself alone. In addition, he had a large radio located in the living room – and it was always turned on, and tuned into, at a quiet volume, one of those American gospel music and preaching stations. Very early during our stay, therefore, I asked Uncle Joe whether he was a practising 'Methodist' - like his brother, my father, had been brought up to be. To my surprise, he answered in the negative and told me that he was, in fact, a practising 'Seventh Day Adventist' and that he was bringing up his son, Melvin, to be the same. I then asked him what some of the main tenets of his faith were. Alas, the only thing I can recall from his answer, now, is that 'Adventists' like him believed that the 'Sabbath Day' was not Sunday - as Catholics like Philomena and myself did, as well as former Methodists like my dad had done - but, rather, Saturday. Accordingly, he alerted me to the fact that he and Melvin would be going to church on the next Saturday coming.

Given his then religious nature, therefore, I was very surprised by what he subsequently told me about the background to the 'advent' of his son, Melvin. As part of that history, he reminded me that he had spent more than 20 years living and working in the Dutch West Indian island of Aruba - in the oil industry. Perhaps, it had been with the famous petroleum company called 'Shell'. At any rate, Uncle Joe told me that, although he had been married in Montserrat prior to emigrating to Aruba, his wife had not wanted to accompany him to that Dutch island. Consequently, he had, reluctantly, left her behind in Dyers. He then recounted how the highly predictable breakdown had occurred and how he had met another lady during his sojourn in Aruba. He went on to reveal how that later relationship had led to the birth of a daughter –named 'Violet' – who was to grow up to become a school teacher in her native Caribbean island. I was delighted to tell Uncle Joe that I had actually met Violet – in England, years before, when she had come to Swindon, during a holiday in Europe in the 1970s, to visit her 'Uncle Jim' and his family at my then home in 'Alexandra Road' – but that I had not understood, at that time, quite how she was related to my own, then, nuclear family.

Uncle Joe's recounting of his family history became even more complicated, however, when he went to tell me that his relationship with Violet's mother did not last, and that, when he eventually decided to return to live in Montserrat, he had left both her and Violet behind in Aruba. Worse still, he then confessed to me that, even before deserting Violet and her mother, he had met, and had started up a relationship with, yet another woman – then also living in Aruba, but who was from Montserrat's neighbouring island of St Kitts. That third lady had later returned to live in her native St Kitts, and, my uncle told me, instead of returning directly from Aruba to Montserrat when he finally retired from the petroleum industry, he had stopped off in St Kitts to look up his former, but most recent, lady friend. Again, he told me, the 'inevitable' happened and she ended up becoming pregnant with Melvin! At the time of our holiday with him in Montserrat, therefore, his son had already grown up to be a young pre-teenager – who was then currently living, and being educated, in Montserrat - though his mother was still alive and well in their native St Kitts.

I must have thought to myself - after hearing Uncle Joe's story about the origins of his children, Violet and Melvin - that my father's elder brother had been on his own 'Road to Damascus' and was then living a 'God-fearing life', according to the tenets of his Adventist religion, in order to atone for what he might have considered to be his sinful past. Certainly, there was no woman living with him at his home during our time visiting with him that Christmas season – not even the wife that he had left behind when he had first emigrated to Aruba. I can no longer recall what had happened to her by that time, and it is possible that she had either emigrated from Montserrat herself or, perhaps, even have died. But whether 'atoning' or not, Uncle Joe seemed to have won the respect of all the neighbours around him, so far as I could see. For, he seemed to me, every inch the master of all he surveyed around his home – and he had plots of land producing crops which surrounded his house, as well as a number of livestock in parts of the same. Furthermore, his neighbours all seemed to greet, and pay their respects to, him as he went to and fro about his property.

Such deference may have been accorded to Uncle Joe because many of those near neighbours were, in fact, relatives of his. Certainly, he was at pains to introduce me, Philomena and our children to the inhabitants of the house just a few plots away from his on the same Dyers land. That turned out to be owned by another first cousin of mine, named 'Thomas', and his small family. That close relative, I was soon told, was one of the many offspring of yet another uncle of mine - Uncle Tom, back in Swindon – the younger brother of my own late father, who had first gone to live in that Wiltshire town with Dad, from their homes in London, after their respective emigration from Montserrat in the early 1950s. However, I was also told that 'Cousin Thomas' was a child whom Uncle Tom had fathered even before emigrating from Montserrat. Moreover, that Thomas had been born before his father had married his wife - the lady whom I called 'Auntie Catherine', back in Swindon - and had produced his first batch of seven legitimate children whom I had known as my childhood cousins, and playmates, then living in the 'Walcot' district of that Wiltshire town (and of whom I wrote about in *Swimming without mangoes*[37]). That newly-discovered Montserrat cousin of mine, Thomas, however, I was pleased to learn, was not only one of my native island's best cricketers – who, indeed, had already represented Montserrat in several Caribbean regional competitions – but he was also one of its leading builders of new houses. I liked Thomas, from the start, and had nothing but respect for him in relation to how well he had done in his life - given that he had grown up without his father, Uncle Tom, being present in that journey to maturity very much, if at all.

But, perhaps, the 'illegitimacy thing' explained why Uncle Joe was so much respected in and around that Dyers district, notwithstanding his non-monogamous past. For, as I have shown in *Growing up BAREFOOT*,[38] he and his siblings (including my father, Jim, as well as Uncle Tom) had been illegitimate themselves. Their own father, Joseph Leacock, had been the *paterfamilias* of two families – one with his wife, 'Catherine', and the other with his partner, 'Mary Susanna Ryan' (more commonly known as 'Miss Baby'). Uncle Joe and his siblings had been the children of Miss Baby. Thus, perhaps, it would not have mattered very much to his immediate neighbours, who were also relatives from Joseph Leacock Bradshaw's bloodline, that Uncle Joe had sired illegitimate children, such as Violet in Aruba and Melvin in St Kitts, and that he was bringing one of them up right in front of the eyes of those neighbours. After all, Uncle Joe himself was illegitimate too – as were some of those very neighbours (and relatives), including Cousin Thomas.

In telling me about his bygone Aruba days, however – including about his daughter's conception there and how he had, afterwards, first met the mother of Melvin in that country – Uncle Joe had one very good reason for doing so. That was to call upon my expertise as a lawyer. For, as he subsequently recounted to me, although he had spent more than two decades working for his oil company employer in that particular Dutch Caribbean island, he had never received any pensión from it, since returning to live out his retirement in Montserrat. He, thus, asked me whether I would help him try to obtain what was due to him in that regard. Given that my family and I were already having our Christmas holidays with him in his home, I thought I had little choice but to tell him that I would be happy, indeed, to try to help. And even though, in truth, I really wanted to do no Law at all, during my relatively short absence from Cave Hill and my 'legal duties' at UWI for the 'Festive Season', I had already grown to like my uncle and genuinely wished to do something that would bring some 'justice' into his life - if I possibly could have done.

I, therefore, asked him to provide me with any papers relating to his contract of employment which he still had, and which went back to the time when he worked for the oil company in Aruba. I wanted to see whether there was any provision for any pensión, to be provided to him at the end of such employment, stated in the same. To my amazement, Uncle Joe – after disappearing into his bedroom for a while – then 'pulled a rabbit out of the hat', as far as I was concerned! For he emerged from his inner sanctum with paperwork that was relevant to what I was looking for. Thus, while Philomena and our children amused themselves in the fields with the animals outside, I spent some hours poring over the paperwork - as well as asking my uncle some questions on the same, from time to time. From my findings, it appeared that, during his time in employment in Aruba, he had never paid any of his wages into any pensión pot in order to build up a fund to provide himself with the kind of annuity which he was then hoping to have. I managed, however, to find a provision in the contract which referred to the company having some sort of discretion to provide some funding to help relieve former employees from 'poverty'. I was, therefore, able to tell Uncle Joe that, though I could find no 'right', given to him in his contract of employment, to get a pensión from his former employers (which he might, thus, be able to enforce through a court, for example) there was some sort of discretion available to the company, in the agreement, which he might be able to persuade them to exercise in his favour. Accordingly, I also told him that I would draft a letter, pleading his case as to why the company should do just that, after he had given 20, or more, of the best years of his young life in working for it. I also suggested that, if he was happy with my draft – after we had gone through it together to enable him to make any change he wanted - he get it typed-up, and then sign it before sending it off to the company's personnel department in Aruba. Those steps were, indeed, subsequently followed by myself and Uncle Joe – before my family and I ended our Montserrat sojourn.

I could see that Uncle Joe had become extremely happy about what I had managed to do for him regarding his pensión. In return, it seemed to me that he wanted to do something 'really special' for me and my family as a reward. That was despite the fact that I had been at pains to point out that, basically, we were sending a 'begging letter' to his former employers in Aruba – one to implore for the exercise of a discretion - which meant that a positive answer, or outcome, was far from guaranteed. Nevertheless, he insisted that he really wanted to do something exceptional for my family – to both show his gratitude for what I had done for him regarding his pensión, as well as to mark the very first Christmas, ever, of Philomena and our two young sons in the Caribbean. I, therefore, told Uncle Joe that I accepted whatever special thing he had in mind and wondered, as our stay got closer and closer to the 'big day', just exactly what the surprise was that Uncle Joe had resolved to give as a present to my nuclear family.

Whilst I had been busy with helping my uncle sort out his begging letter to his former employers in the Dutch West Indies, my children and their mother had been introducing themselves to many of the animals which were pastured on our host's land in Dyers. Those included one or two donkeys – which I had warned my family, in advance, not to get too near to, for the reasons given in *Growing up BAREFOOT* relating to my close encounters with my great-grandmother's donkey, at Amersham, Montserrat, back in the late 1950s.[39] There had also been a number of pigs, as well as some goats on the property. The animals which had most attracted Noel and Kim, however, were the small group of sheep which my uncle also reared on his land. The boys liked the lambs, especially, but seemed to be taken with the gentleness of their mothers as well as with the ram which had fathered them.

About two days or so before Christmas, however, I noticed that the ram in question had been relocated and was then tied up immediately outside our bedroom at Uncle Joe's house. It was bleating away - as it seemed to want to be reunited with the rest of its family, which were some distance away in a neighbouring field. It was thus impossible not to hear, and therefore be disturbed by, the cries of the animal, during the night in question, as I was trying to sleep. When, finally, we were all together with my uncle at breakfast the next morning, I took an early opportunity to ask him why the ram had been separated from the rest of his flock and told him how I had been rather disturbed during the night by its sounds of evident distress. Uncle Joe beamed a happy smile at me and replied by saying: 'Well, David - that is the surprise that I was telling you all that I would be giving you for Christmas. I am going to sacrifice my best sheep for our Christmas lunch!'.

Philomena and I immediately looked at each other in shock – and with our mouths open! She seemed to feel exactly like I did at that moment. That is to say, completely horrified at what my uncle had in his mind. He was clearly extremely happy about the decision he had come to and maintained the smile on his face, after telling us how he was going to 'treat us'. Moreover, being the God-fearing, church-going, Adventist that he had then become, he would have encountered many examples of 'sacrificing' sheep, or other animals, for a 'good cause' in the Bible - which he regularly read at home, or listened to broadcasts about on his radio there.

Uncle Joe's announcement to us, therefore, immediately gave Philomena and myself a major headache – one caused by a clash of cultures. What were we two people, raised in the 'First World', going to do about what was, perhaps, a 'Third World' practice (if, admittedly, also a Biblically-approved one)?

Following breakfast, therefore, whilst our children played outside Uncle Joe's house near us – and close to the still-tied ram, with the rest of his flock within his sight and that of our children also – Philomena and I had a discreet conversation. Ordinarily, I knew that she really liked 'lamb with mint sauce', for Sunday lunch, back in England. It had been one of the staples upon which she had often told me that she had been raised by her own mother when growing up in her native Liverpool area and, later on, in Swindon. Like me, however, she said that, having first known the animal that was earmarked for slaughter, there was absolutely no way that she would be able to eat it during a meal – no matter how well it had been cooked after its killing. I felt exactly the same way – and all the more so, since Noel and Kim had got to know, and even play with, the doomed creature and its family over the previous days since our arrival from Barbados.

Accordingly, Philomena and I resolved to go back inside the house to speak to Uncle Joe about our decision – as diplomatically as possible. First of all, we told him that we both felt really honoured that he had decided to sacrifice his best animal in order to celebrate our Christmas with him. We then told him how we felt about the prospect of trying to eat an animal that we, and our children, had previously got to know, and, indeed, had become fond of. We could see that Uncle Joe was no longer smiling, and, moreover, that he was having difficulty seeing things from our point of view. No doubt, his puzzlement was because, for him, there could hardly be any greater honour that he could personally bestow upon my little family that Festive Season. I, therefore, pressed on with the next piece of our argument - which was to propose an alternative to his own honourable idea. That was to tell him that the best present, for Philomena and myself from him that Christmas, would be for him to save the ram's life! Also, that to return it to its family in the field and, thereby, let it live on for many a year to come, is what would give our family of four the most happiness for that Holy Season. Moreover, in return, I offered - on behalf of myself, Philomena and our children - to go into the island's capital in Plymouth to look for, and buy, the biggest (already dead!) turkey that we could find in any of the supermarkets there, for it to become the substituted centrepiece of our Christmas lunch.

Uncle Joe was not happy! He seemed to quickly realise, however, that Philomena and myself were very serious about wanting him to save his best male sheep's life, and that to go ahead with his original 'ram sacrifice' idea would be futile – since Philomena and I would feel unable to eat its flesh, no matter how deliciously my uncle would have tried to cook it before our forthcoming Christmas lunch. Being the good man that he had clearly become in his more recent senior years, he eventually smiled at us both and said that he could, after all, understand our point of view. He also accepted our offer to buy-in a big turkey, instead, and proceeded to tell us which supermarket in Plymouth might be the best place to try to find such a bird (even though he added the spoiler comment that he did not usually have turkey for Christmas, and, perhaps had never done so, since he regarded eating the flesh of that fowl as being more of a tradition from England or America – neither of which place he had ever visited!).

By the next morning therefore - Christmas Eve - our friendly ram had been reunited with the rest of its flock, in a field a little way from Uncle Joe's house, and Philomena, myself and our children found ourselves waiting for a 'bus' on the main road from Dyers to Plymouth. There was no such thing as a bus-timetable for that part of Montserrat in those days. Rather, we all just had to wait, at a certain place at the side of the road, until the correct vehicle of public conveyance came along. Moreover, what did eventually come was not a 'bus' at all, as one would find in England or even Barbados! Rather, it was more of a mini-van – full to bursting with its friendly passengers already inside, who were only too happy to 'squeeze-up' in order to make way for a visiting Montserratian and his White wife and children. After a scenic ride in that packed vehicle, around curve after curve on that very windy road, we eventually arrived in the island's capital of Plymouth.

That main town of Montserrat was somewhat familiar to me, as well as to Philomena

- as we had spent part of our honeymoon trip there, just over three years before, when my great-grandmother, Joanna, had still been alive. There was, still *in situ*, the white-painted band-stand, with its clock-face at the top. A little to the left of that, as one looked towards the sea, was the 'Jetty' – the small pier, from which my brother, John, and myself had embarked in August 1961. That had been in a small boat, or tender, which had taken us out to our ocean liner, anchored temporarily in deeper water, ready to sail with us two small boys, among other passengers, to England in order to be reunited with our mother and father already living there. Accordingly, I would have been quite delighted to be able to show my firstborn son such an historic place for me, and to tell Noel (who was already full of understanding beyond his tender age) something of my memories of that unforgettable night. After indulging in a little nostalgia from our honeymoon trip, however - and from my earliest childhood days, before that, in my case - Philomena and I soon remembered that we had some 'business' to do. We had a certain 'big bird' to find.

Uncle Joe had recommended that we try to accomplish that at a supermarket which he had named and which moniker had seemed really unusual to me. Philomena and I, nevertheless, decided to 'shop around' elsewhere first – to look for both the size of poultry that we really wanted as well as to discover how high were the prices being charged by those other competitors in 'Town'. Alas, we soon found out that there were not many other 'supermarkets' to choose from in Plymouth and Philomena told me that she wished she was, then, shopping in England, or even Barbados, for the errand which we were trying to carry out. In the end, we found only about two other stores, in addition to that recommended by Uncle Joe. Inside of them all, however, I was to be extremely surprised as to how 'popular' turkey seemed to be in Montserrat that Christmas Eve – given what Uncle Joe had told us about his avoidance of that particular kind of poultry for the Festive Season. I resolved the poser for myself by speculating that there must have been many other *émigré* Montserratians revisiting their native island, from England or North America, that particular Christmastime and many of them would have brought back with them a taste for the traditional seasonal poultry of their particular adopted homeland. Despite the obvious demand for the large birds in question, however, the quality which my wife and I found in those other, non-recommended, stores was not good. Those on offer were too small for us. They were, probably, also, much too expensive for whatever was on sale.

Eventually, therefore, Philomena and I decided that it was time to venture into Uncle Joe's recommended 'Rams Emdee' supermarket. There, we found the place packed with shoppers, hoping, it seemed to me, to be able to buy-in their last-minute items for their respective Christmas celebrations. Moreover, such items did, indeed, include many turkeys. Unlike those that would have been available in England, however - where Philomena and I had spent all our Christmases since meeting at school there in 1964 - all the birds were deeply frozen! Who would have known how long the poultry on show had been killed, prior to being put on sale? For all one could tell, it could well have been that the store was making available, for purchase, poultry which had been left over from the previous Christmastime or, as more likely, the American 'Thanksgiving' celebrations of the November month just past. Having recently side-stepped, however, the opportunity to have some very 'fresh' lamb, or mutton, for the then-current Festive Season - out of Uncle Joe's formerly condemned ram - there was nothing for it but to buy the biggest frozen turkey that we could find, from amongst what was, perhaps, a bad lot. Philomena and I, accordingly, did just that and then both agreed to pray that we would not have to wait too long for a 'bus', going north, to enable us to get the bird back to Dyers, and Uncle Joe's place, before it started to thaw.

My wife and I then did the sensible thing and, having paid for our poultry, asked the supermarket to keep it for us to collect a little later. That is because I wanted to show my sons – particularly, Noel – their father's old school of 'St Augustine'. That was situated in upper Plymouth (on the road back to Dyers), as well as was 'St Patrick's RC Church' nearby, where I had been Baptised, and had made my First Communion shortly before emigrating to England in 1961. I also wanted to discover whether one of the nuns, who had taught me during my time at St Augustine – the one named 'Sister Marie Sylvie' – was still in residence at the convent, which was situated across the road from the school. There was every possibility I would have been told that she had already retired and had returned to her native 'Belgium'. After such a disappointment, however, there would still have been one other person, in the environs of Plymouth, whom I would also have wished to look up with my little family on that occasion – namely, one 'Mr Tommy Meade'. For, he it was who had given Philomena and myself a wonderful welcome during our honeymoon trip just over three years before, and I would have wanted to show him just how well our marriage was being blessed with our first God-given offspring. As I write, however, I cannot recall our meeting with Mr Meade on that particular visit to Plymouth and I trust, therefore, that we did not find that he had, like my great-grandmother Joanna, already passed on by the time of our seeking him out that Christmastime.

Prior to leaving Plymouth, to return to Dyers that day, I would have tried to take note of just how 'Christmassy' the capital had looked and felt at that time of year. In so doing, no doubt I decided that there was a huge contrast with what I had been used to in England during such a Festive Period. No Christmas trees, with or without lights, were to be seen on street corners of Plymouth, for example. Neither were there any 'Father Christmases' to be spotted. Nor can I recall any particular 'sparkle' or 'colour' inside the shops of that main town – or outside of them, for that matter. What made the atmosphere seem somewhat festive, however, were the smiling, evidently happy, people all around - particularly, within the stores. Apart from the extra volume of people, however, it seemed to me that Montserratians were usually a cheerful and sunny set of people at most times – so, perhaps, what I had observed in my native capital, during that Christmas Eve visit, had very little to do with the special season in question.

Back at Uncle Joe's home in Dyers, he was kind enough to allow Philomena to take the leading role in defrosting the turkey and, then, preparing it for the special lunch the next day. Normally in England, and, certainly, before our two boys had been born, Philomena and I would have made every effort to go to Midnight Mass on Christmas Eve. Having returned from our 'turkey-hunting' trip to Plymouth, and with the burden of our two small sons (whom we would have felt obliged to try to keep awake during the night-time service), Philomena and I decided that it would have been just too much trouble, and expense, for our family to return later that evening, to St Patrick's in Plymouth, for Midnight Mass. Rather, we agreed that we would just have to give the special service a miss, for that particular year, and take up the practice again when our boys were a little older, in a year or two. Accordingly, with our large turkey duly stuffed, and with Uncle Joe's ram safely alive and doing ram-like things with his sheep family in a field nearby, my own little human one had a relatively early Christmas Eve night. The next day would be the special one, which we had come all the way to Montserrat to celebrate, as one family unit, for the first time in our joint lives.

As it happened, Christmas Day at Uncle Joe's was memorable because it was so unlike what I had been used to for nearly two decades beforehand, since my first Yuletide celebration, in England, in 1961. For one thing, my uncle's home was not decorated with a Christmas tree or any brightly-coloured bunting on his walls, to mark the special time of year. Admittedly, there might have been the odd Christmas card or two, on the table in his living room, but that was about the main concession which he had given to the feast day in question. That may have been because he, personally, did not believe in celebrating on the 25th of December itself, or, perhaps, because his particular Adventist faith did not allow him to do so. At any rate, Philomena got on with cooking our 'Rams Emdee turkey', with Uncle Joe's prior permission to do so in his kitchen, and, from then on, my wife and I tried to treat the day as if we were at home in England again.

Once the turkey was in the oven, we asked my uncle to gather with Melvin and our two sons in his living room and then gave him and his son the presents which we had brought for him from Barbados. Insofar as those would have included items such as a few pairs of socks and some handkerchiefs, we split them into parts, so that one portion could be given to Melvin - whose existence (as seen above) we did not know of until our actual arrival in Montserrat some days earlier. We also gave Noel and Kim the new (but small) toys, which we had brought for them in Barbados but had kept hidden from both until that day. Both Uncle Joe and Melvin seemed happy with the practical gifts which we had given them, and, needless to say perhaps, Noel was delighted with his new playthings even if his younger brother did not yet understand what 'Christmas presents' were all about.

With the sound of Christmas music being broadcast on my uncle's radio – mainly consisting of American carols such as 'O Holy Night' and 'Joy to the World' – a small-scale atmosphere of the festive day in question started to pervade his home. Certainly, if he did not celebrate the 'Big Day" in question himself, his immediate neighbours gave the impression of their doing so – as evidenced by the fact that they all seemed to be staying inside their homes, rather than being out in their fields, tilling them or tending to their respective animals there. Just like those neighbours, also, we stayed put within my uncle's home also, until it was time for our meal of the day – the Christmas turkey lunch. What a triumph that turned out to be - notwithstanding the domestic fowl's original deep-frozen state! Philomena had, once more, produced a wonderful roast bird. And, with the other items which we had also managed to buy in the various stores throughout our visit to Plymouth the previous day – including, 'Irish potatoes' for roasting with the turkey, as well as cranberry sauce which had also been imported from America – my wife managed to produce a celebratory meal which would have been hard for her to have bettered for the occasion, whether we had still been in Leeds or Cambridge at the time.

Somehow, during our Plymouth shopping trip, Philomena and I had also managed to find a Christmas cake – again, most likely with a provenance in America. During that excursion to the capital, we had tried to find a traditional 'Christmas pudding', for our ideal festive dessert but, alas, such a discovery confounded us during our shopping search. Fortunately, however, both my uncle and Melvin seemed satisfied with the elaborate cake, as our 'Plan B', and it made a nice finale to our special meal for that day. After that, it was a case of all the members of our party (with me carrying Kim in my arms) going for a ramble around my uncle's land, in order to digest our big meal. During that outing, we saw my uncle's ram again among his flock of ewes and lambs. For me, that sighting was the highlight of that special day itself – since it meant that the male sheep was where it belonged and was, above all, alive and kicking instead of being in the stomachs of either my nuclear family, Uncle Joe or Melvin, and thereby being, then, digested as part of our very first Christmas meal together!

Philomena and I had planned to stay in Montserrat until the New Year, at least. However, once Christmas Day was over and our little 'celebration' of that day with my uncle and his son had passed, it occurred to the two of us that we might actually enjoy what remained of our precious Christmas holidays, together, by returning to our home in Barbados somewhat earlier than planned. For one thing, we badly missed being by the sea and being able to swim with our sons in it – owing to Dyers being somewhat in the middle of the island and our having no private transport of our own whilst in Montserrat. Moreover, although my uncle was extremely well-meaning and relatively 'easy to live with', Philomena and I both agreed that it felt to us, at times, that she and I had to 'walk on eggshells' within his home, and had to constantly try to ensure that our two small children never got out of hand.

On Boxing Day, therefore, I asked Uncle Joe what he thought of the idea of Philomena and myself returning to Plymouth the following day - when the shops would be open again. I quickly explained that such an outing would not be to look for another turkey at Rams Emdee, for the New Year celebrations ahead, for example, but, rather, to visit the capital's LIAT airline office. I then revealed to him the thinking of my wife and myself, about missing being near the sea with our children whilst based in Dyers with him, and, therefore, our wanting to cure that yearning by returning home to Barbados, somewhat earlier than we had originally agreed with him. Fortunately, just as with the case of our exchanging his ram for a turkey Christmas dinner, he quickly came to understand, and then accept, my family's point of view. Indeed, I even detected that he became quite enthusiastic about our suggestion - after he had reflected on it for a minute or two.

Accordingly, on 27th December, my family took another one of those public mini-buses back to Plymouth. At the LIAT office there, we were fortunate – both to find the place open notwithstanding the holiday season in question, as well as our being able to re-book my family's flight back to Antigua for the following day. We were also successful in getting LIAT to re-book our connecting flight, on British Airways, from Antigua to Barbados. Before returning to Dyers, however, there was just one more thing that I wanted my family to experience before we said our goodbyes to Plymouth for what might have been quite a number of years into the future. That was to go and have a swim nearby, in the bay a few hundred yards away from the Jetty in the town, in the direction of Kinsale. For, it was at that very place, just below Montserrat's Government House on the hill, that my brother John and myself used to regularly disobey our great-grandmother, Joanna, in order to take dips in the sea, on our way home from St Augustine School, in the early 1960s. I wanted Philomena and my boys to experience what the sea, and beach, at that place was like - so that when we returned to our own Maxwell Beach in Barbados, in just a few days' time, they might better understand why our leaving Montserrat, and even its beaches, earlier than planned, was a smart decision. Alas, when we arrived at the beach in question – with its volcanic black sand - the waves were much too rough for Noel, let alone Kim, to swim in safely and, after walking on the sand for a while, Philomena and I felt obliged to cut short, what should have been, for me, a most nostalgic visit.

The following day found us saying our fond farewells to Uncle Joe and Melvin at Blackburne Airport. It had been a memorable return to my native land, and I had achieved my main objective – namely, of introducing my own firstborn sons to the 'land of their immediate forefathers'. I had also met another paternal uncle of mine (and his son), for the very first time, and already knew that, even if only because of his outstanding pensión issue, I would be keeping in touch with him (and Melvin) into the future. As our little LIAT plane took off to get my nuclear family back to Antigua, however, I felt that, perhaps, my wife and myself had chosen the wrong season in which to visit Montserrat. Or, rather, that it had just been a case of the two of us having been unfortunate in choosing my Adventist uncle with whom to 'celebrate' Christmas – when, unbeknown to us, he personally did not wish to 'keep up' that Season or, possibly, because his religious faith did not allow him to do so with any alacrity. Whatever the case, however, I was not sorry about having taken myself and my family on the holiday in question, and I had been delighted to have been able to help Uncle Joe with his Aruba pensión issue. Nevertheless, I was also glad to be going 'home' to Barbados and back to its pristine beaches – and, I was pretty sure, Philomena and my boys were rather of the same mind too!

*Fig 26: Philomena, Noel and Kim on the beach in Antigua – en route from Montserrat back home to Barbados in late December 1979, after they (and the Author) had spent Christmas with the Author's Uncle Joe in Dyers, Montserrat*

*Chapter 8*

# A New Year (and academic term) in Barbados – January to Easter 1980

After an uneventful connecting flight onwards from Antigua, my little family were soon back at Grantley Adams International Airport, Barbados. Our Skoda car was still at the parking area there, where we had left it before our pre-Christmas flights to Antigua and then Montserrat, and, thus, I was able to drive us home fairly quickly. It felt good to be 'in charge' of our own destiny once more. And that feeling included returning to our home at Hygeia, greeting Mrs Payne downstairs, and celebrating our return by, each day up to the New Year and a little beyond, going down to our very own beach at Maxwell – or to the one 'just up the road', at Oistins. Philomena and I had learned a great lesson from our trip to Montserrat – namely, that we must not try, too hard, to celebrate the great Christian festivals of the year! For, what our recent overseas excursion taught us, was that sometimes the best fun is to be had by simply staying 'at home' with the family. And that is exactly what we did in order to 'see in' the New Year, and Decade, starting 1st January 1980. At Hygeia we stayed, and toasted the two major 'milestones' with some champagne bought from our favourite supermarket in Oistins. If our two boys had already been fast asleep in their beds at the time, it mattered not to Philomena and myself. That was because 'we four' – all the members of the same nuclear family – were all safe and sound, for the time being, in our very own home (or, at least, the dwelling that we then possessed, courtesy of my university employers).

Alas, no idyll lasts forever! For, even before I knew it, the holidays were over and those university employers of mine would have been expecting their 'pound of flesh' as part of the *quid pro quo*, or price, for their providing my family and myself with our special 'proximate to the beach' accommodation in Maxwell. Moreover, all too suddenly also, I was back on the seemingly revolving hamster-wheel of giving up most of my waking hours of the New Year, and new academic term, to either preparing my lectures, delivering them, or - at the very least - thinking about them! It did not take long, therefore, for the stress, which I had experienced to almost a breaking point before Christmas, to return to afflict me - even before the month of January 1980 had come to its close. That adverse condition, however, was exacerbated by an event, that particular month, which should have brought a happy diversion – and, thus, some respite - for me.

The occasion in question was the visit to us, for a few weeks' holiday, of Philomena's younger brother and his girlfriend. Like my own immediately younger sibling, he was also named 'John', whilst his partner was called 'Jane'. John had been delighted when he had discovered that we were emigrating to Barbados from Leeds University in the summer of 1979. Indeed, perhaps, he had been the very first of our relatives - on both sides of our families - to ask whether he could come to have a Caribbean vacation at our home near the sea. Philomena and myself had both been thrilled to say 'yes' to his request – and also for him to bring Jane, his future fiancée. That was owing to our being always conscious that we would miss our respective families, back in England, if a number of them did not come to stay with us - from time to time. At any rate, John and Jane came to stay with us at Hygeia, by about the middle of January 1980, and Philomena and I were as over the moon – as much as our visitors seemed to be – when they first arrived.

That must have happened on a weekend, for no weekday lectures or other classes got in the way of my wife and myself swiftly taking them around the various beaches that we knew near our home. In return, John and Jane were very generous to us from the outset. They soon bought Noel a huge toy tractor, which he was able to sit on and pedal around the rectangle pathway which surrounded our home. In addition, they also bought Philomena and myself a huge 'cool box', for keeping our future beach picnic

*Fig 27: Philomena's brother, John, and his girlfriend, Jane, with Philomena, Noel and Kim at the front entrance of Codrington College, Barbados in January 1980 – probably after visiting the nearby Bath Beach to introduce the holidaying John and Jane to that wonderful seaside picnic and swimming resort*

snacks and drinks fresh and at a low temperature – no matter how far away our *al fresco* eating, and playing, place on the island was located. Accordingly, by the very first Sunday of our visitors' stay, we had treated them to their earliest picnic at Bath Beach with us - and had enjoyed a wonderful time together there eating, drinking, swimming, or just playing about in, perhaps, Barbados' warmest sea water.

The first Monday after our guests' arrival soon arrived, however. That was a full lecturing, and tutorial-giving, day for me – and also the one for the preparation of my Tuesday morning Conflict of Laws lecture. Wishing to be as generous to John and Jane as they were being to us, I suggested that they should take over my family's Skoda for their own use, during the hours that I was working at Cave Hill – in order to get about, with Philomena and our children, as and when they wished to do so during the day. John eagerly accepted that offer - despite our not having discussed whether he would be covered to drive by my insurance - and, in return, kindly agreed not only to drive me to work on those days when I had to teach at UWI, but also to drive the car all the way back from Maxwell to Cave Hill Campus on each such day in order to pick me up from my office in the evening. The arrangement was put into operation that first Monday of our guests' stay, but my morale started to go downhill, in a huge way, from the moment John dropped me and drove off to return to Jane, Philomena and our sons back home in Maxwell. I quickly realised that I was feeling that way because I, too, wanted to be 'at ease', just like our visitors, and 'on holiday' with them too. Or, at least, I wished to be like Philomena, and free to just be at home and able to go down to Maxwell Beach, with my visiting brother-in-law and girlfriend as well as our children, anytime that I liked during the working week. Certainly, the last thing that I wanted to do, that particular Monday, was to enter the Faculty of Law to give my classes. Or, at any rate, even if I did not mind giving my Comparative Law lecture within an hour or so of my arrival at Cave Hill (which I would have previously prepared on the Friday, just gone), or my Law of Torts tutorials that coming afternoon, I was certainly dreading the preparation process, to be undertaken in the evening afterwards. That last bit of 'spadework' was, of course, necessary for the putting together of my Conflicts lecture due to be given the following day. All the more so, since I would not really have been able to 'escape' such painstaking toil until John would come to collect me with the Skoda at the agreed time of 8pm. Although I would normally have remained in my office to prepare my Tuesday lecture until that hour anyway, the fact that I was no longer able to just 'escape' in my car, at an earlier hour if I just chose to do so before 8pm, had a devastating psychological effect on me.

Perhaps the longing to be 'like John and Jane', and be simply 'on vacation', was even greater the next morning. That was when I had to say goodbye to my wife's brother sitting in the driving seat of my car, wave him off as he made his way back to Maxwell and another lovely day at the beach, and then take myself inside the Law Faculty buildings in order to further prepare for, and then deliver, my lecture and tutorials for that Tuesday. Once John had come back to pick me up about 8pm that evening, however, there was the wonderful 'family day off' for me to look forward to. That would have been the Wednesday of John and Jane's first week in Barbados and our party would surely have made a bee-line for Bath Beach, once more, in order to try out our new cool box gift and have another of our favourite picnic days out at that special place for my nuclear family. It might well be easily imagined just how badly I would have felt - after such an exceptional experience of being 'at one' with my brother-in-law, his girlfriend, my wife and our children, in 'relax mode' at Bath - when the very next morning arrived. For, on that fourth weekday, I had to report for duty back at Cave Hill and deliver my Thursday Conflicts lecture, followed by tutorials in that subject, in the afternoon. As the first week of John and Jane's vacation wore on, I longed for the weekend to come. My morale went ever lower until I obtained some respite with my favourite Comparative Law seminar class starting at noon on the Friday. An hour or so later, I was free again to share in the fun that our English guests were having during their first Caribbean holiday– and, for the next couple of days at least, I was at peace with myself again.

Similar 'highs' and 'lows' in my feelings about my teaching at Cave Hill - whilst also hosting my wife's brother and girlfriend - would have been experienced by me during their second week with us. Indeed, if anything, I would have started to feel even deeper 'lows' during that latter period. I managed to pull through, however, and to continue with my 'extensive-hours at Cave Hill' regime. At least, I did so for long enough to enable me to assist Philomena in giving her brother and his partner the best holiday, with us, that we could muster and to eventually see them off, happily, at Grantley Adams International Airport, for their flight back to England at the end of their sojourn.

Alas, however, John and Jane's return to England - and my getting my car back to enable me to commute to and from work at Cave Hill just as I wanted - did not do much for my low morale. Perhaps, I had felt somewhat better for the first few days after they had left, but any such lift in my mood did not last long - as the extensive hours of my preparing for my classes ahead, into the evenings alone in my office, took their toll. It was just a matter of time, therefore, before, one day, about midway during that Second Term, I decided that I just could not face going into the Faculty to give my classes – for the time being, at any rate. Accordingly, I rang up my secretary, Audrey, and asked her to please tell the Head of the Teaching Department that I was ill and would not be coming in for a few days. Perhaps, I gave my having been struck down by 'the flu' as my reason, but, certainly, I would not have mentioned feeling excessively 'stressed' – which, of course, was the true cause.

When I did return to my give my classes the following week, I felt obliged to speak about that true reason for my taking time off with one or two of my colleagues – in case they, too, had felt similar pressures in their own careers and might have some words of guidance or advice for me. Thus, I surely would have mentioned my issue to my 'tea time' visiting-lecturer friend, Peter Morton. And whilst I would have found him to be extremely sympathetic and a great listener, he also regretfully admitted that he, himself, had not sustained any similar experience in his lecturing career so far and, thus, was not really able to help me very much. On the contrary, if anything, he had a working life not so dissimilar to my own, and also spent long hours in the evening in his office preparing for his future classes to come – without any adverse physical or mental affects, it seemed to me.

More practical help and advice, however, came instead from a rather unexpected source. For it emanated from another male colleague – one located right next door to me! That person was Michael Castagne – the young man of Trinidadian origins, of about the same age as me or, perhaps, one or two years my junior. He was like me in one other way also, in that he was a practising Catholic. After I told him about my low morale interfering with my ability to prepare for, and then give, my classes as enthusiastically as when I had first started at Cave Hill the previous term, he said that he had sometimes felt like that during his career too. Just as importantly, he went on to tell me that he had found a positive way forward, namely by his 'getting closer to God' and putting all his troubles and negative feelings into 'the Lord's hands' and asking 'Him for help at all times – especially during crisis episodes caused by low morale'. One of the best ways, he also told me, that he felt that he was able to keep that closeness with his Creator – apart from attending Mass in church every Sunday – was to attend a weekly 'Prayer Meeting Group' every Monday night. He went on to reveal to me that such a gathering took place in the 'Strathclyde' district of Bridgetown – about 15 minutes' drive from Cave Hill - and started at 7pm.

Because I was desperate to try anything reasonable, to help me feel better about my teaching life at Cave Hill, I told Michael that I would like to go with him to the next meeting of his Prayer Group. I figured that, if I started working on my Tuesday Conflicts of Laws lecture a little earlier on Monday afternoons, then I should be in a position to be able to get to the Prayer Meeting by 7pm, on a regular basis - if I found Michael's solution worked for me too.

That is exactly what I did, therefore - on the second Monday of my return to the office from illness. I went to my initial Prayer Meeting Group session with Michael – the two of us taking our own separate cars from Cave Hill to Strathclyde and neither of us, so far as I knew, mentioning our 'spiritual date', or the special aspect of our respective private lives, to any of our other colleagues in the Faculty. The venue of the Meeting in question, much to my surprise, was a large private home – one belonging to, and presided over by, a White Bajan lady! I immediately liked the atmosphere which I encountered inside, however – for the Meeting was taking place in the main living room of the house, and it was already quite full - with about 25 to 30 adults, when Michael and I first arrived. About one third of those present were White, like the hostess - and the rest Black, or brown-skinned like Michael and myself. The other wonderful thing, to me, was that quite a few of those other attendees had their guitars with them and, just as Michael and I entered the room, the hostess began the Meeting by asking everyone to sing, with her, the uplifting hymn 'Come, Bless the Lord'.

We were all given a booklet of such holy songs, and it was very easy to sing along with the rest of the Group - even if, now and again, we were led into singing one or two spiritual tunes which I had not come across before. Every song, to me, was emotional, and, thus, rather helped me to 'tune in to God' – just as Michael (back at the Law Faculty) had suggested that I should try to do. Whilst so focussed, I found that it was much easier for me to be fervent in my prayers to the Almighty in asking Him to help me get over my then current difficulties with my lack of enthusiasm for my teaching vocation at Cave Hill in order to prevent me from putting my family's new life in Barbados into any jeopardy. And though there were several periods, during the Meeting, where we listened to passages being read from the Bible, or to 'testaments' of some of the attendees relating to how God had acted in their respective lives in recent days, most of the session was dominated by lots of spiritually-uplifting songs accompanied by several of the guitar players present.

When the Meeting broke up at about 9pm, tears were in my eyes - owing to how 'moved' I had been. A whole new experience had overtaken me. As a result, I told Michael that I was already resolved to return to the Meetings, with him, on a regular basis in future. Needless to say, I could see that he was happy with my decision. Moreover, one further pleasant surprise for me was that I discovered that there was no cost involved in such regular attendances, nor even any particular religious denominational requirement. I had rather imagined that most people at the Meeting were fellow Catholics, like Michael and myself – but, speaking with one or two attendees afterwards, I discovered that at least a few of them were, in fact, Anglicans. Everyone seemed friendly and to be present and participating for the same reason – namely, to bring a greater focus of the Almighty into their daily lives.

And, so, it came to pass that every Monday thereafter, for the rest of my Second Term at Cave Hill, I would go to the Strathclyde Prayer Meeting – with or without Michael (who sometimes had conflicting commitments with his Amnesty International duties, for he represented that organisation in Barbados, in addition to lecturing at Cave Hill). Little by little, therefore, I did find myself developing the fortitude to 'survive' my difficult teaching regime at the Law Faculty that term. When the going got toughest, I put my problems in the hands of the Lord – at least metaphorically, through prayer. Attending the Strathclyde gathering on a regular basis, without fail, enabled me to keep Him as my focus - for both times of crisis as well as more generally, in my everyday life, either domestically with my family or whilst at the university.

Thus, I even became mentally strong enough again to be able to accomplish the difficult task of drafting my first examination papers at Cave Hill - for both my Comparative Law course and my Conflict of Laws one. Moreover, I found it relatively easy to compose a question or two for Norma Forde's Law of Torts exam paper, which subject I also tutored in. In addition, before too much longer, it was time to look forward to the end of my Second Term at Cave Hill and the coming Easter vacation. That was to be another break which I, not unsurprisingly, was very much looking forward to. That was not because my household had planned to travel outside Barbados again, for the coming major holidays - to a member of my Caribbean extended family or otherwise. Rather, it was because another family – as opposed to a couple of single people, as John and Jane had been - was coming to stay with us! That family was none other than that of my 'Best Man', 'Bernhard Schuhmacher' or 'Berndt', and his wife, 'Monika' or 'Moni', who were due to visit us from West Germany. Moreover, they were bringing their little daughter, 'Miriam', with them too – a toddler who just happened to be my goddaughter and who would be having her very first birthday whilst with us on the island. And, as if one other nuclear family coming to holiday with us was not already enough cause for joy, the visiting party was also to include Berndt's oldest and best male (and livewire) friend - one 'Hubert Pfeiffer', or 'Hupsi'!

*Chapter 9*

# Some Dear Friends from West Germany holiday with us in Barbados - May 1980

I was extremely excited about the visit of our West German friends to stay with us at Hygeia. That was not merely because it was an opportunity to forget about all my 'troubles' at Cave Hill. For, ever since starting my Prayer Meetings at Strathclyde, I had come to realise that I had to stop 'regretting' my Barbados teaching duties whilst discharging them and, instead, be thankful for the opportunity which they gave me to enjoy the lovely lifestyle in Barbados which performing those obligations gave me. Moreover, my teaching responsibilities were almost over for that first UWI academic year of mine in any case – apart from a few post-Easter 'revision classes'. I still needed to stay relatively focussed, however – mainly because of the examination period which would follow those remaining sessions. My mounting excitement nevertheless continued to bubble away and arose from the fact that Philomena and I had not seen Berndt and Moni since the July of the year before - when they had visited Swindon with Berndt's mother, 'Frau Schuhmacher', for the Christening of our then very new baby, Kim. Indeed, Berndt had been Kim's godfather on that occasion – a neat reciprocation of the honour which he and Moni had given me a few months before, in West Germany, when they had made me the godfather of their own first child, Miriam. I was also keen to show Berndt, his family and Hupsi, a little of my native Caribbean region. For it would be the very first visit, to that exotic part of the world, for any of them. It was my great desire, therefore, that their stay in my own '*Heimat*' (the German word for 'Homeland' or 'Area of one's birth') would be as memorable, and as happy, for them as possible.

Berndt was fortunate enough to work in the international transport industry in West Germany. He had trained in 'Bremen' as an international 'forwarding agent' which required him to professionally arrange for goods to get from one part of Europe to another, or, indeed, to places across the globe outside Europe (including, perhaps, the Caribbean - even if he had never visited that latter region). Moreover, it could well have been that one of his clients was treating him and his family to the Barbados trip in question – a first time adventure which I had also played a part in bringing about. That is because I had been able to tell him about the honeymoon trip of Philomena and myself in 1976 to the island and about how we had flown there from London with Caribbean Airways, which had included a stop-over in Luxembourg. Consequently, between the two of us, Berndt and I had been able to work out that the relatively short drive from his, then, home in 'Siegen', West Germany to Luxembourg in order to catch the Caribbean Airways flight to Barbados was the easiest way for him and his family to get to us from Europe. Hupsi, however, had a bit further to come as he would first have to get to Siegen to join the Schuhmachers there, since he still lived in 'Salzgitter' (the twin town, or city, of Swindon back in England where Berndt's godson, Kim, had been Baptised the previous year).

Accordingly, my happy feverishness knew no bounds as Philomena, myself and our boys drove to the back of Grantley Adams Airport to watch the Caribbean Airways flight from Luxembourg land – hopefully, with our West German visitors on board. We knew that it would take us no longer than 10 to 15 minutes to get round to the front of the airport, and its 'Arrivals' section, and also that it would take somewhat longer than that for our visitors to clear passport control and customs - once they had disembarked from their aircraft.

We need not have worried about failing to reach the front of the airport in time to meet and greet our West German guests as they exited the Arrivals doors. For, they must have been one of the last set of passengers, on the flight from Luxembourg, to clear the passport and then customs area within the terminal. Unfortunately, we could not see them trying to do so. Thus, Philomena and myself began to worry, after our would-be guests failed to appear for more than 30 minutes to an hour after we had first arrived at the doors to await them. At worst, we speculated to each other, that, perhaps, they had missed their flight! Finally, however, the familiar face of my Best Man and his wife, Moni - as well as their friend, Hupsi - emerged pushing quite a bit of luggage. One of the 'items' being propelled along – by Moni – was her daughter Miriam, sitting in a Baby Buggy. Very soon after that exit, all five of us adult 'meeters and greeters' and visitors, combined, were in a huddle - either giving a welcome to Barbados to our West German guests, or their happily receiving the same. And then it was the turn of Philomena and myself to make a fuss of Miriam – and exclaim to her parents about how much she had grown since we had last seen her – followed by our three adult guests doing likewise in relation to Noel and Kim. For me, in particular, it was already the start of a dream coming true – an ambition to get one of my dearest friends, and his family and best mate, to visit my own family in my native region of the world.

Within a few more minutes, Philomena and myself had managed to pack ourselves and our sons, as well as our three adult visitors and little Miriam, into our Skoda. It was only built for a driver and four passengers – so, I cannot imagine now how we ever managed to accomplish all that was necessary (with luggage and Baby Buggy, to boot)! It could only have been with a lot of squeezing together of the adults, plus each of the children sitting on the laps of one or other of their laps (apart from that of the driver, who was myself), that we managed to get everyone in. The baggage (including Miriam's pushchair) we, somehow, also managed to fit into the 'trunk' of the car – which, in the Skoda, was at front of the car since the engine was at its rear. I doubt now, however, whether (in view of the bulk which our visitors had flown in with) I was able to fully close the cover of the trunk. Perhaps Berndt and I only managed to partially do so, and then we were forced to tie the cover with a piece of string in order to stop it from flying open as we drove along. At any rate, however, our entire party was soon driving, excitedly, along the road to Oistins from the airport and then onwards to our home at Maxwell – as Philomena and myself asked our adult visitors about the highlights of their flight on Caribbean Airways, and their journey from their homes in West Germany generally, and with Berndt, Moni and Hupsi, in turn, responding in their own respective and animated ways.

Unlike the situation from a few months earlier when Philomena's brother, John, and his girlfriend, Jane, had visited us, our West German guests had arrived at a good time in relation to my university duties. For, I was effectively on holiday myself. That was either because the Second Term had just come to an end and it was already the Easter 'vacation' for staff and students. Alternatively, it was because it was already the start of the Third Term and, basically, there was little or no teaching to be done and the students just had to revise for their forthcoming examinations later that trimester. Accordingly, unlike the period when our English visitors – John and Jane - had come to stay a few months before, I was in a 'good mood' most of the time. My UWI responsibilities, generally, would not be getting in the way of my being able to be a cheerful host to – and spend a great deal of time with – my West German guests.

Once, therefore, the first welcoming dinner at Hygeia was out of the way for the new arrivals, I very much wanted to show off our nearby beaches to our guests the next morning. Top of the list would have been the one at Oistins. For, not only was that just a short car ride away, it had that wonderful half-moon strand which was gently lapped by the shallow waters of the Caribbean Sea. That would be the ideal place to introduce not only our adult visitors to that body of warm water for the first time, but also my goddaughter, Miriam. She had already grown into a 'little girl' instead of the 'baby' I had last seen just after her Christening Day in West Germany nearly one year before. Moreover, she was already managing to toddle about, if not quite being able to walk without falling over - as well as make sounds such as 'mam-ma'. I was, thus, delighted to be able to witness, for myself, such welcome developments from the infancy stage in which I had last seen her. With her own armbands, or swim wings, Miriam took to the Caribbean waters at Oistins just as well, and happily, as my own two sons. The latter, in particular, stayed close to her - floating in the placid sea, and doing their best to make her splash and laugh – whilst her mum, Moni, was more at pains to stop her little daughter from trying to drink the salty water from time to time.

The other nice thing about choosing Oistins, for our first beach outing, was the fact that nearby - within the village but on the main road back to Maxwell and Bridgetown - was a fish market. Returning home from our sea baths, and first picnic – elongated, naturally, by a post-swim visit to the Back of the Airport to watch a few Jumbo Jets fly in from, or take off for, England, Canada and the United States – our party of eight was able to stop at that seafood outlet and choose some flying fish for our supper that evening at home. For that purpose, I, personally, would have put myself forward to do the buying. That is because I had been advised by our neighbour back at Hygeia, Mrs Payne, that if Philomena ever tried to do so by herself, the sellers would assume that she was some 'rich, White, tourist' and so might well try to charge her a higher price than that asked for from the 'local inhabitants'. Accordingly, in my best mock-Bajan accent, which I had already developed after about nine months of living on the island - and in the vernacular - I would ask one of the fishmongers (who happened to be all women, incidentally): 'How you selling the flying fish today?'. On that particular occasion, perhaps I had been answered with a stern: 'Three for a dollar!'. If so, I would already have known, from previous buying experiences at Oistins, that such a price was a good, or fair, one. That would have been notwithstanding the fact that I had been at the market on days when a catch was plentiful and when, therefore, I might get four, or even five, fishes for one Bajan dollar.

At any rate, on that first occasion of our West German guests' visit to the Oistins market, I showed them my 'expertise' as a fish-buying customer and we then went home to Hygeia with more than enough for a fine supper for us five adults - and even for Noel and, to a lesser extent, the toddlers, Kim and Miriam. My experience with flying fish, however, did not end at the buying stage. For, thanks to the ever-helpful Mrs Payne, I had been taught how to 'clean' such a sea creature for the frying pan. Our neighbour had shown me, soon after our arrival at Hygeia, just how one should start - by first turning the fish onto its back. Then, with a sharp knife, make a cut, from the hole to be found near its tail, all the way up past the middle of the stomach to the midpoint of its gills, near its head. You then had to turn the fish over, and draw the knife all the way along one side of the fish's spine to a depth of about half an inch – followed by a repeat of that process on the other side of the creature's backbone. The fish was then ready to be turned unto its back once more, and opened up by putting both thumbs into the first incision, previously made in the creature's abdomen, and prising the belly of the fish apart. The stomach and other innards of the creature were then exposed and could easily be ripped out and thrown away. One would thus be left with two sides of the flying fish, still joined together by its spine and with its head and tail still intact. By lifting the tail and pulling it up slowly, the whole backbone would come away from the fillet, all the way up to, and including, the head. With just the fillet remaining, there were only a few final processes left to do. These were to remove the two lateral bones found on its underside, as well as the two 'wings' on its upper(by which means it had been able to 'fly', or glide (more precisely), above the sea whilst it had been alive). After all those steps had been undertaken, I was left with one flying fish fillet ready for the frying pan. I then merely needed to go over the same operation 10 to 15 more times, in order to have enough quantity for our fish supper - and I was delighted to be able to do so, watched by my intrigued friends from West Germany.

One of the earliest things that Hupsi did for us all, after our guests' arrival at Hygeia, was to tell us that he wished to treat our enlarged household – by buying us all 'something special'. He would not tell us what he had in mind, but asked me to drive him – along with Berndt – to the supermarket at Oistins, whilst Philomena and Moni stayed at home to cook the fish supper or just play with the children. At the supermarket, Hupsi asked Berndt and myself to simply wait for him outside until he returned. About 10 minutes later he was back - accompanied by a huge crate of beer! It must have been one holding about two dozen bottles or more – and, certainly, a good deal more than I have ever bought for myself, in one go (or, perhaps, even in total!), during all the time that I had lived on the island. The brand of the brew in question was 'Banks' – which I had often seen advertised on billboards around island as 'The beer of Barbados'. To me, it seemed to be clearly the best among the competition as far as Bajans were concerned, and, given that West German (or even English) beer was just not available anywhere on the island, Hupsi's gesture was very much appreciated by both Berndt and myself. And whilst I was then unsure as to whether Moni liked the ale in question as much as Hupsi or her husband, I already knew that Philomena would be happy to join in with the many 'beer evenings' that would now lie ahead at our home, during our visitors' sojourn, thanks to Hupsi's largesse (if only by herself, and perhaps Moni, partaking in drinking some of the red wine which we kept a few bottles of at Hygeia for such celebratory times).

That first flying fish evening was an undoubted success for Philomena and myself, and (as far as I could tell) for our West German guests too. We had dined on fresh fish - taken straight out of the sea, near the place where our party had spent our first beach day together on the island. That food product had first been bought, and then prepared for the frying pan, by my own fair hand, and then cooked to perfection by Philomena's. Lastly, we had imbibed plenty of booze to wash our dinner down with, thanks to Hupsi's generosity regarding the crateful of Banks (and to our little 'cellar' of wine for the ladies in the house). Our visitors' stay had begun on a very positive note and it was my sincerest wish that the remainder of their time with us would follow suit.

During one of those earliest days of our guests' stay, I was obliged to go into the Law Faculty for a day. Perhaps, I just had to give a revision class or meet one or two of my students there in order to go over a few queries which they had respectively encountered during their revision. Accordingly, I put into operation the procedure which I had used during the earlier visit of John and Jane and - again without discussing any motor insurance issues that might arise - asked Hupsi if he would drive, with me, to Cave Hill and then return to the others with the Skoda so that the rest of the enlarged household could make use of the vehicle during the day ahead, with him driving it. He readily agreed and, having taken me to the UWI campus, also consented to come back for me at about 6pm that evening. When that hour came, I went out to the Faculty car park to find Berndt waiting in my car for me. With much surprise in my voice, I asked what had happened to Hupsi. Berndt laughed out loud and then answered that he would tell me when we got home. I was very curious to find out what had transpired with Hupsi, but kept my impatience in check until we reached Hygeia.

There we found Hupsi in bed – looking much the worse for wear! Berndt then revealed that when Hupsi had arrived back from Cave Hill that morning with the Skoda, he and Hupsi had decided to go on a special tourist excursion – since Philomena and Moni just wanted to have another day with the children at the beach. The 'boys' had, therefore, gone into Bridgetown, alone, and had booked for the four-hour, or so, sailing trip on the 'pirate ship' which cruised along to the West Coast of the island from the capital, and back again. That vessel was named the 'Jolly Roger' and one of the highlights of the excursion on it was that passengers could 'drink as much as they wanted' - once they had paid their ticket money. It seems that Hupsi had taken that 'special bonus' of the trip a little too literally and had made a bee-line for the innocuous-looking, colourful, and sweet-tasting 'rum punch' as soon as the Jolly Roger had set sail. Berndt went on to tell me that, by the time the ship had anchored off Barbados' second largest municipality of 'Holetown', on its West Coast, to allow the passengers to have their lunch (and a swim if they wished), it had already been too late for Hupsi. He did not have much room left, nor any appetite, for any food!

Hupsi had therefore given both the lunch, and the chance of a lunchtime swim in the Caribbean, a big miss and began instead to try to sleep off his excesses from his morning's binge drinking session. By the time the Jolly Roger had returned to Bridgetown, he was still slumbering and in no fit state to drive himself and Berndt back to Hygeia in my car. Berndt, therefore, had been obliged to do the honours of getting both of them back to the home of their hosts in order to get Hupsi to bed. That is why, therefore, Berndt had been compelled to come to fetch me at Cave Hill that evening instead of my agreed driver, and why that driver gave 'the rum of Barbados' (or from anywhere else in the Caribbean, or the world, for that matter) a very wide berth for the rest of his stay on the island!

A much happier event took place a few days later at our home. That was the hosting of a birthday party for my goddaughter, Miriam - her very first anywhere in the world. I felt extremely honoured that Berndt and Moni had decided to come to celebrate that significant event in their firstborn's life with my own family in Barbados. For, surely, they could easily have come a little bit before, or after, the birthday - so that they could have been present in West Germany, with Miriam's grandparents and other close relatives, to 'keep up' (with those relatives) her first really 'big day' since her birth? On the contrary, however, Miriam's parents had chosen her godfather, and his family in their new Caribbean island home, as the special people and place for the celebrations - and, for that, I was extremely touched.

Accordingly, Philomena and myself went to some trouble to make the birthday party for Miriam as special as possible. We could have tried to have baked our own cake for her, but neither of us were experienced in that matter. Instead, the two of us left Noel and Kim in the care of our visitors on Maxwell Beach on the afternoon of the birthday and went in our Skoda to Supercentre at Oistins. There, we chose the biggest birthday cake that we could find among quite a selection in the store – one with lots of pink icing surrounding it. Choosing the one candle needed, to complement it for the event in question, was relatively easy after that. Finding a suitable gift for Miriam was also a 'must'. And though I can no longer recall what my wife and I finally decided on for that purpose, it was more than likely some kind of toy. That is because we had once bought my little goddaughter a 'Paddington Bear' teddy - when we last visited her in West Germany for her Christening the previous year - and we had since been given to understand, by her parents, that she had really enjoyed that toy back at home in Siegen. Consequently, I am pretty sure that Philomena and I would have played safe and bought her something else along the lines of one of her favourite playthings in her West German nursery.

The one thing, however, which I could help Philomena make for my goddaughter's party, and which we guessed that she (as well our own children) would enjoy at the coming party, was lots of jelly – or 'jello' as many Bajans called the dessert, as per their neighbours in relatively nearby America. Accordingly, the two of us bought a variety of different colours and flavours for the event – as well as the largest tub of vanilla ice cream that we could find in our local Oistins supermarket. Back at home, I set about helping Philomena to make the red, yellow and green jellies which would complement the frozen dessert. Unusually, the latter was manufactured within the island itself, and not imported from somewhere in North America - as so many other 'goodies' to be found in the local Supercentre were.

And well before the sun went down at about 6.30pm on the May 1980 day in question, our enlarged household was ready for the party. We held it on the veranda at the front of our house. That ran almost the entire length of Hygeia, but was raised up above the garden and paved path which went right around the house. That particular location meant that people on buses passing by on Highway 7, to Bridgetown in one direction or Oistins in the other, could look out of their windows and spot us celebrating Miriam's big day. Any such witnessing being observed by curious onlookers would have been momentary and I, for one, did not mind that at all. Neither, it seemed, did the 'birthday girl', nor Noel and Kim, as they tucked into their jelly and ice cream, among other things. If the children were happy with the fare specially made, or bought in, for them, then so, too, were the adults at the party with their own. For, among the latter, was the remainder of the many bottles of Banks Beer which Hupsi had bought in for us some days before – although Philomena and myself made sure that there was not a drop of rum anywhere in sight!

Of course, no visit to us by our West German friends, at that time in our life on our new island, would have been complete without a trip to my family's most favourite beach at Bath in St John parish on the East Coast. We would have made a very full day of it for that special excursion, by starting out early so that we could also take in a few other sights on the way to our final destination. For, Philomena and I would have planned to arrive at that treasured place at a suitable time for us to have our picnic lunch by the beach. Thus, other interesting places *en route* before that meal would have included

*Fig 28: Miriam Schuhmacher's 1st birthday tea party at our family's 'Hygeia' home in Barbados in May 1980 – with her parents, Berndt and Moni, and fellow-West German family friend, Hupsi Pfeiffer (far right), as well as Noel, appearing in this photo. The 'jello' and ice-cream came later!*

'Crane Beach' – located not too far from the airport in Christ Church, but already 'over the border' in the neighbouring parish of St Philip. That particular strand was a very rough one with lots of crashing waves – breakers which once turned Philomena over so much, during our honeymoon trip to the island four years before, that she had resolved on that occasion never to re-enter the sea at that place again. A little further along the St Philip coastline, however, in the direction of neighbouring St John and Bath, was the more attractive – at least as far as my wife was concerned – venue of 'Sam Lord's Castle'. That locale, despite its name, was an upmarket hotel – perhaps the second best in the entire island, only beaten by the reputedly even more luxurious resort of 'Sandy Lane Hotel' on the West Coast near Holetown. Even if we had not wished to have actually tarried long at Sam Lords, however, Philomena and I would have felt able to treat our visitors to some refreshing drinks at one of that hotel's beach bars. In so doing, we would have been able to show our guests the standard of beachside life at one of the island's top tourist resorts.

That last stop would have been important for me, since I wanted our West German friends to have some background with which to better appreciate seeing just how wonderful Bath Beach was. When we all finally arrived at our main destination for that day, the West German guests would already have seen other Bajan beaches with which to compare that favourite place of my family – such as other strands which included that attached to one of Barbados' top hotels, at Sam Lords. Thus, I am pretty sure that our adult visitors would have better understood that, in Bath, we had probably found the very best beach, for a family with young children, on the whole of the island. At any rate, we all shared an excellent picnic lunch there on that first visit together, and Berndt and Moni were kind enough to ask Philomena and myself whether we could all repeat the experience, at least one more time, before they would finally have to leave the island to return home, via Luxembourg.

*Fig 29: A picnic lunch at Bath Beach, Barbados in May 1980, shared by (from left to right): Hupsi Pfeiffer, Noel, Philomena, Kim, Moni Schuhmacher, Miriam Schuhmacher and the Author. Berndt Schuhmacher was also there, but was operating as the taker of the photo on that occasion. The calmness, and shallowness, of the sea on that eastern coast might be appreciated from the background of the photo, as well as why our family regarded Bath Beach as one of the most child-friendly on the island*

Alas, after what was one of the best non-work interludes in my new life in Barbados, since arriving there to teach at the university the previous year, Berndt and his family had, of necessity, to return home to Europe. His work beckoned him in Siegen, as well as that of Hupsi in Salzgitter! It was, therefore, with a very heavy heart that I, along with my family, saw them, accompanied by Moni and Miriam, off at Grantley Adams International Airport - one evening about two weeks or so after they had first arrived at that terminal. Once they had gone through the doors for departing passengers, we knew that we would not be able to see them again inside the building itself. Nevertheless, we told them that, after they had disappeared from our sight within the terminal's bowels, we would drive quickly around to the Back of the Airport to see their Caribbean Airways flight take off for Luxembourg. We, thus, asked them to look out for us waving to the flight – and hoped that they would all get seats sitting on the right-hand side of the plane before it speeded down the take-off runway. That is what my family and I did, therefore - once our West Germany friends had 'gone through'. Arriving at the Back of the Airport, with plenty of time to spare, we eventually saw the Caribbean Airways plane trundle down the runway from where it had been parked next to the terminal. Then, as it turned onto the take-off runway, my entire family and I waved our hands, holding whatever pieces of cloth that we could find – including one or two beach towels from our last trip to Bath – so as to do our best to ensure that our guests might see something of our 'farewell-wishing' efforts for them, as their aircraft took to the skies and headed for Europe. I, for one, would have had a tear or two in my eyes. For, I would not, then, have known if - and when - I would ever see Berndt and his family again. Nor, indeed, Hupsi - for that matter. In addition, our West German guests' departure meant that I would no longer have the legitimate distraction of 'looking after my foreign visitors' to take my mind off my work and, thereby, keep myself from going into the Law Faculty with good reason. Rather, I would once more have to re-concentrate on my university duties and the main reason for my being in Barbados!

*Chapter 10*

# My First Summer Term at UWI – May to July 1980

In fact, 'returning to work' was not as difficult an experience as I had first imagined it might be. That was mainly because most of my teaching had already been done and it was the period when the students were mainly revising for their exams – commencing from about the end of May, or early June. Of course, I had to be in and around the Faculty on weekdays in case any of my students wanted to see me to ask me about issues he or she might have encountered during their exam-preparation process – and, thus, I tried to come to Cave Hill on the same days as those of my teaching ones during the earlier two terms. The huge difference in that third session, however, was that I no longer felt obliged to stay until about 8pm each time. Moreover, I made sure that I continued to have my sacrosanct 'family day out' each Wednesday until the exams began to take place. However, by continuing to attend Cave Hill on those normal 'teaching days', I found that I needed to adopt something which would keep my mind occupied. That is, therefore, when I began to research for, and then write my very first legal article - for possible publication in a Law journal somewhere in the Caribbean, England or elsewhere in the world.

At that time it was always being emphasised to me, by other colleagues in the Law Faculty, that in order to obtain 'tenure' – a long-term position - in that UWI teaching department, one had to 'get published'. From what I had gathered, it did not matter very much about the quality, or length, of the intended publication. Or, indeed, whether it was a whole book or just an 'article' in a journal. That latter situation suited me well - for an entire book was out of the question, for myself, at that early stage of my career. I did, however, have in mind trying to write an article about a West Indian case which I had encountered in my researches in the Law Faculty Library and which was still unreported anywhere (as far as I could see). From my earliest days of teaching at Cave Hill, I had been struck by how very much my long-standing colleagues had been forced to rely on English Law cases as 'authority' for legal propositions, in the West Indian context, when teaching their various subjects. What I really wanted to do, in relation to those subjects which I taught and which had a good deal of 'case Law', was to find as many local West Indian cases, or authorities, as I could to back up the major propositions of Law which I was teaching in those subjects. That approach I considered as most necessary in relation to the Law of Torts (which I only tutored) and The Conflict of Laws (which, as seen,

I had been at pains to tutor, and lecture on, during my first UWI academic year in question). And, by good fortune, perhaps, I managed to discover one such 'precedent' in my search of unreported cases in the Law Library at Cave Hill.

That had been in the Torts area of my teaching subjects. It concerned the question of when does a 'duty of care', or an obligation to take reasonable care, arise in a situation where a person is giving financial advice to another person – without any contract between them being present – and that advice leads to 'damage' which is financial only (that is to say, non-physical and, thus, 'pure economic'). In England, during the 1979-80 academic year in question, the best authority, or precedent, on this area of the Law was a case from its then highest court. That highest tribunal was then the 'Appellate Committee of the House of Lords' (usually referred to simply as the 'House of Lords', but it has since been replaced by a new 'Supreme Court'[40]). That case is named '*Hedley Byrne v Heller and Partners*',[41] but it had been decided nearly two decades before in 1963. The judges in that litigation had ruled, or 'held', that such a duty of care could arise if certain conditions were satisfied, and that, if such duty was breached, then the adviser could be made liable for the pure economic loss which reliance on his advice had caused. Through my researches among the unreported cases of West Indian courts, stockpiled in the UWI Law Library, I was fortunate to find a decision with similar facts to the *Hedley Byrne* one – but which was of much more recent vintage - decided by the 'Court of Appeal of Trinidad and Tobago'. Insofar as it applied the Law as laid down by the English case, it seemed to me that, for the future, it would be much more significant for legal development in the English-speaking jurisdictions of the Caribbean territories if the courts therein relied more on the Trinidad case. To me, that would be a more locally-apt legal approach than to slavishly 'follow' the *Hedley Byrne* precedent from the 'Motherland' situated some four or five thousand miles away. I, therefore, set about trying to write my article on that local Caribbean case. That was done with a view to letting my future students in the Law of Torts know of its existence – as well as my colleagues at UWI (such as Norma Forde, the Director of the Torts course) and practitioners in the Caribbean legal systems which sent their Law Students to us at Cave Hill – so that, in time, that local Trinidadian case might become just as much a West Indian precedent as the much older, and distant, *Hedley Byrne* decision was an English one.

By such researches and writing, I occupied my days leading up to my students' examination papers, in my main two subjects, landing on the desk in my office in later June, or early July, 1980. I read, and re-read, the Trinidadian legal case – which was named '*Pampellone v The Royal Bank Trust (Trinidad) Ltd*'[42] - and tried to write about it as simply, and as clearly, as I could. Ironically, perhaps - given that I was setting out to urge a move away from simply copying English precedent - in drafting my article, I took pains to write in the style of my hero in the legal world back in England! That person was 'Lord Denning' - the former 'Master of the Rolls', by whom I had been 'Called to the Bar of England and Wales' at 'Lincoln's Inn' in 1978.

Little by little, therefore, and starting by my stating of the facts of that Trinidadian case as simply as possible, I then went on to show how closely the legal issues in it resembled that of the *Hedley Byrne* case. With such a positive opening, I was then able to proceed with a close analysis of the three individual judgments in the case, and then set out the essential parts of the reasoning of each such judgment within the body of the draft article. Thereafter, I presented my own assessments of the merits of what the judges had said in the West Indian case and, thereby, was able to finalise my efforts with a conclusion. Such verdict was that the Trinidadian justices had indeed done a good job with their decision-making and reasoning in the case. So much so, indeed, that I was able to propose that *the case itself* should, in the future, be regarded as a 'local' West Indian precedent which could, and should, be cited as an authority for the legal issue in question within in the courts of Commonwealth Caribbean - just as much as (if not *more often than*) the English, 'out of region', *Hedley Byrne* one.

I had been pleased with my first efforts to get published and, after polishing my draft and asking a few other colleagues in the Law Faculty with expertise in the Law of Torts – including my senior colleague in the Faculty, Professor Ralph Carnegie – I began to start thinking about which Law journal I should send my article to for possible publication. One of those, with arguably the highest reputation of all in the Common Law world around the Commonwealth, was back in England and based at my old university in Cambridge. The Law Faculty, in that ancient city, published the '*Cambridge Law Journal*' and I still had connections with lecturers there, such as 'Mr John Collier', who might well have been on the editorial board of the Journal at that time. There were also other famous English legal journals then in existence, such as '*The Law Quarterly Review*' or '*The Modern Law Review*' – both of which were then published in London.

Notwithstanding the fame of such England-based legal journals, however, I avoided sending my draft article on the *Pampellone* case to either Cambridge or London. That was because of what I hoped my article would do – namely, make that Trinidadian decision become a 'household name' among the lawyers of the English–speaking West Indian territories. For that purpose, therefore, I needed to go for a publication which most such legally-connected, or interested, persons in the Caribbean region would be likely to see and read. Sending it to even the most famous Law journal in Cambridge, England – or even to one of those in London – would risk missing my target audience by thousands of miles. Fortunately for me, there was in existence at the time a suitable 'more local' Law journal whose intended readership was based mainly in the Caribbean territories in question – one based in Jamaica and published by the (West Indian) 'Council of Legal Education'. That institution (based at the 'Norman Manley Law School' at UWI's Mona Campus in that island's capital of 'Kingston') was responsible, with its Trinidadian counterpart (situated at the 'Hugh Wooding Law School'), for the practical training of future West Indian lawyers, after they had graduated with their LL.B Law degrees from my own UWI Law Faculty at Cave Hill Campus in Barbados. (After completing, successfully, such practical legal training, they are usually called 'Attorneys-at-Law' in most of the English-speaking Caribbean territories). The journal in question was called, somewhat unsurprisingly, '*The West Indian Law Journal*' –which name was often abbreviated to '*WILJ*'.

Off, therefore, I duly sent the draft of my *Pampellone* case article, to the Editor at the *WILJ* in Jamaica, asking him whether he would be willing to accept it for publication in his journal. To my delight, within a week or so - which was amazingly quick by Caribbean standards, in my limited experiences to date – I had received a letter from him accepting my draft, without the need for any editing! I was, thus, delighted by that outcome – even though the Editor also disclosed that (unlike publication in one or other of the English legal journals which I had considered) I would get no payment for the eventual appearance of the said 'published work'. Financial reward, however, was totally irrelevant to me at that stage. Rather, what mattered, much more, was my 'getting published' and seeing my work, and my ideas about the development of an aspect of Caribbean Law, 'broadcasted' to the West Indian legal community via the *WILJ*. All in all, therefore, I was, with the news from Jamaica, much more content about my working life at UWI by that period, in the Third Term of my first academic year there - and as I excitedly looked forward to actually seeing my article 'in print' in the pages of the *WILJ* in due course.[43]

Something completely different, however, was around the corner which risked shaking my contentment at that time. For it was the start of the examinations for the students at the Law Faculty – including, of course, class members of my respective subjects in Comparative Law, The Conflict of Laws and the Law of Torts. Despite my setting what I considered to be very fair exam papers in the first two subjects, and my contributing one or two such questions for the Torts one of Norma Forde (for which subject assessment she, as Course Director, was primarily responsible for drawing up) I found myself to be extremely nervous for my students. I guessed that I was feeling that way owing to my empathising with them all rather too much. Perhaps, that was because I had been a Law student, myself, only two years before in England when I had sat my 'Bar Finals' examinations in London, as a precursor to my becoming a Barrister-at-Law of Lincoln's Inn in that capital city. Such a relatively short time later meant that I could still fully identify with what my students were about to undergo – as part of passing their Final Year, and qualifying for their Law degrees, in the case of my Comparative Law and Conflicts students. Such nervousness, on my part, was made all the worse by UWI's requirement that the Course Director, of the subject being examined on any particular morning or afternoon during the exam period, had to be present in the room at the start of the exam in question – and for the first 30 minutes of its three-hour duration (for both sets of participants). That meant that your students would see you as they came into the room – which gave me the opportunity to nod to each of mine, smile and wish them a silent 'good luck'. That nerve-wracking occasion, however, also meant that if, once the students were asked to turn over their paper and begin the exam, any of them looked alarmed and, perhaps, then decided to make a dash to escape the room, you would be there to witness such a nightmarish moment. Fortunately, such a scenario never came to pass - at either the start of the Comparative Law or Conflicts exam. I was, thus, able to leave the room, which was situated in the main 'Administrative Block' of Cave Hill Campus, and walk back to my office in the Law Faculty - feeling rather sorry for the 'ordeal' which my students were then undergoing, and for which I was responsible. All I could do then was await the completed papers – or 'scripts' as they were called – to later arrive on my desk.

Those scripts duly appeared, within an hour or so of the completion of each of the Comparative and Conflicts exams, on the different days that they were respectively taken. Regarding those for the Law of Torts, Norma Forde, as Course Director, would be getting them first and I would only see them one week or so later, as 'second marker'. Actually receiving my Comparative Law and Conflicts scripts, however, made me very nervous - all over again. For, the reception moment of those, for each subject, caused me to be extremely aware of the fact that I had the future of each of my students in my hands - as I, thereafter, proceeded to mark and assess what they had each written in their respective answer book. I, thus, felt a huge burden on my shoulders to treat the marking process with as much seriousness, concentration and fairness (between one student and another) as I possibly could. Just as I had done at Leeds University one year earlier, therefore – and, there, I had merely been a second marker for my Torts and 'English Legal System' tutorial subjects - I would be locking myself away in my office, with the door closed, in order to discharge that (perhaps, largely self-imposed) duty to the very best of my ability. It was, thus, the start of a period of confinement for me – not unlike what I had done in the first two terms of the academic year in question when composing my lectures for Comparative Law, and especially those for The Conflict of Laws course.

Accordingly, I had to tell Philomena and the children that I would be working late into the evenings ahead, once more – after the first of the scripts had arrived. Moreover, as there was also a time limit within which the marks had to be back to Faculty's 'Board of Examiners', I also had to work at the weekends. That meant going into my office, or my 'UWI Cave' as I then called it to Philomena, for the rest of the day - even on a Sunday after our foursome had first gone to morning Mass together at St Dominic's near our home. Little by little, however, I got through all the scripts for the larger student group which had taken The Conflict of Laws examination, and then those for the lesser one which had sat my Comparative Law paper. And, finally, I was able to turn my attention to the second-marking in the Law of Torts – which, because the scripts in that subject had already been supposedly analysed thoroughly by its Course Director, Norma, I could treat somewhat more lightly.

If truth be told, however, I was rather more concerned for my Comparative Law and Conflicts students than I was for my Torts tutorial ones. Some in the first two cohorts did very well and a good number managed to obtain 'First Class' marks in my (generous marking) view. The majority would have obtained average marks ranging from 'Lower Second' (or '2.2') to 'Upper Second' (or '2.1') and the worst ones (of which there would only have been a few) would have obtained a 'Third Class'. To the best of my memory, I failed no one in the two subjects for which I was Course Director that year. If any of the scripts had been borderline 'Fails', I always gave the student in question the benefit of the doubt and awarded him or her the bare minimum Third Class pass.

Fortunately, the exam system at UWI at that time had some 'quality control checks' in it and the scripts, and my marks, had to go to a second marker – as well as an 'External Examiner' from a UK University. In that first Comparative Law exam of mine at Cave Hill, I seem to recall that the second marker was Dorcas White, my fellow Montserratian and Faculty colleague based at UWI's Mona Campus in Jamaica. (Alas, I can no longer recall who my second marker for The Conflict of Laws scripts was). My External Examiner, for both subjects, was a lady professor from the 'University of Manchester'. And, much to my relief, neither of my second markers, nor the External Examiner, seem to think that the marks, which I had given to my Comparative Law or Conflicts students, had been unfair or not merited and, at any rate, were prepared to go along with the 'first mark' which I had given to each of my respective students in the subject in question. That was not necessarily the case with Norma Forde's first marks which she had respectively allocated to the scripts in her Law of Torts examination and I worked hard, during my second marking, to try to 'bring up' the marks of any student which she had failed on her initial assessment. Fortunately, too, when the two of us met to resolve the difference between our respective marks in such cases, she nearly always agreed with my 'upgrading' and, therefore, to our jointly giving a 'Bare Pass' to the students in question.

Eventually, all the marking processes, and meetings between first and second examiners and then with the relevant External Examiners, were complete. And sometime about mid-June or, perhaps, a little later, a huge 'Faculty Board of Law' was convened, in which all the lecturers in the Faculty, the External Examiners and several members from the Administrative Staff at Cave Hill Campus came together, one Saturday morning. The task of that Board was to rubber stamp, among other things, the final marks for the students in all the Law subjects that academic year. Moreover, and most importantly, in relation to the Final Year students, the Board had the powerful task of deciding what 'Class' of degree would be awarded to each such 'Finalist' at their forthcoming graduation. Perhaps, at some stage in the proceedings, the Faculty Board had constituted itself into a formal 'Board of Examiners'. As a new member to the Law Faculty, however, I did not feel able to contribute very much to the, sometimes heated, discussions where someone was a borderline case. That happened, for instance, where only four First Class marks had been obtained in the nine subjects sat by a student during his, or her, Second and Final year at Cave Hill. Rather, I was content that I had done as much as I reasonably could have for each of my Final Year students in Comparative Law and Conflicts (and, in some cases, in saving some of my Torts ones from failure, as second marker, during my 'negotiations' with Norma Forde). What Class of degree each such Final Year student would obtain, I was more or less happy to leave to the 'consensus' being distilled by the body of lecturers and professors in the Law Faculty –

which 'jury' comprised, perhaps, up to 20 or 25 persons.

In the end, all the examinations business of the meeting in question was concluded and, in essence, the lecturers in the Faculty of Law were free to have their holidays. The Administrative Staff would take matters on from there, regarding writing to each student concerning their marks, Class of degree obtained, graduation day details, and the like. Perhaps, the professors still had some minimal duties to perform - such as the signing off of the degree certificates, in certain cases. In my case, however, I knew that I was then 'free' to have a holiday. And a vacation with my family – far from Cave Hill – was exactly what I intended to do next, and as soon as possible!

*Chapter 11*

# The End of my First Academic Year at UWI and Summer Holidays 1980

The 1979-1980 academic year at Cave Hill had been a difficult and arduous year for me. It had been my first - and, thus, a sort of real 'Baptism of fire'. I had needed to compose most of my lecture notes for the classes which I had given in two Final Year subjects, and which I had taught as Course Director for each. For future academic years, I would have those transcriptions to start from when preparing my classes – and, thus, should normally only have to update and revise them in accordance with developments in the Law. I was able to speculate, therefore, as my first Caribbean academic year ended, that, perhaps, I would never have such an arduous three-term period of teaching again whilst at UWI. Whether that would prove to be so or not, however, I just needed – and wanted very much - to recharge my batteries for the time being.

'Where was my Bradshaw family quartet to go for their summer holidays 1980?' was, rather, my main preoccupation at that time. We had some options. That is because one of the terms of the contract on which I had been recruited by UWI, whilst still living in England (and teaching at Leeds University at the time), had been that UWI would give me a 'travel grant', at the end of each academic year. That was intended, and supposedly enough, to pay for me and my family to revisit the UK, for a holiday there, and then return. As, in fact, that grant, effectively, only amounted to the price of the air fares from Barbados to London and back, I had (soon after my first arrival at Cave Hill) been advised, by one colleague or another, that it was a much better idea to 'save up', or carry-over, the grant for another year or two. That was so that, when the UWI lecturer in question finally claimed the grant, he or she would obtain more than one year's worth at that later time. By so doing, the lecturer would be able to 'do' something meaningful, with the enlarged amount of grant moneys, whilst back in Europe - over and above merely having only barely enough to pay for arriving at London's Heathrow Airport and later flying back to Barbados.

Accordingly, although Philomena and myself would have loved to have taken our two children back to England to visit their two grandmothers and other relatives in Swindon, Wiltshire – and to let our kinfolk in that railway town see how well the boys had developed since we had left Britain the previous year – we had both decided to err on the side of caution. Instead, we had saved the 1980 travel grant due - for at least one more year. That had not been an easy decision for us to arrive at - since we both missed our respective mothers and siblings living back in England's 'West Country'. All the more so since, so far as we both then knew, neither of us had any relatives at all living in Barbados at that time. Moreover, we knew that even though the grant would only just about cover our family's four sets of air fares to England and back, our respective mothers would each have been more than delighted to house, and feed, us - for free - whilst we would have been with them for the summer of 1980. In my own case, however, I also wanted to have enough financial resources to enable our family to travel in Continental Europe in order to see friends living there, such as Berndt and Moni in West Germany, after first arriving in England. Consequently, in order to have the economic freedom to be able to do so, the better decision seemed to be the one to 'save' the travel grant then due to me – and, thereby, add it to the one which would be coming my way the following year, so that our family could enjoy a more extensive European holiday at that later time.

If we did not travel to Europe in the summer of 1980, what, instead, were Philomena and I to do with ourselves and our children for the forthcoming 'long vacation'? The answer lay in what I had earlier promised my wife - when we were first thinking of emigrating to Barbados from England a year, or two, before. That was to enable us to 'explore' the Caribbean region whenever, and as reasonably often as we could, whilst living in Barbados. In line with that undertaking, I had already taken Philomena to Montserrat, again, for our Christmas 1979 holiday – along with our boys, for their first visit to their father's native island. Moreover, because we had all been 'grounded' in Barbados for the Easter holidays, owing to the visit of Berndt, Moni, Miriam and Hupsi from West Germany, some six months on or so from our last one it was high time for another Caribbean regional trip. But whereabouts – in that large archipelago of hundreds of islands? Since we had such a huge range of islands to choose from - including Jamaica some four hours flying time away - for reasons of economy Philomena and I decided on somewhere which neither of us had ever visited, but which was also fairly near to Barbados (and, therefore, less expensive for the four members of our family to fly to). The two nearest islands to Barbados are St Lucia, to the west, and 'St Vincent' – also to the west but south of the former. And since Philomena and I had once landed in St Lucia, and had spent an unexpected, but eventful, number of hours there during our honeymoon trip in 1976 - when the plane taking us from Barbados to Antigua had broken down (as further described in *Fledging and Learning to Fly*[44]) - that left us with only one other realistic choice. St Vincent, accordingly, it would be - for our summer holidays 1980!

But what kind of Caribbean holiday would it be – for that second one of ours in about half a year? For, unlike our previous Christmas trip to Montserrat, neither Philomena nor I had any relatives in St Vincent. Nor did we even have any friends or acquaintances there. And, to the best of my knowledge, I had never taught any student from that particular island during my first academic year at Cave Hill just ending. Accordingly, Philomena and I agreed that our family would just have to go on a 'budget' vacation – given no relatives, friends or acquaintances to stay with, or to 'assist' us with lifts or the odd meal or two, during our St Vincent sojourn. Moreover, there was the handicap of me not taking my travel grant for 1980 - which would have been of assistance with the travel and living expenses we would incur whilst on our holiday island. Any such outlays, therefore, would have to come out of my current salary from UWI – given that Philomena and myself had no savings put by to speak of.

My wife and I, therefore, decided that, rather than try to book a hotel or guest house in advance, we would just buy our air tickets to St Vincent and back, and then look for accommodation once we had actually arrived on that island. Looking back now, it is clear that we took a risk of failing to find anything available, within our budget, once we had reached St Vincent. I remembered, however, Philomena and myself being once stuck in Antigua, on our way to Montserrat during our previously mentioned 1976 honeymoon trip, and our having to spend the night in a guest house on the former island without our occasioning any difficulty. Admittedly, that overnight accommodation had been found for us by LIAT – the local airline which had caused us to be late in arriving on time from St Lucia and, thus, ahead of schedule to catch our connecting flight to Montserrat. Accordingly, in relation to that summer vacation of 1980, I may have thought that, if necessary, my family and I could always ask the LIAT desk, at the airport in St Vincent, to help us. Perhaps, it could do so by perusing its list of local guest houses which it used for its passengers who were unavoidably delayed overnight - as my wife and I had been in Antigua in 1976. Naturally, that would have been on the basis that we would have had to pay for any such accommodation ourselves. Moreover, in my mind at least, I had one other 'fail-safe' idea for obtaining some emergency accommodation for our family – should it have proved necessary. That notion was founded on the basis that Philomena and myself were good practising Catholics in Barbados and it being most likely that the priest at the main Catholic church in St Vincent would probably know some of his counterpart colleagues in our home island, and, perhaps, even Father Dan of St Dominic's, Maxwell. If it became necessary, therefore, I had in mind showing up with my family to the presbytery of that main Catholic St Vincent church, telling the priest there exactly who we were, and then asking him to help us find some local accommodation – either at the presbytery itself or, perhaps, with another 'good Catholic family' in his parish.

That, therefore, was the full - or, rather, 'sketchy' – extent of our family's summer 1980 holiday planning by Philomena and myself. With our basic project in mind, my wife and I, with our two boys, left Barbados for St Vincent, on a small LIAT plane, one summer's day in 1980, by the middle of July. We four were thereby embarked on a true 'adventure'. For, even though we had return tickets - for a day about two weeks after our departure date - the adults in our party had no real idea of where we would be spending those two weeks!

After an uneventful flight from Barbados of less than one hour, we duly arrived in St Vincent's small 'Arnos Vale' airport. Fortunately for us, and our budget, that terminal was located much closer to the island's capital of 'Kingstown' than the 10 miles or so between our home island's airport of Grantley Adams and its capital at Bridgetown. It was, thus, fairly inexpensive for us to take a taxi into Kingstown, but that short ride gave us a good opportunity to ask the driver to recommend an inexpensive hotel, or guesthouse, for the first part of our stay. He enthusiastically did so and, within about 15 minutes or so of our getting into his vehicle, he was dropping us outside a largish establishment in the middle of our current island's capital. To me, our potential accommodation looked rather run down - and I guessed that it had, perhaps, seen much better days. The dishevelled appearance of the place did not worry me too much, however, as its uninspiring condition suggested to me that it just might be a 'low budget' concern and, thus, all the more 'affordable' for my family's pocketbook.

The taxi driver took us inside and introduced us to the woman at the reception - who was obviously known to him. Most likely, therefore, he would be getting an extra 'tip' for such introduction later on. I was then able to explain our 'plight' to the receptionist and, above all, emphasise to her that we did not have much money and only really needed a roof over head for a relatively small number of days. I also pressed the point that we only needed one large room with a double bed – since our elder son could always sleep in the middle of it between my wife and myself, whilst his younger brother could slumber in his carrycot (which we had brought from Barbados with us, since it also doubled as a Baby Buggy, or pushchair, for taking him out and about). I also tried to bargain with the receptionist by suggesting to her that the cheaper the daily rate price she quoted us, the longer would we be able to afford to stay in her 'hotel' (which, arguably, could also have been classed as a large guesthouse).

Our attendant must have liked us – or, perhaps, simply had some pity for my family. Certainly, it seemed to me that not many tourists came to her establishment who found themselves in a situation like our foursome - and for whom, therefore, she might have some 'set prices' ready to offer them for such unusual circumstances. Rather, I perceived her to have a wide discretion about how much to charge us and, in the end, she did indeed offer Philomena and myself such a reasonable daily rate that we decided to book for five days.

My wife and myself did not take a reservation for the whole of our holiday period for good reason. That was because St Vincent is only the main island in a group of islands which formed the, then, newly independent state of 'St Vincent and the Grenadines'. Philomena and I, therefore, wanted to also see something of one, or more, of the Grenadines - those smaller islands which were linked to the main one on which we had just arrived – along with our boys, during our holiday. Again, however, such a 'side-trip' would depend on how affordable that would prove to be for us. Accordingly, we did not think it wise to book our hotel for the entirety of our vacation – at least, not until we had taken the opportunity to ask around regarding getting transport to, and from, one or more of the Grenadines during our sojourn.

Before all that, however, we just wanted to explore Kingstown a little. Neither Philomena nor I had ever been to St Vincent before, so our then current capital was a real novelty for us. Accordingly, even on that first day, we were eager to see as much of it as we reasonably could, with our boys in tow, and, after putting our suitcases inside our large, and comfortable-enough room and then freshening ourselves up, we placed Kim in his pushchair, took Noel by the hand and went 'abroad' into 'Downtown Kingstown'.

The place immediately struck me as being very much like Plymouth in Montserrat (where, as previously established, I had been born and had gone to my first school up to the age of eight). There we found shops and domestic homes, side by side, throughout the town. Most seemed to be made of wood and looked somewhat run-down – just as I had found my native Plymouth to be some six months or so earlier. There were also open drains at the side of the roads, which made pushing Kim along in his Baby Buggy rather precarious, at times, for Philomena or myself - as we took turns in doing so. Any negative impressions about the island's capital, however, were soon to be more than balanced by the local inhabitants whom we encountered. For, just like in Montserrat's main town, the vast majority were friendly, polite and willing to give us ready smiles as we passed along. Many also gave us the time of day and, after greeting us with a warm 'Good afternoon', might ask us whether we were enjoying our holiday, followed by a curious: 'And where do you come from?'. More than a few would have been surprised when we answered 'Barbados' - since, apparently, not many 'Bajans' chose St Vincent as the place for their summer holidays.

Like Plymouth, I also found the 'Vincentian' capital, and largest town, to be quite a small place. Most of its 'essential venues', such as the cathedral, the main post office, the courts and the government buildings, seemed to be contained within a relatively compact, and somewhat square or oblong, space – which was, perhaps, a quarter of the size of central Bridgetown back in Barbados. To me, therefore, it certainly would not have done to have to spent the entire 14 days or so of my family's precious summer holiday in that relatively confined location. We needed to get out and about on that main island and, before too much longer, go further afield, to one or more of the Grenadines, if it proved economically possible for my family to do so.

Prior to that, however, Philomena and I had to find somewhere to buy some food. That was because we had only booked our hotel on a 'room only' basis. Our meals there were not included in the price we had paid - although we were free to order some there, whenever we wished, by just paying extra for them. Accordingly, my wife and I, took our boys to the central market in Kingstown during that first afternoon and, there, bought lots of fruit which we thought our boys would like – not least, some bananas (looking green, but perfectly ripe inside) and mangoes. We were also able to purchase some locally-made bread, some fried fish and some fizzy drinks like 'Pepsi Cola'. Those beverages were something of a holiday treat for our boys, since they were not ordinarily the kind of liquid refreshments that we would ever buy for them back home in Barbados.

The next morning came soon enough. Philomena and I decided that we would treat our family to a cooked breakfast of ripe plantain and fried eggs, prepared for us by the hotel kitchen staff – since the price they gave us for those 'extras' was a very reasonable one. After that, our foursome set out to see something of St Vincent - beyond Kingstown. As far as I could perceive, the island was not a popular place for tourists. Consequently, there were no 'sightseeing tours' being advertised, in any of the places we had passed the previous afternoon during our first walk around the capital. Our family, therefore, had to choose, for ourselves, just how to see something of the island by using whatever else looked available. For one thing, we could have tried to hire a taxi for just one day, or part thereof, and to have asked the driver to take our family, exclusively, to the 'sights' around the isle. Owing to our limited budget, however, Philomena and I ruled out that idea from the start - without even bothering to approach any Kingstown taxi driver to give us a quote for such a tour. Instead, we both agreed on a different plan. That was to go to the main bus depot nearby to try to find out which route, from the capital, went furthest away from it to reach its destination - and at what fare. An essential thing for us in our 'research', however, was also to discover whether such bus would also be returning that day, or evening, back to Kingstown – since we did not want our family to be 'marooned' somewhere out in the wilds of the island, or have to call a taxi to take us many miles (at great expense, perhaps) back to our hotel in the capital.

That, therefore, was the plan which Philomena and myself put into effect. When we arrived at the bus depot with our boys, however, we were in for a surprise. That was because, unlike Barbados, there were no large, high-sided, vehicles with seats inside for, perhaps, 30 to 40 people – what Philomena and myself knew to be 'buses' in our home island – to be seen anywhere in that terminus. Rather, what we found were only the much less roomy, and uncomfortable-looking, 'mini-vans'. It also seemed that those so-called local 'buses' did not run to any set timetable. Instead, their drivers were advertising that they were going to a certain town or village in the countryside, and were then waiting until they had attracted enough would-be passengers to fill up their respective vehicle before embarking on the journey in question. After a short discussion, however, Philomena and I agreed that taking a 'magical mystery tour', into the St Vincent countryside with our boys, would be a suitable adventure for our family that day – even if, we already guessed, it would not be the most comfortable one we had ever experienced. We also decided that we just had to first make sure that whichever 'long trip' we opted for, the driver would guarantee to return with us to Kingstown that same day. Once we had discovered, by asking various drivers in the depot, that a trip to 'Mesopotamia' would be the furthest away from the capital that morning, our foursome joined the mini-van that was going to that ancient-sounding place (having first obtained the same-day-return-journey guarantee from its driver).

Because of the connotations with the Bible which it brought to my mind, I was rather excited to be going to a town or village named 'Mesopotamia'. And the initial stages of our van ride did not disappoint - since we soon left the capital and drove up into the hills. As we progressed along the journey, I found myself enjoying the views of the countryside more and more – since it was so unlike our relatively-flat Barbados and much more like my native Montserrat (especially the native Dyers region of my father's side of my family). However, as much as I, and evidently the rest of my family, enjoyed observing life in the villages along the way to our Biblical-sounding destination, I soon found our excursion coming to an end all too quickly! For I had envisaged my family and I being taken somewhere really far from Kingstown – perhaps, to a place right on the other side of the island. Indeed, my ideal sightseeing trip would have been a coastal journey right around St Vincent. Alas, however, Mesopotamia turned out to be not more than about 20 miles, at the most, inland from the capital. Our mini-van took us nowhere near any coastal road – and, in fact, I later discovered that (at that time) there was actually no road in existence which went all the way around the island, such as one can find in Barbados.

Worst still, when we finally arrived in the village of Mesopotamia, there was nothing very much to see or do there which could entertain my family and myself for long. In any event, Philomena and myself were reluctant to venture too far from our van, in case it filled up with passengers again – who were wanting to go down the hills to Kingstown – and it left as soon as it was full, without us. Had it done so, we could not have been sure whether another van 'to town' would ever become available for us to catch later that day. Accordingly, my family and I had to be content with merely admiring the wonderful views of the hills and valleys around us, as we picnicked with the left overs of our food, fruit and drinks bought from the Kingstown market the day before, whilst we waited for enough would-be passengers to turn up so that our van could set off on its return journey with our family on board.

Our outing that day to Mesopotamia had certainly given my family the opportunity to see something of life outside St Vincent's capital. For me, however, I had been far from satisfied with the short trip. I needed to see more of the country's main island, if possible – and, in due course, even get away from it altogether by taking my family into the Grenadines.

Before all that, however, Philomena and myself decided that we would see something of greater Kingstown first, beginning with the following day – whilst also make some inquiries about the cost of, and regularities for, getting a ferry into the chain of islands to the south. For, the latter formed part of the relatively new independent state in which we found ourselves – and were what constituted 'the Grenadines' part of the country's total, and lengthy, name. In fact, we did the required research first - through our friendly lady receptionist at our hotel. From her, we discovered that there was a 'postal packet', or small ship, which was either run, or organised by, the local government to take (and pick up) the post from St Vincent to the islands of the Grenadines - all the way down south to the last in the chain, near a northerly island belonging to the neighbouring state of Grenada, named 'Carriacou'. It was just as well that we had made enquiries with our hostess, since she was also to tell us that the vessel only ran twice a week and that the next one was the following day – and then, not another for some four days! With that vital information, and after a short discussion with Philomena, we were able to go back to her with a plea that she kindly allow us to shorten our original five days' booking at the hotel – if we could obtain tickets for our family on the ship for the next day, at a price which we could afford. Much to our relief, our hostess kindly agreed to that contingency.

After another splendid breakfast of plantain and fried eggs, therefore, my family followed the directions of our hostess on how to get to the relevant office of the government maritime postal service in question. Within a few minutes of leaving the hotel, we were there - since the office was situated by the 'Port of the Kingstown', not even a quarter of a mile distance from the centre of the capital. There, Philomena and I saw a large ship with the first name of 'Geest', followed by some word or other. Philomena and I knew, from our days in England, that the first word had something to do with a specific tropical fruit and that such appellation suggested, therefore, that we were literally looking at a 'banana boat' - which took the exotic produce in question from the Caribbean region, where we then found ourselves, to our former home country and its neighbours in Continental Europe. Moreover, nearby in the office of the postal packet, we were soon able to book 'passages' for our family to sail on it into the Grenadines – at a very reasonable price for our budget, since Noel and Kim were allowed, owing to their young ages, to travel for free. More of where exactly we booked our tickets to in due course, but, armed with those travel authorisations, we were able to return to our friendly hostess at the hotel and arrange to check out the very next day - in order to go 'island hopping', almost literally, southwards.

With some peace of mind - after obtaining our tickets, and being allowed to leave our hotel earlier than originally booked (with the blessing of its management) - I was extremely happy to proceed to explore 'non-central Kingstown', on foot, with my wife and our sons. The main tourist place, within that larger vicinity, seemed to be the capital's 'Botanical Gardens'. These were a distant jaunt away from its centre but, reputedly, interesting enough to justify the longish walk that it would take my family to reach them (including by Philomena or myself pushing Kim along in his Baby Buggy, as we proceeded along). To the best of my memory, it was about one mile or so from our hotel - going inland and away from the port. It was also uphill, quite steep, and somewhat like the walk I remember doing in Montserrat from my native Plymouth to my great-grandmother Joanna's village in Amersham when I was at school there, during the late 1950s and early 1960s. It was, however, a pleasant enough excursion - notwithstanding the heat of a Caribbean summer's day.

I, for one, was extremely pleased, when we finally arrived at the Gardens, that we had decided to make the effort to reach. For we soon discovered, from a notice board at the entrance, that they were in fact 'the oldest botanical gardens in the Western Hemisphere'. We had come to a place that was truly historic, therefore - since the guide, who was assigned to us upon our paying the required entrance fees, told us that the place was in fact established in the later 1700s! For our sons, however, the main points of interest inside the Gardens, perhaps, were not so much the hundreds of plants and trees to be found there, but rather the aviary in which some species of local birds were kept in captivity. Among those was the spectacularly-coloured, and extremely rare, 'St

Vincent Parrot' – a breed only to be found on the island where we were then sojourning. For Noel and Kim, the rarity of the parrot species would have been lost on them, but to see such brightly-coloured specimens, closely flying about in front of them, would have been a delight.

For myself, however, even more special were a few astonishing facts which I only learned, after actually arriving at the Gardens, from our guide. The first was that 'Captain William Bligh' – of the 'Mutiny on the Bounty' fame[45] - had once visited the Gardens himself, in 1793. Comprehending that, was quite an educational surprise for me. Even more so, however, was our guide then informing us that Captain Bligh had brought with him, during that late 18th century St Vincent visit, and all the way from 'Tahiti, Polynesia' on the other side of the world, the very first 'breadfruit' plant ever to reach the Caribbean! That original species of flora was exhibited to us inside the Gardens – where much was made, by our guide, of the fact that it was from that very plant that one of the main staples of Caribbean foodstuffs spread from St Vincent throughout the rest of the West Indian territories. I myself rather like the taste of breadfruit – which I had always regarded as being more of a vegetable, and thus, perhaps, the Caribbean equivalent of the English (or Irish) potato which is, seemingly, grown (and eaten) everywhere in Europe. Until my visit to the St Vincent Gardens, therefore, I had always thought that breadfruit was one of the finest examples of something that was most definitely of a West Indian origin.

If my family's visit to the Botanical Gardens, outside Kingstown, had managed to teach me that 'One is never too old to learn something new', by the time that the next day came I was more than willing to do so again in the 'new' (for me and my family) territories of the Grenadines. When booking our tickets for that trip, we had been told that the postal packet in question would be travelling southwards - all the way to the last island in the chain before Grenada's Carriacou. We were also informed that, because it would not reach that final Vincentian island until late in the evening (after leaving Kingstown in the morning), it would be better for our family to get off the boat at an island or two beforehand. That was so that we could disembark during daylight hours, and whilst there was still time for us to easily find ourselves a guest house for the night. Philomena and myself followed that advice and that is how it came to pass that we booked our tickets to 'Union Island', in the southern Grenadines, as opposed to, say, 'Palm Island' or 'Petit St Vincent' - which were even further south and, thus, even closer to Carriacou and Grenada.

And what a 'voyage' for my family and myself that first day of our trip south turned out to be! The first surprise was how relatively small our ship was. Nothing at all like the large ferry boats which Philomena and I had been used to taking, during our student days in the 1970s, from 'Dover', in England, to 'Calais', in France, in order to cross the English Channel to begin one Continental European holiday or another. Rather, our St Vincent postal vessel was, perhaps, only about 10 per cent of the size of such typical European ones of our former experience. The Vincentian watercraft seemed to be

*Fig 30: Philomena, Noel and Kim outside the port of Kingstown, St Vincent in the summer of 1980 – possibly en route, with the Author, to book the family's tickets on the ferry, or postal packet boat, for a 'cruise' among the islands of the Grenadines and return. The large ship in the background was many times larger than the vessel on which the family was to travel for their holiday sailing*

*Fig 31: Philomena holding Kim, and beside Noel, on board the rather small ferry, or postal packet boat, during the family's 'cruise' among some of the islands the Grenadines during the summer of 1980. Kim seems to be more interested in 'plane spotting' than enjoying the beauty of the St Vincent island chain in question, although Noel seems to have the right idea*

mainly designed for carrying mail, and not people – the latter seeming, to me at least, to be mere 'afterthoughts', if the mail did not take up too much room and make the accommodation of passengers impossible. Accordingly, although there was one toilet on board our vessel, as well as a 'below deck' part where we could obtain drinks and heat up some baby food for Kim during our journey, most of the space on it was to be found 'upstairs, on deck' and we were joined there by only about four of five other voyagers – two of whom were White tourists from England.

The captain and his younger 'mate' were very friendly, however, and they fostered a very relaxing atmosphere on board as we sailed from one island to the next. The first, at which we stopped and moored up, was called 'Bequia'. I remember the delight which I felt as we slowly pulled into the small jetty of some village or other on that island – and moored up at a landing stage, peopled by a number of expectant persons (mainly men). They seemed to be eagerly anticipating the mail, as well as other items arriving from the 'greater world out there' which the captain was preparing to unload from his ship. Our ferry's master seemed to know everyone waiting on the jetty for him, and shouts of mutual greeting were exchanged before we eventually tied up in order for the discharge of deliverables to be made. That was a process which was followed by the collection of items due for the other islands further south. We did not, however, remain tied up to the Bequia jetty for very long. For there were several more islands to visit - even before our vessel reached my family's destination, which was still much further south in the Grenadines chain.

The next island which we were due to temporarily halt at – and there seemed to be dozens of tiny, uninhabited, islets that we passed during our journey - was one that even I had heard of prior to our setting off from Kingstown. That was 'Mustique'. In fact, it was a world-famous place owing to a particular individual who (as I understood matters) owned property on it and who regularly holidayed there with her famous film star friends and the like. The person in question was none other than 'Princess Margaret' – the younger sister of 'Queen Elizabeth the Second' of England. Jokingly, I asked Philomena and Noel to look out for the princess, when we had docked for a short time at the jetty in Mustique. Alas, none of us was able to spot a lady with a crown on her head – either on the jetty or further away on land. Perhaps, I told them, she only came to that particular island during the winter months in Europe and now it was high summer - both there and in the Grenadines. At any rate, I added for my wife's and elder son's amusement that, even if she had been staying in her holiday home at the time, it would have been most unlikely that she would have come to collect her mail 'in person' as opposed to sending one of her 'footmen' for the same.

After the passing of even less time than we had spent docked at the previous island, we were off again. Within another hour or so, we had reached yet one more island in the Grenadines chain which I had never heard of. On that second occasion, it was 'Canouan' – a name which I liked, for bringing to my mind the idea of some 'unknown' tropical island being discovered and given that exotic moniker by the indigenous 'Carib Indians' many centuries before. However, if I was being continually captivated by the voyage from Kingstown thus far, I was not so sure that my little boys – or even my wife, for that matter – were feeling quite so happy about things. For one thing, the sea was not always so very calm as we sailed along. Not that there was any real 'choppiness' to speak of. Rather, it was more that, every now and then, my family and I were certainly made aware that we were not on 'terra firma' - every time that our diminutive ship hit a large wave or two. Worst still, apart from the possibility of proceeding to the toilet on deck, or in the kitchen area down below, there was not much possibility for us to move about the upper part of the vessel with the children – let alone let them run around and play on it. There just was not enough room for that – given the minimal size of the craft and the other passengers on board who needed to occupy their own 'space'. Thus, by the time we had been into Canouan and unloaded the items for that island, as well as collected what was destined from there for other territories in the state, both Philomena and myself were starting to wish for that first part of our sailing venture to come to an end.

There was still one more island to visit, however, before we arrived at my family's overnight terminus. That was, what seemed to me like, an even smaller territory than Canouan had been – namely, the equally exotically-named 'Mayreau'. Again, the procedure was the same – with our ship pulling into a jetty located in some small village development on the island in question and then exchanging bags of mail and packages. And, once more, within about half an hour of doing so, our boat was off again and soon onto the 'high seas'. By that time, I had begun discussing with Philomena my idea that, if we ever did such a trip again, with any of our small children, it would be much better if we got off our boat at each of the territories that we called at - for a day or so at each place. For, by so doing, that would enable us to explore each place a little bit, and also to give our children (and ourselves) some relief from the sea and an opportunity to play, or otherwise exercise, for a while, at each new stop. I soon remembered, however, that since the mail boat did not pass through the islands every day, the suggestion would not work - since we might have to stay, in each of the places we stopped at, for about half a week before we could get another ferry to continue on with the rest of our journey.

So, after Mayreau, we found ourselves on the high seas again – but in the southern Grenadines by then – many hours after we had first left Kingstown on the northern-most island of the country, about 9am that day. It was already about 4pm by then, but our next stop, thankfully, would be our intended destination for that part of our trip. Union Island was ahead of us and we were scheduled to be there by 5pm. However, just as when we had first arrived at Arnos Vale, St Vincent on the first day of our holiday, there was a worry in my stomach as we pulled into the jetty at Union. Would we be able to find some accommodation there and, if so, how would we get to it from our landing point?

I (and perhaps Philomena too, in her silence) need not have been so anxious. For, once we had tied up, the captain took me and my family to meet a man whom he knew and who was standing near the jetty. The first man introduced us to the second as being a family in need of somewhere to stay for the night. The stranger on the landing stage smiled and told us that he would certainly be able to help us - as he owned a guest house nearby. He also revealed that he often assisted casual tourists, just like ourselves, who had not pre-booked any accommodation, which is why he always came to meet the mail boat – as the captain well knew. Before I could fully relax, however, I needed to discuss the price of our potential stay with our would-be host. Once more, however, I was able to agree a reasonable price for our room and breakfast and, soon, my family and I were in his car being driven to the man's lodging place – which was situated on a hill overlooking the sea and the jetty where we had landed during the hour just past. It was still daylight – just!

We were shown into what was a very large room in a relatively modern house. Our host was evidently a man of property since, he told us, the house contained a number of other such guest rooms. Philomena and myself, however, were content with our situation for that evening. For it meant that our boys could, at last, run around the room, and outside the guesthouse in its garden, to their hearts' content. They were clearly even happier than their parents to finally get off the mail boat, after nearly one whole day of being confined on it – notwithstanding the beauty of the islands and seascapes that we had passed along the Grenadines chain to get so far south.

It was only after we had eaten our evening meal – prepared by our host, and paid for as an extra by Philomena and myself in order to treat ourselves and our boys for safely accomplishing the first part of our 'adventure' - that I spotted a potential problem. I had just been lying down and relaxing on the large double bed in the room – which Philomena and I would, again, share with Noel that night whilst Kim slept in his carrycot – when I looked up to the very top of the high, wooden, ceiling there. To my horror, I could see two to three white nests, belonging to 'jackspanners', which were attached to that ceiling and hanging below it – with some of their occupants flying around near them, up at the same lofty level. Quietly, I told Philomena about what I had seen. Unlike me, however, she had never had a bad encounter with such wasp-like, potentially aggressively-stinging, insects – as I, unfortunately, had done in my earliest past, as described in *Growing up BAREFOOT*.[46] Yes, indeed, I had been severely stung by some of those red-coloured, often vicious (when disturbed), creatures whilst maturing as a boy in Montserrat in the late 1950s when 'mango-hunting'! I certainly did not wish for a repeat of that experience - either for myself, my wife or our little sons.

Because Philomena was somewhat calmer about the presence of the jackspanners in our room, and as they were very high up in its ceiling, she was able to persuade me that I should not make a fuss with our host guesthouse-owner by demanding a change of bedchamber for us all. Moreover, she reasoned with me that any other guestroom in the place probably also had one or two jackspanner nests as well – and, having by then settled into our accommodation with our children for the night, she did not, at that point, want us to have to look for an entirely new guest house (even assuming that a 'jackspanner-free' one was available somewhere else on the island). She also wisely suggested that if we did not trouble the creatures – as I had repeatedly done whilst foraging for mangoes as a boy in Montserrat – they should not trouble us. Despite, my wife's reasoning, however, I, for one, did not sleep well that night – and, possibly, only did so with one eye open!

All was well, however, when the morning finally came. None of our foursome had come to any harm. And, after a leisurely breakfast at the guest house followed by a drive by our host back to the seaside near the jetty from where we would be catching our mail boat on its way back to St Vincent later, we were soon in the Caribbean Sea again to enjoy our very first swim since we had left Barbados. The previous evening, the captain and his mail boat had gone on to one or two more of the Grenadines islands south of Union Island. He would, however, have eventually stopped his voyaging for the day, perhaps gone to stay in his own home situated on his most-southerly destination in order to rest and sleep, and then started out on his return journey back to Kingstown, St Vincent at about the same 9am hour that we had commenced our trip from the capital the previous day. Thus, he and his mail boat would not be getting back to Union Island to pick up his northbound passengers (including my own family) until sometime after 10am. We, therefore, had a little time to frolic in the sea, near the jetty on our host island, before the vessel came back for us. I, for one, wanted our two boys to exercise themselves, in the water, as much as possible. For I knew how relatively immobile they would have to be again - once they were back on board the boat returning to St Vincent.

The homeward journey to Kingstown was uneventful – and we saw no princesses on that leg either. It was hard going for Philomena and myself, however, in our trying to keep our sons mentally engaged - when they were not actually sleeping during our 'cruise' northwards. And even Noel, as well as his toddler younger brother, did sleep an awful lot until we eventually reached St Vincent again. For they, as well as their parents, had 'seen it all before'. The calling-in at the many larger islands of the Grenadines chain, and the exchanging of mailbags and packages, had lost its ability to stimulate their minds as much as those of their parents. And whilst their mum and myself could find their compensation in just looking at the beauty of the changing seascapes all around us as we progressed northwards, such delightfulness was lost on our little ones. Many sheets of paper, and crayons, were therefore used up as Philomena tried to stimulate the boys by getting each of them to draw our mail boat, or the captain, or one or other of the islands as we got close to docking with it. There was no doubting, therefore, that all four of us were extremely happy to eventually get back to 'old familiar' Kingstown again - and to feel the firmness of the land under our feet there, once more, as we walked away from the port. We were also glad to be able to return to our homely hotel in the centre of the capital, to see our friendly hostess there once more, and to get back our old room for the rest of our stay on that main island. What is more, there was not even one jackspanner to be seen inside it!

During the remainder of our stay, Philomena and I had decided that we had undergone enough, for a while at least, of travelling about with our children. What we wanted to do for the immediate future, and what we both thought that the boys would appreciate much more than going from place to place, was to concentrate on a beach holiday. But which beach? We had seen, when leaving, and later returning to, the Kingstown port during the few days just past, that there were not really any pleasure beaches to speak of near that harbour. And, indeed, that such beaches as there were seemed to consist of black sand – somewhat like those we had found in my native Montserrat during our Christmas holidays some months before. Our boys were much more used to, and seemed to prefer, the white sandy beaches of Barbados where they now lived. But were there any in St Vincent and, if so, were those near enough to our hotel such that it would not break our budget to travel to one or other of them?

Once more, our friendly hostess came up trumps. For she was to tell us that there was a wonderful – if only 'semi-public' – place about a 10-minute taxi ride away from the hotel called 'Young Island'. She said that though it was a 'private resort', once you had paid the ferryman to take you across to the island, any member of the public could use the beaches there and that, moreover, those consisted of white sand!

Our hostess had never failed us with her tips during our holiday at her hotel, thus far, so Philomena and I could hardly wait to try out Young Island the following day. We managed to find the friendly taxi driver who had brought us from the airport to the hotel on our first arrival in St Vincent. We were then able to successfully negotiate a deal with him to take us, for a cheap price, to the ferry embarkation point for Young Island. That was on the basis that we would probably want to go there each day, for the rest of our holiday, and also that we would use him to go there and back each time. He seemed happy with that 'deal' and, soon, we were with the ferryman, in his very small rowing boat, as he shuttled just myself and my family, for a few minutes only, across a small stretch of sea to a very diminutive island. We duly arrived at the 'exclusive resort' of Young Island - and although we could see some direction signs there - to the reception of the hotel, its bars and various other amenities on the island - my family and I were content to ignore them and, instead, make a beeline for the pristine white sands of the beach which attracted us as soon as we had disembarked from the little ferryboat. There we joined several guests from the hotel on the white sands, as well as, presumably, other non-residents like ourselves who had simply been ferried across just for the day. We had found our perfect place to see out the rest of our vacation in St Vincent!

No one from the hotel on Young Island bothered us - as we returned to the beach there, day after day, for the remainder of our stay. Philomena and myself just had to make sure that we came armed with plenty of food and drink each day, so that we would never have to go to buy any refreshments inside the resort itself. Like Bath, back in Barbados, the sea on the miniature islet was gentle, where it met the white sandy beach, and was, therefore, very 'child-friendly' for Noel and as well as his one-year-old brother. Accordingly, Young Island was an almost idyllic place from which we could spend the last part of our time in St Vincent and the Grenadines and where both Philomena and myself could truly relax by reading, picnicking and swimming – whilst always keeping an eye on our two boys as they spent most of their days floating, or splashing about, in the Caribbean Sea.

*Fig 32: Kim and Noel, in their armbands, floating in the Caribbean Sea off the beach at Young Island, near Kingstown, St Vincent, duly supervised by their mother, Philomena – during the family's 1980 summer holiday*

*Chapter 12*

# A Not-expected (and Non-UWI) Assignment – Summer to Autumn, 1980

All too soon, however, our lovely days at Young Island, and at our hotel in nearby Kingstown, were over. Before I knew it, we were back at Hygeia in Maxwell, Barbados. But it was still August and, so, I did not yet have to start dropping into Cave Hill in order to prepare for the forthcoming 1980-81 academic year. Or, at least, that is what I had been thinking until I received a phone call, out of the blue, one morning soon after our return from St Vincent. It was Professor Carnegie! He had a proposition for me. One that would involve some extra teaching – of a subject which I had never taught before! My heart sank.

Such a depressing feeling was caused, firstly, by the fact that my senior, and much respected, colleague - who had, I seem to recall, taken over from Professor Telford Georges as Dean of the Law Faculty by then – had a request to put to me. He asked me if I would be willing to teach the Law of Trusts, over several weeks ahead, to two would-be Attorneys-at-Law who were based at a particular legal firm in Bridgetown, named 'Cottle Catford & Co'. Trusts Law was a subject which I had not particularly liked as an undergraduate student back in England in the early 1970s – although I had done well enough in the final exams relating to it and it had helped me to get a good first degree eventually. Secondly, somehow I had felt rather 'trapped' and constrained to give an affirmative answer to Professor Carnegie's proposition - despite my real inclination being to say 'No' - simply because I did not want to let my esteemed colleague down. From our conversation, it seemed to me that he knew one or more of the partners in Cottle Catford and had been approached by one of them to help the firm out of a difficult situation. Professor Carnegie was, thus, now turning to me to help him out of an awkward circumstance in which he found himself – namely, his, or his Law Faculty, being relied upon by a leading Bridgetown legal practice to prove his, or its, mettle.

What was that 'difficult situation' within the Bridgetown firm? It had to do with the fact that the practice had invested many hundreds of Barbadian dollars in the two would-be Attorneys in question, by taking them on as 'articled clerks', some years before, without either of the two having gone to UWI to obtain a Law degree first. In other words, they had been taken on to learn, 'on the job', their would-be profession in the Law. Such a process had once been the usual way of becoming a 'Solicitor' in England in the years, decades, and even centuries before I ever became a Law undergraduate in that country, but that long-established 'apprenticeship process' had, by then, almost died out. Similarly, such a traineeship process was, by 1980, coming to an end in Barbados too. The two articled clerks in question had been given just one last chance to take, and pass, the English Solicitors' 'Law Society' exam in the Law of Trusts. Such exam success would then be recognised by the Barbados legal system, as entitling the two candidates to become Attorneys-at-Law therein. For they had both already passed all their other required English Law Society subjects for the English Solicitors' qualification, but had failed the Trusts Law paper - several times, each. Given that final opportunity provided to both of them to re-sit the paper in question, and to prevent the Law firm's investment in them over the years coming to nothing, Cottle Catford had turned to Professor Carnegie for help and he had approached me, in turn, to help him out - and, thereby, the said Law firm and its two articled clerks. Feeling thus constrained, I gave a reluctant 'Yes' to my senior colleague.

Professor Carnegie, at the end of that first phone call on the matter, thanked me for accepting the assignment. He also told me that he would arrange a time for the articled clerks to meet me at my Cave Hill office within the next few days - and that he would ask them to bring, to that meeting, everything I would need to know about the syllabus for the forthcoming exam paper as well as the recommended study materials for it. Within a day or two, accordingly, he had called me again. That was to tell me that a meeting had been arranged for the last day of that week - in my office, and after the articled clerks had finished their working day. On the Friday in question, therefore, I found myself waiting in my Cave Hill room, with not a little trepidation, when there was knock on my already opened door. I looked up and saw two mature persons – who were both, perhaps, in their early to mid-30s. One was a male and he quickly introduced himself as one 'Asquith Jules'. His female colleague was even more forthcoming on entering my office. She proffered her hand with a smile and told me that her name was 'Laureen'. She added that her surname was: 'Waterman'.

After I had introduced myself to them in return, I quickly put my cards on the table - by letting them know that I was in no sense an 'expert' on the subject in question (which, I also admitted to them, I well understood they needed to pass, at the next sitting of the exam in October 1980, in order to attain their eventual Attorney-at-Law qualification). I did add, however, that although I was an England-qualified Barrister, and not a Solicitor from that country who had had been required to take and pass the Law Society's Trusts Law paper in question, I had passed their 'bogey subject' during my undergraduate years for my first Law degree and, also, knew how to prepare for Law exams generally. I, thus, added that I would do my best to help them with such preparation – if they were prepared to help me as much as possible on their side, by following my guidance and assiduously completing the assignments which I would be giving them as our classes progressed. My would-be Trusts Law students seemed to be happy with my approach and we, thus, immediately started to discuss together the best strategy for approaching their preparation for their forthcoming 'Final' - literally - given the short time we had available to us before the date of that exam, about six to eight weeks hence.

The first thing that the three of us did, therefore, was to go through the syllabus which they had brought with them for me. I also wanted to see which 'set books', or textbooks, the Law Society had recommended to all would-be takers of the exam - for them to study from, when preparing themselves for it. For I planned to get hold of such primers from my own Law Library at Cave Hill - so that I could, at least, keep one chapter ahead of Asquith and Laureen when meeting them the two times a week which we had agreed over the next two months or so until their Final. Above all, however, I wanted very much to see the Law Society's past exam papers for the subject - and I was, thus, happy to see that my two students had also brought with them not only the past papers that they themselves had taken, during their recent previous unsuccessful attempts at passing the Trusts paper in question, but also all the earlier ones going back for, perhaps, the previous five years.

From that first happy meeting in my office with Jules and Laureen, I was resolved to tackle my unexpected teaching assignment in a completely different way from how I had taught my two university lecture courses at Cave Hill, so far – in Comparative Law and The Conflict of Laws. In the latter cases, I had always given a general excursus of each subject, across the number of teaching weeks available in the academic year in question. That approach had been a relatively leisurely process (at least for Comparative Law), through the whole syllabus, with an exam in the relevant subject, at the end of the academic year, coming along in due course and almost as an afterthought – at least to me, the lecturer, as opposed to my students, perhaps. With Asquith and Laureen, however, I just did not have the luxury of the whole academic year to enable me to adopt such a leisurely approach. Accordingly, I decided that I would only teach them to the exam paper to be passed! That is to say: teach them how to pass the exam paper.

By adopting such a 'different process' I mean that I decided to first go through the past exam papers - which my students had given me - with a fine-tooth comb. I wanted to see what topics the Law Society examiners had asked questions on, in those papers – so that I could restrict myself to only teaching my two charges on those topics alone! And, in so doing, I soon discovered that those assessors, back in England, had certain favourite areas of Trusts Law which they liked to base their exam questions on. Moreover, to my delight, I also gleaned that certain questions were often repeated in a different academic year – perhaps, with only one or two small variations on a theme.

Armed with such discoveries from my own researches, I was able to start my teaching of Asquith and Laureen, at our next meeting, in a most un-academic way. For, I was in a position to tell them about what I had uncovered about certain themes, or even wholesale questions, re-occurring from year to year in the past papers. I, therefore, began Professor Carnegie's mandate to me by teaching on one of those themes - as guided by the treatment of it in the recommended textbooks (which I would have read up on, before my class and, thus, based my teaching notes upon). At the end of my class, I would then ask the two articled clerks to kindly look at all the past questions on the theme in question, which I would refer to them with care, and to actually prepare a written answer to at least one of those questions for me to look at during the next class. I asked for such written 'homework' because I already knew, from my limited experience as a Law teacher, that it was one thing to understand the principles applicable in a particular area of Law; but that it was quite another to be able to express oneself in writing, clearly, about that area of Law, especially under exam conditions.

Accordingly, our twice-a-week meetings continued in my office during the latter weeks of my long (summer) vacation – always, only after Asquith and Laureen had finished their office work in Bridgetown. Each of them became quite proficient at answering the past questions, in writing – after a shaky and unsatisfactory start on both their parts. By my asking them to read out what they had respectively written on a given assignment, we were able to compare and contrast their individual attempts. More than that, I was able to help them to cut out any waffle and to just stick to giving the Law Society examiners the kind of answer which, my experience suggested, they were looking for to any given question.

As the weeks went by, I had managed to help my two students to polish up their exam preparation processes. So much so that, by the end of our first month of meetings, Asquith and Laureen already knew that they were not to concern themselves with the Law Society's Trust Law syllabus as a whole. Rather, each knew that he or she would be concentrating on, perhaps, about six to eight of the areas, or themes, of the subject in question – for the four questions, only, that they would have to answer in the forthcoming exam. Moreover, with just a week or so to go, I could ask each of them to practise writing out answers to questions on the six to eight areas in question, during my class itself under exam timing – and we would all be satisfied with the quality of the answers eventually produced in such setting. In other words, both they and myself became fairly confident that they were both 'ready' to face the real examination ordeal the following week – and, certainly, more ready than they themselves had felt when they had each sat the exam in question, several times, during a number of recent past years.

On the afternoon of our final meeting before their exam, the three of us went over to the Senior Common Room (or SCR) on Cave Hill Campus to have a farewell drink. Both Jules and Laureen seemed happy with how things had gone with my teaching of them over the past two months or so. I was certainly both content and relieved – for things had turned out much better than I had anticipated when I had first said 'Yes', to Professor Carnegie, regarding taking on his unusual, and unexpected, teaching proposition to me. At least, I was satisfied that, in accepting that assignment, I had first of all not let down my senior colleague's faith in me as a teacher. Nor, in the way I had tried to prepare my charges, did I feel I could have fulfilled my duty to them any better – and I had a good feeling about myself in how I had gone about discharging that task. After that SCR meeting, it would be down to the two of them to perform, under exam conditions, as close to the way that they had managed to do, of late, in their writing assignments completed in my office during our final classes there.

To jump forward in time – perhaps, by one month to six weeks - I was to receive a phone call in my UWI office, one day during the First Term of the new academic year 1980-81. It was from Asquith. He came straight to the point. He had just received his Trusts Law exam result from the Law Society in London. With baited breath I asked him to please tell me that result. 'I passed', he shouted down the phone! 'Well done! And Congratulations', I excitedly replied. Immediately thereafter, however, a terrible thought entered my head. 'Why is he calling me alone? What if, he has passed, but…?'. So, I quickly asked Asquith: 'What about, Laureen?'. He side-stepped that question by saying: 'She will be calling you herself – soon'. For the next few minutes, therefore, I sat in my office waiting for my phone to ring again and wondering what words I could use to try to console Laureen - if a certain outcome, which, by then, I was starting to really anticipate, had occurred.

Eventually, the call came. It was Laureen, greeting me as follows: 'Hi David! Guess what? I passed my Trusts exam too!'. That was all I needed to hear. Having also congratulated her as warmly as I could, the two of us started to make provisional plans to meet up again for a celebratory drink - with Asquith in Bridgetown - in the very near future. She agreed to liaise with him and arrange, for one or other of them to get back to me again, to let me know the time and venue.

In the meantime, there were just two people in the world with whom I most wanted to share the good news, which I had just heard. The first was my wife – for I had needed to be apart from her and our sons during those twice-a-week exam preparation sessions with Asquith and Laureen. The second was Professor Carnegie. For I wanted him to know that I had duly discharged the obligation which I had undertaken, from him, to coach the two articled clerks for their outstanding exam – which constituted their 'final of all Finals'. Moreover, I wanted to let him know the successful outcome, for both of them – which result might not only increase his standing in the eyes of his partner friends in the Bridgetown Law firm in question, but also the stature of UWI's Law Faculty as a whole.

*Chapter 13*

# The Start of my Second Academic Year at UWI (1980-81) – including my first trip to another UWI Campus outside Barbados

By the time I had heard the wonderful news from Asquith and Laureen about their both having passed their outstanding Trusts Law examination, which they had needed to do in order to become Attorneys-at-Law in Barbados, I had already begun my second teaching year in the Law Faculty at Cave Hill. Owing to the positive way my teaching of the two Bridgetown articled clerks had progressed - and, more importantly, because of the fact that I already had a full set of lecture notes for the Comparative Law course of which I was the Course Director - I had begun the new academic year in an upbeat, positive and confident frame of mind. That was added to by the fact that Tony Bland had returned from his sabbatical year away at Birmingham University in England and was once more in charge, as Course Director, of The Conflict of Laws Final Year course. That latter consideration meant that a huge weight had been lifted off my shoulders, and, though I still had a full set of lecture notes from the previous academic year for the Conflicts course, I then only needed to use them in my 'revising', just before holding my tutorials in that subject - which I would be continuing to provide (in parallel with Tony, who would also be doing so for his different tutorial groups).

*Fig. 33: Photo of Tony Bland – '...in the 70's [on] his wedding day' according to his daughter, 'Disa Allsopp' (in an email to the Author dated 21st February 2024). Perhaps, therefore, Tony had married in 1979, just before the Author took up his post at the UWI Law Faculty, and had treated his sabbatical year at Birmingham University during the 1979/80 academic year, as something an elongated honeymoon trip – with a little lecturing thrown into now and again*

Fortunately, too, I had managed to persuade Andrew Burgess - my colleague responsible for devising the Law lecturers' respective timetables – to keep my own teaching schedule more or less the same as it had been the previous year, with a 'family day off' for me on a Wednesday. If anything, my new timetable was even kinder to me in that second UWI academic year of mine, since I no longer had to give a dreaded Conflict of Laws lecture on Tuesday and Thursday mornings! Accordingly, it was a much more relaxed lecturer and tutor which my new students found when they entered my respective classes – either in the Seminar Room, for their Comparative Law lectures and discussion sessions on a 'Paper' prepared by one or other of them, or in my office (still situated in Room 4 of the main Law Faculty building) for their Conflicts or Law of Torts tutorials. Owing to my dropping my former lectures in Conflicts, I was given two hours of tutorials in a subject called 'Legal Research and Writing' in order 'to compensate'. For that new course (for me), I had to help Second Year students learn how to better research and find legal materials in the Law Library and, then, how to use such discoveries more efficiently in writing their essays. That substitute obligation I found to be not too taxing, since the latter part was not so very different from what I had already been doing with Asquith and Laureen in order to prepare them for their Trusts Law exam during the weeks leading up to the start of the new academic year.

There was one other very significant event in my private life, however, which redounded to my being happier in my work life at Cave Hill. That was the fact that, by the start of the new academic year commencing by early October 1980, Philomena had discovered the reasons why she had been experiencing mild morning sickness ever since we had returned from our summer holidays in St Vincent and the Grenadines. For, as a result, she had felt compelled to finally visit her family doctor in Maxwell - and he was soon able to provisionally diagnose that she was pregnant again!

With that joyful news, we both assumed that the occasion which had led to her conception had occurred during the relaxing days of our holiday in St Vincent – perhaps during the non-travelling period at the end of the trip when we had merely been calmly refreshing ourselves by playing daily with our sons on the beach at Young Island. My wife and I were to be in for a shock, however. By the time that her doctor had given her confirmation of his initial opinion, he had also added that she was then already about five months pregnant! He was finally able to add that the approximate due date of the baby would be in early January of the coming New Year. That meant, therefore, that my wife must have become pregnant in, or about, April 1980! That was an amazing fact to both of us - for neither she nor I had had been given any inkling (by changes in her body's shape or the like) of her expectant state when we had embarked on our summer holidays in St Vincent in late July or early August that year. Indeed, if we had even suspected her expectant condition, then even though we might still have decided to continue with our flight and holiday to St Vincent, we certainly would not have made the (sometimes turbulent) two-day sea journey by compact mail boat to the southern Grenadines and back.

Philomena's doctor's news was welcome to the two of us would-be 'new parents for the third time', however – even though, by traditional standards, we were rather late in learning her 'with child' condition. Being the good Catholics that we were at that time, although we were not actively seeking to add to the number of our offspring – by that still early period of our immigration to Barbados – nevertheless, we certainly had not been taking any of the usual steps to assiduously prevent such an occurrence from happening. Indeed, the two of us always hoped that, after the birth of our second son, the Almighty would - one day in the future - bless us again with another child which would be a daughter on that third occasion.

Accordingly, it was with a spring in my step that I embarked on my teaching duties at Cave Hill during the First Term of the 1980-81 academic year. Given Philomena's condition during that time - as well the fact that she needed help with our two existing children who were proving to be more of a 'handful' as they were growing up from month to month - I tried not to stay late in my office at Cave Hill on my teaching days unless that was really necessary. Moreover, unless I had to remain later than usual – in order, for example, to finish marking some essays received from my students in my three old subjects of Comparative, Conflicts or Torts, or in my new one of Legal Writing and Research - there was usually no need for me to stay at the Campus beyond, say, 6pm. For, as stated, even in my then sole lecture course of Comparative Law, I already had a full set of notes for such purpose from the previous academic year. In addition, and fortunately for me, revising from such notes the night before the next day's lecture I found to be much, much easier, and less time-consuming, than composing those notes from scratch in the first place.

Accordingly, I could usually be home by about 6.30pm on those four teaching days a week when I had to go to the Law Faculty. Such an evening return hour would be prior to the bedtime of either Kim or Noel - which meant that I could see, and play with, them a little before they had to say 'goodnight' to their mum and myself. Indeed, I could usually be home in good enough time to enable all four of us to have dinner at the table as a family, before the pre-bedtime playing and the reading of nursery rhymes or stories would begin. What is more, there were always the wonderful family Wednesdays – when we would still all delight in making the trip in our Skoda to the warm, gentle beach at Bath on the eastern side of the island. It was, indeed, a most happy time for me and my family.

And, even before I realised it, the Christmas holidays of my second academic year at Cave Hill were just a few weeks away. More evidence of just how self-confident and content I had become, in my still relatively new teaching life at Cave Hill by that time, can be gleaned from the fact that I had even planned a pre-End of Term trip - overseas from Barbados. Unlike my jaunt with my whole family to my Uncle Joe in Montserrat about one year before, however, on that later occasion I was travelling with just one other member thereof – namely, my firstborn son, Noel. Moreover, we were going to be travelling southwards in the Caribbean region that December 1980 - instead of in the opposite direction to where my native island is situated. In fact, my latest foreign excursion entailed both part work and part pleasure for me. That was because Noel and myself first had to travel to Trinidad where I had some UWI business to perform.

Those overseas university duties came about as a direct result of my growing self-confidence at that period of my UWI career. For, with such a positive feeling about my life in my new university by that time, I had dared to stand as a candidate to be, and had been elected as, the Law Faculty's representative upon a university-wide committee called the 'Board for Postgraduate Studies'. That committee met once every academic term - respectively, at the following UWI campuses: St Augustine in Trinidad; Mona in Jamaica; and Cave Hill in Barbados. Accordingly, towards the end of the Autumn Term of 1980, it was the turn of the Trinidad Campus to host the committee in question. I decided to tack on a 'pleasure' aspect to that 'duty visit' by not only taking my elder son along with me to St Augustine, but also paying an extra fare for the two of us to travel on from Trinidad to a neighbouring South American country and back.

It was to be the very first trip to either of two overseas countries in question for both Noel and myself. Fortunately, as far as Trinidad was concerned, we had a family friend to stay with there. That was none other than the colleague at Cave Hill who had helped me mentally, and spiritually, during my initial ('Baptism of fire') year there - by introducing me to the Prayer Meetings that he was already attending in the Strathclyde district of Bridgetown in order to maintain his own emotional and intellectual equilibrium. As mentioned previously, that person was Michael Castagne - and, as luck would have it, since our joint Prayer Meeting days he had transferred his Law lectureship post from Cave Hill to St Augustine in order to teach First Year Law students at the latter (before they had to transfer to the Barbados Campus to enable them to follow the Second and Final Years of their LL.B Law degree programme). I had corresponded with Michael before Noel and I left for Trinidad that December, and not only did he tell me that he was delighted for my son and myself to stay at his home in the St Augustine area during our visit, but he had also confirmed that he would be happy to 'baby sit' Noel for me whilst I attended my Board for Postgraduate Studies meeting at his new Campus.

With much excitement in my heart, therefore, as well as a certain amount of pride at taking my elder son off on his first international trip alone with me, I held Noel's hand as we boarded the British Airways flight from Grantley Adams Airport in Barbados to 'Piarco International', Trinidad – situated not far from that latter island's capital city of Port of Spain. What a shock awaited me as we arrived. The two of us were overwhelmed by the crowds of people at the airport – both inside the arrivals terminal, as well as after we had successfully passed through immigration control and customs. Even more unexpected for me, however, was the great contrast between the local population and that which we had so recently left behind in Barbados. For, it seemed to me that at least half of the peoples I was seeing around Noel and myself were of East Indian stock (as evidenced, typically, by their dark complexions and straight, shiny-black, hair). Most of the remainder seemed to be of 'normal' Afro-Caribbean heritage (which I, myself, claim and which ethnicity I was used to being among, from my time of living in Barbados and recent visits to Montserrat, Antigua and St Vincent). That was so, apart from the odd smattering of 'White people' - who might well have been tourists, for all I could tell. (I was to learn later, from Michael, that, just like Barbados, Trinidad too has a very small percentage of 'White natives' in its population - who are descended, mainly, from the plantation-owning class of previous centuries). And although, during my then 16 months or so at Cave Hill, I must have taught one or two Trinidadian students - whose forefathers very likely originated from the sub-continent of India - I had just not been prepared for the amazing population mix which I found upon landing at Piarco Airport. Most remarkable of all, however, was that it seemed to me that the two main ethnicities of Trinidad were (at least superficially) interacting together quite happily. For, there seemed to be no gathering of Afro-Caribbeans on one side, and Indians on another. Rather, I perceived that the society around me seemed to be in a state of flux and, on the face of it, one race was intermingling very smoothly (and indeed even sharing laughs, from time to time) with the other. Thus, my first impression of Michael's native land was a happy, if surprising, one.

In a similar way, the drive to Michael's home from Piarco Airport, after he had picked Noel and myself up, left me pleasantly astounded. For, though it was already dark as we drove along, the streets were much busier with people, as well as noisier and more colourful than their counterparts would have been back in Barbados. And a common theme seemed to be: lots of fast-food outlets or small rum (and beer) shops - everywhere! By the time that we had reached the St Augustine area, however, most of the hustle and bustle was behind us and Michael's home seemed to be situated in a quiet street of mainly wooden houses. Such a setting was not so unlike that to be found in the Strathclyde district of Bridgetown, where we had previously attended our Prayer Meetings together.

As delightful as I had found my first blush with Trinidad to be, however, I was also very aware that I was visiting that island for 'business' reasons. I had, thus, not arrived with any plans to do any major sightseeing with Michael on that first trip - especially as I had every expectation of returning again, perhaps with my entire family, in the not-too-future. Rather, I was more preoccupied with thoughts of my forthcoming first meeting the next day, with many of the non-Law professors of UWI who would also be sitting on the postgraduate awards committee in question which I had come to Trinidad to attend. One of the main purposes of that body was to decide who, among a number of student applicants, deserved to be awarded scholarships or bursaries to further their postgraduate studies. I, therefore, had a deal of paperwork to read, concerning such applications, prior to the following day's meeting. Thanks to Michael's kind offer to look after Noel the next morning, I was happy to get on to so prepare for that meeting - with a view to attending it in due course (without any qualms about my son's well-being during my temporary absence from him).

The next day, after leaving Noel in the safe hands of Michael, I made my way to St

Augustine Campus for my very first time. I was excited to see the place - in order for me to gauge how it compared with my own base at Cave Hill. I was not to be disappointed, for it did have the feeling of a 'proper university' - with lots of buildings situated around the perimeter of a 'campus', or field. Behind those edifices of the institution, however, were to be seen high hills, or even small mountains, which were features that would not be found in the relatively flat landscape around Barbados' Cave Hill site.

I soon found the Administration Building at St Augustine and, from there, obtained directions to the room in which my first Board for Postgraduate Studies was due to be held. Another excitement then lay immediately ahead of me. That was founded on the prospect of meeting, in the flesh, some of the other 'famous' teachers, within the university as a whole, who were not based in Barbados but who were also members of the committee in question. Those included such senior educators as the person who would soon become knighted and renamed as 'Professor Sir Roy Augier'. I was not to be disappointed - for, despite one after another of such distinguished individuals coming into the meeting room only in a piecemeal fashion, the atmosphere within remained full of Caribbean informality.

I witnessed no 'prima donna-ish' behaviour on the part of any of the attendees. Indeed, if anything, I was rather shocked by the laughter and jollity which pervaded the gathering - given that we were there to decide upon the academic future careers of a number of, evidently, talented student applicants for scholarships and bursaries. I soon reminded myself, however, that I was then in the Caribbean and not at the University of Cambridge, for example, or even that of Leeds where I had most recently taught. Moreover, if anything, Trinidad was, it seemed to me – even from my 24 hours or less on the island – a much more 'laid-back' country than relatively 'straight-laced' Barbados. Accordingly, it should have been little wonder to me (I soon told myself) that the atmosphere in the meeting reflected the informal atmosphere of the West Indian country in which it was taking place. At any rate, we duly transacted the 'business' that the session had been called to deal with and I found the whole experience to be a rather pleasant one – not least because I was never called upon to explain why I, personally, felt any one candidate should succeed to an award over any other competitor. The whole proceedings advanced extremely smoothly and in good humour, with junior members like me seemingly deferring to more senior ones, like Roy Augier, if ever there was any initial non-consensus in relation to any particular award. Thus, much before I expected it, the important cross-UWI Campuses meeting was over and I was free to enjoy Trinidad. That was as a result of just one morning's work - and thanks to UWI having paid my airfare to attend and participate in such 'exertion'. What an extremely good deal, I thought to myself, as I exited from my very first UWI Board meeting!

As stated, however, I had not totally focussed on trying to see much of Trinidad during that particular trip. For Noel and I were booked to fly on to a country on the South American continent on the very next day after my UWI meeting. Perhaps, it had been Michael who had insisted on the three of us visiting the island's capital of Port of Spain before my son and I departed for our new country. That main city was situated about 10 miles away from St Augustine. I can no longer recall, however, whether it was during that first trip of mine to Michael's native land that I got to see that particular metropolis (in some detail) for my initial time. If so, perhaps that was when I had been introduced to the charms of the 'Hilton Hotel' above the city, with its views overlooking the 'Queen's Park Savannah' and its 'Oval'. If so, also, Michael would no doubt have told Noel and myself that it was at the Savannah that Trinidad's famous annual 'Carnival' culminated each 'Shrove Tuesday' - just before 'Lent' started in February or March. And he would also have pointed out to us that it was at the Oval that the West Indies cricket team played its 'Test Matches'. Those would have been against one touring team, at least, from among those belonging to England, India, Australia and other Commonwealth counties – no less than once a year, from about April time.

*Chapter 14*

# A First trip to South America

If Michael had offered Noel and myself some kind of greater tour of his native island – which might then have included a visit to Trinidad's second city 'down south', named 'San Fernando' – during the remainder of the time we had left before setting off for South America the next day, I would not have accepted it. For, as stated, not only did I fully expect to return to Trinidad - for a longer visit in the not-too-distant future - but I was also already starting to look beyond the borders of that Caribbean island once my meeting at St Augustine had ended so satisfactorily for me. But where were Noel and myself going on to in South America? The answer is: 'Venezuela'!

That response begs another question, however – namely: 'Why Venezuela?'. The short answer, to that second inquiry, is: Because of my job at Cave Hill as a Comparative Law lecturer - which role involved me teaching my students about the comparing of different legal systems. Venezuela was a country situated relatively near to Barbados but which had a most dissimilar juristic regime from that of my adopted home island – namely, one based upon 'Roman Law' which was inherited from its former rulers in Spain. Thus, the Venezuelan legal system could be greatly contrasted with the 'Common Law' system which my students in Barbados knew, all too well, was the basis of the Law of that country and those of the other Commonwealth Caribbean islands or territories. My idea, therefore – and, indeed, dream – was to visit 'Caracas', the capital of Venezuela, and, there, seek out its main university in order to find its Law faculty or department, and then try to have a meeting with a fellow teacher of Comparative Law there. And although I had not written to him or her in advance, I already knew - from researching a publication entitled the '*Encyclopedia of Comparative Law*' kept in the Cave Hill Law Library - that there was such a person attached to the 'Universidad Central de Venezuela' (the 'Central University of Venezuela') situated in Caracas. That individual was a professor of Comparative Law, but what I did not know, upon embarking with Noel on our flight from Piarco, Trinidad to 'Simon Bolivar International Airport' in Caracas, was whether the professor in question was in residence that December month - and not away from his university, perhaps on sabbatical leave. Or whether, indeed, even if he was in residence, he would be willing to meet with me for a discussion with him about a certain collaboration which I had in mind for our two universities.

Another answer to the 'Why Venezuela?' question, stems from the fact that - as part of my general feeling of well-being about my life at Cave Hill in that early part of my second academic year there - I had decided that I really wanted to explore at least some parts of South and/or Central America. I desired to do so with my family, during our future holidays. That was owing to the fact that we were rather nearer to those countries of Latin America than a return to England or Continental Europe would entail for us. For example, Caracas was only about one hour's direct flying time from Barbados.

Moreover, owing to the fact that the main language of most of the countries of Latin America – apart from Portuguese in 'Brazil', of course – was Spanish, I had decided that I wanted to learn that language better, by attending classes in Barbados to that end. When, therefore, I had also discovered that there was a 'Venezuelan Cultural Institute' in Bridgetown which offered free, or relatively cheap, Spanish lessons during certain weekdays (at times which did not clash with my own lectures or tutorials), I had signed up for the same. And it had not taken me long to fully engage myself with those language classes and with my lady teacher at the Institute. It was a help that I already had a smattering of Spanish from my two trips to Spain to visit Philomena whilst she had been a student and/or 'au pair' there in 'León' in 1972 and in 'Valencia' in 1973. By that December 1980, however, I was in a formal learning situation with other 'mature students' and I had not only learned such things as the Venezuelan national anthem by heart, but also a small number of Venezuelan Christmas carols such as '*Niño Lindo*' – all of which I can still remember as I write these memoirs over 40 years later.

Yet one more answer to the question 'Why Venezuela?' stems from the fact that I had made, in Barbados, a Venezuelan 'acquaintance' by that December. I would not go as far as to call him a 'friend' by that stage, but I had encountered the individual – a mature man, who had told me that he had a wife and children back in Caracas – on Maxwell Beach one day. I have long since forgotten his name, as well as lost such contact as I had with him, but let us call him 'Luis' for these purposes. In our first conversation at my family's closest seaside spot, Luis had told me that the reason he was then living temporarily in Barbados was in order to follow a course of English at some language school in Bridgetown – perhaps, in order to become proficient in the language for the purposes of his employment back in Venezuela. Very likely, his employers were sponsoring him during his time in Barbados - for he seemed to have accommodation in one of the larger homes on Maxwell Coast Road. I only came across him a few more times on the beach before he had returned to his homeland – but I managed to exchange home addresses and telephone numbers with him prior to his so doing. When later I knew that I would be visiting his native country in early December, I wrote to him to let him know and to ask if, at least, he would be willing to meet my son and myself during our stay in his city. Perhaps, I had been hoping that he might even have offered the two of us some accommodation at his home whilst we were in Caracas, but I cannot recall ever getting a reply to my letter. Nevertheless, I took both his address and his telephone number with me when Noel and I had left Barbados for our two-country trip that December.

Venezuela, therefore, had quite a pull for me when Noel and I said goodbye to Michael at Piarco International Airport that last month of 1980 and also thanked him for all his hospitality during our short, first ever, visit to Trinidad. As part of my excitement of going to the second 'new country' of our trip, I had even been sure to have booked our extra onward trip to Caracas and back (paid for out of my own money, just as Noel's travel costs for the entire trip had been) on Venezuela's own national airlines. In those days, that was called 'VIASA' - which stood for 'Venezolana Internacional de Aviación Sociedad Anónima' in Spanish, but simply referred to as 'Venezuelan International Airways' in English. Thus, I already experienced a little taste of Latin America by simply checking in at the VIASA desk at Piarco for exotic-sounding Caracas - and, even more so, by the time that Noel and I had boarded our orange and white liveried aeroplane staffed by smart, and mainly European-looking, air stewards and stewardesses. Surely, I thought to myself, exciting adventures awaited us in my, and my young son's, very first encounter with the continent of South America. And my expectations were in no way lessened when we landed, less than an hour later, at Caracas's International Airport - some 10 or so miles outside that capital city, in a district named 'Maiquetia'. The colour scheme of that airport was orange and white too, and it seemed so clean and well-kept, to me, that I really thought that it had only recently been opened. That very favourable impression made me think that we were in for quite an auspicious visit.

The first thing which I had to do was to find somewhere for Noel and myself to stay in the city. Fortunately, there was a tourist bureau in the airport which we visited as soon as we had cleared customs and immigration. That enabled me to speak to someone there who could converse with me in English (since my Spanish was still not yet good enough for transacting business) about the possibilities of obtaining some kind of cheap transport into the capital city – as well as ask about a budget bed and breakfast hotel, or *pensión*, situated there. I must have been successful in my quest, since I can still recall going out to the main road nearby, just outside the airport's perimeter, crossing over to the other side and then waiting for a small mini-bus (such as that which my family had travelled on during our holidays in St Vincent the previous summer). The half-hour journey into Caracas, thereafter, was a delight for me, as I contrasted the red-earth landscape of that particular Venezuelan region with the darker, hillier and tree-filled topography which Noel and I had so recently left behind in Trinidad. Moreover, as we motored along towards the capital, I could see, on the hillside to my left, a very extensive 'shanty town' – with little, box-like, dwelling houses seemingly piled, terrace-like, one above another. I was to learn, later on, that I had been observing the one area on the outskirts of Caracas which was the equivalent to the many '*favelas*' which are to be found around 'Rio de Janeiro' in Brazil. I was also to discover that, in Venezuela, the name for that particular place, where hundreds (if not thousands) of migrants from the countryside gravitate to in order to find somewhere to live near the capital city, was '*ranchito*'.

At any rate, after a pleasant ride in our combi-bus 'into town' with my being absorbed with the features of my fellow passengers and their rapid-fire Spanish (full of hard-sounding rollings of the letter 'R' as they conversed with each other), we eventually reached our terminus in the city centre. Even that arrival was a delight for me too. For the bus station happened to be right outside the '*Plaza de toros*' – the bullfighting arena of Caracas. What a lovely surprise that was for me! For, it just had never dawned on me, prior to arriving there, that not only had the Spanish '*conquistadores*' brought over their language and their Law to Venezuela in bygone centuries, but so also had they transported their 'national sport'! The thought struck me that, perhaps, I would get an opportunity to take Noel to see his first bullfight during our visit – just as his mother had taken me to my initial, and only previous, one some years before. That had happened during my stay with her in Valencia, Spain in 1973, whilst she had been working as an *au pair* there. The exploration of such an opportunity, however, would have to wait since my first duty to him (and myself) at that time had to be to find the *pensión* which we had been recommended at the airport's tourist office.

Caracas seemed, at first glance, to be a 'long', extensive, city from east to west – as it appeared, to me, to be squeezed between two mountain ranges on its northern and southern sides and therefore could only grow, and expand laterally, in the other two directions. Owing to that perceived extensiveness, I decided that there was little chance of Noel and I trying to find our own way from the bus terminal to the recommended *pensión*. For, in my mind, it might have been the equivalent of being deposited at 'Victoria Coach Station' on the west side of London and trying to walk to an endorsed hotel in 'Stratford' in the 'East End' of the British capital. Accordingly, I took Noel to the nearest taxi which I could see and asked the driver to take us to the recommended place of accommodation – which was written on a piece of paper provided to me following my touristic inquiry at the airport. That step turned out to be a prudent one, since even the taxi driver had to visit a few different locations before we finally reached the front door of our officially-approved lodgings.

The room which Noel and I were given turned out to be quite a small one. It was, however, adequate for our purposes since I had no intention of the two of us spending very much time inside it during our stay. Rather, the first thing that I did was to phone Luis in order to let him know that Noel and I were already in his city and to ask him whether the three of us might meet up within the next day or two. I made the call with the help of the receptionist at the *pensión* and, thus, was able to give Luis our precise location and also arrange for him to come and pick us up the following day - in order to give us a small tour of his native city. My having succeeded in making such an appointment with my Venezuelan acquaintance already felt like an achievement in itself. Much more important for my trip to Caracas, however, was my goal of securing a future international arrangement between two universities - for which I still had no appointment at all. Thus, I still had to try to visit my Comparative Law counterpart at one of the local universities in order to try to establish some kind of partnership with him and his faculty. I already knew, however, that my target person was an individual based at, arguably, the most famous and prestigious university in Caracas, if not the whole of his native country – namely, the Universidad Central de Venezuela, or 'UCV' (as, I was soon to discover, it was more popularly known as). As I also learnt (from the receptionist at our *pensión*) that the revered institution was only a relatively short taxi ride away, within an hour or two of our first checking in at our latest lodging place Noel and I were on our way by cab to UCV.

I was not to be disappointed when we arrived at the university. Despite the campus being a large one - full of buildings, but with no 'field', or other green space, that I could see - once our taxi had deposited my son and myself at its main entrance it was relatively easy to find the '*Facultad de Derecho*', where my desired Law teacher was based. His name was 'Professor Allan Brewer-Carias'. And, much to my great delight, when I had introduced myself at the reception of UCV's Law Faculty and requested a meeting with him, then - after waiting a few minutes whilst enquiries were made on my behalf - I was informed that he had just finished lecturing for the day and would, thus, be very happy to meet with me immediately.

*Fig 34: Photo of Professor Allan Brewer-Carias looking a little older, and greyer, than the Author remembers him at the Universidad Central de Venezuela (UCV), Caracas in December 1980 – but still sporting his trade mark 'Salvador-Dali-like' moustache from those earlier days*

I could not have asked for a better welcome from the professor. He told me that because of his specialisation in Comparative Law, he too had spent time visiting (and even teaching in) other Law faculties around the world, including some in England. Accordingly, he was more than a little sympathetic to my initiative in coming from Barbados to try to meet up with him – including my having included my son in my 'scouting party' for the encounter! Most importantly, however, was the fact that he was more than willing to help me try to arrange to bring my Comparative Law students over to UCV for a one week's visit, during one or other of the two remaining terms of UWI's current academic year. That was especially the case when I told him that the maximum numbers involved would be no more than about 15 students (assuming that all members of my class would be willing, and able to afford, to come). His big question to me was: 'When would you all be wanting to come?'. My answer to that was based on the fact that most of my students would be having their exams (in all of their subjects) during the Third Term of UWI's academic year. That would be after Easter, and I anticipated that most of them would have really preferred to have had all of that Final Term to simply revise - with no distractions such as foreign 'field trips' being involved - in order to be best prepared to write their exams. Accordingly, my confirmed answer to the professor's question was that it therefore seemed to me that the best time for my students and myself to come would be just as the Easter holidays were beginning at UWI, at the end of the Second Term. My UCV counterpart seemed more than happy with my suggested timetable, as he replied that it did not interfere with either his future teaching schedule or travel plans. I was, thus, able to eventually leave our long introductory meeting more than a little delighted. For, in 'scouting out' the particular Venezuelan professor in question, it seemed to me that I had clearly chosen an excellent Comparative Law colleague and future collaborator.

It is even possible for me to give an exact date to that auspicious meeting with UCV's Professor of Comparative Law. For, whilst walking back with Noel to our *pensión* afterwards, I saw a billboard with words in Spanish which brought my post-meeting happy heart almost to a standstill. It said something like: '*John Lennon asesinado a tiros en Nuevo York!*'. Even with my basic grasp of the national language of Venezuela, I could well understand that the breaking news was that, perhaps, the best-known member of 'The Beatles' pop-group – whose music I had grown up with, as a teenager in the 1960s – had been killed by a shooting in USA's largest city. What an unexpected shock! I knew no details at that stage, but nevertheless I would never forget in which city Noel and myself happened to be visiting when we first saw the news that John Lennon had been assassinated in 'New York City'. That unforgettable date was 8th December 1980!

The following morning, after Noel and I had eaten breakfast - which had included a lot of fried corn flour with shredded beef - Luis came for us as he had promised. I was rather taken aback by his car - which turned out to be a large American model and, perhaps, some kind of 'Cadillac'. In his own land, therefore, Luis came across to me as 'a man of substance' – to contrast with the impression he had given me when I had first met him earlier in Barbados as a mere 'language student'. Moreover, he had arrived with his own young son in tow – who seemed to me to be just a year or two older than Noel. Luis greeted me warmly with a hug, introduced his boy and then allowed me to introduce my own. After a bit, he offered to show my son and myself around some of the main sights of his city, and then to take us back to his home for a meal with the rest of his family. I readily accepted his kind offer, and soon we were driving in his limousine along some of Caracas's urban highways which were full of traffic. I had never visited New York City by that stage in my life, but, in my imagination, driving in Luis's own metropolis was how I imagined doing the same thing in America's largest city must have been like at the time. Massive cars and buses all around us, going in our direction as well as in the opposite one, on several lanes of the highway which we happened to be on at any particular moment. Moreover, as I looked out of our car's windows beyond any such highway, I could see 'skyscrapers' everywhere – high-rise residential apartment blocks as well as office buildings, seemingly intermingled at random. Perhaps those particular edifices were not as high as those which one would have found in New York during that era, but they left an unforgettable impression on me – as a visitor who had just recently arrived from relatively low-rise Bridgetown and Port of Spain in the Caribbean. I was enjoying the contrast in the topographical (and, to a lesser extent, the traffic) situation - immensely!

Apart from those highways, towering buildings and the mountains to the north and south of us as we drove around the city, however, the actual 'touristic sights' which we visited left little lasting impression on me. That was so, except for one particular location situated in a large park. For, I still have some faded photographs of our four-person visit to that particular outdoor space and the monument that was to be found in the middle of it – perhaps, as a memorial to Venezuela's, or its capital city's, war dead. The photos feature Noel prominently, wearing a yellow rain-jacket which went nicely with his similarly coloured sun-bleached hair which he still possessed at that age.

*Fig 35: The Author and Noel in Caracas, Venezuela in December 1980. The other small boy, on the left of the photo, is the son of 'Luis' – the Venezuelan acquaintance of the Author who kindly gave the two visitors from Barbados a tour of his home city*

Eventually, it became time for Noel and I to go with Luis and his son to visit their home. That was situated some way outside the centre of Caracas, back in the direction of Maiquetia and the airport. Perhaps, like most residents of the Caracas area, his residence was situated in an apartment in one of those high-rise blocks that pervaded the city centre which we had just left behind. Moreover, he and his family lived quite high up in his particular block - perhaps, as much as 10 floors up or even higher. Accordingly, the views out of his living room windows, when he welcomed Noel and myself there in order to meet the rest of his family, were stunning. Inside, we met his wife and two of his other children and got treated to some delicious local food and drinks. By the end of our time with Luis and his clan therefore, I had come to the conclusion that he was indeed a 'man of substance' who enjoyed a very good lifestyle with his family, by Venezuelan standards. They were, to my mind, at least 'middle class' – and, certainly, had a standard of living well above what life might have been like for those living in the *ranchito* we had passed during our journey from the airport after our arrival. It is likely, however, that the lifestyle of Luis and his household would still have been below that which was enjoyed by someone like Professor Brewer-Carias (who, I dared to imagine, would surely have lived in a house - somewhere in the suburbs of Caracas).

After our time in Luis's family home had come to its natural end, he kindly offered to drive Noel and myself back to our accommodation in central Caracas. On behalf of my own family, I pressed an offer on Luis, and his wife, to come, with their children, to visit me and my family at our home in Barbados in order to enable me to repay their much-appreciated Venezuelan hospitality. Luis's wife especially thanked me, in Spanish only, for my offer but gave me a wry smile as if to say that she could not see that ever happening – perhaps, because of the cost of travel to the Caribbean for her whole family, or because of other practical considerations such as the need to acquire expensive passports for herself and children as a prerequisite to such an international trip. At that time of my life, however, I was full of optimism and fully expected to see, in the future and once more, Luis and his family, as a whole, whether in Barbados or in their own homeland. Only time would tell, however, and I said '*Hasta la vista*', or 'Until the next time', to the family as we left their apartment. I repeated those words of temporary parting to Luis himself, once he had dropped us at our *pensión* and I had given him my fervent thanks for all he had done for Noel and myself that day. I genuinely could not wait for an opportunity to return his kindness (and that of his family), back at our own family's home in Barbados, sometime in the not-too-distant future.

From the next day, Noel and I were free to do as we wished. We had some choices of how to utilise our last full days in Venezuela. One was to further explore the possibilities of taking him to see his first bullfight. From what I remembered about my experience of such event in Spain seven years previously, such 'sport' always took place in the afternoon as the sun was going down from the hottest part of the day. That would have meant wasting a morning in the city whilst we waited for the post-lunch period to come. Accordingly, I decided to check on how much it would cost us to travel to another city nearby. Such a side trip would enable the two of us to see something of the Venezuelan countryside, *en route*, as well as visit some other regional municipality which I could compare with the country's biggest city (which I, for one, had already started to become somewhat familiar with).

As it happened, the place to get the requisite information from was at the same bus terminal where we had arrived when coming from the airport a few days before. Moreover, and as stated, that was located right next to the *Plaza de toros*. Thus, if my enquiries had proved our proposed travel to be too expensive, I could have decided to stay in Caracas with Noel to watch some bullfighting, as a second-best option, after all. Upon inquiry, however, I happily discovered that travel to the next big city, west of Caracas – in the direction of the 'Andes Mountains' – was very cheap. That city, coincidentally, was also named 'Valencia' – just like the Spanish city of my first bullfight, previously mentioned. It was, perhaps, about two hours away from Caracas on the 'bus' – that is to say, making use of a proper, and long-distance ride, in a 'coach' (as we would call such a vehicle in England). And the pleasant surprise for me was that the fare for Noel and myself was little more than the cost of our transport from the airport into downtown Caracas - which latter we had paid on our first day of arrival in Venezuela.

Valencia it would be, therefore - and, shortly after I had bought our tickets, Noel and I took our seats on a packed bus which was to take us there from the Caracas terminal. Whilst waiting for departure, I enjoyed looking out of the windows at the teeming life outside - as scores of would-be passengers tried to find the vehicles that would be driving them to their intended destinations, and as drivers and conductors were shouting out the places they were proposing to terminate at, or otherwise stop at on the way.

The journey to Valencia itself proved to be fairly uneventful, however – at least, after our bus had managed to make its slow, traffic-congested, way out of the centre of the capital. Once we had left the big city behind, we were on a motorway and speeding through relatively flat countryside. The temperature in our non-air-conditioned vehicle seemed to get hotter as we went along. It is likely, therefore, that we were also leaving the elevation in which Caracas finds itself and which enables it to enjoy a temperature that is neither too hot nor cold at most times of the day or night. I noticed, as we went westwards to our destination, that we were travelling on a plain and that there were no mountains to be seen in any direction around us. It thus beggared belief, to me at least, that we were really travelling towards to the Andes Mountains and the neighbouring country of 'Colombia' which they continued on into. Perhaps, therefore it had been during that particular phase of my first trip to Venezuela that I resolved to return to that part of the country and that, when I did so, I would not stop until I had arrived at that world-famous mountain range. For the time being, however, all that I could hope for, in the short period that remained before our pre-booked return flight home, was to get a first flavour of 'somewhere else in Venezuela that was outside Caracas'.

When we arrived at 'sweltering' Valencia, I was not to be disappointed with the choice that I had made, for Noel and myself - regarding how we should spend our 'free' day. My initial perception of the city was that it was very much smaller than Caracas and, certainly, there were no urban motorways all around it which prevented a visitor from crossing roads, and easily seeing something of the place on foot. Indeed, the latter is exactly what Noel and I set out to do - after our arrival at the much less busy bus terminal than the one which we had left behind in the capital a couple of hours before. And, at first blush, the place seemed to me to have a distinct feel of Spain – or, at least, somewhat redolent of the few cities which I had visited in that European country such as León in the north, or, even, the exact namesake of the city which my son and I were then visiting, situated on its south-eastern Mediterranean coast.

Once we had our feet on the ground in Venezuela's Valencia, Noel and I had a good wander around the area nearest to its bus station. That was the district that had a distinctive 'old Spanish' feel, to me. For, on the horizon during the walk, I could detect a newer part of the city - situated about a mile or two away - from the higher rise buildings that I was able to spot there. I was neither interested in going such a distance, especially in the heat of the day in which we found ourselves, nor thought it wise to tire Noel out by attempting the required trek. Accordingly, after only a short time of rambling around that more ancient district of Valencia under the unrelenting sun, the two of us had a break and I bought some drinks for ourselves from one of the multiple kiosks which seem to pervade the streets of both the Venezuelan cities which we had encountered, thus far, on our trip.

We sat down on a bench, which I had spotted in the yard of a nearby church, whilst we quenched our thirsts. During that respite stop, I noticed something which piqued my interest: little by little, other people were going past us and into the church itself. Moreover, they were all neatly dressed – both the men and the women in question, as well as the children arriving with some of them. Consequently, it did not take me long to figure out that some sort of celebration was about to take place inside the church and, at first, I thought that, perhaps, we had arrived in Valencia on some sort of feast day. Could it even have been the birthday of the patron saint of the city itself? However, when one of those large cars, which Noel and I were by then used to seeing in both the Venezuelan cities we had spent time in, turned up and a young woman (dressed in white) exited along with an older man, there could no longer be any doubt in my mind as to the event which was about to unfold.

Since my son and I had 'no appointments' for the rest of our day in Valencia, I decided that I would take him to witness his first international wedding – indeed, his very first marriage ceremony anywhere in the world. Even at the age of three years and two months of age, Noel was already interested in seeing new things and, accordingly, was game to go inside the church with me in order to observe what was about to take place there. I was not to be disappointed when the nuptial Mass began – and although the language of the proceedings was in Spanish, naturally, the general structure of the rites being performed at the altar in front of us was extremely familiar to me. The singing, and the wardrobe of the bride and groom as well as their guests, had a Latin flamboyance, however, which went beyond anything which I had ever encountered at similar events in England or even in nearer Barbados.

I made Noel sit with me at the back of the church, since we were uninvited persons at the event. When the wedding ceremony was over, however, and everyone was milling about outside the front of the church, I was bold enough to take Noel and myself up to the bride and groom and say 'Congratulations' to them - in English. That single word, in a foreign language to the newly-weds, was to be the catalyst for the unexpected development which was to occur afterwards. For the bridegroom replied to me with a 'Thank you!'. He then went on to ask me: 'Where are you from?'. When I replied that my son and I were from the nearby Caribbean island of Barbados, he seemed most interested since he was then to reveal to me that he himself was from a nearby Caribbean island too – namely, the Venezuelan one of 'Isla de Margarita'. I told him that I had heard of that particular place – since, at the time, I was able to pick up on my home wireless set in Barbados, and sometimes listened to, the Venezuelan 'pop music' station of 'Radio Margarita' which, I added, that I loved for the vibrancy of its output. My enthusiastic response about my knowledge of 'Margarita Island', and its radio station, seemed to be the trigger for what came next: 'Would you like to come to the wedding party, in the hall behind this church, which is going to start in the next half hour or so?'. Without even bothering to ask Noel if he would like to do that, I immediately accepted the bridegroom's kind invitation and thanked him and his new wife for their very kind gesture. I could hardly believe what had just happened - since I did not even know the names of the newly-weds, nor had Noel and myself arrived at the church in any sense 'prepared for a wedding'. Certainly, neither of us was 'all dressed-up' like all the happy couple's other guests - but if they had not minded extending their invitation to us, despite our ordinary travelling clothes, then I was not going to turn that surprise invitation down.

After a few more minutes of polite conversation with the newly-weds, they moved along from Noel and myself, in order for them to greet some of their more-legitimately invited guests. Once I saw some of those others starting to file into the hall behind the church, however, I took Noel by the hand and followed them inside the building. Fortunately, once within, I found that some of the tables around the perimeter of the room did not have nameplates and so I took Noel to one that was well out of the way of the bridal party's area. Within a relatively short time afterwards, the proceedings had begun with a number of formal speeches - which, surprisingly to me, included that of the bride (as well as her father). That session may have lasted a good hour or so. Thereafter, however, those at the nuptial assembly were invited to serve themselves from the buffet of wonderful foodstuffs which were set out in a lavish spread in one part of the room. Much as I would have loved to have charged up to the front of the queue for what was on offer, as I (and, I daresay, my son) was extremely hungry by that time - having not eaten since our arrival in Valencia earlier that day - I held Noel and myself back until a good number of the 'regular' guests had already procured their own platefuls of food, before I took forward the two of us 'outsiders at the wedding banquet' to select our own.

And what a feast we both had then! I took the opportunity to try things I had not yet come across anywhere else during our Venezuelan sojourn thus far. Noel, would no doubt have been more conservative in his choices but he, too, was to have his fill - even if that had mainly consisted of chicken and rice, chased down with an even greater quantity of ice cream afterwards. There was also lots of drink available to the wedding guests. And though I do not remember 'champagne' itself being on offer, other South American sparkling (and still) wines had certainly made up for that - in abundance.

And then the dancing began! I remember the infectious Latin American beat which pervaded the room that evening and the wonderful rhythmical steps which most of the guests executed on the dance floor during that stage of the celebrations. It seemed to me that nearly everyone there was some sort of practised performer – especially among the adults - and knew well how to contort themselves in time with the 'salsa' beat of the music. How I envied their confidence, and ease of movement - and my witnessing of those delightful gyrations made me resolve to register for salsa dancing lessons when I returned to Barbados (especially if I was to discover, on my homecoming, that they were also offered by the Venezuelan Cultural Centre in Bridgetown).

Before I knew it, night time had arrived - and yet the wedding festivities were still in full flow. It was clearly much too late for Noel and myself to try to catch a bus back to Caracas – for, even if they had still been running at that late hour, which I doubted, I, for one, was having too much fun to want to return to the capital city, in the middle of the night. Moreover, Noel was, by then, fast asleep on my lap near our table – where I had sat observing the dancing (and continued eating and drinking) - and it would have been a shame to have disturbed his slumber for what might have been a wild goose chase back to Valencia's bus station in order to seek a possible non-existent night bus back to Caracas. Fortunately for Noel and myself, the party went on into the night and then the wee hours of the morning. Moreover, there were many a guest (mainly male ones, admittedly) who had imbibed a little too much of the free alcohol to want to make the effort of finding their way home and who were happy to 'sleep off' the celebrations, right there in the hall, along with Noel and his father. For me, the place had everything which my son and myself needed 'for one night only' – a comfortable chair for the two of us (even if not a bed) and a toilet not many steps away from our 'berth'.

The next morning, after a quick wash in the hall's bathroom facilities, Noel and I were able to take our leave of the place even if we left a few, still-sleeping, guests behind as we did so. Naturally, there was no sign of the bride and groom by that stage and, so, I was unable to thank them, again, for inviting Noel and myself to their wonderful celebration. Perhaps, they had even already arrived on the Isla de Margarita for their honeymoon by that hour! All I could do, therefore, was to say a silent prayer for them by asking God to give them a very happy married life together and to keep them as generous-hearted, in the future, as they had been to us the previous day in inviting us two strangers to their nuptials. Only afterwards did it strike me that the invitation might well have been a piece of luck for the newly-weds too – not unlike the Scottish tradition of 'First Footing', by 'a dark stranger' bringing a piece of black coal, and other gifts, into a household and being the first visitor there on New Year's Day. It is even possible that, as far as the bride and groom were concerned in inviting me (and Noel), I was the equivalent of 'the dark stranger', first footing it to their wedding party during the first hour or two of their married life the previous day. Certainly, as far as I can recall, I had been the only Black person at the wedding celebrations all that day – and night!

Noel and I were, thus, able to easily get a very early bus back to Caracas and be there in good time to visit our former *pensión* in that city to enable us to retrieve our suitcase before lunchtime. Fortunately, the manager did not charge us for the previous night's accommodation - which we had pre-booked, but not used owing to our over-stay in Valencia. And, soon afterwards, my son and I were back at the *Plaza de toros*, and its neighbouring bus station, in good time to catch one of the many minibuses going that early afternoon from the terminus to Maiquetia - and the main road there, just up from Simon Bolivar International Airport. An uneventful flight back to Piarco, Trinidad then followed - with a short stay on the ground there, before we caught our connecting flight on to Barbados. After an absence of about one week, my Skoda car (left parked near Grantley Adams International) started first time for me, fortunately, and soon Noel and I were back in the bosom of our family at Hygeia in Maxwell. Christmas was not far very away by then – and nor was the imminent arrival of Noel's new little sibling awaiting to escape the, already, very prominent tummy of its mum.

*Chapter 15*

# A New Sibling for Noel and Kim

Given Philomena's heavily pregnant condition by the Christmas 1980 holidays in question, there was no way that we wanted to repeat the precedent of an overseas Christmas holiday trip which we had made the previous year – whether to my native Montserrat or elsewhere in the Caribbean. By that time, our expected new baby had been further confirmed by Philomena's doctor as being due in the fourth week of the following January. Accordingly, our main focus of the end-of-year holidays at that time was to concentrate on the things which we would be needing for the new baby – although we made sure that we also obtained suitable presents for 'Santa' to bring for Noel and Kim for their Christmas. Indeed, that late December might have been the very first year in our family's history where the four of us went to Midnight Mass together on Christmas Eve. We did that at nearby St Dominic's RC Church, Maxwell – whilst leaving Mrs Payne, our elderly neighbour downstairs, to play Santa for us by putting out our sons' Christmas presents whilst we were away attending the service.

Once Christmas was over, New Year's Day 1981 seemingly arrived, for me, excessively quickly. And even before I had 'caught myself', that latter special milestone, too, had passed by and I soon found myself back at work at Cave Hill in the second week of January – preparing for some classes that would be starting again from the following Monday. I was certainly at the Law Faculty on Thursday, 8th January and, for once, I was rather late in arriving back at Hygeia. During the drive home, I had noticed that the fuel gauge in our family's car was showing that the petrol tank was very low. I had not particularly worried about that, however, since Philomena and I had already planned that I would take the following day off to go out with her and our boys in the Skoda to do our weekly grocery-buying at the Oistins supermarket. That would be one day before our usual 'shopping Saturday' – and I had also planned to fill up the car with petrol during that outing. I arrived home in a completely calm frame of mind and Philomena met me in her normal welcoming and relaxed condition too. The following day would be a shopping and petrol-acquiring day and we would mainly have discussed what items needed to be added to the buying-in list which she had already drawn up. Two weeks hence, approximately, would be the time of arrival of our new baby.

To paraphrase a well-known Scottish saying: 'The best made plans of mice and men often go awry'. And 'awry' is certainly how my (and Philomena's) plans were to transpire during the night and day ahead. For, after we had enjoyed our normal family supper, put our sons to bed and then watched the news on television prior to setting off to our own room to turn in for the night, Philomena began to tell me that she was starting to feel somewhat unwell. She added that she was experiencing a kind of sensation which she had only encountered twice before! Our slow realisation of what was starting to happen to her was confirmed when she, very soon afterwards, exclaimed to me that her 'waters had just broken' and that she thought she was then aware of some mild 'contractions' in her stomach.

Although, I had been in a similar situation with Philomena before - just prior to arrival of both Noel (at home, in the village of Coton, near Cambridge in England) and then Kim (in the middle of Leeds city centre in the same country) I must admit that, as per those two previous occasions, I had rather panicked at my wife's unexpected news. She, however, kept her head much better than me and suggested that I should call the hospital in Bridgetown - where it had been pre-planned with her doctor that she would be having our new baby. The name of that place was the 'Queen Elizabeth Hospital'. I made the suggested phone call and was told by the maternity ward person ('the midwife'), to whom I eventually spoke, that I should bring my wife in immediately – given that her waters had already broken. I was unpanicked enough, however, to ask the same person whether I would be allowed to be with my wife during the birth of our new child. The reply was that such a possibility would only be allowed if my wife's doctor (who had previously agreed, with Philomena only, to be present at our baby's birth and to help deliver it) gave his permission for me to be so present. I then asked the midwife to kindly get in touch with my wife's doctor to let him know that I was very shortly about to bring my wife into the hospital, and that we needed him to be there to attend to the birth (as previously agreed with Philomena in her pre-natal visits with him) - as well as to give his permission for me to be at my wife's side during the event.

The other thing that I, unexpectedly, felt obliged to do that night was to rouse our neighbour downstairs from her sleep to tell her our surprise news and to ask her to kindly perform a favour for us. Thankfully, as a retired midwife herself, Mrs Payne immediately, and fully, realised the seriousness of the situation in which Philomena, and our family, were in. Moreover, she straight away agreed to come upstairs to us in order to sleep with Noel and Kim in their bedroom, so as to be there for them when they each awoke in the morning – and, thereafter, to look after them until we (or, at least, I myself) returned home from the hospital.

Accordingly, after then hastily packing a small suitcase of a few clothes and nightdresses for Philomena as well as her bag of toiletries, it was off in our Skoda for the relatively short drive to Queen Elizabeth Hospital – about a mere five or six miles away, on our side of Bridgetown. And then it hit me, as we got into the car. It was very low on fuel. That was something that, as I have stated, I had planned to put right during our planned shopping trip to Oistins the following day, near our supermarket one mile or so away. Nevertheless, I made the 'executive decision' to take the gamble of the car's fuel tank having enough in it to get us to the Bridgetown hospital – rather than 'waste time' in driving the Skoda in the opposite direction towards Oistins in order to fill-up first. That hazardous choice was based on Philomena's evident closeness to giving birth as well as on the fact that I did not even know whether the Oistins 'gas-station' would still be open at that late hour and whether a trip there would have been a futile one in any event.

Thus, with me trying to keep Philomena calm with comforting words and caresses – and always being mindful that our previous baby, Kim, had arrived extremely quickly in Leeds, England after her waters had broken an hour or so before his birth[47] – we set off in our car towards Bridgetown. It was then that one of the worst possible things, in those particular circumstances, occurred. For, just as we passed the turning from the main road to St Lawrence Gap – the road in which was located the Sandhurst Hotel base for our honeymoon trip to Barbados in 1976 – the Skoda's engine's cut out! I was, therefore, forced to quickly attempt to bring it to as safe a stopping-place, at the left-hand side of the road, as I could. Try as I might after doing that, however, I just could not get the engine to re-start. The car's fuel tank was clearly empty!

That, surely, had to be the worst moment of my life! My wife was in labour and soon to give birth (if the precedent of Kim's speedy arrival in Leeds, 18 months before, had been anything to go by). It was close to midnight and there were no public buses still running at that hour. The hospital was still about five miles away – so trying to walk there would have been out of the question. Taxis did, naturally, exist on the island. Unlike London, however, they did not ply the streets empty hoping to be hailed for hire just about anywhere in the locality. Rather, in Barbados, one took a taxi from a specific fixed location or rank, such as the airport or 'Trafalgar Square' in Bridgetown, and I certainly did not know of such a staging post in the St Lawrence Gap area. What, therefore, in the name God, was I to do in my moment of desperation? That was the question which I internally screamed to myself.

And then it struck me! Do something that I had never seen anyone else try to attempt in Barbados in all the months that I had been living there. Do something which was a throwback to my student days – and which, if any of my colleagues or students at Cave Hill had seen me doing, would have caused me no end of embarrassment. Do something that would depend wholly on the goodwill of some 'Good Samaritan'. What, therefore, was that deed? The answer was: something that involved nothing no more onerous than putting out my left thumb and waving it slowly at passing motorists heading in the direction of Bridgetown. Yes, I started to 'hitchhike'! Right next to my 'broken down' Skoda, and with Philomena standing right beside me looking somewhat bewildered – not just because of her very imminent birthing condition but also, no doubt, because of the transportation catastrophe which I had reduced the two of us to.

Despite it being a Thursday night and a full 24 hours or so before the weekend would begin, there was nevertheless a good deal of traffic on Highway 7 at that time. Some drivers, no doubt, would have been on their way to, or from, some nightclub or other in that touristic district of St Lawrence Gap (where we ourselves had honeymooned not many years before) - or even proceeding to (or from) the downtown area of the island's capital. The Almighty must have decided to smile upon Philomena and myself, pretty soon after I started using my thumbs, however, despite (or, perhaps, because of) our dire situation. For, within a minute or so of my commencing doing so, a yellow 'Mini Moke' screeched to a halt beside the two of us. That particular make of automobile was the classic hire vehicle which tourists to Barbados rented, at that time, as their normal first choice – for the looked-for relaxed stylishness which would emanate from one, and its usually well-to-do passengers, as it motored along the small roads of the island. It was something like a half-sized 'Land Rover' or 'Jeep', but without a roof – though a canvass one could be erected quickly, if it ever began to rain during use. Notwithstanding its diminutive size, however, a Moke contained four seats – two in front and two behind.

When the Moke in question pulled up, Philomena and I could see that it was being driven by a White middle-aged man and that he had a passenger, of similar description, sitting beside him. The driver spoke to us first, and, from what he said, it was immediately clear to us two stranded 'hitchhikers' that he was drunk! 'We are from Mars! How can we help?'. His first statement and question were accompanied by laughter between himself and his fellow passenger - as well as by a waft of strong alcoholic fumes emanating from his breath towards our direction. I, therefore, had to do a quick calculation on whether it was safe to negotiate with such a driver in order for my wife and myself to try to obtain a lift to the hospital. And coming to the speedy decision that 'beggars cannot be choosers', I decided to tell him that we had just run out of petrol, my wife was in labour and we were desperately in need of a lift to the maternity unit at Queen Elizabeth Hospital - before she gave birth to our new baby by the roadside of Highway 7!

'Hop in!', is what he directed us to do - without a moment's delay - after hearing of our plight. Indeed, Philomena really had to 'hop' - in order to get into the vehicle - since Mokes do not have doors! I was able to simply swing myself onto the final vacant seat, at the back of the vehicle, and then we were off. As might be expected, it was thereafter not the smoothest of rides for us all - as our 'Martian' jerkily manoeuvred the Moke along the windy coastal road towards Bridgetown. His two hitchhikers were able to get enough sense out of him, and his original passenger, however, to learn that the latter pair were both pilots working for Caribbean Airways who were just coming from a night out in the Oistins area when they had spotted me trying to 'bum a lift'. Philomena and I were also told that, after piloting a flight from London, they always got a few days on the island in order to recover before working again on the return leg, and that the Friday night in question had been occurring during their current time off period. My wife and I were then able to tell them that we ourselves had previously flown with Caribbean Airways - for our honeymoon trip to Barbados - and how extremely grateful we then were to have encountered two of their pilots at that crucial moment in our family's history – even if they had journeyed via Mars in order to be able to find us and perform their rescue!

Within 10 minutes or so of Philomena and myself getting into the Moke, our interesting conversation (coupled with our anxiousness about the way the vehicle was being driven) had come to an end. That was not owing to a dreaded, but much anticipated, crash into another vehicle or some sea wall along Highway 7, but, rather, because our driver had successfully 'piloted' us to the front entrance of the Queen Elizabeth Hospital without incident. He was clearly a very competent motorist - even when 'under the influence' - and it made me wonder whether he ever flirted, or got away, with piloting any of his Caribbean Airways planes in such a condition!

Having said our profuse 'thank yous' to our two 'Martians', Philomena and I were soon inside the hospital itself and had the new challenge of trying to find which ward she was going to be admitted into. The latter turned out to be surprisingly straightforward once we had reached the reception area on the ground floor, and, soon, we were both making our way, on foot, to a lift which took us to an upper level where the maternity unit was situated. Unbelievably, however, another unexpected, and tragic (so far as I was concerned), thing then occurred. That was after the nurse, who met us at the entrance of the unit, had readily received Philomena and told her that she was expected. For, when the hospital employee then requested my wife to follow her to a delivery bed further inside the unit and I then naturally tried to follow along, the former woman (whom I suddenly realised was probably the midwife on duty for the night) told me, in no uncertain terms, to 'Wait there!'.

I was so surprised at the nurse's command to me that I was only able to stutter out a few words in response such as: 'But I am her husband!'. I then caught my senses and was able to add that the family doctor, who was looking after my wife during her pregnancy, had assured her that I could be at her bedside during the birth. Without budging from her stance, the nurse replied along the following lines:

'That's the problem. Here at Queen Elizabeth's, husbands and partners can only accompany their wives and partners at the birth, if the doctor who has looked after them is also present and gives such permission.

Your wife's doctor, Dr McConney, is not here to give his permission!'.

I then replied that Dr McConney promised my wife that he would attend at her birthing and had already assured her that I could be at her side during the event – just as I had been when our first two children, our sons, had been born in England just a few years earlier.

To my absolute horror and disgust, however, the nurse (or midwife, perhaps) was having none of it! She further responded with something like:

'Whatever the practices are like in England, the position is very different here in Barbados. Without your doctor's presence and permission, you cannot come into the delivery room and that is that! More than that, and despite Dr McConney's earlier promises to your wife, given the late hour of the night, I do not think he is going to come to the hospital now!'.

With that, she took Philomena off to a delivery room which was somewhere out of my sight – but not before I managed to steal a kiss from my wife in an attempt to soothe her (and myself, indeed) from our second, totally unexpected, development of the night.

Philomena looked very worried as she left me - as she must have realised, as I had, that our then latest difficulty (regarding our 'best laid plans') was one that even 'Martians' working for Caribbean Airways would not have been able to help us overcome. I felt utterly deflated and helpless. There was absolutely nothing I could do, it seemed to me – save, possibly, try to appeal to someone higher in rank to the nurse in question. Not only, however, was there no other nurse or midwife to be seen in the unit at the time of night in question, it also seemed futile for me to try to change what seemed to be a national (but, to me, backward-looking) Barbadian policy that childbirth was a 'women-only-business' – except, perhaps, in emergency 'life-or-death' circumstances. The other thought which occurred to me, as I tried to think of some way of getting into the delivery room to be with Philomena, was to call Dr McConney at his home to try to get him to immediately come to the hospital in order to attend Philomena's childbirth – as he had promised that he would do. To take that bold step, however, would have required the assistance of the obstructive nurse in question, in order for me to have obtained the necessary residential telephone number of Philomena's physician – and, even if I could have wandered 'behind the scenes' to try to find out where she was, I was already pretty sure she would not have wanted to help me succeed in obtaining the required number.

As I waited and waited, without knowing what was happening to Philomena at any particular moment, I became angrier by the minute. In fact, I started to regret ever coming to a 'backward-looking' country like Barbados. For, it seemed to me, that everything had been so very different with the arrival of Noel and Kim at the Cambridge and Leeds Maternity Hospitals, respectively. In both of those earlier cases, I had been more than welcomed to be with Philomena as she had gone through the travails of childbirth – in Noel's case, during a very lengthy labour endured without the presence of any doctor, in the main.[48] Soon, the time came when my anger, aroused because of my excluded situation, was reaching its peak and starting to get the better of my rational judgment. But, just as I had more or less decided that I was going to go back down to the hospital's main reception and ask for the Barbados telephone directory in order to look up Dr McConney's number and call him, I heard the cry of a baby!

Moments later, the most hateful woman in the world that night, as far as I was concerned, appeared from the direction in which she had last vanished from my sight with Philomena. She was smiling then, as she said:

'Mr Bradshaw, you may now go and see your wife. She has just given birth to a healthy baby girl!'.

With that last word – 'girl' – my anger melted away at once! It was a magical expression, as far as I was concerned. For, suddenly, I realised that the child that Philomena and myself most wanted, in order to complete our family, had just arrived. Being the pessimist that I had become during my exclusionary minutes just past, I replied to the news with:

'Really?! Are you quite sure it is a girl?!'

I could hardly wait to see the two of them and asked the midwife to quickly lead me to the room in which they were located. When I got there very soon after, I saw Philomena first of all. She looked absolutely shell-shocked. Smilingly, I rushed to her side, hugged and kissed her and said: 'Well done, my Love!'. She forced a smile back to me and whispered something along the lines of: 'I have just had a most awful time! I almost delivered our baby all alone! No one was with me as she was being born!'. I hugged her all the more, and tried to reassure her that all was then well as her ordeal was over. I told her that she had safely delivered the daughter that we had both wanted so much and that our little family was then complete. It was only, as I said those words, that I realised that I had not looked for our new baby yet!

I, thus, changed my focus to the little mite in the crib beside Philomena's bed, and there, for the first time, saw our infant daughter. She was well wrapped up in a blanket. What caught my immediate attention, however, was her mass of curly black hair. Accordingly, I was already delighted that she had seemingly inherited at least one prominent feature from her father's side of her family. I was still so ecstatic about her arrival, however, that I would not have cared at that moment, which of her parents she most looked like. In fact, to me, she was already a beautiful little girl – not unlike how I remembered seeing my sister, her 'Aunt Sylvia', just after the latter had been born, similarly, in the wee hours of the night nearly 20 years before. I could see that Philomena was, then, still too overwrought from the awful experience that she had just undergone - in bringing our daughter into the world - that she could not yet fully appreciate just what a momentous thing she had just done for our family. It was left to me, therefore, to check that our new little child girl possessed all her fingers and toes, and to tell my wife that such, indeed, was the case. She responded by surreptitiously telling me, whilst the midwife was temporarily out of the room, that her latest childbirth was the worst that she had experienced of the three to date and that she had found the care given to her 'primitive' compared to that which had she had received in England for the arrival of Noel and then Kim. I myself, however – being the mere 'daddy' in the scenario - was already only thinking positive thoughts, by that stage, about what had 'come to pass' that night. For, owing to Philomena and myself being blessed with our longed-for daughter, I was then even prepared to forgive Dr McConney for not keeping his word to attend on Philomena at the hospital during the birth – as well as the nurse in question for applying the hospital's 'policy', to the letter, and, thereby, keeping me out of my wife's delivery room. To my mind already, I was being properly philosophical in thinking: 'You cannot change the past, but you can influence your future. Now that we have a daughter to go with our two lovely sons, our family's future looks both completed as well as rosy!'.

After, perhaps, an hour or so of my commiserating with Philomena regarding the trauma she had just undergone, and then both of us starting to come to terms with the reality of our brand-new baby daughter, as well as surveying her in detail to double-check that everything was in order with her, reluctantly I took my leave of the two 'girls' in my life. That was because I needed to return home in order to relieve Mrs Payne of her babysitting duties which she had kindly undertaken for my family. I promised Philomena, however, that I would be back just as soon as I was allowed to do so later that day, according to the hospital's rules regarding visiting hours. I also urged her to try to get some rest after the very trying set of experiences she, primarily had been challenged to overcome since the previous evening. And, a short time afterwards, I was 'walking on air' out of the door from the main entrance of the hospital and into the night. It was only then that it really began to hit me that I was, from that day on, the father of *three* children – namely, two lovely boys and, the 'pink icing on the cake' (as it were), a pretty little curly-haired daughter. That meant that from just being a newly-wed couple less than five years before, Philomena and myself were then part of a 'family of five'! 'What a blessing!', I thought to myself. 'What a responsibility too!', was the notion which also crossed my mind immediately after.

It was most likely that added sense of an increased responsibility on my shoulders which gave me the incentive to get my car working again as soon as possible. 'We five' would soon need to be able to get around, together, and the easiest way for us to do that would be in our Skoda. It having been left abandoned on Highway 7, a mile or so from our home, would not help us. I, therefore, needed to get some petrol – or 'gas' as Bajans invariably called that fuel, from its fuller name of 'gasoline' – and then take it to the vehicle in order to get it running again for us. Moreover, it was going to cost me much-needed family funds to walk back to the taxi rank in central Bridgetown and take a taxi home from there, or even just as far as where our Skoda had been left near St Lawrence Gap. It seemed to me, therefore, that the best thing to do was to walk the five miles or so back to the car – during which process I would pass at least two gas stations along Highway 7 at the English-sounding districts of Hastings and Worthing. And, thus, it came to pass that one new 'papa' (of three), that night, found himself happily walking along the coast road - with the sound of the Caribbean Sea, breaking on the beaches he was passing, echoing in his ears as if in applause.

I can no longer recall which of the Highway 7 stations I eventually obtained a can of fuel from – or whether I found it already opened, or had to wait a while for it to become so. By daybreak, however, I had returned to my temporarily deserted vehicle and emptied the can of gas into its fuel tank. After that, it was just a case of getting the car to start - which eventually happened, after several attempts - and then return the empty container to the gas station, before driving home.

Mrs Payne looked relieved when she saw me – perhaps, because my reappearance meant that she no longer had any further babysitting duties and could 'stand down' from her temporary responsibility for my sons. She seemed to acquire even more peace of mind when I told her the news that Philomena had given birth to a sister for the boys and that mother and baby were both doing well. I certainly did not go on to tell her about Philomena's bad experience in the delivery room since, as a retired midwife herself, Mrs Payne would most likely have immediately concluded that 'best practice' had not been observed by the individual attention (or lack of it) which my wife had received that night from the maternity staff at the hospital. Soon after my arrival back home, it was time for me to wake my boys up and tell them the wonderful news that they then had a new baby sister and that we three would be going to see her, and their mum, a little later that day at the hospital. They, too, seemed very pleased to receive the glad tidings - even if, perhaps, it caused them to wonder what it would be like to have an infant girl in the house and how long it would take her to be able to join them in their existing games.

After my own 'adventures' of the night just passed, I needed to catch up on my lost sleep for a couple of hours. Bless her soul, therefore – because Mrs Payne realised that and kindly offered to take the boys downstairs to her place and keep an eye on them, whilst they played in the garden in order to allow me to go to bed for a while. She also volunteered to make some breakfast for them whilst I did so – which I gladly accepted.

A few hours later, however - somewhat refreshed - I found myself driving up to the Oistins gas station, with Noel and Kim, to fill up the Skoda with the fuel which could, and should, have been better inserted some 24 hours or more before. I reasoned to myself, however, that, if I had done so, Philomena and myself would not have had the 'pleasure' of meeting the 'Martians' the previous night – which was an episode we would both remember for the rest of our lives! And then the three males in my very recently enlarged family headed in our car to the Queen Elizabeth Hospital, and, soon after arrival there, into a ward within its maternity unit. There, we found Philomena and several other new mums lying in bed - with their respective new-borns beside them in cradles, or in their arms being fed.

The boys seemed overwhelmed to see their tiny sibling in the flesh. Perhaps, that was because, during her pregnancy, Philomena and myself, were both in the habit of telling them regularly that their new baby brother or sister was 'inside Mummy's tummy'. We had even allowed each of them to feel the baby moving inside their mother's stomach, as it grew ever larger in the course of its prenatal development. During that first introduction, however, it seemed to me that both Noel and Kim were delighted with the end product and by the fact that they no longer had to imagine what he or she would look like any more. 'Now, at last', they both seemed to be thinking, 'I can see my baby sister for myself!'.

Philomena, too, was looking much better than how I had left her the previous night. She had, by then, come to terms with the reality of what she had so very recently accomplished and was clearly pleased with her 'production' – or 'our co-production', more precisely. Moreover, just as she and I had discussed in relation to 'big brother Noel', when Kim was about to be born some 18 months before, she was at pains to make a fuss of our two boys during the visit. Thus, she was able to reassure them that she and I loved them very much indeed and that the new addition to our family was 'their baby'! For, in no way did we want either Noel or Kim to feel any sense of jealousy in relation to the new arrival – particularly during those moments when Philomena would be breastfeeding their infant sister in the course of the first year of her life, just as she had respectively done with each of her boys up to a year or two before.

It was during that first outing to visit their mum and new sister, that we, as a family, seriously began to think about names for the baby. Philomena and I had already decided that just as our firstborn son would have the name of each of his grandfathers, so it would be that our firstborn daughter (if we were ever blessed with one) would bear the names of her grandmothers. Accordingly, just as Noel had been given 'Basil', after Philomena's father, and 'James' after my own, so it would be that our little girl would have, among her names, 'Margaret', after my mum, and 'Maureen' after Philomena's. In the case of Noel, however, we had chosen a completely new first Christian name – one that did not come from any predecessor on either side of his family, as far as we knew. 'Noel' was a French name, which we both happened to like and which, by coincidence, was also an Irish moniker which would, therefore, pay homage to Philomena's (and my own supposed) Irish heritage. What, therefore, would the two of us parents do in the case of our firstborn girl?

We went as far as to ask Noel and Kim for some ideas. Indeed, perhaps it had even been one or the other of them who had first suggested the name, *'Claire'* or *'Clare'*. Certainly, there was a well-known song being often played on the radio at that time which was entitled *'Clair'*, and Noel would surely have heard it - both whilst we had lived in Leeds and even after our family's first arrival in Barbados. If the suggestion of such a name had come from him, it would have been most fitting, since the singer-songwriter of the No.1 song in question was one 'Gilbert O'Sullivan' – a man of Irish birth who had not only grown up in Swindon, Wiltshire but who had also attended Philomena's and my old *alma mater*, St Joseph's School, in that English country town. Just as in the case of naming our first son, however, Philomena and myself wanted a name for our new baby that was not only Irish-sounding but which also possessed a bit of French flair. For myself, I had always liked female Gallic names such as 'Marie-Claire' – but I ruled that out as being, perhaps, a little too popular and well known. Rather, I preferred something more distinctive or even unique – something suitable for our only daughter (for even at that stage I was sure that Philomena and I would never have another 'child' in Barbados after the ordeal she had been through the previous night, let alone another hard-to-get 'daughter'!). And, as I had always liked the French name of 'Louise', with Philomena's and our sons' blessing - or, rather, without too loud a protest from any of them - I proposed the name of 'Claire-Louise' for our new baby. Thus, as the *paterfamilias* or male head of the family, with some kind of unspoken 'casting vote', that was the name she was registered with, as her first 'given' one, at the Registry in the Courts of Justice, Bridgetown by myself a few days later. For 'belt and braces' reasons, and to proclaim her UK nationality at birth in addition, I also took the trouble to do the same thing at the British High Commission in that capital. Her 'middle names' of 'Margaret' and 'Maureen', after her two grandmothers back in Swindon, were also registered at each such place.

*Chapter 16*

# Claire-Louise Comes Home – and some 'Fall-Out' therefrom

By about two days after that first visit to Queen Elizabeth's with Noel and Kim to meet their new sister, and temporarily see their mum again, Philomena and Claire-Louise were both declared well enough to be discharged from the hospital. Another red-letter day in the family's history had just dawned, therefore, as we three 'boys' drove down Highway 7 to Bridgetown in order to pick up the 'girls' and bring them home. Our excitement should have been palpable and, from the moment the five of us got into our Skoda for the drive home, Kim 'took charge' of his little sister by holding her tenderly on his part of the back seat as we drove along – with me piloting the car with exceptional care and unusual slowness.

Mrs Payne seemed equally excited, when our growing Bradshaw family all finally arrived back at Hygeia. Naturally, she wanted to see what Claire-Louise looked like – and, no doubt, as an experienced (but then retired) midwife, silently check whether, in her long-established professional opinion, everything seemed fine with the baby. When she gave Claire-Louise back to us, after first lifting her out of Kim's tight embrace of her, the smile on the ex-midwife's face told us that all was well with the new addition to our family, as far as she was concerned. Perhaps, she had also passed some fleeting comment at the time such as 'your baby is beautiful', or, more likely, 'the baby looks like its father, with its broad nose!'. I, for one, was still so happy - at finally being the dad of our longed-for little girl - that I would not have even minded such a comment from Mrs Payne, had she been cheeky enough to make it!.

Once we had Claire-Louise home, there were some practical things to do relating to her arrival in the world – in addition to the registrations of her birth which had already been seen to. 'Telegrams' – the possibility for sending which still existed in those days – had also already been despatched (an hour or two after the 'agreement' of her name by the family in the hospital, during the first visit of Noel and Kim to see her). That had been done by me, to both of our baby's grandmothers back home in Swindon, England, in order to announce her safe arrival - as well as her long list of names. I can still remember the gist of what the identical text of the telegram to both ladies had stated: 'Beautiful Claire-Louise Margaret Maureen arrived this morning at 2am. Both Mum and baby are doing well'. There was one other thing that I needed to do, however, in order to preserve the 'precedent' which Philomena and I had instituted with Noel's arrival some three to four years before – namely, get some birth announcement cards printed for the purpose of sending out to our family and friends, mainly back in Europe on that particular occasion.

As I, accordingly, researched the matter I quickly found a printer in Bridgetown who could do the job for me. Whereas Noel's birth announcement card had been a blue one, and Kim's white with blue lettering, for Claire-Louise's I chose a pink card with blue lettering. The resulting draft design by the compositor looked fine to Philomena and myself and contained wording along the following lines:

'Noel and Kristian Kim Bradshaw are pleased to announce birth of their baby sister ...CLAIRE-LOUISE... on Friday, 9th January 1981'.

The card would also have contained some reference to the names of our children's mother and father as well as our full address and phone number at Hygeia - in case any addressee wished to write to us, or ring, about Claire-Louise's birth. Fishing for congratulations, however, was not the point of the card. Rather, it was more to announce to the world that our two sons now had their baby sister, too – as a sibling and potential playmate!

Of course, Claire-Louise sort of arrived at what might have been considered an 'inconvenient moment', as far as my teaching year at the UWI Law Faculty was concerned. Not that I had minded in any way – since my priority in life was much more to have a daughter to complete my family than to enjoy uninterrupted 'convenience' in my teaching life. Nevertheless, I reluctantly had to return to teaching at Cave Hill just as Claire-Louise and Philomena came home from hospital – so could not physically have been around very much, during my teaching week, to help my wife with caring for our then three small children.

Philomena, however, had been quite happy for me to leave her each morning as that new Spring Term had got under way at the university. Indeed, no one in the Law Faculty (whether the Dean or otherwise) even suggested that I should take some 'paternity leave' to help my wife during her first few weeks at home with our new baby. The taking of such leave just did not occur to me - and it is very likely that such a common 21st century concept, in England and other economically developed countries of the earth, was still a relatively unknown one in the third world region of the West Indies in the later 20th one. In any case, I quite liked the idea of returning to my Faculty at UWI on the very first new working week after Claire-Louise's birth – since it allowed me the opportunity to give out my pink birth announcement cards to my colleagues to let them all know that I was a 'Dad' again!

Indeed, it had been one of those printed declarations that was to lead to a 'spot of bother' between myself and one such colleague. That had occurred with my 'friend', Margaret DeMerieux, who had somewhat taken me under her wings during the previous academic year when I had experienced so much trauma about the heavy work load I then had from having to lecture two Final Year subjects and work such long hours in order to discharge that burden. Margaret, like Michael Castagne, my other friend

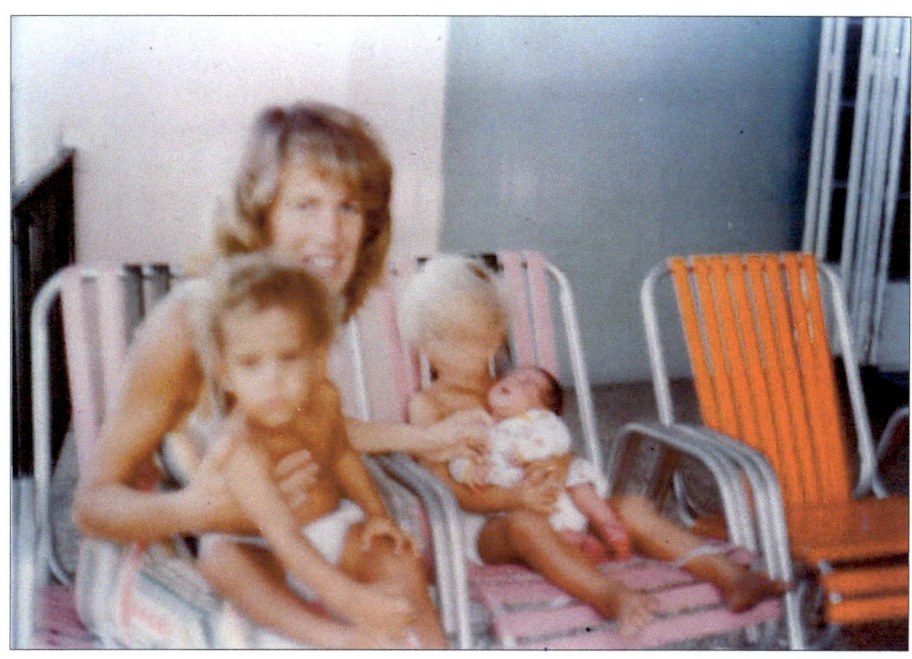

*Fig. 36: Claire-Louise's first day at home in 'Hygeia', Maxwell, Barbados - following her birth a few days before, on 9th January 1981. The photo shows her being held by Noel, and very close to Kim (as well as Philomena), in the effort of the newborn's parents to show the two brothers that their new baby sister very much belonged to them*

*Fig. 37: Philomena and the Author holding Claire-Louise - within a few weeks of her birth in January 1981. The photo is taken at Grantley Adams International Airport, Barbados by 'Mary Bernadette Norman' - one of Philomena's bridesmaids at our 1976 wedding in Swindon - who had just flown in from Jamaica to spend a few days' holiday with our family at our 'Hygeia' home*

and colleague next door to my office at the time, was a native of Trinidad. Whereas Michael had given me spiritual help, however, by introducing me to the weekly Prayer Meeting group he attended and which held fellowship meetings in the Strathclyde area of Bridgetown, Margaret was more of just a social friend. The two of us seemed to have a lot in common, for she had also studied and worked in England – at Manchester University and as a Magistrate's legally-qualified 'clerk' in London – prior to taking up her appointment as Lecturer in Law at Cave Hill. Accordingly, she would often stop by for a chat with me - *en route* to her office further down the stairs from the Secretariat above our respective rooms. Moreover, she regularly amused me with her, often acidic, views about some of our colleagues – including two other female ones, namely, my fellow native country person, Miss Dorcas White, and the local Bajan, Miss Norma Forde. For indeed, Margaret was never one to sit on the fence with her opinions – and though she was, to me, far from being perfect in lots of ways, those views were usually scathingly negative ones.

As a result of our regular chats in my Cave Hill office during my first year at UWI, Margaret eventually started to invite me to stop by her home on my way back to Hygeia. That was an easy thing for me to do, as she lived in Hastings, Christ Church – not very far inland from the Highway 7 coast road which I had to take to get to my home in Maxwell, further along that main road. I would never stay very long during such visits, but it always gave me a chance to see Margaret in 'civvies' and in totally relaxed mode – perhaps practising with her violin, which she told me she had learnt to play in Trinidad prior to emigrating to study at Manchester University. It was also during such visits to her flat in Hastings that Margaret was to tell me more about her family – including about her younger brother, who also happened to be named 'David'. Perhaps, it was that common moniker that had led me to believe that Margaret had developed some kind of 'soft spot' for me and it was also clear to me that, of my female colleagues in the UWI Law Faculty, Margaret was the one whom I most liked. Indeed, I regarded her as not only a colleague but also as a 'friend'.

I was, thus, extremely surprised by Margaret's reaction when I happily handed her one of Claire-Louise's birth announcement cards - on my first teaching day back at the Law Faculty after my daughter's arrival. Certainly, she did not offer me the hearty congratulations that I had expected from such a buddy. Rather, she perused the wording on the card carefully and then said something along the lines of:

'Bradshaw, the name you have chosen for your daughter makes her sound like a member of French or Russian royalty. Delusions of grandeur, Bradshaw?!'.

Not unnaturally, perhaps, I was rather taken aback by such an outburst from my 'friend'. I was immediately prepared to laugh it off, however, as being typical of Margaret to put a negative slant on the best of things. Nevertheless, it was what happened next that left me absolutely gobsmacked. Margaret proceeded to hold the card in both hands and started ripping it into small pieces. I could hardly believe my eyes – and, certainly, it was not an action which I could have predicted from my worst enemy let alone from someone whom I had, until that moment, regarded as an honorary 'big sister'. From being just totally flabbergasted, I then became angry and repaired to my office, from the passage outside it where we had been having our conversation, and shut my door. And, at least for the rest of that day, Margaret and I had no further communication with each other.

All might have been well – eventually – between us, had it not been for what Margaret did next. For, on the day following her tearing up Claire-Louise's card to smithereens outside my office, I got home to Hygeia late in the evening - after preparing for my next classes at Cave Hill - to find Philomena somewhat agitated and keen to tell me about her day. To my horror and surprise, my wife then related to me how she had recently experienced an unannounced visit from none other than Miss DeMerieux herself – who had called by to see the baby! I was shocked by that news. That was not only because Margaret had never visited my house before, but also because of what had happened the previous day with Claire-Louise's card (which had suggested to me that Margaret could not have cared less about the fact that our new daughter had recently come into the world). My feelings of being stunned turned to anger, as I reflected on the fact that she had 'just turned up' when she could easily have telephoned the house first, in order to make an appointment with Philomena - even if she (Margaret) had not wanted to arrange her proposed visit through me at the Law Faculty. So, little by little, my anger turned to feelings of getting really 'mad'. There was no way that I was going to allow the then 'sleeping dog' matter of Margaret's uninvited and unannounced visit to 'simply lie'. Rather, I was going to 'confront' her at the Law Faculty the very next day!

The following morning could not have come soon enough for me. I kept my door open whilst I was in my office between classes, and maintained a vigilant eye on the passage immediately outside in order to see if, and when, Margaret would pass by. Alas, that did not occur until there was already a tutorial going on next door in Mrs Stanford-Johnson's office. Accordingly, some of her tutees were able to witness what then transpired between myself and Margaret in the corridor outside their tutor's door. As soon as I saw her, I flew out of my room and stopped her in her tracks. I am ashamed to report that I did that in both a physical way by restraining her by the arm, as well as by words which came out both loudly and incoherently owing to my anger. I shouted at her, in a volume which the students in Mrs Stanford-Johnson's room must easily have heard, words to the effect:

'Margaret, what the hell do you think you were doing calling round to my house both uninvited and unannounced?!'.

My female colleague was clearly taken aback by the altercation which I had engendered. I cannot now recall the full details of what she answered back to me, but that response did not include any words of apology. Knowing her as I did, her reply would have been something along the lines of defending her right to do whatever she had done – without the need to clear her proposed action with me beforehand. Margaret, like my other female colleagues in the UWI Law Faculty, was a 'women's libber' – by which I mean, someone who stood up for the rights of women and who wished them to have 'equality' with their male counterparts. She would therefore have believed, and more than likely would have told me during our stand-up argument, that my wife had a right to receive visitors whether there was a previous appointment or not, and that she (Margaret) as a woman, and colleague of that wife's husband, had every right to make such a visit. I vehemently disagreed with her and when she pushed me away with a shove, I regret to say that I retaliated by pushing her back in a much more violent manner. It was a case, perhaps, of an immovable object jousting with an irresistible force. Arguably, however, the saddest part of the whole episode was that it was witnessed by the eyes of at least some of Mrs Stanford-Johnson's tutees, and by the ears of perhaps all of them as well as by my fellow tutor herself!

When Margaret walked away and thereby signalled that, as far as she was concerned, the two of us would just have to agree to differ about her 'right' to have made the visit in question, one might have thought that, perhaps, the matter would have been at an end. From my own point of view, I was satisfied that, after seeing my negative reaction to her attempt to, uninvitedly and in an unannounced way, 'socialise' with my wife and our new baby, Margaret would never wish to do so again. Alas for me, however, either Margaret herself complained about what I had done, to the Dean of the Faculty - or she and Mrs Stanford-Johnson made such a complaint, in concert - on the basis that I had disturbed one of the latter's classes with my shouting in the corridor and 'violent behaviour'.

*Fig. 38: Photo of Professor Woodville Marshall, looking a little older than the Author remembers him from their early 1980s days together at the Cave Hill Campus of UWI – but still wearing one of his 'trade mark' flowery-patterned, short-sleeved, shirts and giving the appearance of being 'anything but a learned and venerable university professor'*

Within a short period after the altercation, therefore – perhaps even before the week in question had ended – I had been 'served' with papers which told me that there would be an inquiry by Professor Woodville Marshall. He was the Cambridge educated doyen of the Faculty of History at UWI of whom I previously referred as being a *habitué* of the Senior Common Room at Cave Hill Campus, and dominoes player there – and he was given the task of deciding whether I had committed a disciplinary offence in relation to Margaret!

Thus, within a week or so of my daughter's birth, one of the happiest events in my life had, almost seamlessly, led to one of the direst ones. Surprisingly enough, however, deep within my soul I felt that Margaret was in the wrong and that I would be vindicated in my reaction to what she had done. I can still recall putting part of my defence to Professor Marshall's inquiry, in writing beforehand, in words along the following lines:

'Margaret cannot do what she did, in visiting my wife and new baby at our home whilst the former was still recovering from giving birth – in an unannounced and uninvited way – then shove me for taking her to task about that *faux pas* and thereafter rely on the saying that "A gentleman never hits back".'

When Professor Marshall's inquiry took place, a week or two subsequent to the altercation in question, it was held over at the main Administrative Buildings of the campus – down the hill from the Law Faculty itself. I did not see Margaret either inside the room in which the inquiry took place, or whilst waiting outside. I, thus, assumed that he was 'taking evidence' from each of us (and, perhaps, also Mrs Stanford-Johnson and/or some of her tutees) in a piecemeal way. I can recall, however, that there were other persons in the room, in addition to the professor himself, taking notes of the proceedings. Accordingly, in theory, it was a 'formal' situation and I suppose that only with hindsight did I come to realise what a potentially serious situation I was in – with, perhaps, my post at Cave Hill being 'on the line'.

My naiveté about my situation served me well, however. For, whilst Professor Marshall's verdict was pending, I did not lose sleep at night worrying about which way it would go, and thus had more energy by day for my new daughter, her brothers and their Mum at home - as well as for my teaching duties, whilst at Cave Hill Campus. Obviously, however, during that waiting period, Margaret and I studiously avoided contact with each and did not speak – whether face to face or on the telephone. The whole situation with my former 'friend' made me think of the days of my Sixth Form years at school when Philomena and myself had fallen out over a present which I had given her. In fact, it was a little like history repeating itself – since the 1969-70 'stand-off' with my future wife had occurred because I had thought that I had been doing a 'good deed' in giving Philomena a present from my holidays in London.[49] Similarly, with Margaret, I had thought that I had been doing something laudable in giving her the card announcing Claire-Louise's birth. I had only reacted badly when she had torn up the card, in front of my face, and then, almost immediately afterwards, made a visit to the baby in question, and its mother, without asking my (or the mother's) leave to do so in advance. Because of the historical precedent with Philomena, who later forgave me for my 'silent treatment' of her so completely as to wish to marry me, I had every hope that Margaret, too, would become my friend again (short of wanting to marry me, of course) – even if I could not see, then, how that would ever be possible as a result of the formal inquiry against me that, I presumed, she had played a part in engendering.

My 'confidence' in a positive outcome for me, from Professor Marshall's inquiry, was thus greater than that in Margaret and myself ever becoming friends again. When the letter arrived for me, from the powers that be in UWI, though nervous prior to opening it, I was relieved but not altogether surprised by its contents. It stated that Professor Marshall had found and decided that, in view of the whole history leading up to the altercation in the corridor outside Mrs Stanford-Johnson's office and my own, I had not committed a disciplinary offence either in the confronting Ms DeMerieux *per se*, or in the manner in which I had done so. Thus, there was to be no finding of an offence committed by me – nor even a formal, or informal, warning to watch my conduct for the future. I, thus, had a 'clean slate' on my employment record at UWI!

With hindsight, perhaps, such an 'official absolution' was a bad thing for my future career at Cave Hill. For, in a way, it could well have sowed the seed that, maybe, I could even 'get away with murder' in due course – meaning, do things which strictly were not advisable or of which I (or my family) would not be proud, in the expectation (or at least hope) that I would be able to 'survive' such actions or activities.

After Professor Marshall's inquiry was over, and the possible 'close shave' concerning my UWI career was behind me, it was back to my work-a-day life teaching in the Law Faculty as well as helping Philomena to 'bring up baby' at home. And, certainly, there were also some positively high points in my family's life at that time which were to break up the mundaneness of our everyday existence. Not least of those were the preparations which we were making for the Christening of our new daughter. Naturally, a major discussion had to take place between my wife and myself regarding whom we should choose as godparents. For me, there could only be one person who was 'worthy' enough, among our friends, for the role of godfather. That was my former office neighbour, and confidant, at Cave Hill, Mr Michael Castagne. For, I could not think of a more spiritual and 'good' person than him – outside members of the priesthood, such as Philomena's uncle, 'Father Paddy', back in England - whom I had encountered during my life. To me, therefore, Michael would have been the ideal Caribbean person to help bring our little girl up in the Christian (and, indeed, Catholic) way of living her life – and somehow, for me, that mattered even more for my daughter than it had done for my two sons.

There was, however, one major problem in Philomena and myself choosing Michael to be Claire-Louise's godfather – namely, a logistical one of geography. For Michael, as we have seen, was then living in Trinidad – one hour's plane ride south of Barbados. That potential spatial roadblock, however, was ameliorated by the facts that Michael's parents – including his father, 'Pat Castagne', who was famous in the Caribbean for having composed the national anthem of Trinidad and Tobago – were then living in retirement in Barbados and Michael often came over from Trinidad to visit them. All my wife and I had to do, therefore, was to liaise closely with Michael in order to see when he had next planned to make such a 'duty visit' to Barbados to see his dad and mum and then book Claire-Louise's Baptism, with Father Daniel Gennerelli in nearby St Dominic's RC Church for one forthcoming Sunday chosen to coincide with such visit. That is exactly what we did, therefore – after being fortunate enough to discover, from our parish priest, that no one else had made a booking for another Baptism on our wished-for Sunday. Father Dan even agreed to carry out the Baptism during our usual 11am Mass – rather than have a separate ceremony outside our normal service times, which privilege suited my family very well indeed.

But what of a Godmother for Claire-Louise? Whom could Philomena and myself choose? It seemed to me that it had to be someone as spiritual, and as good, a person as Michael was – that is to say, his female equivalent. Again, there was little argument between my wife and myself about whom the ideal candidate should be. In that instance, however, it would be someone inside our Catholic religious establishment – namely, a feminine equivalent of someone like Philomena's uncle (and priest), Father Paddy. Accordingly, Philomena and I chose a person whom we had known for several months, if not somewhat longer, as the leader of the weekly prayer sessions which both of us had begun attending. Those took place on a weekday evening, at a school known as the 'Ursuline Convent' in Bridgetown - once Philomena's pregnancy with Claire-Louise had been confirmed. Our ideal female candidate was actually a teacher of senior girls at that school, who was an American of French descent and who spoke her English with a slight Gallic accent. As suggested by the name of her educational institution, she was a nun in Holy Orders – as were many, if not most, of the teachers on the staff there. Her name was 'Sister Michelle'.

In our choice for Claire-Louise's godmother, Philomena and I could not have picked a more lovely person. She was still a relatively young woman – perhaps only in her early 30s by then – with the most attractive, but modest, personality. She was also deeply spiritual, it seemed to both my wife and myself, and was, thus, definitely an equivalent of Michael as far as we were concerned. Moreover, being female, it seemed to my wife and myself that she would make an excellent role model for our daughter in the latter's future life. Much to our delight, therefore – since my wife and I did not even know whether nuns were allowed, by our Church, to act as godparents for babies – Sister Michelle accepted our invitation to be such a spiritual sponsor for Claire-Louise immediately upon our asking her.

Accordingly, everything was able to be put in place pretty quickly - once we knew, from Michael, the date of when he would next be over from Trinidad to visit his parents during a weekend in late January or early February 1981. For, by that period, we had a lovely new baby, wonderfully spiritual godparents in Michael and Michelle, a handsome and young American priest to conduct the proceedings, and, last but not least, a doting mother and father. All was, thus, set fair for a wonderful celebration. Everything, that is, except for a few major outstanding issues – namely, which guests to invite to the Christening and, then, which place to take them to after the important proceedings at St Dominic's were over and what to provide for them there.

Of all the headaches encountered in arranging Claire-Louise's Baptism, determining the guest lists and the catering arrangements constituted the biggest ones for me (and, perhaps, for Philomena also). In contrast, it struck me as being ironic that the central event of the day – the Christening of Claire-Louise itself - was the simplest part to organise. I wondered, however, as to whether 'it was ever thus' as I recalled just how much sleep I had lost on the night before my wedding day some five years before in England worrying about whether the disco man would turn up to the post-nuptial evening celebrations at the 'Blunsdon House Hotel', Wiltshire – and even up to several hours after the wedding itself had already been smoothly carried out by Philomena's uncle, Father Paddy.[50] As far as potential guests were concerned, I remember considering inviting some of my colleagues from the Law Faculty at Cave Hill. One of those, however, would have been a *persona non grata*, to me, at that time owing to the recent Professor Marshall inquiry – namely, Margaret DeMerieux. On the other hand, I did ask along our colleague, Andrew Burgess – a Bajan who taught the Law of Trusts, among other subjects, and who, I happened to know, also lived in Christ Church parish. To my disappointment however, Andrew declined my invitation. His so doing, thereby, confirmed the impression that I was starting to develop, after living in Barbados for over a year, namely, that many Bajans tended to be very 'inward looking'. It seemed to me that the majority were not inclined to invite 'foreigners' to their family gatherings - and, the corollary: that they were also not keen to accept invitations from foreigners to come to the latter's family gatherings either.

At any rate, if no one else from the Law Faculty apart from Michael eventually came – and even he was from UWI's 'foreign' St Augustine Campus, Trinidad – Philomena and I certainly ended up with enough guests to fill the main living room of our Hygeia home. That was the room in which, as stated earlier, one could easily play a good game of badminton, since it had a very high ceiling as well as a full-size court space for that racquet sport to take place on. At last, therefore, Philomena and I had found a better, more tasteful, use for the huge chamber - beside mainly watching television in the evenings there. And, among the guests who eventually came to fill it up that Baptism day were included Mrs Payne from downstairs, the godparents, Father Dan, and several other parishioners whom my wife and I had got to know over the 16 months or so that my family and I had been parishioners at St Dominic's.

And what of the catering? Thanks to suggestions, and then practical help, of some of the invited ladies from our parish church, Philomena was able to do most of that herself from our home. Perhaps, however, we had been obliged to borrow some extra crockery and cutlery from some of those ladies – and even depend on a number of them for extra dishes of food to be brought from their own homes to ours to be shared out on the day. Somehow, nonetheless, everything fell into place for the 'house party' following the

Baptism of our daughter itself at nearby St Dominic's. As far as that earlier main event of the day was concerned, Claire-Louise did not cry, as far as I can remember, when Father Dan poured water on her head as the sign that she – at only about the age of about one month – had been 're-born' as a newly-hatched 'follower of Christ' for the remainder of her life. In other words, that she, like the other four members of her immediate family, had then become a 'Christian' too.

*Chapter 17*

# Claire-Louise's First Trip outside Barbados – February 1981

As if Claire-Louise's Baptism had not been excitement enough in my family's life at that time, however, there was yet one more event (which occurred just a week or two later) which I, if not everyone else in the family - apart from Claire-Louise herself, ironically – would recall for the rest of our lives. That unforgettable happening was Claire-Louise's very first flight overseas at the age of just six weeks old! The episode is memorable firstly because our baby daughter – just like her younger brother, Kim, at about the same very young age (but from London's Heathrow Airport, in his case) – was about to take to the international skies for the very first time. It was also unforgettable owing to where, and for what purpose, Claire-Louise and the other members of her family were leaving Barbados' Grantley Adams International Airport on the occasion in question.

The answers were none other than: Trinidad; and the second best-known 'Carnival' in the world (after the undoubted leading one of Rio de Janiero's in Brazil which was about to take place at the same time). I personally was so excited to be returning to Trinidad again, having only visited it for the very first time a mere two months previously (just before John Lennon had been shot dead in New York City) – with my entire family during that February 1981 time, and not just my first son, Noel, as in December 1980 – that I had hardly been able to sleep in the days leading up to the trip. Moreover, that later occasion would be no 'whistle–stop' UWI-business sojourn of a day or two, on my way to arrange a Comparative Law trip for some of my students at Cave Hill. Rather, it would be a proper one-week holiday stay - during which my family and myself would be able to relax, somewhat, and actually see something of Trinidad itself outside the confines of the capital city of Port of Spain (where, admittedly, most of the Carnival activities which we were off to see would be centred).

But how had that Bradshaw Family trip to Carnival in Trinidad been arranged? It might well have been through connections with the new godfather of our baby daughter, Michael Castagne. Whatever his role may have been, however, in assisting with the initiative in question, it had certainly been primarily arranged through the 'Marriage Encounter' movement within the Catholic Church in Barbados (of which Philomena and myself had become new members during her pregnancy with our daughter) and especially via its leader there, one 'Father Pat'. At any rate, a Catholic couple (and their small number of young children) who lived in small town of 'San Juan', situated somewhere between the St Augustine Campus of UWI in Trinidad and that that island's capital city, disliked the annual 'fuss' which, they thought, the island in general had to 'endure' every year at Carnival time. The pair, therefore, 'wanted out' for themselves and their children during the annual 'confusion', as they saw things. That particular wish coming from Trinidad, therefore, suited very well indeed another Catholic couple located in another Caribbean island (with their own small number of children – one of whom was very diminutive indeed!) who wanted 'in', as far as their experiencing a Trinidadian Carnival was concerned.

That other couple and their kids were, of course, the Bradshaws of Barbados! And so, it came to pass that letters were exchanged, through the good offices of Father Pat and the Marriage Encounter movement in Barbados. As a result, an 'exchange of homes' was arranged and agreed, for one week only, between the two families in question. Moreover, someone suggested that both couples could also throw their respective family car into the deal, in addition – so that the visitors to each respective island would have a means of exploring the island of their temporary home in a touristic kind of way. After all, Philomena and myself did not wish to 'see' and experience Carnival for ourselves, and our children, on a non-stop basis in Port of Spain for the whole of the week that we would be in Trinidad. Rather, we also wished our family to get to know something of that island outside the capital city itself. And the same applied to our counterparts from Trinidad. For, even if the parents in that family had visited Barbados before, nevertheless they surely would have wanted to explore it again, if merely for the benefit of showing their children not only Maxwell or Oistins beaches, but also the charms of Bridgetown, Bathsheba and other places further afield from Christ Church parish.

Alas, the name of the Trinidad family in question has long since disappeared from my head. But I seem to recall that they had something of a French surname – such as 'De Voeux' – so let us use that name for these purposes. In any case, De Voeux is, perhaps, a most suitable candidate for the surname in question since the father of the family was a White Trinidadian – presumably, from a French immigrant family stock. He was a business man and was to tell me that he often travelled to Europe for his work, including Continental countries such as Switzerland. His wife, too, was White – we were to discover when the couple picked my family up on our arrival at Piarco Airport, Trinidad. That happened on the weekend before the week leading up to the climax of the country's Carnival the following Monday and Tuesday. The plan was that the De Voeux family would install us Bradshaws into their home on our first night there, show us how everything inside it functioned, as well as their car, and then depart for our home in Hygeia, Barbados the following day.

Everything in that proposed arrangement ran smoothly, including us Bradshaws catching a British Airways Jumbo from Barbados to Trinidad. That flight, however, included several of my students from Cave Hill Campus (who had all been given a 'reading week off', since most of the lecturers in the Law Faculty realised that many of the students there would also be heading for Carnival during the week in question). That would have been so whether they were from Trinidad themselves, or from any of the other English-speaking Caribbean islands who sent their would-be lawyers to the Barbados Faculty.

Thus, after one night's sharing the De Voeux's home in San Juan, our host family departed for Barbados and we were left to discover the joys of Carnival, and Trinidad generally, for ourselves. One of the first things that I personally very much wanted to do was touch base with an old acquaintance from my Cambridge University student days. That person was none other than the son of the then-serving President - indeed, the very FIRST AND ONLY President, to date - of Trinidad and Tobago, whose name was 'Dr Ellis Clarke'. His offspring was named 'Peter' and I had encountered him several times at Cambridge, since he had come there to study Law also – perhaps, as a postgraduate after graduating from a North American university, in some non-Law discipline. I had not succeeded in getting to know Peter really well whilst we were both at Cambridge, even though Philomena and myself had, at least once, invited him to dinner at our flat on the 'Wychfield' site of my College, 'Trinity Hall'. Peter himself was then at 'Downing College', if memory serves me correctly, and if he had ever returned the invitation it would have been to lunch or dinner in the hall of Downing, rather than a meal in his private rooms elsewhere inside his Cambridge base.

At any rate, Peter and I had been fellow-Caribbean persons and acquaintances, rather than close friends, studying the same subject at the same prestigious Oxbridge university. Nevertheless, I had not been at all confident that he would even remember me when I looked him up in the Trinidad telephone directory, found his number and called him. To my relief, he did, indeed, recall both myself and Philomena and immediately said 'Yes' to my suggestion that the three of us, and our three small Bradshaw children, all meet up during the next day or two before the Carnival really began in earnest on the coming Monday and Tuesday. Moreover, it was even at his suggestion that the venue was set to be at a drinks bar in the very same San Juan neighbourhood in which the De Voeux family's house was situated. In addition, he chose the time of such rendezvous to be sometime in the evening of the very day of my call. Peter was clearly keen to see me - and, more than likely, as curious to see how I had turned out after Cambridge, as I was to discover how he had fared in life with the help of his 'Cantab' Law degree (to say nothing about the cachet he must have had as being the son of the then-current, and first, President of Trinidad and Tobago).

My family and I turned up early at Peter's designated venue in San Juan, given that we did not know the place or how long it would take us to find it. Minutes later, Peter arrived in a sports car - with the roof down and relatively loud music emanating from its innards. A young man – wearing dark sunglasses (though the sun was already down!) emerged from the car with a broad smile and hand extended out to me.

'David, how are you doing?'.

My initial thought of a true reply to the manifestation which had just appeared in front of me, with all the trappings, was:

'Clearly, not as well as you, "Mr Playboy of Trinidad"!'. Instead, however, I kept my counsel, and merely replied by uttering something along the lines of:

'Fine, Peter! Thank you for agreeing to meet me and my family at such short notice. It's great to see you again after so long!'.

Despite his outward trappings of living the fast life, however, Peter turned out to be much as I remembered him from our Cambridge days – namely, a guy with a good heart. I believe that, like Philomena and myself, he was a practising Roman Catholic too, so that a Christian way of life, if nothing else, would have kept him 'grounded'. Certainly, he was most interested not only in meeting Philomena again, but also in asking how we were both finding married life together and bringing up three young offspring. Moreover, he took a great deal of interest in the children themselves – including our babe in arms, Claire-Louise. We were also able to discuss our very different career paths since leaving Cambridge and I got the opportunity to tell him about my life as a Law lecturer at UWI and how much I then preferred teaching the Law rather than the idea of practising it, even though I had qualified as a Barrister after graduating from Cambridge. He himself told me that he had no ambitions for a career in academic life. That, rather, he was much more interested in making money and that whilst he had also qualified for the Bar in England after Cambridge, and indeed was then practising as an Attorney-at-Law in Trinidad, he was seriously thinking about leaving his Law practice in order to become a stockbroker! Looking at his fast 'Porsche' car – or whatever model it was – I was not at all surprised that he wanted to speed his career off in that particular direction.

After about an hour of drinking and chatting with Peter about our very different lives and careers in the legal field, our time together came to an end. Alas, my secret wish of contacting him and, thereby, getting an invitation to also meet his father at the 'President's Palace' – or whatever the name for Trinidad's Head of State official residence was named – did not come to pass. Indeed, Peter did not suggest that we might meet again - whether the venue be in Trinidad again during my family's then-current visit, or maybe in Barbados after we returned to our home there after Carnival. And it is sad to relate that, after that one meeting in San Juan just before the climax of Carnival 1981, Peter and I were never to meet again. I did learn, however, that he subsequently went on to marry a former beauty queen from his island, who had even perhaps been a 'Miss Universe' winner or finalist. Such information did not surprise me one little bit - after what I had seen of my 'Life in the fast lane' acquaintance at our February 1981 San Juan meeting!

With the meet-up with Peter Clarke behind us, my family and I could concentrate more fully on what we had primarily come to Trinidad for. That was, in the local parlance of our host island, to 'Play Mas'. Accordingly, with the De Voeux family home in San Juan as our temporary base near the island's capital, it was then full speed ahead to do just that!

When we had first arrived in Trinidad on the Friday evening before the grand finale of the Carnival on the following Monday and Tuesday, my family and I really did not know what to expect. All that I had been told beforehand was that those climatic two days to come were a 'big deal'! Something that was to be participated in, or (failing that) witnessed at close range, at least once before you 'slipped off your mortal coil'. It was, thus, the Caribbean equivalent of the 'See Naples and die' - a saying which I had known in Europe during my student days. Moreover, even whilst living in Barbados for the past two academic years, I had heard it said that the Trinidad Carnival was the best in the world – apart from one other which almost every adult alive knew about, namely that in Rio de Janiero, Brazil. It was the Caribbean event that thousands in the region seemed to flock to Trinidad for – and which even justified the 'unofficial' shutting down of the Faculty of Law back at Cave Hill, Barbados for at least the two days in question, if not the entire week in which they fell.

Despite my knowing all of the foregoing, however, about the reputation and spectacle of the Trinidad Carnival, I still did not know what to expect when my family and myself actually arrived on the island. I, therefore, sought to rely on the guidance of the De Voeux family, who had seen the island's Carnival play out before them many times before. So much so, indeed, that they were, by that 1981 year, heartily tired of the spectacle and wanted to escape to my family's more sedate adopted island home of Barbados. On the night of our arrival at their home in San Juan, our hosts – thankfully – were extremely keen to offer us guidance and advice about what to see and do. One of the things that they emphasised was that the coming Monday and Tuesday were, indeed, the ones to prioritise as far as our Carnival events planning was concerned. That was because the day after the latter was 'Ash Wednesday'. That was when Lent, and the season of fasting, began according to the Catholic religion, which was the dominant one in Trinidad and Tobago. Accordingly, the two days of revelry in question were the 'last chance' for the populace and visitors to 'party' before the strictures of the Lenten season began in earnest.

In relation to the said 'Carnival Monday and Tuesday', Mr and Mrs De Voeux mentioned a French word which I had not heard of until our arrival at their home – namely *'J'ouvert'*, which I understood to be the Trinidadian contraction of the French words *'Jour ouvert'* (meaning 'day open' or simply, 'daybreak'). Mr De Voeux told us that both days had such a start – or 'opening' to the events of the day – but that such commencement began as early as perhaps 5 or 6 am each morning, and in Port of Spain itself! He therefore advised us to take his family's car to drive into the capital city, some 10 miles or so away, on each of the two special days. To avoid any excessive traffic jams, however, he suggested that we park some distance away from the Queen's Park Savannah – where most of the events, including the 'bands', parading past the grandstands there, would be taking place. If we, thus, parked on the San Juan side of the capital, he recommended that we simply walk the mile or so from our parking place to the Savannah. He stressed, however, that we would have to get up really early to be able to leave his home by about 5am - in order to get to the Savannah in good time to get a seat in one of the grandstands before 'the show' really began in earnest.

Mr De Voeux also advised that most people coming to Carnival in Trinidad wanted to 'Play Mas". He explained that the expression meant, first of all, being part of a huge band of people - all dressed in the same, or similar, way for the theme of their particular band that year. Alternatively, it also had the meaning of dancing in the street behind such a band - as it progressed through the streets of Port of Spain and eventually arrived, as one of many others, before the grandstands in the Queen's Park Savannah. He then went on to strongly advise Philomena and myself that, given that we would have a baby in arms as part of our family group when attending the festivities in the capital on the Monday and Tuesday to come, we should not even think about following a band as typical Carnival tourist-revellers from outside Trinidad would normally do. Rather, he suggested that we should simply take our pram for our baby to be able to sleep in throughout the days in question – if and whenever she wanted to do so – and make ourselves as comfortable as possible in one of the grandstands, with plenty of food and drink brought along with us for each day.

The De Voeux family also mentioned another aspect of the Trinidadian Carnival experience - which would have interested me if I had been on the island without the rest of my family. That was the singing competition, between the various 'calypsonians', for which their island was world famous – with, perhaps, the 'Mighty Sparrow' being the very best known of all. During the celebration time in question, our hosts had added, there would be lots of competitions at so-called 'Calypso Tents' located in many different places around the island itself, and not just the capital city. The purpose of those contests was to decide who would go forward to the final sing-off to determine who would be that year's 'Calypso King' and, also 'Queen'. However, I was not alone in Trinidad and, as I understood that such competitions took place quite late at night, I reluctantly ruled out trying to attend any such contest during that particular Carnival visit - either for myself alone, or with the rest of my family.

Accordingly, instead of trying to get immersed into Carnival as soon as the De Voeux family had departed for Barbados the following day, Philomena and I decided to 'take things easy' for that day, and the Sunday following, and simply play ourselves into Trinidadian life gently. There was to be no rushing up to Port of Spain with our children, therefore - in order to see what activities relating to the festivities were going on there during those earliest days of ours in our new island. Instead, we decided to get to know our local area a little bit – especially the shops, where we would need to buy the provisions to sustain us during our week-long stay ahead. Prudently, also, I had tried out the De Voeux family's car in order to make sure that I was confident, and proficient, at driving it on the Trinidadian roads. In that quest, therefore, my family and I ventured in the vehicle as far as UWI's St Augustine Campus during those first days. We also drove to Michael Castagne's home near the Campus. Perhaps, it had been during that particular visit that Michael had introduced my family and myself to 'Andrea' - the beautiful young woman of, evidently, East Indian ethnicity who would soon become his devoted wife and mother of their several children. Our family would certainly also have gone to the De Voeux's local Catholic parish church on the Sunday morning. No doubt, our hosts – prior to departing for Barbados - would have told us the name of their parish priest and who else, in their local congregation, we should look for at the Mass in order to introduce ourselves to them.

Before I realised it, however, that particular Sunday had turned into the wee hours of 'Carnival Monday' and, thus, *'J'ouvert* time' in the twin-island republic. Our family had, however, prepared for the latter by all of us going to bed early on the Sunday evening. According to the plan of Philomena and myself, that was to ensure that each member would not find it too difficult to wake up very early the following morning - and also be refreshed enough to have sufficient energy to see us though what would surely be one of the longest days, ever, for us all. Naturally, such precautions did not apply so much to our babe-in-arms, Claire-Louise. That was because we would be taking her carrycot along with us in the car and then on to the Queen's Park Savannah in Port of Spain. By so doing, she would then be able to have long sleeps or just short 'cat naps', throughout our Carnival Monday - just as she felt like.

I had raised myself as early as 4am on that special Monday, to wash and shave. Soon after, I had woken Philomena with a cup of tea - to get her going too, and for her to then help me rouse and prepare our children for our family's 'big day out'. Given the 'regimentation' which I would have started for the whole process, we would all have been washed, dressed and breakfasted by 5am and would have set off for Port of Spain in the De Voeux's car very soon afterwards.

No doubt, I would have been very surprised at how many other cars, full of other would-be revellers, we encountered on the dual carriage highway from San Juan to the capital city that morning. Just as much so by the noise that some of them were making - even at that early hour when, presumably, some people in the neighbourhoods we were passing would have been trying to complete their sleep before having to work, as normal, that first business day of the new week. Nevertheless, I would already have started to get a flavour of *'J'ouvert'*, even before we had arrived in Port of Spain and I would have seen that some of the revellers – evident in their cars accompanying us on the highway, as well as from the many hundreds of pedestrians making their way on foot to the capital as we passed them – were covered in oil, mud or, perhaps, just coloured paint. (I was to learn, later, that such body ornamentation had historical roots at Carnival time in Trinidad. Indeed, that they related to riots occurring in earlier times of slavery, by being the means by which the rioters hid, or disguised their identities, in order to prevent themselves from getting into trouble with the Law, subsequently, for being participants in illegal demonstrations and, perhaps, even worse activities).

Soon, however, the car containing our family had arrived in the capital itself – on the 'wrong side' of the city, as far as Queen's Park Savannah was concerned. I nevertheless followed Mr De Voeux's advice and left his family's vehicle on that eastern suburb and our family then made our way to the Savannah on foot (apart from Claire-Louise, whom Philomena and I took turns to push in her carrycot along the crowded streets of Port of Spain). Those thoroughfares were becoming more and more congested as the day was breaking and the sun was ever rising in the sky. Either my wife or myself (when not pushing our daughter along) had to hold Kim's hands to help him walk along with us (he himself being only about 18 or 19 months old at the time). Less than an hour later we had reached our 'Mecca'. That was the fine, green, open space the name of which included the word 'Savannah' as part of its title – just like its smaller counterpart back in Barbados, popularly known as just 'The Garrison'. Like the Garrison Savannah, which was still used as a place of horse racing in Barbados, perhaps the Queen's Park counterpart in Trinidad had also originally been used just for 'the sport of kings'. At that February 1981 time, however, the latter's normal grassy, campus-like, space was full of grandstands, marquees where food could be bought and sold, and temporary toilet cubicles, among other things. What would, therefore, normally have been a huge, empty, green expanse looked more like what I would have imagined an 'Eastern bazaar' in a country like Morocco to have been like, when my family first encountered Queen's Park Savannah that Carnival Monday. Moreover, in addition to the temporary 'structures' that were dotted all about the former open space of the venue, there were hundreds more 'temporary bodies' moving about on the soil of the place. These were mainly the revellers - or would-be ones like my family and myself who had come to 'Play Mas' (or simply 'Watch Mas'). After we had paid for, and found, our seats in one of the many grandstands which faced away from the sun at its hottest times of the day, there would be hundreds more such revellers adding themselves to the throng than when we had first arrived. And that was not even counting those passing members of the bands that would file by, in procession before us, during our time in the grandstand.

And, slowly but surely, the tempo of our day began to change. Perhaps, for me, there had even been a disappointing 'lull' after we had first arrived at the Savannah and found our seats - as nothing much had appeared to be happening in front of us to witness at that time. I had, thus, wondered whether most of the would-be revellers, having risen extremely early for *J'ouvert* - had then returned home to catch up on their sleep with a view to getting up later to start the 'partying' again when the sun was properly up. I also asked myself whether my family had just arrived somewhat too late and whether we had missed *J'ouvert* altogether by arriving in our seats by 6am that morning! The latter conclusion seemed too unrealistic to be true but the lack of activity passing before us made the thought a plausible one.

By the time that Philomena and I had given Noel and Kim a snack and a drink for their 'second breakfast', however, things started to 'hot up' – as they might have said in the local vernacular – just as was the sun was rising above our grandstand. By, say, 9 or 10am the sound of steel band music approaching the 'road' in front of us could be heard - getting ever louder, and excitingly hypnotic to me, as it got nearer. And associated with this 'pan' music, as my family and I could see, was the first of the bands approaching. These were led by large, open-topped, trucks - where persons in similar-themed costumes (skimpy ones often, in the case of the ladies participating) could be seen gyrating about and generally having fun, whilst 'putting on a show' for anyone who cared to look their way. And behind each moving vehicle, containing its gyrators and steel band players and their companions, would be even more persons, on foot, who 'belonged' to the band in front of them. Such pedestrians wore costumes (such as they were, in the case of many of the ladies) which were identical, or similar in theme, to those lucky enough to be riding on the vehicle in front of them – so that one could easily discern that they were all part of the same troupe.

One thing became clear to me quite quickly: once the line of moving vehicles, with their gyrators and pan-musicians, began passing where we were seated, there would be little or no gap between one passing band and another. Indeed, one could see just a slow procession of bands - one behind the other. All in all, with the colour of the costumes, the gyrations of those wearing them and the loud volume of the accompanying music as each band passed along – slowly - the experience was mind-blowing for the senses. That was so even if the noise may have prevented our baby daughter, when she was napping, from ever remaining asleep for very long that day.

*Fig. 39: Noel, Kim and Philomena in a grandstand at the Trinidad Carnival in Port of Spain during February 1981, watching one of the many 'bands' parading in front of them. Claire-Louise is also there – probably fast asleep in her carrycot (in the bottom left of the photo), notwithstanding the riot of music and movement surrounding her*

And because the spectacle of Carnival Monday, and its aftermath the following day which Philomena and I were anticipating, were international events, peoples from other countries, far and near, flocked to it. Accordingly, it was somewhat like the Carnival in Rio de Janeiro, Brazil. The setting, therefore, gave the two of us parents a chance to play 'spot the famous person' among the throng of any particular passing band. And it was during that game that either Philomena or myself was able to first identify 'Sir Norman Parkinson' - in a leopard-skin outfit cladding his extremely tall body, and sporting his unmistakeable 'Salvador-Dali'-like upturned moustache. At the time, he was the well-known dressmaker to 'Queen Elizabeth II' in England! (I only learnt, later, that he owned a house in the neighbouring island of Tobago, and lived there for part of the year when not fashion-designing for the English Queen and other 'high society' patrons). It was definitely Philomena, however, who spotted a joyous 'Mick Jagger' engaged in 'strutting his stuff' dancing performance behind a band that, for once, was not his own 'Rolling Stones'. I had last seen him with that group - with himself as the lead singer thereof - some 12 years before, at the famous 'Stones in Hyde Park' concert in 1969, which experience I wrote about in *Swimming without mangoes*.[51]

To be totally honest, I can no longer recall what were the qualitative differences between my family's experience of Carnival Monday and those which we also witnessed, in more or less the same grandstand in Queen's Park Savannah, the following day. The five of us certainly went back on the Tuesday for more of what we had witnessed on that very long day some 24 hours or so before. Perhaps we had just been presented with 'more of the same' – but, if that was the case, I cannot recall that I ever felt that Carnival Tuesday was just '*déjà vu*, all over again!'. On the contrary, when the final band passed my family by on that last day of Carnival 1981 – in the late afternoon, or evening - and we had to return to the De Voeux family home in San Juan in their car, I still felt ready for more. And yet, that for me was the magic of what I had experienced. There would be no 'more' the next day – for that would be Ash Wednesday, a time for us Catholics to go to Church and get our ashes to remind us that: 'All mortal things (including gyrating in the Streets of Port of Spain and around the Queen's Park Savannah) will pass!' And that from dust we were formed, and to dust we shall all return one day'. In other words, that after the craziness and excesses of Carnival, the season of serious things – including 'fasting' – was upon us. That, indeed, Lent had begun!

For my family, however, if Carnival was over we, nevertheless, still had some days left of our Trinidadian holiday and, so, did not need to be totally 'serious'. After all, we still had the De Voeux family car and, as they would not be back for another three days or so, we had the opportunity to explore the island in it – far away from the (former) Carnival fleshpot of Port of Spain. On that initiative, my family would certainly embark – immediately after attending Mass and having ashes placed on our respective foreheads (in the Sign of the Cross) by the De Voeux family's parish priest during the service at their Catholic church.

Accordingly, on that Ash Wednesday, we all set off in our hosts' car 'down south' -

after breakfast and following the Mass with the distribution of ashes. Our first target was San Fernando – Trinidad's second city. I, for one, was most curious to see how unlike it was in scale to the capital city and how alike it might have been to Barbados' second-biggest populated municipality of Holetown, in relation to its own capital of Bridgetown. I was not to be disappointed, for San Fernando turned out to be a much easier place for my family and myself to walk around and 'get the measure of' than any such attempt in Port of Spain would ever have been. *En route* to that second city, I was rather surprised at how relatively undeveloped the countryside between the island's two biggest conurbations appeared to be - but, nevertheless, delighted to see what looked like water buffalo, in some of the fields which we passed, working together with people on land which seemed to be cultivated with rice! Such phenomena were quite unexpected, for me at least, as being so out of place in my mind for a 'Caribbean scene'. Rather, although I had never been to Asia, it is how I would have imagined the paddy fields of India or places like Burma or Thailand to be at that time. Then I remembered that Trinidad was populated with about 50% or so of persons whose ethnic origins were, indeed, from Asia – namely, the sub-continent of India itself. Thus, I told myself, I should have anticipated – even before embarking on that journey to southern Trinidad - that the original immigrants from that part of the world may well have brought some of their land cultivation practices with them. And such agricultural operations would have been handed on to succeeding generations - right down to the present time, when my family and I were passing the fields in question.

After the hot, long drive from San Juan to the South of the island, however, the last thing that my children wanted, or needed, was to spend time walking around another city – and, maybe, stopping at a museum or two there to look at the exhibits inside. Rather, both Noel and Kim, especially, were ready to let off some steam and burn some calories. That was not least because, for the past two days of the Carnival's climactic shows, they had basically spent all their time sitting in one place in a grandstand at the Queen's Park Savannah watching, or listening to, a riotous world of colour, dance, and music go by. Before we took them away from our little walk around the centre of San Fernando to some nearby beach for a swim and a play, however, there was one more 'touristic attraction' which Philomena and I agreed that we should all see before we relaxed for the day on the sand and in the Caribbean Sea. That was to visit the world famous 'Pitch Lake', which was located just a relatively few miles further south from the second city – near a town named 'La Brea'.

I had researched, before our visit, that special place on the island. Accordingly, I expected that our family would find there 'the world's largest natural deposit of asphalt'. That is to say, a lake of black, sticky pitch – which could be used for surfacing roads, for example. Such large pool, I had read, had first been discovered as long before as the days of England's 'Sir Walter Raleigh' in the 16th century (who was supposed to have used some of the asphalt found in the large pool to caulk, or seal the joints of, the hull of his ship). When our family arrived at the venue, I, for one, was not to be disappointed. We found something of a nascent visitor centre and, for a few local dollars, my family and I could enter the compound in question. There, we were not only able to observe the tar-like, substance, but also play with it too – in the sense of prod some sticks into it, and then try to pull some of the asphalt up with them. In attempting to do so, time and again, Noel and Kim were fully diverted for quite a few minutes. Eventually, however, our firstborn eventually reminded us that it was high time we took him and his two siblings on for the promised beach visit, so that they could finally have their swim.

Alas, from my own pre '*Tour de Trinidad*' researches, I had discovered that, perhaps, one of the best beaches 'Down South' was located on the other side of the island from San Fernando and La Brea – namely, at a place called 'Mayaro Bay' on the South-East coast. There, as I understood things, we would find a beach that was many miles long and relatively unpopulated too. That meant, however, another hour or more of driving my, by now, rather impatient sons – and wife, too, if the truth be known – from the west to the east side of the island. Thankfully, once we had reached the seaside just south of the town of Mayaro itself, we all seemed to be delighted with our discovery – even baby Claire-Louise, to whom Philomena and I had already introduced to the joys of 'sea bathing' at both Oistins and Maxwell beaches, back home in Barbados, during her earliest days after her first coming home from the Queen Elizabeth Hospital where she had been born.

To be honest, however, the stretch of the beach that we all finally ended up on at Mayaro Bay was not as good as our own favourite one at Oistins back in Barbados. That was because, visiting the former place, situated on Trinidad's east coast, was comparable to trying to swim at Bathsheba on Barbados' equivalent seaboard. The water was equally choppy in both places – and more suitable, therefore, for surfers who like high waves, rather than for children and their mums who, usually, much prefer placid conditions in which to take their sea baths. For, just like Bathsheba, Mayaro Bay was located on the Atlantic Ocean coast of its respective island. Accordingly, what our family really needed was a beach on, or near, the more calm Caribbean Sea side of the island – and one that was much nearer to our base in San Juan and Port of Spain in the 'North'. Philomena and myself, therefore, agreed that such would be the quest for the Bradshaw-five during our day out of the following day, during which we would be continuing to 'explore Trinidad'. Accordingly, after our time at Mayaro Bay our family headed back to the North, via such exotic-sounding places as 'Manzanilla' and 'Sangre Grande' – the latter place name being one which I knew from my (former?) friendship with my Trinidad-born UWI colleague, Margaret DeMerieux, was actually pronounced by locals as 'Sandy Grandy'! That knowledge had come about because she had once or twice, during my visits to her home, sang me a verse or two from a Mighty Sparrow calypso which went something along the lines of:

'Tell you sister to come down quick
… and meet Mr Benwood Dick
…de Man from Sangre Grande'.

The place name in the verse, however, was never pronounced by Margaret as a French person might have done but, rather, with the special Trinidadian creole of her native land.

Then it was a case of Philomena, myself and our boys each taking our showers (and baby Claire-Louise having her bath) in order to wash away the saltiness of our Atlantic seaside dips. We then each had our dinner (or last feed) and went to our beds (or carry cot) for the night, so as to be ready to continue with our explorations early the next morning - during what would be our last full day in Trinidad. The De Voeux family would be coming back to their home on the day after that – that is to say, on the Friday, and, after returning their house keys and their car to them, we would be flying back home to Barbados that very evening.

Next morning Philomena and I agreed that we would be going as near as we could, in Trinidad, to the South American continent. That is to say, that we would travel to the nearest point to the Latin American country of Venezuela – which, I had been told, was only about nine miles away from Trinidad at the closest point situated in the island's north-west peninsula called 'Chaguaramas'. To actually reach that point was really no 'big deal' for myself – or, perhaps, even for my eldest child, Noel. For, as seen before, the two of us had already been upon the territory of Venezuela itself (and, therefore, the South American continent) just a few months before – and had not merely espied it from afar or even from a mere nine miles away. Going to the peninsula in question, however, clearly meant something to Philomena - since it would enable her to see, for herself, the 'start of Latin American' from the viewpoint of Trinidad. Moreover, we would not be limiting ourselves to merely 'continent spotting' that final full day of ours on our holiday island. Rather, we would also be seeking out some nice beach or other on the Caribbean Sea side of the island - even if it was situated more on the northern extremities thereof. For, that should have been rather more placid than the Atlantic coast beach which we had sampled the previous day at Mayaro Bay.

In actual fact, when we first arrived at the most north-western end of the island that we could drive the De Voeux family's car to in our quest to 'spot Venezuela' - a few miles further west from the largish town of 'Diego Martin' - we discovered that there were a number of small islands off the coast which were also part of Trinidad and Tobago territory. Only later did I learn that the government of the twin island state used at least one of those islands as the 'local Alcatraz prison', and another as a leper colony. In that discovery, I was also to find out that Trinidad was actually part of the South American mainland, in the past, and that the said islands are all that now remain, above the Caribbean Sea, of the former 'land bridge' between, what is now, Venezuela and mainland Trinidad. During my family's visit to the peninsula in question, some locals informed us that the so-called nine miles' distance to Venezuela was only calculated from the last of those islands, as you went from east to west starting at Chaguaramas. Only then, we were also told, did the 'gap' begin between the two states in question – a gap known in English as 'The Dragon's Mouths' and in Venezuelan-Spanish as '*Las*

*Bocas del Dragón*'. Those '*Bocas*' were, in fact, the northern most part of a greater stretch of sea between the two countries known as the 'Gulf of Paria'. As a result of Philomena and myself learning those new geographical facts during our visit that morning, there would be no longer any wish by Philomena and myself for our family to hire a boat to get us to the furthest of the islands from Chaguaramas, in order to see whether we could actually spot the South American mainland in Venezuela on that particular occasion. Rather, the two of us decided that we would have to postpone that objective for another time and, meanwhile, set off to find our much more sought-after target (by the children and Philomena, at least) of a 'placid Caribbean beach'.

We had been told – perhaps by the De Voeux family or even by my UWI colleague and friend, Michael Castagne - that the place to go, for the best seaside hangout on the north coast of Trinidad, was 'Maracas Beach'. Whoever recommended it to us may have gone so far as to say that it was 'Trinidad's most popular beach', but had warned that, though only about one hour's drive from Port of Spain, it entailed a very hilly journey through the mountains north of the capital. For us Bradshaws, coming from even further west of the island after our stillborn quest to 'see Venezuela', our car journey to Maracas took us even longer. We had to pass through places with exotic sounding names such as Diego Martin itself, 'Petit Valley' and 'Maraval'. Philomena, myself and our sons were, however, certainly delighted with our view of the bay, and the beach itself, as we drove down from the mountains for our destination. That particular Trinidadian paradise would serve all five of our family well for the remainder of our sojourn on the North Coast. No more exploring. No more 'Continent spotting'! Just 'liming' as the Trinidadians (and their neighbours, the Bajans) say – meaning: doing nothing, or very little, and fully enjoying it! One could add to such 'activity' – as our Bradshaw clan did that day - lots of eating and drinking thrown in, as well as a dip or two in the calm Caribbean Sea, just a few steps away from our picnic place under the shade of the coconut trees. An idyll for my family, indeed – which we fully enjoyed whilst it lasted. That was because the following morning would be the start of another day. One which meant going back home to Barbados to continue my work at UWI and, generally for my family, back to the trials of (Caribbean) life!

*Chapter 18*

# Comparative Law Trip to Venezuela – Eastertide 1981

After trading mutual 'thank yous' for the exchanges of each other's homes and cars (and discovering that they had liked ours as much as we had enjoyed theirs), my family and I said our farewells to the De Voeux family and returned to our routine lives in Barbados (including my work-a-day one at the Cave Hill Campus Law Faculty). Just a few weeks later, however, I found myself back in Trinidad again! On that later occasion, that was because I was *en route* from Barbados to Caracas, Venezuela - along with some of my Comparative Law students - and the flight had made a short stop there. Be that as it may, I did not disembark, however, on that particular occasion. Rather, my journey with my students had a non-Caribbean island destination and it was the culmination of several months' planning for that later trip. As previously seen, such preparation had even involved an earlier excursion to Caracas (with my firstborn son, Noel) to find a university, and a Law school within it, to try to establish mutual relations with my own back at UWI in Barbados, and, more specifically, with my Comparative Law class for the 1980-81 academic year in question. Despite my original idea for a full-exchange of students, however, such a reciprocal arrangement was not about to happen for that particular year. That was because no students from the Universidad Central de Venezuela (the Central University of Venezuela) – or 'UCV' – would be coming back to us at Cave Hill, for the time being. Nevertheless, there had been nothing to prevent our small group, of about 16 persons, from making an initial unilateral legal (and cultural) visit to the UCV in Caracas - and from aiming to have a great time whilst doing so.

The host for our arrival in the Venezuelan capital was my counterpart at UCV, Professor Allan Brewer-Carias. He had given me (and Noel) a wonderful welcome when we had visited his Law Faculty in Caracas the previous December – around the time that John Lennon had been assassinated in New York. And, true to form, he and his seemingly very efficient lady secretary, or PA (whom I shall name 'Agnes' for these purposes) were there to meet and greet us, after we had left our VIASA Venezuela Airlines plane at Simon Bolivar International Airport in Maiquetia, Caracas. That had happened after my Barbados group had cleared immigration and customs to emerge into the orange-liveried 'Llegados' (or 'Arrivals') part of that airport.

Professor Allan had even arranged some wonderful accommodation for us in downtown Caracas – just about 20 minutes' safe walking distance from his UCV Faculty, and even nearer to the capital's main bus station and its bullring or *Plaza de toros*. That base of ours was part of the 'Hilton' chain. Just from that name, therefore, my students and myself knew that we could expect to be extremely comfortable during our stay. The actual name of our hotel was the 'Anauco Hilton'. When we were shown our rooms, I for one had been absolutely delighted. That was because we were only given about three or four of them in total - to be shared between ourselves - with each such room being an apartment containing three or four bedrooms, a living room and a kitchen (where we could, therefore, do our own cooking if we so wished). The main thing, however, was that several members of our group would be sharing each of the rooms together – with myself included in such division of our 16-person (or so) group – which collective arrangement gave the promise for a very cohesive 'touring party'. Moreover, because our rooms – or 'sets of apartments', if you will – were all next to each other on a fairly high floor, we all had excellent views, out of our respective bedroom or living room windows, which allowed us all to take in the high mountains which enclosed Caracas between its northern and southern sides.

The students and I would be paying for own accommodation. However, owing to what Professor Allan had done in arranging for my group to be accommodated in just a relatively small number of rooms, and the cost to us all being on a 'per room' basis (to be shared among the occupants thereof), somehow the actual cost 'per person' came down to a very small amount indeed! Perhaps, it had been no more than about the equivalent of £50 (in total for the entire stay) per person, in the 'Venezuelan Bolivar' local currency. My students, and therefore, myself were, accordingly, extremely delighted at the state of things as we checked into, and explored the amenities of, our respective rooms – and, also, slowly realised how relatively little the whole adventure of our 'field trip' would be costing us financially.

Left to our own devices after Professor Allan and Agnes had temporarily departed from us to enable us to settle into our surroundings at the hotel, one of the first things which most of the group wanted to do was explore the surrounding area which was in close vicinity to our base. For most of my students, that visit to Caracas was also their very first trip to 'Latin' America – although two of them, at least, were natives of the neighbouring country to Venezuela on the 'South American' mainland, namely Guyana. One of those Guyanese students was a pretty young lady who went by the unforgettable Christian name of 'Petal'! She was merely one of a number of attractive young women belonging to my Comparative Law class that year. Moreover, whereas I well remember quite a few of them from that cohort – especially all those who came on the 'field trip to Caracas' - I struggle to recall the names of the young men in the class of 1980-81 (apart from one 'Kurt Rattray' of Jamaica). Guyana, however, did not have the monopoly of pretty young women who were interested in Comparative Law at that time, and I was to always retain the memory of another fine example thereof – but from Trinidad, this time. Her Christian name was 'Jennifer' (or 'Jenny') and, because she had studied the Spanish language at A-level whilst at school prior to studying Law at UWI, she had been extremely keen to act as my group's 'official' translator from that second language of hers to English, and vice versa, during our sojourn in Caracas. I had been more than happy for Jenny to fulfil that volunteered role of hers. That is because it had saved me from a lot of embarrassment owing to the fact that, as 'leader of the visiting group', my own command of Spanish (despite my classes at the Venezuelan Cultural Institute back in Barbados) had been extremely basic (compared to hers), to say the very least!

One of the first places that we tried to find that afternoon, after being left to our own devices by our Venezuelan welcoming party, was whereabouts in the hotel the swimming pool was located. That was because several of the young ladies in our group seemed to find Caracas, during that first daytime, somewhat 'hot' in temperature and seemed keen to either have a cool dip or to simply shed some of the more formal attire which they were wearing on the plane journey from Barbados to Venezuela. I, for one, had not been too averse to the suggestion that anyone in our party, who wanted to do so, could simply relax for the remainder of that first day – whether by the poolside or otherwise – and I was quite happy to join the majority of the cohort in seeking out the hotel's pool. When I made inquiries on our behalf at the reception, however, it turned out that the Anauco Hilton itself did not have its own swimming pool on site. Rather, its guests were allowed to use the outdoor, heated one, of the 'Caracas Hilton' (proper) – a much more low-rise edifice, which was located across the road from our own hotel. We were, however, able to easily get to the latter property by means of a simple bridge linking the two establishments - which was situated above the busy roadway we would otherwise have had to attempt to cross at street level, with some difficulty.

At any rate, perhaps about eight to 10 members of my visiting group managed to get over to the Caracas Hilton's pool and, before long, we were all either swimming and/or otherwise relaxing by the poolside and discussing the days ahead in that 'new' country, and capital, for everyone in the party except myself. With the discovery of such a wonderful amenity so near to our own Anauco accommodation, I had begun to feel extremely content with my group's induction to Caracas and to conclude that, perhaps, things for us could not have begun more swimmingly. If anything, however, the 'undressed' nature of myself and my, almost 100%, cohort of female Comparative Law students (apart from Kurt) was, perhaps, the beginning of the 'thin end of the wedge' for me. By that quoted expression I mean to state the following. Namely, that it is arguable that the said initial, and relatively-intimate, scenario with my students made me want to be more 'one of them' – instead of my resolving to maintain a respectful, but friendly, distance as their teacher and mentor. Would such a situation have repercussions which might come back to haunt me? The answer must wait, but, at that particular moment in my life and in my group's visit, I was so happy about the way things were going that I would not have been able to see any dark clouds on the horizon for myself.

After our swim, those of us taking part in that particular excursion all returned to our rooms together, in order to meet up with the minority of the group who had decided to do other things. When we had done so, we found out that some members of that minority were able to confirm a memory of mine. That had been from my early recce visit to Caracas a few months previously – namely, that the cost of eating out in the Venezuelan capital, compared to doing so in Barbados, was very much lower. Moreover, with the rate of exchange of the US dollar (and, therefore, the Barbados dollar, which was fixed in relation to the former at the rate of 2:1) being extremely favourable against the local currency – the Venezuelan Bolivar – my students and I found ourselves relatively well-off. That was vis-à-vis the 'pocket money' we had each brought on the trip with us, in either US or Bajan dollars. Accordingly, although we all had cooking facilities in each of our respective shared apartments, we unanimously decided, that evening back at the Anauco Hilton, that we would have all our meals outside! There was to be no cooking for us on that particular trip, therefore – though most of us seemed to appreciate that it was wonderful to have had a choice in case any of us became 'peckish' in the middle of the night, for example, and wanted to knock something up quickly in the kitchen of his or her apartment! Accordingly, that first evening we all went out, *en masse*, to one of the first street café-restaurants that we could find close to our hotel. In fact, there were many around - since almost every other place, in that particular neighbourhood of Caracas, seemed to be some kind of eating establishment or other - with black beans, shredded beef, and bread-like items (evidently made with maize, and always bright yellow in colour) seeming to be on offer in each of them!

The next morning was the start of our first full, and proper, day in the Venezuelan capital. It was a date when, as I anticipated and told my group, we would be linking up with our counterpart Law Faculty and Comparative Law students at the UCV – and I felt that it was, therefore, a relatively formal occasion. Accordingly, I put that thought over to all the students in my party and asked them to dress relatively formally – for that first visit to the UCV Campus, at least – since I wanted us all to present a good impression of our UWI selves. No jeans for any of us that morning, therefore, and I for myself, as leader of the group, felt obliged to even wear a suit and a tie - despite the heat of the Caracas forenoon (which was close to what it might well have been in Barbados at the same time of day). Fortunately, I had brought several suits with me on the trip – suits which I had been gifted by my great friend, Berndt Schuhmacher in West Germany, who had himself obtained them for me via his male cousin in the city of 'Limburg' in that country (which cousin had happened to be the manager of the menswear department in one of the well-known department stores in their country and who was, therefore, entitled to free suits from time to time! I was the beneficiary of the cousin's cast-offs, therefore – but very glad of them, nevertheless). Little did I know, at the time, that one member of our cohort, in particular, noticed how smart the German suit made me look, apparently – and that she would also note that I changed my suit to a different one every single day on which we visited the UCV, and approved of that fact!

We all walked from the Anauco Hilton that first morning - to the UCV, some 20 to 30 minutes away. That turned out to be a pleasant experience as there was a safe pedestrianised way, passing by some parks and other smaller green areas. We were, thus, safe from the fast, multi-laned traffic whizzing past on a variety of roads and flyovers, on both sides of us as well as above. That was so, as we perambulated along in the pleasantly-warm, blue-skied, morning to meet our hosts – Professor Allan, Agnes and some of his students.

When we first arrived at the UCV, Agnes – who seemed to have been given just one duty for the week in question, namely, to look after the visiting group from Barbados – was there to meet us and welcome us to the campus. She could not have been more accommodating and I, for one, felt that already we were being treated as 'VIPs'. Soon afterwards, we were all taken to Professor Allan's huge office - to meet with him and be offered some refreshments there. It was during that time that he made an important revelation to us – in his lovely English in which he rolled his 'R's' in the typical Venezuelan manner of speaking the Spanish language. That was the fact that the UCV did not actually offer a class called 'Comparative Law' as we did at UWI, or as other English-speaking universities also provided such as those at my old Law faculties at Cambridge and Leeds. Nevertheless, he told us that he had a number of students in his Faculty who were very interested in the English Common Law legal systems (perhaps, because of their particular areas of legal research), including those in the West Indian islands such as neighbouring Trinidad and Tobago and Barbados, and who, therefore, would be happy to meet with us and be our counterparts during my group's sojourn at UCV. He also told us that he would be delighted to have our party come to witness one of his lectures to his students that morning.

At that first meeting, he also gave us the splendid news that Agnes had arranged for us all to have a welcome lunch together – that very day after the first part of our visit was over - at a high-class restaurant in downtown Caracas. Also, that Agnes had even hired a 'bus' – meaning what I might have called a 'coach' – to take us to the eatery in question. Professor Allan went on to tell us that the next day, he had arranged for some of his students to take us from the UCV – again by hired bus – to one of the Law courts in the city in order to see the 'administration of justice' at work in the Venezuelan capital. He added that, for the day after that, he had organised a day away from Caracas for my group. To my amazement – because it had been completely unprompted by me – he revealed that the 'away day' would be to the very same city which my son and I had visited for our outside-Caracas excursion a few months before. As may be recalled, that had been to the city of Valencia, in 'Carabobo State', situated to the west of the capital. Professor Allan had not, that morning, gone on to also tell us what we would be doing in that third largest city of Venezuela and would only do so later. I already knew, however, from my experiences with Noel there the previous December, that it was a very good place for weddings! Accordingly, I guessed that it was likely to be a great place, also, for visiting other lawyers, Law courts and the like!

That particular morning, our UWI group took up Professor Allan's invitation to attend his very next lecture – to commence about half an hour or so after we had arrived in his office. It was to be held in one of the largest lecture theatres that I had ever seen

– the so-called 'Aula Magna' of his Law Faculty, which had seating for, perhaps, one thousand students or more. There were many hundreds less in attendance when my group made up part of his audience that particular morning. Moreover, the subject matter of his discourse was not Comparative Law at all but, rather, some topic that did not particular excite me (or many members of my group, perhaps) such as Constitutional Law (of which Professor Allan was also something of an expert). During the event in question, we witnessed at first hand the classical theory of how legal education is carried out at Law faculties throughout the 'Civil Law World'. The latter included jurisdictions in Continental Europe such as France and Germany, as well as in the Latin American countries including Venezuela and its next-door neighbour, Colombia. Such method classically utilises the 'magisterial lecture' in which the professor stands above the students, like a very god, and delivers his 'testimony' from on high without a word of interruption from his subservient, submissive and ever-attentive students.

Accordingly, Professor Allan presented a very different scenario from the 'Harvard Law School' approach, involving inter-active Law teaching, known as using the 'Socratic Method' – which entailed teaching by means of the questioning, by the professor, of individual students in the class and extracting an answer, or not, sometimes to the embarrassment of any such interrogated student. Thus, according to such method at Harvard – a university in USA which is part of the 'Common Law World' - the focus is likely to be on the individual student, particularly if he gets his or her answer to his professor wrong. What Professor Allan's audience witnessed, however, in his 'Civil Law Tradition' class that morning, was that the focus of the session was solely on him - the teacher and professor. And he did, indeed, look god-like during his lecture of an hour or so – with his very distinguished-looking face made even more so by his tortoiseshell spectacles and his 'Salvador Dali'-like moustache. 'What a role model for me!', I silently thought to myself - as I watched him in action on the dais of the *Aula Magna* that morning declaiming in front of his 200 or so undergraduates and his visitors from Barbados. On the other hand, however, I soon realised that I also valued the 'intimate' touch which I had managed to develop with my very much smaller group of less than 20 Comparative Law students back at UWI, Cave Hill that particular academic year – about two-thirds of which were interested enough in my subject to want to accompany me on my then current Comparative Law field trip to Caracas.

After Professor Allan's class, it was soon time to be going off with him, Agnes and some of his students – including a few from the very lecture which we had just listened to – to the pre-booked restaurant, in the centre of Caracas, for lunch. That 'international gathering' of Law students and their teachers - as well as Agnes, the great organiser of the event - turned out to be one of the highlights of my group's visit, when viewed in hindsight. The venue was top class. So was the food which was on offer - from a very wide menu of choices. And so, too, was the company – including Professor Allan on my own table. It seemed to me that most of the professor's own, specially invited, students all knew enough English to be able to converse relatively easily with their counterparts from Barbados in that language. Certainly, they were much capable of doing so in comparison to our lot being able to do likewise with their Venezuelan hosts in the Spanish language. From what I could see and hear taking place at the other student-with-student tables in the restaurant, my original 'student exchange' idea was already being forged extremely well. Moreover, and, even if the UCV cohort present at the lunch that day would not have been coming back to Barbados with us in the very near future – in order to experience some 'Bajan hospitality' as well as some comparative legal perspectives - there was already an excellent interaction, or exchange indeed, going on that lunchtime if only one relating to 'ideas'. From my point of view, therefore, the trip was already turning out to be a successful one – and it was, then, only our very first proper morning of doing 'academic' things with our Venezuelan counterparts!

After the wonderful – and extremely long – lunch of some two to three hours, which, of course, had to include some alcoholic drinks such as Venezuelan wine and rum, there seemed to be only one, realistic, option regarding how my group should spend the remainder of our first full 'academic' afternoon in Caracas. By the consensus of my UWI party - following my thanking, profusely, Professor Allan, his students and Agnes for the magnificent lunch they had just treated us to - that was to head back to our hotel, and cross over to the Caracas Hilton's pool for a swim or just a relaxation session on the sun loungers nearby. Those few of my group who did not fancy swimming, or to merely sunbathe by the poolside, were (under my very benign leadership) given my blessing to do whatever else they wished, including simply return to their respective apartments and to 'sleep off' the prandial feast which they had just enjoyed in downtown Caracas.

Our second full day as visiting Comparative Law students (and their teacher) came soon enough. Once more we made the enjoyable journey between the Anauco Hilton and the UCV on foot, past the 'Venezuelan National Gallery of Fine Arts' on our left as we went, as well as many trees beautifying several small parks nearby. Once again, I put on a fresh suit for that new day, in order to stand out as the 'leader of the pack' – that is to say, as the head of my small band of visiting Comparatists, mainly consisting of young women. One of these, as stated, was Jenny – our volunteer interpreter from English to Spanish, and vice versa. I relied on her to get myself fully understood to our counterparts at the UCV - and for fully understanding what our counterparts were trying to say to us in full-Spanish or even broken English (not including Professor Allan, whose command of the Anglo-Saxon language was pretty much fluent). As a result, she and I seemed to establish a closer working rapport than I had yet managed with the rest of the group. Certainly, she, above all the rest, was the one to go out of her way to compliment me on how smart I looked in my 'new' (to her and the others) suit. Naturally, I had been much too embarrassed to let on to her, or any of the others, that I was in fact only wearing 'hand-me-downs' from friends or acquaintances in West Germany!

Be that as it may, when we arrived at the UCV that morning, we knew already that we would not be staying there to witness any lectures or other classes, as per the previous day. Rather, there was already a mini bus waiting to take us off to the Law courts further inside the centre of Caracas – along with some of Professor Allan students. The esteemed Law teacher did not accompany us - as he told us that he was too tied up with other matters to be able to do so. For myself, however, I was hoping that we might be taken to some dramatic criminal trial, going on at that time in the country's capital – something like what a journalist might consider to be a juicy murder case. That was so, even though in my own Comparative Law course we did not study any substantive *Criminal* Law at all. Rather, we merely looked at comparative aspects of the *civil* 'Law of Obligations' – which could basically be split between the Law of Contract and the Law of Tort (with my course covering, in the Second Term, actual cases decided by the French Law courts (mainly those in Paris) in those two legal areas.

When we arrived at the court in question, I, for one, was to be rather disappointed. For, notwithstanding that my own course back in Barbados being more concerned with non-Criminal Law, there was absolutely no Criminal Law on the menu at the legal establishment where we were taken. That was because it was, indeed, only a civil court which dealt with legal disputes in contracts between litigants, and the like. Indeed, we were not even taken to see what a Venezuelan court room looked liked. Rather, our group was shepherded into offices within the building in question and, there, shown 'dossiers' which had been built up by the judges hearing the cases, when new matters relating to them came up from time to time. At least, by looking at such dossiers, however, my students got to understand the reality of the theory I had taught them back at Cave Hill – namely, that in Civil Law countries (of which number Venezuela was included) the English Common Law idea of 'the day in Court' is largely non-existent. That is to say, the English Law tradition – in either criminal or civil cases - of two opposing sides fighting it out against each other, with the judge sitting between them as umpire, is not to be found in countries of the, old Roman-Law-based, Civil Law Tradition such as France, Germany or the Latin American countries including Venezuela.

Thus, the point would have been brought home to them that morning – as much as it was reinforced to me - that in such latter countries, the judge is much more like a 'seeker of truth'. Also, that, accordingly, there is no room for the 'jousting', accusatory process of the English Common Law Tradition -which is played out in a public court room, over one or more days. As a result of our visit that day, therefore, my students would have seen evidence of the theory that in Civil Law countries, like Venezuela, that Common Law process which they were so familiar with in their home territories, of Barbados and elsewhere in the Caribbean, was replaced by the very different 'Inquisitorial Process'. Moreover, they would have appreciated that such latter approach could be operated even outside a formal courtroom and in a regular office, for example – just as they had witnessed for themselves that day. They would, thus, have better understood the Civil Law Tradition being evidenced in the Venezuelan court that we visited, which required the parties to be called in, from time to time, to answer questions of the *judge/ inquisitor* (as opposed to interrogations coming from their own, or their opponent's, *lawyer(s)* in a formal court room, as in the Common Law Tradition). Also, that such Civil Law

Tradition process thereby allowed the Venezuelan adjudicator to 'build a dossier' of the case in question - with a view to, eventually, finding out the 'truth' relating to the dispute in question (and ultimately come to the 'right' judgment in the case).

Lessons learned, despite the absence of any particular 'fireworks' in a courtroom (or other 'drama' witnessed inside the Caracas court buildings to which we had been taken that day), our visiting party came away from the legal establishment in the early afternoon ready to eat and to have some other mental stimulation. On that second full day, my UWI group would have to arrange our middle of the day meal for ourselves, instead of being treated by the UCV as on the previous day. Things would be very different the following day, however. For not only would we be going, as a group, to another city quite far from Caracas, we would also be treated to lunch there, to boot!

After the educational part of our day, in the downtown Caracas courthouse, was over our group returned to our base at the Anauco. The majority of us then had another swim and relaxation session in, or around, the pool back at the nearby Caracas Hilton. Eventually, the whole cohort repaired to a nearby restaurant for dinner together. After an early night, all members of my UWI visiting party seemed well-rested after a good night's sleep the following morning and ready for our 'away day' outside the capital city. That was just as well as, for once, we had to make our own arrangements to travel to the place in question. Fortunately for me, however, I had made the necessary journey, and purchased the tickets for it, once before – with my elder son, Noel – to my group's destination. As earlier seen, that was to be to the city of Valencia – Venezuela's third largest city. It was, thus, easy for me to be a 'fully-in-charge group leader' once more - for I even knew the way to the bus station in question, from which our public transportation to Valencia would start. That terminus, thankfully, was to be, once more, the one right beside the *Plaza de toros* in Caracas – not more than 500 yards or so from our hotel! Accordingly, after a good breakfast together at one of the nearby street cafes just outside our base - which included lots of bright, freshly-squeezed orange juice - I led the way in my latest 'new' suit. That involved for an even shorter walk than our usual one to the UCV – namely, to the bullring in question. It was also a very straightforward job to take my students to the requisite kiosk at the bus station for each of them to purchase their return tickets to 'the third-city'. I could tell that, like me, most of them were excited about the prospect of leaving the capital – beautiful as I, for one, found it with its special situation between the mountains – and embarking on a trip to somewhere which promised to be somewhat 'quieter'.

My students seemed to enjoy the journey along the relatively flat plains of the Carabobo province which we passed along on the highway between the two cities. Upon our arrival at the relatively sparsely-populated bus station in Valencia (compared to the 'heaving with humanity' one which we had recently left behind back in Caracas), the ladies in the group were able to take their leisurely time in using its 'bathroom' facilities. One of those individuals I will always remember from that excursion - owing to her taking so long in those toilets that I had to send a 'search party' for her. That had resulted in her not being best pleased with me when she had finally emerged from the same - to enable our reunited entire group to set off together on its mission to find its way to the 'Chamber of Commerce' headquarters in the city. The lady in question was one of the senior librarians employed at the Law Library in our Faculty in Barbados – who was either only working part-time whilst she also pursued her Law degree at Cave Hill, or who had taken leave of absence from her librarian's post for the necessary two or three years needed to complete her Batchelor of Laws degree on a full-time basis. The student's name was 'Sylvia' – the same as my only sister, therefore, and all the more memorable for that – who was married, at the time, to a fellow lecturer at Cave Hill, a non-lawyer, named 'Alan Moss'. After the incident in question, Sylvia and I were only to enjoy a somewhat prickly, but respectful, relationship for the remainder of our Venezuela trip.

Quite a contrast, therefore, between Sylvia's 'regard' of me and that of her fellow student, on that Valencia visit, Jenny. Once more, the latter fully came into her own since, when we all eventually walked into the city and found the Chamber of Commerce venue which we were seeking, we discovered that most of the welcoming party awaiting us there had little or no English. Accordingly, after my group and I were taken inside the headquarters building to a very plush 'state room', as 'honoured guests' from the overseas Caribbean region, we were treated to several speeches welcoming us – but, whilst some were quite long and others shorter, they were all delivered in the Spanish language! Jenny, therefore, saved the day for us by acting as our group's translator, once more. She did so in relation to what was being said to us during such speeches – as well as by translating, to our hosts, my somewhat much briefer reply, in English, thanking the spokesman, and the Valencia Chamber of Commerce in general, for the wonderful reception which they were giving my group and myself that day.

Perhaps, the best thing of all for my students on that occasion was that our whole experience, since leaving our hotel that morning, had related very little to Comparative, or any other, Law! For it had turned out to be truly a 'day off' – or one which had involved no legal pursuits, but, rather, some much appreciated cultural ones. And though the venue we were then visiting belonged to an institution which possessed the word 'commerce' in its title, very little was said to us about commercial matters. That was so, despite our party being treated to a magnificent, and veritable, banquet from early afternoon for some two to three hours by that local business association. Moreover, neither myself nor any of my group were called upon to engage in discussions about business, Law or any comparative aspects thereof. In the end, it had seemed to me that, very likely, Professor Allan, back in Caracas, had known someone high up in the Valencia Chamber of Commerce – perhaps a relative or an ex-student of his – and he had asked that person to 'Give the visitors from Barbados a good time' and, perhaps even, 'Do me a favour and take them off my hands, and out of Caracas, for one full day at least!'.

Whatever 'inspiration' had caused Professor Allan to arrange the banquet lunch for us in Valencia that day, it had been a much appreciated one - not only by myself but also by all the members of my group (or so it had seemed to me, at least). And when the meal was over – eventually – it became time for me to get up on my feet again, with Jenny translating alongside, to make another little speech of thanks to the Chamber members attending for all their much-appreciated hospitality to my little group of visiting West Indians. Extremely well-fed and 'watered' (with, perhaps, something mixed with H2O which was even more potent), it was, indeed, a very happy and content bunch of 'Comparatists' – comparers and analysts of fine lunches in Venezuela by that stage of our stay in the country – who made their way, on foot, back to the Valencia bus station that afternoon.

Accordingly, my group and I found ourselves back in Caracas later that evening. Too late indeed for another session at the Hilton Hotel pool, once we had reached our neighbouring apartments in the Anauco establishment. A relatively early night could, however, be profitably enjoyed by us all after our long day out to Valencia. Moreover, although the following day would be a 'free' one, we had to prepare ourselves for a 'party' – to be held inside the largest of our several Anauco apartments in the evening - to which Professor Allan, Agnes and several UCV students, selected by our hosts, had been invited to attend.

I, thus, gave my students a free reign regarding what they wanted to do with their spare time during our last full day in Caracas the following morning. Most of them were like me, and content to spend it once more at the Hilton Hotel pool either swimming, reading or just chatting. Some might have taken the opportunity to visit the 'Museum of Fine Arts' relatively nearby, or to go further into the centre of the city, beyond the UCV, to do some shopping. The time to prepare for our approaching party was soon upon us, however. Members of our visiting UWI group were the prime movers behind that farewell gesture and, as such, took on the responsibility of buying-in, and cooking, suitable amounts of food – as well as purchasing the important accompanying drinks. In doing so, I seem to remember that as well as Caribbean fare, such as chicken and rice featuring on the menu, so too did rum and cola (albeit the alcohol was that produced in Venezuela itself, as opposed to the variety imported from nearby Trinidad for example). And, once more, owing to the flowing goodwill of our Caracas hosts, the event between themselves and their UWI visiting guests went off swimmingly – even if it had very little to do with 'Comparative Law', as such.

It had probably been during the build-up to the party in question that afternoon that Jenny, whilst sunbathing next to me at Hilton Hotel pool, had told me that one of her hobbies was to give haircuts to her male friends. I had been most surprised by that revelation but had complimented her on being so multi-talented. She had retorted by suggesting that she would very much have liked to have given me such a trim - prior to our returning to Barbados. And although I had not felt that I was in need of such a service just at that particular time, I had already placed much trust in Jenny for all the translation help which she had given me during our time in Caracas. Accordingly, I had little problem in also putting my faith in her to do a good job on my hair - even though

I had never seen any previous results of her work. I, thus, found myself agreeing to be the subjected to Jenny's tonsorial skills.

In so submitting myself to my student's work upon my hair, in some way my arm's-length relationship with her undoubtedly became fractured. Indeed, it is arguable that our roles as teacher and student became reversed as I was having to trust her to take the lead during the operation in question, as well as in her producing a good outcome at the end of the day. Moreover, there had to be contact between the two of us – if only via the medium of the pair of scissors that she was using during the cutting operation. Be that as it may, the former professional distance between the two of us would never be as far apart again for the remainder of the evening - the last full day of our Venezuelan sojourn - or for the rest of her time as my student back in Barbados.

The next day came all too soon, however, and by mid-morning our visiting group was back at Maiquetia Airport - along with Professor Allan, Agnes and a few of our hosts' UCV students who seemed keen to see us off safely. It was as much as I have ever had to do to try to convey to the professor, and his team, how very much myself and my students had appreciated all that they had done for us during our time in Caracas. I also begged the dapper academic to try his best to invite some of the students whom he was then currently teaching, to form a similar group of about 20 or so, who were interested in legal systems belonging to the English Common Law tradition, to come to visit me and my Comparative Law students at UWI in Barbados. I also told him that, by his so doing, it would enable me to try to return some of the wonderful hospitality which he and his UCV team had most kindly bestowed on my UWI party during our Venezuela visit.

Before long therefore, my students and I found ourselves on our VIASA plane heading back to Barbados. The remainder of the Easter holidays at UWI would have to run their course, but very soon it would be back to Cave Hill Campus for the Third Term. For myself and my students, that meant very little new teaching and learning ahead but, rather, preparation for the coming examinations. And it would be during that 'revision period' that Jenny and I would renew the less-than-arm's-length relationship which had begun during the trip to Caracas. For, on one occasion, whilst I was already marking the earliest of the examination papers that had come to me – from my Second Year Law of Tort cohort – she paid me a visit in my office at the Law Faculty. She was to tell me how very low she was then feeling about her very imminent exams in 'Administrative Law'. I did my best to give her the most ardent 'pep talk' that I could manage - about how exams were merely an opportunity to show one's examiners just how well one knows his or her subject, and so forth. Alas, my exhortations did not seem to be working too well and when she eventually left my room, thanking me for my company and my efforts to cheer her up, I had felt for her as I might have done for my own child - rather than for a 'mere' student of mine, suffering from such a predicament. Little did I know that feeling of 'caring' on my part was a somewhat mutual one at the time.

*Chapter 19*

# The Third Term of my Second Year at UWI – Summer 1981

Going back to the start of the previously mentioned Third Term of my second academic year at UWI, which had commenced after Easter 1981, I need to recount some information about a 'movement' which Philomena and myself were involved with in Barbados for some months by that time. It was called 'Marriage Encounter', or just 'ME', and - as may be recalled - my wife and myself were already involved in it at the time of our family's trip to the Carnival in Trinidad in February 1981. Indeed, it had been the ME movement which had facilitated that particular trip of ours and the exchanges of homes and cars with our counterpart family in Trinidad. The prime mover behind the movement in Barbados, as stated before, was a priest named Father Pat. He was a White Canadian – a short man with a lovely, bubbly and smiling personality. The key element behind the organisation was the desire to keep marriages fresh and alive.

Accordingly, a relatively small number of married couples – perhaps up to about five or six – would meet regularly at each other's home in turn. Such get-togethers occurred every week, or fortnightly, in the evening. Father Pat would participate in such meetings also, as the coordinator and spiritual adviser. The essential process in these meetings was that each couple would communicate with each other – not merely by speaking to one another but also by writing to the other in a book which each would bring to the meeting for the purpose of creating such 'love letters'. Father Pat might start a particular evening off with a question to all of the couples, such as: 'How do you feel when your spouse rejects your suggestion regarding whether you should invite your parents to stay with you?'. He would then give each of the couples, perhaps, 10 to 15 minutes to write about their feelings in their own respective book - for their spouse to read later. At the end of that the writing period, each couple would exchange their books and read their own spouse's feelings – as expressed on the pages of such spouse's book. The idea, therefore, was, to some extent, to return to era of the 'love letters', which might once have been written to each other by the two people involved in each marriage in question. That is to say: use the writing procedure to reveal, to the other party, how the writer was really feeling inside, and not simply leave those feelings to be guessed at (or not adverted to at all).

Communication between spouses was, therefore, the key element behind the initiative. After the exchanges of books, each couple would be given time to reflect verbally, with each other, about what they had each read about the other's feelings – often with a mutual reaction such as: 'I did not know you felt that way!'. Such realisation, therefore, had the benefit, presumably, of making a spouse think carefully about acting differently, about the situation in question, the next time it occurred in the marriage – in order to protect their partner from feeling so negatively, perhaps, about the given situation. If better communication between spouses was the main aim of the movement, however, Father Pat would also ask members of the group to volunteer, if they wished, to share, with the whole group, what each couple had written to the other. As time went on, and as the members of the group got to know and trust each other more, we all tended to be ever happy to share our writings among the group as a whole – and not merely restrict the same to our own respective spouse. By such means, we tended to find similar trends and feelings in each other's marriages for any given situation provided by Father Pat at the start of an evening – and, thereby, allowed him to give us all a general spiritual lesson, from the whole proceedings, to take into our respective married lives for another week or two.

Just how Philomena and myself managed to be able to attend such ME evenings, on a regular basis, without our three children is now something of a mystery to me. That is because there were certainly no offspring present at any of the meetings. Presumably, therefore, we must have had a standing arrangement with Mrs Payne – living downstairs below our home in Hygeia - whereby she would come up to our bigger part of the house to babysit for us whilst we went to the home of one of the other couples. When it was our turn to host an evening at Hygeia, I assume that the children would either have been taken down to Mrs Payne's dwelling quarters or (more likely) she would have come up to stay with the three of them, all asleep (hopefully), in the boys' bedroom – with the door open.

If, however, the babysitting arrangements for our ME evenings can now no longer be precisely recalled, I can certainly remember some of the other members of our group – in addition to Father Pat. The most memorable must be a couple named 'David and Margaret Wilson'. That is because they were a gentle partnership with four small children. Their first three were all girls, however, and their son was their last. Nevertheless, our two families were similar in that their last three children were approximately the same ages as the trio of Philomena and myself. Moreover, whilst David was brown-skinned like me (but a business man in Bridgetown), Margaret was a White lady. I was to discover, after many of our ME meetings had taken place, that Margaret's roots lay in Guyana and, earlier, in the Portuguese island of 'Madeira'. Amazingly, though he had been dead by that period of 1981, most likely, Philomena and I had met her father during the first part of our honeymoon trip to Barbados in 1976. For it had been from his shop named 'De Freitas and Co', situated in Roebuck Street, Bridgetown, that we had hired the small motor bike with which we had toured the island during our first marital holiday there.[52] Moreover, Margaret ran a small kindergarten on the outskirts of the island's capital in the Belleville district, and with our firstborn son, Noel, then going on four years old with his pre-schooling on the horizon, she seemed to be a good person for Philomena and myself to get to know better during that period.

*Fig. 40: Noel's first day at the pre-school kindergarten of Mrs Margaret Wilson, situated in the Belleville district of Bridgetown, Barbados, sometime in 1981. Margaret is the only adult in the photo and Noel is on the far right*

Another couple from our Marriage Encounter group was 'Wendell and Irma Lawrence'. Unlike David and Margaret, that pair were Black Caribbean folk – or, perhaps, more Brown, like myself. Moreover, their origins were not in Barbados at all – but, rather, the island of Dominica. Accordingly, they emanated from just two main islands south of my native Montserrat and, with their own distinctive non-Bajan accents, I felt particularly drawn to them. That attraction was even more so, perhaps, than in relation to any of the other couples in our group. For those others all tended to be, mainly, White Bajans – or contained one partner, at least, from my family's adopted new island. Nevertheless, of the latter cohort, my wife and I found each member thereof to be equally loving and trustworthy - in relation to keeping confidential, any sensitivities disclosed by members of the gathering to one another generally, during our ME sessions.

The foregoing, therefore, sets the scene for the social setting in which I had found myself after Easter of 1981. A close family unit at home with our three healthy and thriving children, buttressed by the regular meetings of my ME group, including Father Pat as spiritual adviser and coordinator. At the Law Faculty also, I felt on top of things

- especially after the successful trip with my Comparative Law group to one of the best universities in Caracas, Venezuela, and with my lectures more or less completed and my merely awaiting UWI's examination processes to start. What could possibly go wrong, therefore?

The answer, it seems, relates to the closeness that I had developed with Jenny during the Venezuela trip. And although, in the end, 'nothing happened' between us prior to her completing her exams and departing back to her homeland in Trinidad, I had clearly let my guard down in relation to getting too close to my students, or at least some of them.

And that guard reached a particularly low point one day in relation to a different female student. She was just one year behind Jenny – and I had merely tutored her in the Law of Torts during the academic year in question. Her name was 'Vere' and I had particularly noticed her since she had been a little older than most of the others in her tutorial group – having already completed a first degree, at UWI, in Finance, Accounting or some other such 'Business-related' subject (just as I was to learn that she was three years younger than me, almost exactly). She had thus appeared to me to be extremely self-confident, *vis-à-vis* many of her peers who had come to the Law Faculty straight out of school. Nevertheless, I can remember taking the wind of out her sails one day in one of my tutorial classes with her group, when I had selected her to answer my question: 'What is the leading case under the Tort area known as "The Rule in *Rylands v Fletcher*" '? I recalled that she hummed and hawed and eventually came up with an English House of Lords case decided under the said Rule. I then replied: 'How about *Rylands v Fletcher* itself – the case which gave rise to the Rule?'. I remember that she had been rather embarrassed by my announcement (to her and her classmates) of the answer which I had been seeking - and I surmised that she might have turned red in the face, had she not been a Black Bajan.

*Fig. 41: Vere, as she was photographed some years before the Author first met her in one of his Law of Torts tutorial classes in the First Term of the 1980-81 academic year at UWI, Cave Hill Campus, Barbados*

Vere, however, must have forgiven me for showing her up, a little, in that particular tutorial session - for she kept on coming to my classes in Tort and I found her always well-prepared for those future ones. I guessed, therefore, that she must have appreciated my teaching in the subject. I, too, valued her participation in those subsequent classes – which continued until the end of the Second Term of that 1980-81 academic year, and the examination period had begun, soon after the commencement of the Third.

Then, one day - out of the blue - whilst I happened to be at home in the bosom of my family, I received a phone call from Vere. How she had obtained my home number I can no longer recall but, perhaps, that had been possible to do via the Secretariat at the Law Faculty in the case of an emergency. And, as far as Vere was concerned, it had been an 'emergency'. What was that matter? Nothing more or less than the fact that she was then at the home of her friend and classmate, 'Angela', on the outskirts of Bridgetown, and had forgotten one of her Torts textbooks at her own home in St Philip parish, perhaps some 10 miles away. The crisis for her was that her Torts examination was the following day and she had felt that she needed to have the textbook for her final revision (perhaps because the book contained annotations made by her within its pages, which were vital as far as she was concerned). Then came the moment when my closeness to my students – brought on by recent experiences with Jenny – let me down, it might well be argued. For, rather than tell Vere that she should try to get Angela to help her out, take a taxi to St Philip to retrieve the book, or even reprimand her for disturbing me at home for what many would not consider to be an emergency at all, I empathised with her in her predicament.

Worse than that, I told her that I would come to Angela's home to pick her up and drive her to St Philip to recover her vitally-needed book. In doing so, I had Philomena's blessing - since nothing had occurred in our marriage up to that time to cause my wife to think anything untoward in relation to my wanting to help one of my students so close to an examination.

Within the next half hour or so, Vere was sitting in my car directing me to her (and her mother's) home in the most south-eastern parish of Barbados. I found that, during the journey, we were chatting away like old friends, rather than as teacher and student, and that it was a most pleasant drive for me across the island. In the course of that part of the outing, she told me how she and her mother – named 'Joyce', who was a midwife working for the government – had recently moved to a new home in St Philip, situated on a new housing estate. Also, about how she so missed her old district in St Michael parish near the Garrison Savannah and the coast nearby, as well as friends there like Angela, that she found herself staying over with Angela often – and especially during the fraught UWI examination revision period.

Having duly reached Vere's new home in 'Union Hall', St Philip, and been introduced to her mother briefly, I found myself driving my student back towards Bridgetown, via the part of Highway 7 which ran past the airport. Just before we reached Oistins, she seemed to me to revert to the sad mood with which I had perceived her having when she had phoned me earlier that day – as she seemed to recommence her contemplation of the ordeal ahead regarding her Torts exam the next day (notwithstanding the fact that she then had the vital tool which she was wanting in order to help her fully prepare for that process). I had felt particularly empathetic towards her at that moment as I recalled my own negative 'fear of failing' feelings which I had experienced just before my Bar Final examinations in England just three summers before. Accordingly, I put out my non-driving hand and stroked her forehead – telling her not to worry, and that her exam was just an opportunity to show her examiners, like 'Andrew Huxley' (deputising for Norma Forde as Course Director in the Law of Torts that academic year), and myself, just how well she knew her subject. I added that the whole ordeal would be behind her before very long. Little did I know, then, that those few seconds or so of communing with my student would have a lasting effect on the rest of my life!

*Fig. 41: Photo of Andrew Huxley who taught, with the Author, on the Law of Torts course at the UWI Law Faculty, Cave Hill Campus, Barbados during the 1980-81 Academic Year – possibly whilst Norma Forde was on sabbatical leave. The image shows him looking much as the Author remembers his 'hippy-like' appearance – but with somewhat shorter locks than the Author recalls him sporting at the time*

Shortly afterwards, I had dropped off my student back at her friend's – Angela's - place near Bridgetown and wished her all the very best for her next day's trials. I soon put her out of mind, as I returned home to my family - since I also had my own obligations to think about. Firstly, there was the marking that I would soon have to do in relation to my own course of Comparative Law – in addition to being the second marker of The Conflict of Laws exam papers as well as those of the Law of Torts itself. Moreover, Philomena and I were then planning to take my travel grant for that summer's forthcoming long vacation (as we would then have amassed two years' worth, after carrying over one of those from the previous year when, as seen, we had decided to save it and pay, out of our own pockets, for our family's local holiday to St Vincent and the Grenadines). Doing so would enable us to use the money to return to England for the first time since we had arrived as a family in Barbados in 1979.

Consequently, I had much on my mind, on both the domestic and employment fronts at that time, and I buckled down, as usual, in my office at the Law Faculty with my door closed in order to tackle the exam papers landing on my desk, course by course. Naturally, it was a little easier than the previous academic year's marking of scripts – when I had been Course Director of two Final Year subjects, Comparative Law and Conflicts, and, thus, the first marker for each. Nevertheless, as I was always mindful that each script which I marked could affect someone's future life in a major way, I continued to take my examiner's duties extremely seriously.

And then, out of the blue once more - but whilst absorbed with some of those examination papers in my office at Cave Hill Campus - I received a phone call. It was Vere! She was ringing to find out how I was doing and to tell me that she had managed to survive the ordeal of the Torts exam some days before. She thanked me, once more, for helping her out by taking her to fetch her book at her St Philip home. She added that she had been so touched by what I had done that she had resolved to try to return my kindness in some way. She then, in the middle of our exchange of pleasantries, suddenly and unexpectedly (to me) invited me to come to have some coffee with her at Angela's home. At first, I parried her invitation. That was because I was then up to my ears in exam script marking and had planned to complete a certain quota that day – with my subsidiary focus being on my family's holiday to England, when all my marking was over. After a few more efforts on her part to persuade me to 'take a short break' from my examiner's duties, I managed to convince myself that such a brief interruption would be good for me and also refresh me to return to the fray with more enthusiasm afterwards.

Accordingly, a few minutes after my call with Vere ended, I found myself driving down from Cave Hill and on towards Bridgetown - in order to get to the far side of the capital, near the Garrison Savannah Racecourse. When I reached Angela's home nearby and knocked on the door, it was opened by Vere. She was standing there in a yellow one-piece swimming suit! Although, we did start our time together that morning by having the offered coffee together in the living room of Angela's home – Angela and her family being nowhere to be seen at the time – alas, it did not stop there. As Vere was quick to tell me after I had entered her friend's home, her swimsuit 'felt like a second skin'. And during the coffee, even that second skin was discarded when we repaired to another chamber nearby – which was, presumably, Angela's bedroom. The rest, as they say, is history – and for the first time in my married life, I broke my vow of faithfulness to Philomena!

*Chapter 20*

# A Family Holiday in England (and Continental Europe) – Midsummer 1981

After the said fateful day on which my assessment of examination scripts was so critically interrupted, I did not see Vere again for the rest of the summer. That was because, soon afterwards, I had completed all my marking, the Law Faculty Board of Examiners had met at Cave Hill, and it was time for my family and myself to take our first long-haul flight since we had arrived in Barbados some two summers before. Philomena and myself had booked a British Airways flight to take us, and our three children, to London in order to enable us to visit our respective families not far from there in Swindon, Wiltshire. Naturally, I was still reeling inside from what had occurred between myself and Vere prior to our departure. However, even without telling Philomena about the matter, I had resolved to immerse myself into our marriage with greater intensity for the future. In making such a resolution, I confidently imagined that it would be buttressed by our regular ME meetings with Father Pat, David and Margaret Wilson, Wendell and Irma Lawrence, and the others in our group - once Philomena and I had returned to Barbados after our holidays. The six weeks or so that we would be spending in Europe would, I managed to persuade myself, be enough to get Vere out of my system.

And so it started to prove. With no contact at all with my former Law of Torts student, I threw myself into my family's holiday to the full. We were met at London's Heathrow Airport by the elder of Philomena's two younger brothers, John – whom we had hosted in Barbados just the year before, along with his girlfriend, Jane. There was neither of our children's two grandmothers in sight at that stage, since John's car was only a five-seater and, with him as driver, he needed to accommodate two more adults (Philomena and myself) and our three small children. With our accompanying baggage, we all somehow managed to squeeze into John's 'Ford Fiesta' and the vehicle was soon making its way, with us all, westwards along the M4 motorway which connects London to South Wales. I can still remember marvelling at how green, and full of trees in their tremendous summer foliage, the English countryside appeared to be in my view. I had only been away for two years or so, but I realised, during that journey, that I had missed my former adopted country – the one in which I had grown up from the age of 8 years, after first arriving there from my native Montserrat nearly two decades before.[53]

Our family of five had already arranged to stay at the home of 'Mrs Harrison' –

Philomena's mother - in the 'Southbrook' district of Swindon. It was in that Wiltshire town that Philomena and myself had grown up, had gone to school together and had subsequently married some five years before – as described in *Swimming without mangoes* (2013)[54] and *Fledging and Learning to Fly* (2017),[55] respectively. My own widowed mother, 'Margaret', still lived in the town at that time – along with my own younger brothers, John and George, and our younger sister, Sylvia. Given the fact, however, that our daughter, Claire-Louise, was still only about six months old at the time, it had seemed to Philomena and myself that staying with her mother, and our little girl's maternal grandmother, was the right way to play things. Nevertheless, during the first few days after our arrival in Swindon, our holidaying 'fivesome' from Barbados made regular visits to my own mother's home in Alexandra Road near the town's railway station. For both grandmothers, however, our arrival in the former hometown of Philomena and myself would have brought great joy since it would have been the first time that either of them would have been meeting their first, and only, granddaughter! Moreover, although the grandmothers had known both of their only grandsons Noel and Kim, prior to our family's departure for Barbados in the summer of 1979, Kim had only been six weeks old at that time and was, by the time of our return, already over two years old - and Noel himself was going on four by then. Major changes in both boys would, thus, have been easily perceivable by both grannies since they had last seen their grandsons.

I had plans, moreover, to allow my mother-in-law, at least, to get much better acquainted with all three of her grandchildren during our holiday. I, thus, hoped that deploying them would make up, in some way, for my being responsible for depriving her of the physical contact with those very close relations of hers, as well as her only daughter, during the two years we had been away in Barbados. That project involved me leaving Philomena and our children alone with Mrs Harrison - for a week or so - whilst I travelled to Continental Europe during that time. That was, naturally, on the basis that Philomena would take the children to also visit my mother in Alexandra Road, from time to time, during my absence.

And how did the opportunity to travel to Europe arise, it may well be asked? That had been as a result of the fact that, shortly before I had left Barbados, I had attended, on behalf of UWI, a conference on the island hosted by the 'World Intellectual Property Organisation' - or 'WIPO' – which was based in 'Geneva, Switzerland'. That body dealt with such matters as trade marks, copyright and patent rights (which matters are generally included in the area of Law called, or dealing with, 'Intellectual Property'). During the conference, I got to know one member of the WIPO team quite well and, through him, I was to receive an invitation to another such convention, in Geneva itself, for teachers of Intellectual Property – which was to take place shortly after our arrival in England in mid-July. Moreover, the WIPO member in question offered to get his organisation to pay for my hotel expenses in Geneva during the conference period – and, possibly, also my travel expenses from London.

As luck would have it, upon my arrival back in Swindon I had quickly met up again with my old travelling companion in Continental Europe from 1973 - where we had journeyed, by train, through Scandinavia and Finland - and I had told him about my invitation to Switzerland for the WIPO conference. That friend was 'Raffaele Finelli', my 'Inter-Rail' partner from nearly 10 years before with whom I had shared many adventures as detailed in *Fledging and Learning to Fly*.[56] To my surprise and delight, Raffaele was keen to come to Geneva with me - as he told me that he had a friend from nearby 'Sion' with whom he would be able to stay whilst I was attending my conference. By what means, however, were the two of us going to get to Switzerland together? Inter-Rail once more, perhaps? In a somewhat similar spirit of adventure between us – as well as nostalgia for our 1973 exploits - we decided to hitchhike!

*Fig. 43: Photos showing Raffaele – he with the long, black, hair on the right of the group – in Salzgitter, West Germany in the summer of 1973 – together with Hupsi Pfeiffer, Berndt Schuhmacher, Moni Lork (as she then was) and the Author (per the photo at the top left). The photos were taken at Hupsi's home – who was always one for an impromptu party – at the end of the Inter-Rail tour by Raffaele and the Author around Scandinavia and Finland*

I am pretty sure that we did not tell Philomena, or either of the two Swindon grandmothers, that Raffaele and myself were going to try to reach Switzerland by the use of our thumbs. Rather, I would have let them all assume that, as in 1973, my old Swindon pal and I were going to travel to Europe by train. Be that as it may, however, it was easy enough for the two of us to get, by bus, to the start of the M4 motorway from Swindon to London, at the Junction 15. It was also straightforward to get our first lift to the English capital – all the way to the end of the motorway near 'Chiswick' in its western suburbs. We then took underground trains to get ourselves across London to the south-eastern area thereof – and specifically to 'New Cross Gate'. That station was near the A2 main road - which latter led on to the M2 motorway and, eventually, to 'Dover' in the county of 'Kent', from where we should have been able to catch a ferry to France. And, once more, Raffaele and I found it relatively easy-going to get lifts – as far as 'Canterbury', where we decided to have a break in order to go to seek out some food somewhere in the centre of that city.

After that 'refuelling stop', a wonderful thing occurred - as we were trying to make our way back to the A2 main road from Canterbury to Dover. We happened to be passing a car park in the city when Raffaele spotted inside it a vehicle sporting Italian number plates. The driver seemed to be tidying up inside the car at that moment and Raffaele, in his usual sociable way, started a conversation, in Italian, with the young man in question. To my delight, after a minute or two, Raffaele broke off from his Italian banter and turned to me with the news that the driver was travelling alone – all the way back to Italy, after having just made a driving holiday to England. Immediately, I asked Raffaele to execute what must have been on my old friend's mind also. That was to ask the young man, whom I shall call 'Mauro' for these purposes, whether he would be willing to take the two of us hitchhikers with him, as far as Switzerland. After not much more than a moment's thought, Mauro agreed to do so – perhaps prompted a little by my offer to pay for some of his petrol expenses along the way.

Accordingly, what may have seemed like a very hazardous enterprise of hitchhiking all the way from Swindon to Geneva, in fact turned into a relatively straightforward 'excursion'. Since Mauro had already bought his return ferry ticket for himself and his vehicle to cross the English Channel from Dover to Calais in France, his change of plans only required Raffaele and myself to buy our own tickets in order to make the sailing with him and his car. Apart from that major expense to Mauro's unexpected passengers, it was easy going thereafter as the three of us travelled south-eastwards through France, from Calais, towards Switzerland. We, thus, avoided Paris altogether and spent the night sleeping in the car, south of the French capital in the city of 'Orleans'. Moreover, we took dinner before we settled down for the night, for which I would have taken it on myself to pay for Mauro's meal – and Raffaele's also – so happy would I have been to be back 'on the road' again, and travelling through Continental Europe, as per my former student days from not so many years before.

The next day, however, saw us reach the final destination of myself only – namely,

Geneva. *En route*, however, Raffaele had discussed with Mauro the possibility of the former being driven onwards to Sion - so that my pal could spend time with his old Italian friend there, whilst I was attending my conference. True to form, Mauro also readily agreed to that suggestion. In any case, the bait for Mauro had been that Raffaele would ensure that our kind driver would be able to stay at least one night in Sion, with Raffaele at his friend's house, in order to recover a little from the long drive we had all just made through France. It then only remained for Raffaele and myself to agree a time and place where we two would meet up again, after my conference, to start our return journey home. That was straightforward enough as far as the 'place' was concerned – namely, the 'Hotel Bristol' where I had been booked for the duration of the forthcoming event. As my stay there was for the three days that the convention would last, my pal and I agreed to meet in four days' time, at 12 noon, in the lobby of the hotel in question. The major contingency, therefore, was whether Raffaele would be able to successfully get back from Sion by that agreed time – when hitchhiking alone. I gave him some comfort by simply telling him to do his best to meet the rendezvous time slot, and that I would simply wait at the hotel for him on the agreed day - in the reception area, and for as long as was necessary.

*Fig. 44: Postcard of Geneva, Switzerland – showing 'Lake Geneva' and the 'Jet d'Eau' – as sent by the Author to his matrimonial family back in Swindon, Wiltshire, England, on 15th July 1981, whilst in that beautiful city for a conference at the World Intellectual Property Organisation ('WIPO') – one of the specialised agencies of the United Nations ('UN')*

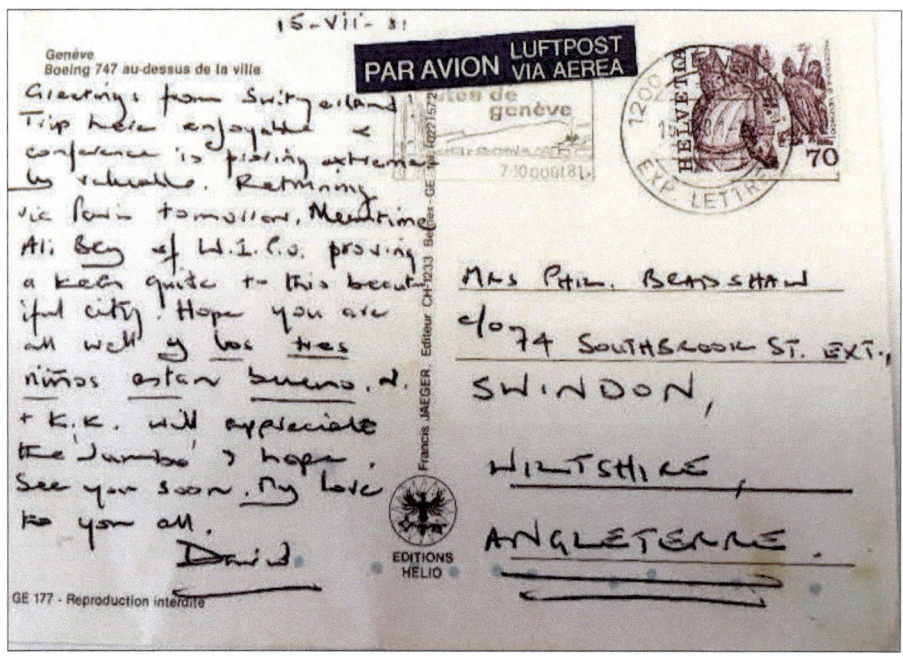

*Fig. 45: The reverse side of the postcard of Geneva, Switzerland – the front side of which shows 'Lake Geneva' and the 'Jet d'Eau' – as sent by the Author to his matrimonial family back in Swindon, Wiltshire, England, on 15th July 1981, whilst in that beautiful city for a conference at the World Intellectual Property Organisation ('WIPO') – one of the specialised agencies of the United Nations ('UN'). Part of the message on the card is an attempt, by the Author, to write in Spanish – a language that he knew his mother-in-law, Mrs Harrison, with whom Philomena and their children were staying at the time, could not understand whereas Philomena, who had been an au pair in Valencia, Spain, in the summer of 1973, could.*

Having thanked Mauro profusely for the lift to Switzerland – both on behalf of myself and Raffaele – I said goodbye to my travelling companions of the past few days and found myself in a very nice hotel in the centre of a city which I was visiting for the first time. As WIPO was paying for my stay in that city, I mentally urged myself on to have some fun – since the whole Swiss enterprise for me was that it was part of my holidays that summer. I was, at that time, free from my relatively arduous teaching duties in Barbados - and even from my domestic fatherly ones for a while - and I simply had to make the best of such a respite. Accordingly, having checked into my room, the first thing that I wanted to do was to go out to have a walk around the city in order to get a 'feel' of it and find my bearings. When I began that adventure, what struck me immediately was the lovely situation of my hotel. It was right outside a huge lake containing a magnificent, and very high, water spray (or fountain) situated about half way across its width from my viewpoint. I was to learn that the expanse of water in question was officially known as 'Lac Leman', though it was often popularly just called 'Lake Geneva', and that the constant stream of water in question was called *'Jet d'Eau'* in French.

And what a thrill it was for me just to walk alongside the lake next to my hotel. The air was wonderful, the sun was shining, the local inhabitants whom I was passing seemed happy, and not only could I see the vast expanse of water to the side of me but I was also able to get a view of the snow-capped mountains of the 'Alps' beyond. What a beautiful city, I thought to myself. I just had to send my wife and family a postcard from it - to let them know that I had safely arrived there and was finding the place to be even better than I had anticipated. Fortunately, I found the perfect postcard quite quickly - in one of the kiosks near the lakeside. It contained a colour photo of a 'Swissair' Jumbo Jet in the skies above Lake Geneva and its main city – and even included the huge water spout to which my attention had first been drawn. I wrote effusively about the city on the back of the card, and asked after them all, and sent them all my love. Having completed that major step of communicating with Philomena and the children, I repaired to my fine room at the Hotel Bristol to relax and then have some dinner in preparation for the immediate days ahead.

When the next morning arrived, I found myself somewhat anxious. That was because, in a sense, I did not feel that I was properly qualified to attend the conference in question. As stated, I had been asked to attend owing to the acquaintanceship which I had struck up with a certain WIPO official. He had come to Barbados, earlier in the year, to give a basic introduction on Intellectual Property to that island's government officials , academics, and other relevant persons whose work brought them into contact with that area of the Law. As far as I remember, I had been the only member of the Law Faculty at Cave Hill who had been interested enough to want to attend. The WIPO official in question – let us call him 'Jay', for such (as far as I remember) was indeed his Christian name - perhaps had taken a liking to me for showing such thirst for knowledge regarding the legal area in question. And it was a result of Jay's positivity towards me that he had subsequently invited me to participate at the WIPO's convention in question – the first-ever meeting of 'ATRIP'. Those letters stood for 'Association of Teachers & Researchers in Intellectual Property'. I was certainly not a teacher of the specialist area of Law in question. Nor could I call myself a 'researcher' in the subject, though I had once been especially interested in Trade Mark Law. Indeed, earlier in the year, I had even given some feedback to government officials in Barbados on that country's draft Act of Parliament, or 'Bill', in that particular legal area. Nevertheless, I was a real novice in the general legal area of Intellectual Property and, thus, I worried that I would feel that I did not truly belong alongside many real 'experts' - who were bound to be attending the convention in question.

And so it proved. Though I had brought at least one suit, as well as some shirts and ties with me for the trip. I did so in a small suitcase - despite the hitchhiking enterprise upon which I had just recently engaged in with Raffaele. However, although I had been suitably dressed, and looked the part, on the first morning of the convention, I did feel somewhat like a 'fish out of water' from the outset. Fortunately, for me, I did not have to take an active role in any of the sessions in question and I was happy enough to go along with all the coffee, lunch and other breaks which took place during the day, as well as listen to papers given by some of the experts – mainly in English as I recall – from Scandinavia, Germany and other countries around Europe. It was also good to meet up with Jay again and be able to thank him for inviting me to the event, as well as for arranging my stay at Hotel Bristol.

And even though there must also have been representatives from some non-European territories, I am pretty sure that I was the only one from any of the Caribbean ones (whether English-speaking or otherwise). Perhaps the hardest part of the day for me, therefore, was my having to ward off curious questions from some of the other participants, with whom I rubbed shoulders during the breaks, about my speciality in Intellectual Property. To such curiosity, I merely had to be honest and answer that though I was an academic lawyer at the University of the West Indies in Barbados, I was still very new to the legal area in question but was at the conference to deepen my interest in it for future work thereon when I returned to my university.

Accordingly, I was able to survive all three days of the inaugural ATRIP meeting in question, by my thus taking very much of a background role throughout the proceedings. The most mortifying part for me, however, was when each of the invitees to the proceedings was asked, during the last session of the final day, to come up, one by one, to sign the charter establishing ATRIP as an official division of WIPO. That had been done in front of the Head of WIPO – one of the top officials in the entire United Nations organisation! I did as I had been bidden, however, but I had felt most uncomfortable about doing so – given my very little learning in the area of Law in question.

Be that as it may, I managed to survive the 'official' part of my coming to Switzerland that summer. And before I knew it, it was time to think about returning to my family back in Wiltshire, England. On my last morning at the Hotel Bristol, I had my breakfast as usual and then decided to have one final walk by Lac Leman to view its massive fountain and mountains beyond. Whilst doing so, I was preoccupied with thoughts of how well, or otherwise, Raffaele might have been doing on his proposed journey back from Sion to Geneva and whether he was having any luck in that enterprise. That was particularly because I knew that he would have been trying to hitchhike as a sole male – and that, in my experience, it was always easier to get lifts with a pretty girl alongside leading the venture with her thumbs. I need not have worried, however. For, by the time that I had returned from my walk, my old pal was already there in the lobby of my hotel – waiting for me with a broad smile on his face! He was quick to tell me that he had encountered very little problem in getting there from Sion and, indeed, had managed to achieve that with just one lift. Consequently, I was then able to promptly check out of my room and, soon afterwards, the two of us were on our way, by bus, to the outskirts of the city to begin our return hitchhike mission back to Swindon.

Whilst I can recall the journey from Canterbury to Geneva fairly easily, it is otherwise in relation to the return to England. It must have been uneventful however, despite involving a series of lifts to get us over the border from Switzerland into France – and then north-westwards to the Channel port of Calais. Nonetheless, I am pretty sure that, once more, the two of us avoided going via Paris – for fear of becoming stuck there, or having to cross that huge city by costly public transport in order to get to the other side to enable us to continue with our hitchhiking journey. At any rate, the two of us did arrive back in Swindon within two days of leaving Geneva. And, for the second time in my life, a major European adventure with my old friend, and former neighbour in that Wiltshire town of my later childhood, had come to an end. That realisation made me rather sad – as I did not know when I would be seeing him again, once I had returned to Barbados at the end of my holidays. Nor, indeed, whether we would ever be able to get up to such an exploit together in our future lives. That air of melancholy, which overcame me, was only broken by the fact of my being reunited with Philomena and our three children. That happened back at her mother's home - on the evening of the return to Swindon of Raffaele and myself.

It might be thought that I should have been content in 'staying put', in one place, with my family – once I had returned from my Swiss adventures. As described in *Fledging and Learning to Fly*[57] however, I had discovered that, when staying with my family at the mother-in-law's home, the best way to avoid confrontations had been not to overstay one's welcome. Or, at least, my welcome! Accordingly, although Philomena and the children had enjoyed a wonderful time with 'Nanna Harrison' whilst I had been away in Switzerland – and probably could have gone on doing so for the remainder of their summer holiday in England 1981 – I had felt, deep down and in advance, that it would not have worked out so happily as long as I was present in the picture too. Accordingly, I had, prior to setting out for England with my family, made plans for an 'exchange of homes' – namely, our Hygeia home in Barbados for one in England. And the other person involved was none other than one of the colleagues whom I had been closest to during my first, somewhat traumatic, year at UWI during the 1979-80 academic year. That person was Peter Morton, who was the Englishman who had been a visiting lecturer at Cave Hill Campus, for that one teaching year only, and who had returned home to his permanent post at the University of Birmingham from the summer of 1980. During the year or so since that time, the two of us had kept in touch by letter. When therefore I had told him that I was planning to come, with my family, to England for the 1981 summer holidays, he had written back to ask whether Philomena and myself would be willing to let him and his partner stay in Hygeia – in exchange for our staying in their home during our time in England. I had gladly accepted that suggestion, though I knew that Philomena would have preferred to have spent all of her holidays based in Swindon – so that her mother, and mine, could see their grandchildren as often as possible during that time. Nevertheless, my wife went along with the plan.

In fact, the arrangement was destined to suit Peter and his partner better than my own family - for they, perhaps, wanted to stay in Barbados and Hygeia for as much as one month during the summer in question. I knew, however, that I had plans to be away in Switzerland, for example, as well as spend a good part of our holiday with the grandparents in Swindon and, thus, would not need Peter's place for one whole month. On behalf of my own family, therefore, I asked only for about two weeks on our side. Moreover, though we were able to offer Peter and his partner the use of our car in Barbados during their stay, neither he nor his partner had one to offer us in return. Despite, the inequality of the arrangement, however, the deal was struck and put into operation. Where exactly, however, did Peter and his partner live at the time? The answer was: a small town, or even large village, somewhere in the middle of England (or the English 'Midlands') called 'Hagley'.

Philomena and I, however, still needed to know the precise location of that rural place – since neither of us had ever heard of Hagley, prior to finalising our plans to holiday with our family in England in that summer of 1981. Peter, however, was to write to us to tell us that it was close to Birmingham – the city of his university – but sufficiently outside that metropolis to be well on the way to another well-known place which also had a cathedral, namely 'Worcester'. That second city made our proposed visit to Hagley all the more attractive - since neither my wife nor myself had ever been there either, and, so, it was definitely on our agenda of places to visit whilst we were based in the home of Peter and his partner.

When it became time for Philomena and myself to make our extensive, but temporary, departure with our children from her mother's home in Swindon for Hagley, predictably Mrs Harrison was not at all happy. Like Philomena, she could not really understand why it was necessary to travel all the way to some small place in the middle of rural 'Worcestershire', for up to a few weeks, when her daughter and grandchildren were all perfectly happy being with her in her comfortable home right there in Wiltshire. Moreover, there were several parks nearby that home, which the children could be taken to, by herself or their parents, from time to time to prevent them from getting bored at her home or otherwise becoming restless. I had to explain to my mother-in-law, more than once, that I had long arranged the house exchange in question with my former colleague at the UWI, Peter, and that my family and I were merely carrying out our part of that arrangement. I argued that Peter and his partner had already taken up residence in our Hygeia home in Barbados, as we were then speaking, and that it would look like a snub to them if my own family had, very belatedly, spurned their kind offer of our going into temporary residence in their own home. Also, that such an insult would be acute as, no doubt - just as we had done at our Barbados home - the two of them would have gone to some trouble to get their home ready (with its 'deep cleaning', changing of bedding, and so on) for us, their temporary guests.

In the end, Philomena's mum reluctantly accepted that we were, indeed, leaving for the Midlands. She may even have accompanied us to Swindon's railway station in order to see us off on our journey to that of 'Birmingham New Street'. Upon arriving at the main railway station in England's second-largest city, I can remember the little difficulty we encountered in making our connection for that of Hagley. As Peter had written to us, his home town or village possessed its own station, but we had to ask at New Street exactly which platform trains for Hagley departed from. In fact, we were to discover that Hagley was situated on the line from New Street to the City of Worcester, and that the relevant train was one which made frequent stops - as it travelled out of Birmingham, into the West Midlands and Worcestershire countryside.

In due course, however, our non-express train arrived at Hagley station. Our family of five were the only passengers to disembark there. The 'halt' was so small that there were certainly no taxis standing outside it - to assist us in reaching the home of Peter and his partner. Fortunately, my former UWI colleague had written to me that the house in question was within walking distance of the station, and had also provided directions on how to reach it. Despite that potential good news, however, and although going on foot might have been straightforward for a Birmingham University Law lecturer who, perhaps, had no more than a briefcase to carry when setting out from Hagley station, doing so was still quite a major challenge for my wife and myself as we had at least two suitcases to carry, as well as Claire-Louise's pram-buggy to push with our daughter lying inside. Nevertheless, the five of members my family eventually reached our destination – if only very slowly, with Philomena doing the pram-buggy pushing and myself carrying the relatively-heavy suitcases.

It is most likely that Peter and his partner had left the keys to their house with one of their immediate neighbours - for us to call for and collect, once we had arrived at our destination. In that way, it would have been somewhat like what Philomena and myself had done for them, in relation to our set for Hygeia and those for our car, back in Barbados – namely, left them with our nearby neighbour (and babysitter from time to time), Mrs Payne.

At any rate, before long after our arrival outside the home of Peter and his partner, my family and I found ourselves within the premises. I breathed a huge sigh of relief on doing so! For, once more, I was master of the home in which my nuclear family and I found ourselves – just as I was back in Barbados. The 'change of scene' had been important to me since I had found that, notwithstanding the kindness of my mother-in-law to my wife, children and myself back in Swindon, I had never been able to fully relax in her home. Rather, I had always felt that I was walking on eggshells – and having to take extra care not to do, or say, anything which might have upset her. Once we were ensconced in our temporary Hagley home, however, I could fully be the 'father of the family', once again.

What kind of home did we find ourselves in at Hagley? It turned out to be nothing too fancy – or large. Just a semi-detached house, with three bedrooms and a bathroom upstairs, and a kitchen and living room below. As far as I was concerned, however, it was a comfortable base, in which I could foresee my family and myself being happy to spend a few weeks. At least, that was as far as the interior of the house was concerned. What my wife and I needed to do, however, was to find our bearings there. And we soon found a working kettle in the kitchen with which to make vital cups of tea, as well as a functioning television in the living room with which to entertain our children whilst we rustled up our first meal in our new base. Thereafter, with the children in tow, we set about exploring the environs beyond the street in which we found ourselves, and even the other side of the railway station at which we had first arrived.

In such initial scouting around the neighbourhood with our offspring, Philomena and I discovered that there was at least one convenience store not too far away from our base. There we would be able to shop for items to make some of the basic meals which we would be having whilst in Hagley. For, not having the luxury of a car, the option of travelling wider afield to, say, Birmingham or Worcester to shop at any of the supermarkets, such as 'Sainsbury's' or 'Tesco', situated in each such city was just not open to us. In straying even further away from our temporary home, however, we discovered a wonderful green space containing a playground where Noel and Kim would be able to let off steam on a regular basis. It also contained an impressive, and old, 'stately home' with extensive grounds. The name of the place was 'Hagley Hall' and it would be to that particular venue that Philomena and myself would find ourselves with our children – at least once a day – throughout the duration of our whole stay in Hagley.

Hagley Hall turned out to be no mere museum, however. Rather, it was occupied by some landed-gentry family or other. Thankfully, the occupants had opened the grounds to members of the public for free – and, thus, my own family and I could go there as often as we wished. We had no desire to enter the Hall itself, however, since the children were quite happy playing on equipment in the playground situated within the precincts of the property, or simply exploring inside the woods on the outskirts of the grounds in the case of Noel and Kim. For me, the most memorable visit we made to the estate in question was that which occurred on the evening of Tuesday, 28th July 1981. For, on that occasion, the powers that be within the Hall gave an extravaganza of lighted torches as well as a musical spectacular. That was for the purpose of celebrating the wedding, the following day, of the heir to the British throne, 'Prince Charles', to his fiancée, 'Lady Diana Spencer'. It had seemed to me that the whole of the small community of Hagley, as well as the residents of the Hall itself, came out to view the grand show that evening - or to participate in the music and other revelry that was put on. For Philomena and myself, it was a wonderful way to prepare our two sons – Claire-Louise being still much too young to be able to understand what was going on around her, and why - for the significance of the huge event that we would be watching, the following day, on the television set located in the front room of our temporary home.

And what a day of non-stop television viewing our family enjoyed that next day in the house of Peter and his partner. I got up earlier than usual to put on the small screen device, as I have always been excited by significant events in the life of the British Royal

Family – and the wedding in question would, perhaps, be the most significant one so far during my adult life (though I could still vaguely remember that of Prince Charles' younger sister, 'Princess Anne', to 'Captain Mark Phillips', which had occurred whilst I had been a student at Kingston Law School in 1973). Having made Philomena her usual cup of tea to get her up a little time later, I then encouraged our two sons to come to join me on the sofa in the living room whilst we watched the coverage of the royal event unfolding on our television screen. That was even to the extent of Philomena and myself exceptionally agreeing to all our family consuming our breakfasts in front of the 'box', instead of at the dining table in the kitchen as usual. I wanted, so far as I could, to pass on the enthusiasm which I had for royalty to my sons also - and to try to get them to understand the great significance of the event which they were about to witness that day. As far as I was concerned, they would not only be learning about what a 'marriage' was. They would also be witnessing, 'live', the nuptials of their future king. For, the bridegroom, Prince Charles, was, we had also told them, the eldest son of their current monarch, Queen Elizabeth II. And they already knew that the latter was the lady whose portrait was on the paper money, and stamps, which they often saw their mother and myself using from time to time - and whom, we had often told them, was the queen of both Barbados and England, among several other places.

At any rate, the boys and their mum stayed the course with me as we watched the proceedings of the Royal Wedding - all day long - in front of the television set in our temporary home. Truth to tell, Philomena had to break away, from time to time, to look after Claire-Louise who still slept a lot in those earliest days of hers. Even whilst my wife was breastfeeding our baby daughter, however, I persuaded her to stay with myself and our sons in order to continue watching the events on the television. I will always remember the exchanges of the marriage vows between the bride and groom, and especially the moment when Lady Diana mixed up the order of her Prince Charles' Christian names when making her own. Perhaps the part which I (and, it seemed, Philomena and our boys) liked the most from the entire wedding day, however, was when the newly-married couple had left the venue of the nuptials at 'St Paul's Cathedral' in London, to drive through the streets of the capital in an open, horse-drawn, carriage back to 'Buckingham Palace'. The streets had been filled with cheering crowds as they had passed along, and such enthusiasm seemed to have transmitted itself to my watching sons – as well as to their mother and myself.

Be as it may, if I had felt rather guilty for keeping my children indoors for most, if not all, of the day of the Royal Wedding to watch the proceedings on television, I soon made up for it by taking the whole family on a major outing – the very next day. That had been by train to the City of Worcester – which was in the same county as that where we were then based, but still further to the west of Birmingham. For some reason, the latter city – England's second biggest after London - just did not enthuse me as a place for my wishing to take the children for a fun day out. Perhaps, that had been because I had envisaged that it would have been quite difficult getting around with them (including having to push Claire-Louise in her pram-buggy from place to place). Worcester, on the other hand, sounded to me like a nicer, and smaller, location in which we would be able to explore as a family much more easily.

And so it proved. The train journey from Hagley's little station was not too long and Noel and Kim seemed to enjoy it as much as I did. If memory serves, it was then just a short walk from the terminus in Worcester to the major point of interest in the city – namely, the Cathedral - and that was where we headed first. Within the precincts of that impressive piece of architecture, we spent, perhaps, a good hour or more. During that time, my sons and I compared some of what we were witnessing in the flesh, with aspects of what we had seen of St Paul's in London on the television, in the course of the Royal Wedding, only the day before. The other place, where I very much wanted to spend time with the children, was the riverside nearby. Accordingly, we all repaired to that location for our picnic lunch soon after our cathedral visit. We found the 'River Severn' to be full of waterfowl, especially swans which all our children seemed to be particularly attracted to, and we spent several happy hours in its vicinity. Feeding the birds seem to give the children a great deal of pleasure. And, even after we had run out of fodder, we were able to spend time playing with all three of them on the swings, in the park, near one of the banks of the river. We ended our day out by doing a little shopping in one of the city's several supermarkets. That was in order for Philomena and myself to buy the children some treats - of a kind which were unobtainable in our little store in Hagley - to take back to our temporary home with us.

In such ways, therefore, we passed our days in the West Midlands in the summer of 1981 – quietly and routinely, with the Royal Wedding and our day-trip to Worcester being the highlight of our sojourn in that region. There came a time, however, when – with about three to four weeks of our holiday remaining before we had to return to Barbados - Philomena and myself had to make a major decision about how we were going to spend the latter part of our European holiday that summer. If truth be known, my wife would really have much preferred to have gone straight back to Swindon to do so with her mum at the latter's home (intermixed with day visits by our family to that of my own mum's in Alexandra Road). I, however, had developed a liking for not having to 'tread on eggshells', whilst in Swindon. Rather, I had been attracted by another option which had been presented to us by one of the former flatmates of Philomena and myself - whilst we had all been students in the London area during the early to mid-1970s. That other person was named 'Mrs Cathy Bannister' – and she was then living in 'Chesterfield, Derbyshire'. That town was located just one or two counties farther north from the Worcestershire borderlands of Hagley where our family was then situated. Accordingly, I argued to my wife that, as 'we five' were already so far north from Swindon in Wiltshire, we should take up Cathy's invitation and travel, by train, to stay with her in Derbyshire for a further week or so – prior to our returning to her mother's home once more.

As detailed in *Fledging and Learning to Fly*,[58] in our student house at 38 Avenue

Road, Highgate, London, N6, Cathy shared her room with her boyfriend, and future husband, 'Richard Bannister' – a fellow undergraduate. Philomena and myself shared flat number 4 within the same house and, in due course, we had invited both Cathy and Richard, among other students in the dwelling, to our wedding in Swindon in the summer of 1976. In return, and whilst I had been a student at Cambridge University doing postgraduate legal studies after our wedding, Cathy and Richard had invited my wife and myself to their own marriage in later 1976. Alas, that latter union was not to last many years and, by the time that my family had returned to England for our holidays in the 1981 summer in question, Cathy and Richard were already living apart – if not actually divorced. Cathy, however, had stayed on in their former marital home in Chesterfield, which is why she possessed enough room to be able to host us there – and Philomena and myself had kept in touch with her, by letter, after her separation from Richard. Moreover, it seemed to me that one of the strong incentives which she had, for inviting us to come and stay with her that summer, was her wish to ask us to return the favour by our offering her the chance to come and stay with us at our own home in Barbados at sometime in the future.

At any rate, after perhaps a little earnest discussion between Philomena and myself, she eventually agreed with my view that we should, indeed, continue further north to Chesterfield, after our two weeks or so in Hagley had drawn to their end. I am pretty sure that we could have stayed on longer in the West Midlands – since Peter, living with his partner in our home in Barbados, was (like me) also an academic and, thus, had no need, ordinarily, to return to his university until shortly before the start of the new teaching year in October. Nevertheless, I was mindful that our own time in England was about half way through – given that my family and myself had fixed dates on our British Airways tickets for our return to Barbados flights – and my children, my wife and myself had more or less seen all the attractions in Hagley and its immediate environs. After our fortnight or so in that middle of England area, therefore, it was more than time enough to move on for some newer stimulation.

Neither Philomena nor myself had spent more than a fleeting time in Chesterfield before and, thus, going there, to meet up and sojourn for a while with Cathy, would be an adventure - not only for our children but also for their parents. My wife and I had passed through that town once before, for Cathy and Richard's wedding – and the nuptial ceremony might even have taken place in a church located within the boundaries of the town. What was more memorable to me, however, had been the reception afterwards. That had taken place in a little mining village some distance away from Chesterfield - near 'Bolsover Castle' - where Cathy's parents still lived and where she had been brought up, if not also the place where she had been born. Moreover, although we had not spent the night in that village, we had done so in a town – situated about halfway between Chesterfield and 'Sheffield' - called 'Dronfield'. Richard's brother and his wife lived in Dronfield and would put us up for the wedding night in question.

Accordingly, despite the earlier visit to the area by Philomena and myself for the marriage in question, the two of us had spent very little time in Chesterfield itself. Effectively, therefore, the town would be a new place for the two of us (as well as for our children, of course). As arranged in advance with Cathy – by exchanges of letter and then a phone call or two – my family and I reversed our train journey of a few weeks before and got ourselves back to Birmingham New Street on a slow train from Hagley Station. At New Street, I bought single tickets for the family - and it is even possible that all of the children were still too young for any of them to have had to pay for a child's ticket - to travel on to Chesterfield Station. Having done so, I phoned Cathy to let her know what train we were about to catch and its time of arrival in her home town - so that she could meet us as we disembarked. At any rate, I was delighted to see her waiting for us - on the platform at Chesterfield - as Philomena, myself and our children exited our train from Birmingham, more or less at the time I had given to our forthcoming hostess over the phone earlier that day.

For the first time since we had left Philomena's mum in Swindon, we had a car to rely on thanks to Cathy. Accordingly, we were soon all packed into her vehicle outside the station and happily driving to her house soon afterwards - as Philomena and myself excitedly exchanged chatter with our former student friend about what we had each been up to since we had last met up at the wedding of herself and Richard a few years before.

I can no longer recall everything that we all did to pass our week or so with Cathy in Chesterfield but one of the highlights, very early into our visit – and, perhaps, even on our very first full day – would have been to the most famous attraction in the town. That was to the 'Church with the crooked spire'. It was an architectural wonder – which could be seen from miles around, since the spire was a rather high one. The proper name of the building was in fact 'St Mary and All Saints' but everyone inside the town, and beyond, seemed to know it by its unofficial name in which the word 'crooked' featured prominently. We first had a very good look, from the outside, at the oddity of the spire. During our visit within the church, we heard several 'myths' of why that highest part of the building was shaped so peculiarly. Perhaps, the one which seemed to be most plausible, to me, had to do with the lead tiles which covered the apex of the building and which heated up, in sunlight, more on one side than the other – with the hotter side tending to 'pull' the cooler side away from its original, 'straight-up', position. Such an explanation might not have meant much to my young sons, but I am pretty sure that they felt happy to be visiting the town's greatest building – perhaps, nearly as much as buying, and eating, some fruit in the market nearby afterwards.

Another of our memorable outings with Cathy, during our week or so with her in Derbyshire, was to a village or small town outside Chesterfield that was famous for a type of cake originally produced there. The name of that particular place was 'Bakewell' and it had given its name to a tart which had been invented there. It had been Cathy's idea that we should visit that smaller municipality - not only to get us outside her home town in order to enjoy the Derbyshire countryside in which Bakewell was located but also to treat the children to some of the product for which that small community was most famous. Philomena and myself were not to be disappointed with the change of scenery rationale for our outing – given the gentle hills and expanses of water which surrounded Bakewell. And Noel and Kim, in particular, seemed delighted with their respective individual slices of the famous tart in question when we all eventually repaired to a tea shop to reward ourselves with several of them during that particular day out. Unlike the small and round 'tart' (with 'a cherry on the top') which one could purchase in many an English supermarket, the 'original version', which my family and I were able to sample that day, was larger and flatter – and had no fruit surmounting it. Moreover, it seemed to me to be a vastly superior and tastier product.

The highlight of our stay with Cathy in Derbyshire, however, must surely have been the visit our family made with her, in her car, to 'Chatsworth House'. That particular place was the vast estate of the 'Duke and Duchess of Devonshire'. It is especially memorable for me because there were lots of things to be found there to entertain our children – in addition to the general beautiful situation of the stately home and its surroundings. For example, there were several different species of farm animals, such as baby goats and chickens, for our sons (and even their baby sister) to see and interact with. Also, a play park which contained, in addition to the usual swings, slides and the like, miniature vehicles such as tractors which they could pedal on by themselves. Noel and Kim, especially, had a wonderful day out, accordingly – even if they (and Claire-Louise) had to put up with the grown-ups going inside the great house to look at the paintings, furniture and other artefacts on show there, for part of their outing.

After a week or so of such excursions in Chesterfield itself and the surrounding Derbyshire countryside, it had seemed to Philomena and myself that we had to avoid overstaying our welcome with Cathy. Accordingly, even I had to accept that, by then, it was high time for my family and myself to return to spend some more time with our children's grandmothers in Swindon – and to rebase ourselves, specifically, at the home of my mother-in-law, Mrs Harrison. We set out to do so, however, only after having arranged with Cathy for her to come and stay with us, soon after our forthcoming return to Barbados, and after our having thanked her, profusely, for giving us such a wonderful time in her native county and her then current home town. Once more, therefore, we bought single tickets for our family to travel, as a unit, on the train – all the way from Chesterfield to Swindon on that latest occasion, with changes at Birmingham New Street and 'Gloucester' stations *en route*.

Both sets of grandmothers would have been delighted to have had their grandchildren back in their home town after our three weeks or so away in the Midlands and then Derbyshire. Once more, however, after the freedom of being able to fully experience myself as 'father of the family', especially whilst in our temporary home in Hagley, I was not altogether happy about having to mind 'stepping on eggshells', once more, whilst under the shelter of my mother-in-law. Accordingly, after a few more days, I finalised plans to do something that was a compromise of my trying to keep Philomena and her mother happy for the remainder of our stay whilst, at the same time, keeping me in that state also. And even though such a step would, nevertheless, involve some 'family travelling' once again, on that latest occasion the participants would only be myself and one other member of my immediate family - namely, my elder son, Noel!

Such a potential further side trip had been in the pipeline for some time. For, even whilst planning our family's visit to Europe from Barbados that summer, I had been in regular touch with my long-time penfriend, Berndt Schuhmacher and his wife, Monika (or Moni), in West Germany, to let them know about our forthcoming travels. As seen, that couple, their first child (and my goddaughter), Miriam, and Berndt's long-time best male friend, Hubert (Hupsi) Pfeiffer, had visited us in Barbados in the month of May the previous year, and we had celebrated Miriam's first birthday whilst they had been with us. Our West German friends would have been disappointed, therefore, when I had written to Berndt to inform them all that Philomena and myself had decided not to return to Europe for our summer holidays of 1980, but had instead decided to travel elsewhere in the Caribbean region for that particular long vacation. Accordingly, there was just no way that I could disappoint our West German friends, one year later, by not making an effort to travel over from England, to the Continent, to see them. At the same time, I had been extremely mindful of the fact that I had been the cause of taking Philomena and our children away from her mother for a large proportion of our English holidays that summer of 1981, and it, thus, did not feel right for me to try to persuade her to leave her mum's home, yet again, to travel to West Germany.

A compromise answer, therefore, seemed to be for me to travel to our family's West German friends without Philomena - and to leave her and our children to stay on, in Swindon with her mother, and with the possibility of them making several visits to my own mum in Alexandra Road during my absence. The only issue, then, was the need for Philomena's agreement to my taking our eldest child, Noel, along with me for the Continental adventure. As our elder son was then going on four years old, it seemed to my wife and myself that he would also get a lot of 'education' out of a trip to West Germany to visit our friends in that country – and even Philomena's mother seemed to agree with that point of view. Younger brother, Kim, really wanting to come along on the trip also, might have caused a potential difficulty. His being only two years old at the time, however, meant that his mum and myself could easily placate him with promises of lots of fun with Nanna Harrison, his mum and baby sister (during the absence of Noel and myself) on days out to places like 'Bristol Zoo' to see lions, tigers and other wild animals – as well as visits to 'Nanny Bradshaw's' home in Alexandra Road for ice cream, sweets and other treats that he liked to receive from her.

And so, with just one phone call to Berndt and Moni - then living in a small village named 'Gerlingen' near the city of 'Siegen', some 100 kilometres or so to the east of 'Cologne' – everything was in place for the trip of Noel and myself to the Continent. It would, of course, be my second trip to the European mainland that summer – after my hitchhiking one with my old Swindon friend, Raffaele, for my conference in Switzerland about a month earlier. On that second occasion, however, with my elder son in my special care, I was not going to take the risk on relying merely on my thumb. Rather, the two of us would be travelling by train.

Exactly how had I arranged the tickets for Noel and myself to use the railway to get to West Germany? I am pretty sure that I would not simply have turned up with my son at Swindon station and tried to ask for a return to Siegen. Rather, it is more likely, that I would just have asked for such a return only to 'London Paddington'. In the English capital, I would then have taken Noel and myself on the underground to 'Victoria Station'. At the 'Transalpino' office nearby, I would then have purchased a specially-discounted-price ticket for the West German city in question. For, I would have recalled, from my student days in England, that Transalpino used to issue such cut-price tickets for 'young people' in general, and for students in particular. And, though by then, I was going on 29 years of age, I would still have been able to purchase such a ticket for my intended journey to the Continent – even if I would have had to pay a little extra for no longer being 'under 26'. To the best of my memory also, since Noel was still only three years old, he would have been able to travel with me on my proposed train trip to Europe entirely for free.

My memory about purchasing my Transalpino ticket to Siegen most likely serves me well, since I can recall buying - in 'Buckingham Palace Road' near Victoria Station and the ticket office in question - lots of 'Charles and Diana Royal Wedding' souvenirs, for Noel and myself to take with us to West Germany to give to Berndt, Moni and their family as presents upon our first arrival with them. Moreover, as we were already in the Victoria station area, after buying the ticket for the return trip to the Continent, we would have started our onward journey to Dover from that very station. I also remember having to change at Canterbury station for the connection to Dover – and taking a little break with Noel in that Kent cathedral city prior to catching our onward train to the coastal terminus. It was in Canterbury that I can distinctly recall, for example, Noel and myself playing together on part of the walls surrounding that city and his running away from me, laughing, and shouting 'I don't like Venezuela!'. Clearly, he was remembering the earlier time, in December 1980, when he had also travelled alone with me to a foreign country for the first time. That was to the South American one which he was laughing about, and in which the two of us had found ourselves at the time when John Lennon had been shot and killed in New York City.

If my elder son really had not liked his visit with me to Venezuela in 1980, that was news to me that particular evening. I rather think that the truth was more that he was already developing his nascent sense of humour and was merely trying to tease me. In any event, I was determined to ensure that I gave him lots of things to 'like' - on what would be only his second ever trip to West Germany. The first had been during the 'mini farewell tour of Europe', which his mother and I had made with him, by car, in May 1979 in order to say '*auf Wiedersehen*' to Berndt, Moni and their families, prior to our emigration to Barbados later in the summer of that year. That had entailed a journey which is detailed in *Fledging and Learning to Fly*.[59]

The first part of the things for Noel to 'like' would be the treat that consisted of his going on his very first ferry ride to Continental Europe - after the two of us had safely disembarked from our onward connecting train from Canterbury to Dover. That boat trip would have been a 'first' for him because, in 1979, our crossing of the English Channel – in our hired car, and with Philomena still pregnant with our second child, the future Kristian Kim – had been inside a vehicle called a 'hovercraft'. As suggested by its name, that vessel had hovered above, and had never in fact entered, the sea - during our then maritime journey from 'Ramsgate', in England, to Calais in France.

On our later crossing of the Channel during that summer of 1981, my son and I journeyed on a ferry from Dover to 'Ostend' in Belgium. It must have left somewhat close to midnight as we only arrived, after a slow crossing, in the Belgian port very early next morning. And then, feasting on sandwiches and other 'goodies' which Philomena had packed to sustain us during the earliest part of our voyage, our Continental train adventure soon began in earnest. During our journey from Ostend to 'Brussels', I pointed out to my son the very flat countryside which we passed along. For, it was so different from the hilly ones which, by then, he would have become used to seeing - even from our relatively short period of staying in Swindon during his summer vacation, thus far. I also brought to his attention the chubby-looking Belgian cows in the fields - which we could spot, from time to time, as we sped along our way eastward. For, again, they were quite a contrast to their leaner counterparts which he would have seen, in England, as recently as during our trip to the farm at Chatsworth House in Derbyshire a week or so before. Perhaps, I told him, the Belgian ones were being reared for meat and therefore needed to be as fat as possible - whilst the ones we had usually seen in England (or even in the Barbados countryside) were being farmed mainly to provide milk.

At any rate, before long, our train had taken us beyond Brussels and was continuing further east past 'Liège', I explained to Noel that the country, which we were then passing through, was divided into two different parts – the 'Flemish'-speaking part where we had started our journey that morning in Ostend, and the French-speaking one where we were then located. I then explained to him that we were soon about to enter another new country, where the people spoke a third language that was new for him – namely, German. And as soon as we were over the border and making our first major stop in the 'City of Aachen', I began to teach my son some basic words of that new language - so that he could surprise our hosts, once we had arrived with them later that day.

Noel and myself had to change trains in the City of Cologne. To give both of us a break from our constant train travel that day, I avoided our getting on the first onward connection to Siegen and, instead, made a note of when the one after that was leaving. By doing so, my son and I had some time in which to make the short walk from the main station to the nearby '*Dom*', or cathedral. That was in order for us to have a short visit to what is, arguably, *the* major attraction in Cologne – and, certainly, one of that city's, if not the whole of West Germany's, most famous (and most visited) landmarks.

Having had a good look at that holy place, both within and without - and after my having pointed out to my son just how black the building was on its outside - we returned to Cologne's main station to continue with the final part of our journey. That was not before I had telephoned with Moni at her home, however, to let her know what train we were about to catch and its arrival time in Siegen. That call would have given her the opportunity to inform her husband, Berndt, at his office to enable him to meet Noel and myself at that city's station at the end of his working day. It was a relatively short trip onwards from Cologne to Siegen and, true to form, Berndt, his wife, and their daughter (my goddaughter) Miriam, were all there, with their car, to meet us off our train.

Be that as it may, it might be imagined how well my long-term penfriend of some 10 years, and his family, gave Noel and myself the warmest of welcomes at their new home. That was situated in the village of Gerlingen – about 20 minutes' drive from the latest city of our arrival. In arriving in Gerlingen, Noel and myself were introduced to our hosts' new house in 'Hallerbergstrasse' - which they had arranged to be built, from scratch, since the last time that I (along with Philomena and Noel) had last visited them in May 1979. As stated, that had been during our mini farewell tour of Europe and, in fact, the major event of that trip had been to attend Miriam's Baptism (at which I had been honoured by being asked to be her godfather). That religious event had taken place in Siegen itself – where Berndt and his family had then been living also. They were, during those earlier days, renting a flat somewhere high above the city centre and had already determined to build their own house somewhere in the region. Three years on, I was not only seeing that particular initiative realised but my son and I were also about to live in our host family's dream home for at least a week or so.

And what sort of things did my son and I do whilst staying with the Schuhmacher family, during our time in that brand new house in Gerlingen? Since Berndt was having to work during the weekdays of our visit, and Moni had no car of her own, we two visitors had to largely entertain ourselves in the immediate neighbourhood, during the working part of each day. One of the more memorable ways by which I was able to do that, was by my taking quite long walks, in the early mornings, with Miriam and Noel, to reach an extensive forest located about a kilometre away. Such outings were not only to provide exercise for the three of us, but they also had a major goal. That was to hunt for mushrooms! Accordingly, soon after breakfast each day the three of us 'fungi seekers' would set out on our quest – with an incentive to see which of us would be able to spot the most on each particular occasion. Surprisingly, Miriam, although only just over two years old at that time, proved to be excellent at spotting our 'treasure'. That was despite the fact that the 'quarry' often grew almost totally hidden in the undergrowth, below the pines of the forest in question. Certainly, she certainly became extremely excited whenever she spotted a *'Pilz'*. And, without a doubt, *'Pilze'*, or mushrooms, was one German word which both my son and I were to have learned - unforgettably - by the time that we had come to the end of our sojourn in that small rural community.

Alas, Moni, being a qualified children's nurse, turned out to be extremely wary of the fungi which we collected in the forest and brought home for her. She knew, only too well, that some of them might be poisonous toadstools rather than edible mushrooms. Moreover, being no expert at being able to distinguish between the two varieties in question, she always took the wisest course and quietly (behind our backs) threw our daily collections away –as well as made us three avid collectors wash our hands, thoroughly, after every hunting trip, to boot! Such a sad end to our booty each day, however, did not put off either Miriam or Noel from wanting to enthusiastically repeat our 'field sport' exercise each new day (especially as they never asked what Moni had done with their 'pickings' from the previous morning). Nor did it demoralise their adult guardian. For not only did I find our hunting experiences delightful, I also regarded it as a learning exercise. That was because, as I told myself, all I had to do was study a book about mushrooms, in the future, to discover how to tell which ones were the 'good' edible ones for my next trip to Gerlingen. All the more so, because my son and goddaughter (as well as myself) certainly knew, by the end of my and Noel's stay in that village, what areas of the forest were the best places to uncover many different varieties of fungi, in general.

That latest trip to West Germany of Noel and myself, however, was never intended by me to be restricted to just the Gerlingen and Siegen areas. That was because there was just no way that I wanted to be somewhere inside my long-term penfriend's country and not also want to visit my favourite lady therein – the woman whom I regarded as my 'second mother in West Germany'. That particular lady I have already written about, fondly, in both *Swimming without mangoes*[60] and *Fledging and Learning to Fly*.[61] Unsurprisingly, that person was Berndt's own mother – 'Frau Gertrud Schuhmacher' – who lived some two to three hours to the north-east of the Siegen area, in a sprawling municipality called Salzgitter. As seen in *Swimming without mangoes*,[62] Salzgitter is the place where I had first met Berndt and his mum, during an arranged trip from its English partner-town of Swindon in the summer of 1971. In that book, it is also seen that it had been owing to that first trip that I had become Berndt's long-term penfriend, and had got to know, and become very fond of, his widowed mother - as well as his maternal grandparents, his then-girlfriend, Moni, and his best male friend, Hupsi.

Accordingly, as soon as Berndt had become free from his work duties in Siegen, during the weekend of our stay, he and his nuclear family, as accompanied by Noel and myself, found ourselves in his car making the drive in a north-easterly direction to Salzgitter. That latter municipality was somewhere quite close to the border with 'East Germany', and also within about 30 minutes' to an hour's drive from both the larger cities of 'Braunschweig' ('Brunswick') and 'Hannover'. It can be imagined, therefore, the happy reunion that myself and my son celebrated with Frau Schuhmacher when we arrived at her home in '*Elbestrasse*', number 10, in Salzgitter after our journey from Gerlingen. For that was the address where she still had her flat – the home, at the top of a block, where I had first stayed on my initial visit to West Germany in 1971 and which I had visited many times since. Indeed, my last visit to my favourite West German lady, in her home, had only been three years before. That had been when Philomena, myself and Noel had also gone out of our way to travel to see, and spend time with, her there - after Miriam's Baptism in Siegen in May 1979.

Frau Schuhmacher was, naturally, disappointed about not seeing Philomena on that latest occasion. Or, indeed, Noel's little brother, Kim. For she had also met the latter once before – even though that had not been in Salzgitter, or anywhere else in West Germany for that matter. Rather, that memorable encounter had occurred during Frau Schuhmacher's only ever visit to England which had taken place during the summer of 1979 – in Swindon! That had been the occasion where she had done my family and myself the greatest honour by 'sumounting' her fear of flying (and of sailing on the sea) in order to attend the Baptism of Kim in the former Wiltshire hometown of Philomena and myself. She had done so by taking the 'compromise vehicle' of a hovercraft from Calais to Ramsgate in Kent and back. Frau Schuhmacher, however, readily understood, as a grandmother herself, how important it would have been, back in Swindon at that very time when Noel and I were with her in Salzgitter, for Philomena's mother to be spending time with her daughter as well as getting to better know her younger grandson and only granddaughter.

Whilst in Salzgitter, Noel and I gave Frau Schuhmacher and her parents - Berndt's 'Oma' and 'Opa', who lived just one floor down in *Elbestrasse*, number 10 - the Charles and Diana Royal Wedding presents which we had bought for them in London and had painstakingly transported with us on our train and ferry journeys starting from the English capital. The recipients of our gifts seemed suitably pleased with them, and certainly, knew about the big fuss which had gone down in England concerning the royal nuptials in question – which may even have also been shown 'live' on West German television. Moreover, upon reflection, the presents could well have been said to have been apposite since Prince Charles, if not also Lady Diana, unquestionably had German blood flowing through his veins, as a result of one his forefathers being 'Prince Albert' – the German prince who had been the husband and consort of his mother's great-great-grandmother, 'Queen Victoria'.

In addition to seeing, and staying with, Frau Schuhmacher - and simply going down the stairs to visit Oma and Opa from time to time during our weekend stay in Salzgitter - Noel and myself also made time to meet up with Hupsi and his mother, 'Frau Pfeiffer'. The last two persons lived just a few minutes' walk away from *Elbestrasse*, in '*Rheinstrasse*'. It is likely that Berndt's best friend and Frau Pfeiffer took some trouble to organise what they usually arranged whenever Philomena and myself had visited Salzgitter in recent times – namely, threw a little house party for their visitors from England, in their own flat (which they shared), even though my wife was not with me on that particular occasion. That would have been all the more fitting since Noel and I had last seen Hupsi when he had been the guest of my family and myself (along with Berndt, Moni and Miriam) just over one year before at our home in Hygeia, Barbados and he would, perhaps, have wanted to return some of my family's hospitality to him from that earlier time. Naturally, to any such house party in *Rheinstrasse* the hosts would also have invited Berndt and Moni and their children - as well as Frau Schuhmacher and Hupsi's sister, 'Christa' (who had been kind enough to have accompanied him to the wedding of Philomena and myself, in Swindon, in 1976).

Soon, however, our weekend in Salzgitter would have come to an end and my son and myself would have had to return with Berndt and his family to Gerlingen - since he would be going back to work at the start of the new week ahead. Before returning to his office, however, he took Noel and myself to Siegen railway station, early on that Monday morning, to enable my son and myself to begin our train trip back to Ostend in Belgium, via Cologne, in order to catch our ferry back to England. Before embarking on that return trip, however, I would have said, at Siegen station, a fervent 'thank you' to my penfriend, Moni and Miriam, my goddaughter, for all the kind hospitality of themselves and their family in Salzgitter during our time with them in West Germany. I would also have said '*Bis bald*' (the German words for 'Until soon') to our Gerlingen hosts. In truth, however, I had absolutely no idea when I would have the chance of ever seeing my closest friends from Continental Europe again – or whether that would be in England, Barbados, or elsewhere in the world. I had every confidence, however, that we would all be meeting up again sometime, somewhere, in the not-too-distant future. With that belief, but also with tears in my eyes, I encouraged Noel to wave with me to Berndt and his family as our train to Cologne pulled out of the station.

With an unremarkable journey back to Ostend from Cologne and then the ferry across the English Channel from that Belgian port to Dover, Noel and myself were back in London by the next day and able to catch our train back to Swindon from Paddington station. Back in Wiltshire, the two of us wanderers were soon, once more, in the Southbrook Street home of my mother-in-law and reunited also with Philomena, Kim and Claire-Louise. Noel and I would be able to tell the other members of my immediate family about our adventures whilst in Gerlingen and Salzgitter – and, not least, about the fun that we had both experienced mushroom hunting with my goddaughter Miriam. Such tales would last us over the few remaining days that we had left in England for our summer holidays 1981. During those final days, Philomena, myself and our children took time to visit and say (or wave, in the case of our baby daughter) goodbye to my own mother back in Alexandra Road, as well as to my sister, Sylvia, who might still have been living at home during that period (though she would have left school and have been working as a secretary by then). We would also have visited my own brother, John, at his home in the 'Toothill' district of Swindon to say goodbye to him and his partner, 'Marion', as well as his three young sons, 'Mark', 'Wayne' and 'Lee'. When so taking our leave of my side of our family, my wife and I did not really know at that stage when 'we five' would be returning to England again, although I for one was fairly confident that it would be, at least, within the next two years or so.

The hardest part of taking our leave from our former home town, however, was when it came to parting from Philomena's mother at her home. Philomena's brother, John, was going to be driving us back to Heathrow Airport for our flight back to Barbados. Accordingly, there was no room in his car to also take Mrs Harrison along with us - in addition to our luggage. Our '*au revoirs*' and final hugs had to be said, and done, at my mother-in-law's home. Moreover, that parting would have been tearful on all sides – since Mrs Harrison had grown very attached to her grandchildren during their stays with her during that summer - and so had they, to her. Philomena, too, would have been mindful of what she had been missing by not having had her mum on the spot from whom to seek advice about childrearing from time to time. Also, of what our children had been missing by not having even one of their grannies in their lives, on a regular basis, whilst we lived in far-away Barbados. What made the situation worse, however, was that Mrs Harrison had no plans to come and visit us in our Caribbean island home in the near future – or at all – and, so, we would all have to wait for another year, or more, before my family could return to England to enable the extended family to be reunited once more.

Be that as it may, our tearful leave was finally, if reluctantly, taken - and Philomena's brother kindly dropped her, myself and our children at the London airport of our departure. After an uneventful cross-Atlantic flight of some eight hours or so, we found ourselves back in Barbados - later that same day. And then it was back to the reality of life for our family on that Caribbean island – and, more forebodingly for me, the teaching duties ahead of me for the forthcoming academic year. Fortunately for me, when my family had returned - sometime in later August 1981 - there were still some weeks to go before I would need to start teaching again at the beginning of October.

*Chapter 21*

# The First Term of my Third Academic Year at UWI – Autumn 1981

After first returning to Barbados in the late summer from our holidays in Europe 1981, there was still enough time for Philomena and myself to play ourselves back into Barbadian life in a gentle way before the pressure would commence for me, in earnest, back at the University. One of the ways in which we did that – in addition to the usual swimming sessions at Oistins, and visits afterwards to the Back of the Airport, with the children - was to get involved, once more, with the Marriage Encounter, or ME, movement as it operated on the island. And during September, the spiritual coordinator of our ME group, Father Pat, announced his having organised a weekend convention at 'St Joseph's Hospital' in the parish of 'St Peter', situated in the north-west of the island. His statement added that the respective spouses in the group would be allowed to stay over in the establishment there (which contained both spare rooms, as well as a Catholic chapel in its grounds).

*Fig. 46: The Author, holding Claire-Louise, and with Noel and Kim, at the Back of the [Grantley Adams International] Airport, Barbados in the Autumn of 1981*

At my urging, Philomena agreed to sign up with me for Father Pat's weekend. Once more, we had come to a babysitting arrangement with our lovely neighbour, Mrs Payne. She would have been delighted to have had our children back from England and be able to spend a lot of exclusive time with them - during which she would have been able to ask our sons about their adventures, that summer, in England (and in West Germany, in Noel's case). At any rate, I particularly wanted to go to the ME event in question since, during my holidays in Europe, I had come to the conclusion that I had made an unforgivable mistake in getting involved with Vere, just prior to leaving Barbados for England. Moreover, I had not been in touch with her, even once, since that time - and I really wanted to re-commit myself to my wife and our marriage once I had returned to the island.

Accordingly, I threw myself into the ME weekend completely. That included my earnestly carrying out, in my notebook, all the writing tasks given to us by Father Pat, exchanging that jotter for Philomena's, and then sharing with her our feelings expressed in those books. That interaction was solely with each other, initially. Then my wife and I did so with a much wider set of other ME couples than would normally be present at our own smaller group's ME evenings that we had regularly attended previously in the south of Barbados. The one thing which never came out during those notebook writings of mine, however, was my indiscretion with Vere. That was because the topics which our then current ME cohort was asked to write, and share, about during the weekend never touched on that of marital infidelity. Moreover, it was because I had buried my one regrettable episode of that sin deep into the recesses of my mind, and I fully expected to be a person 'reborn' when the ME ministrations in question had concluded and I had returned to my regular life back at home and at UWI.

Perhaps it had been as soon as the Monday following the weekend in question that I started returning to my office on a regular basis - in order to 'play myself in', as far as academic life was concerned, and prepare for the new academic year ahead. More than likely, that was one period in which I seriously began work on another article with a view to having it published in the *West Indian Law Journal*. At any rate, the point is that I had returned to work at the University with a feeling of new vigour and professionalism. And then, whilst working in my office with my door open, I had an uninvited and unannounced visitor. It was Vere!

I was shocked to see her - as the new term was still not due to commence for, perhaps, another week or two. Moreover, as stated, I had not been in touch with her – nor she with me - since I had last seen her on the day of our mutual indiscretion. Steeling myself, I invited her to sit down and we exchanged pleasantries about what we had each done during the summer vacation. I then got to the point of telling her that I had just come off an ME weekend in St Peter parish and that, as a result, I had recommitted myself to my marriage to Philomena. Vere reacted by saying that she both understood and respected my decision. At some subsequent point during our meeting, however, I got up from behind my desk in order to go to the bookshelf in my office. That was in order to select a publication which I thought might help her, regarding a legal issue which she had asked me about. Perhaps, it had been one concerning the Conflicts of Laws subject - which she had told me that she was then thinking of choosing as one of her options in the Final Year of her Law degree programme which she was about to commence. I can remember that, whilst so standing, I said to her: 'I am really sorry - but there is nothing that you could do, for the future, that will ever divert me from the right path of my marriage again'.

At that moment, Vere approached me by my bookcase, and looked me in the eyes. Alas, I am afraid to say that we then embraced. I cannot imagine now just how such an occurrence had taken place with my door still wide open. That is because any, and every, person could have witnessed the hug going on inside my office – had they been passing at the time. Be that as it may, we soon parted and quickly discussed what to do next. After a while, and at my suggestion most likely, we agreed to go outside to the Law Faculty car park and then to take a 'little drive' in my Skoda. And what a spin that turned out to be! With my head reeling from my weakness - after all my mental resolutions following my recent ME weekend - our motoring became ever longer. So much so in fact that, within an hour or so, we found ourselves miles away from Cave Hill Campus and on the other side of the island, near Bathsheba - well into the countryside of the eastern parish of St Joseph. And, in that mini-county of Barbados, my second act of marital betrayal took place. Not inside my car - but in one of the fields, close to where we had parked to talk and embrace still further.

And so my life took an entirely new and unexpected turn at the University. Unlike the aftermath of the first act, when we had kept our distance across the Atlantic from each other, and had withheld from communicating with one another, Vere and myself now saw, and spoke to, each other nearly every day of the working week in the run up to the new academic year. And, truth to tell, we did a lot more than merely speak to each other when we did meet up. Worse still, she had decided to take, in her choice of Final Year subjects, not only Comparative Law (of which I was still the Course Director) but also Conflict of Laws (in which I was one of the only two tutors, with Tony Bland as Course Director). As a result, I would not only have to teach her as one of my students - in both subjects - but I was also socialising with her in the evenings, after I had prepared my classes for the following days.

There soon came a time, on some evenings when Vere did not have the use of her mother's car, that I would agree to drive her home. That, as seen earlier, was all the way in St Philip parish, which was situated in the south east of the island (perhaps some 10 or more miles from Cave Hill Campus), just north of my own Christ Church. Accordingly, Vere's mother would surely have known of, or could easily have been able to guess at, the closeness of my relationship with her only daughter, during that earliest period of the new academic year. That would especially be the case, given that I was dropping her off, at their joint home, at least once or twice a week. On the other hand, it was fortunate for me that Philomena suspected nothing. That was because I was arriving home from work at much the same sort of time in the evenings as I often had done in the past at UWI (especially during my first, traumatic, 1979-80 academic year). Owing to the double life which I was starting to lead at that time, however, I began to feel hypocritical about continuing to attend and participate in our ME group's meetings. Quite early into the new academic year, therefore, I managed to persuade Philomena that, owing to the pressure of my work at UWI, we would have to stop attending the meetings - or, at best, only go to them very intermittently in future.

And then the foreseeable – and almost predictable - event came to pass. Vere discovered that she was pregnant! That would have been by about the end of October of that First Term of the 1981-82 academic year. When she had told me of her doctor's determination of her situation - most likely during one of our journey's to her St Philip home after my work one evening - I had been absolutely stunned. That is because I had tried to be extremely 'careful' during our times together. Obviously, however, I had not been vigilant enough - on at least one occasion.

Vere's bombshell news would have made me feel that my life was at a crossroads. For I was still, at that time, a practising Catholic – a member of a church which espoused the 'sanctity of life' and which teaches that 'life begins with conception'. Moreover, and up to the moment of Vere's unexpected announcement, I too had fully believed in those tenets. If, however, the recently-conceived baby was to be allowed to be born, after Vere continued with her pregnancy to term, Philomena, and also UWI, would have to know of the facts in question. I could not possibly envisage either of those two revelations being made – let alone what our friends in the ME group, to which Philomena and myself had so closely collaborated up to recent times, would think.

The dire situation was not so much about me, however. Rather, I was most mindful that the crucial question was: 'What did Vere, the would-be mother, want to do for the future?'. An abortion would have seemed to have been the 'solution' for all concerned – all except for the baby, of course! But could she ever contemplate such a thing – even if I myself had major religious difficulties going down that route. To abort the baby would mean each of us going our separate ways for the future – without Philomena and our immediate families being outwardly affected, and without Vere's student career at UWI being interrupted by a pregnancy (especially in relation to the latter weeks of it, which period was due to occur just as her final examinations in June 1982 would be taking place).

Naturally, my mind, during that first part of the academic year 1981-82, would have been all at sea. No doubt, I struggled to stay on an even keel - as I continued to prepare and give my classes as well as I could. The ability to see Vere more or less every day (except on my 'family Wednesdays') during the working week - as well as to drive her home and discuss what we were going to do about the baby - helped me to sustain my equilibrium somewhat. Moreover, there was one other major factor that served to do that during that fraught period for me. That was a friend of Vere's – a person heavily involved in the Anglican Church and who was, perhaps, even studying at the time to enter its priesthood. His name was 'John' – a married man of middle age, who had a wife but no children (to the best of my memory). He proved to be a jolly individual, prone to laugh very easily, but who was also a musical person (who had been Vere's piano teacher at one time in the past, which is how they might first have met each other). But how was John going to be able to help us?

Vere would introduce me to that Anglican churchman by late October, or early November 1981. That was in order to allow the three of us to discuss, and try to resolve, the dilemma in which Vere and I found ourselves as a result of her pregnancy. As far as I knew, we told no one else about our fraught situation up to that meeting. And, if I had been losing sleep over the matter, no doubt Vere had been suffering the loss of even more. Accordingly, within about two weeks or so of our finding out about our potential parenthood, Vere suggested to me that there was one person on the island whom she trusted, who was close to being in Holy Orders, and whom she thought would be willing to be our spiritual adviser in relation to our worrisome issue. I agreed, very willingly, to her idea. That was because the keeping of our predicament, between the two of us only, I was finding to be most debilitating to my work at the University. And, no doubt, Vere was experiencing much the same with her own UWI legal studies.

As a consequence, and with my agreement, Vere invited John to join the two of us for drinks at the 'Barbados Pizza House'. That was situated in St James parish on the West Coast of the island, and we chose an evening after a work day had ended, and an hour when we might witness the sun setting into the Caribbean Sea. She had simply told him that she wanted him to meet a friend and that the two of us had something of the utmost importance to discuss with him as well as to seek his advice. Living up to being the good Christian person that Vere had told me that John was, he readily made room in his busy schedule to join us at the proposed venue. If the purpose of our meeting had not been quite so serious, where we sat to have our drinks would have been one of the most romantic of locations – since we were right by the sea and were able to watch a sundown that evening, as well as the twilight begin to envelope the surroundings in which we found ourselves. After some jolly banter from John, Vere and I eventually got to the point by telling him the stark facts which had prompted our meeting. Vere was pregnant, we confessed, and the two of us simply did not know what to do about it!

I then took over the discussion by revealing to John that I was a married man with three children. I added that I was a practising Catholic and that I firmly believed in the sanctity of life. After that, I divulged my painstakingly-considered opinion that, despite the ructions which would be caused in both my family's and Vere's lives - by allowing the baby which Vere and I had made to be born - the sanctity of life 'commandment' took priority in my conscience. Finally, I added that I would stand by Vere - if she decided to carry the baby to term. Thankfully, if John had been shocked by the revelations of Vere and myself, he did not show it. Rather, he reacted calmly and told us that he could well see our dilemma. He also thanked us for trusting him to advise about what to do. He quickly revealed, however, that he had no instant solution. He also offered to pray about the matter but seemed to agree with me that, when all was said and done, the final decision would be down to Vere.

When we eventually broke up our meeting with John - after an hour or so, to go to our various homes that evening - I felt somewhat lighter in my mind for having shared our situation with a third party. Moreover, I was rather relieved that our new 'joint spiritual adviser' had not dismissed, as ridiculous, my idea that, somehow, I could keep to my belief in the sanctity of life and still maintain my marriage with Philomena (as well as continue to be a good father to Noel, Kim and Claire-Louise).

Consequently, within a week or two of our evening meeting with John in St James, the die was cast. Vere had heard me offer to support her, if she carried our baby to term – despite my marital situation with Philomena and my existing children – and had witnessed me undertaking, to John, to do just that. An abortion, therefore, would no longer be on the agenda for either of us. All we then had to do – for the future – was live with that decision!

Naturally, it was not going to be an easy road ahead. For one thing, Vere would eventually start to show, by her growing stomach, that she was pregnant. For another, I would have to continue to teach her in my classes, as if she was just another one of the students therein. Above all, however, we would eventually have to tell a limited number of other people - apart from John - about the expected baby. Vere probably told her mother, Joyce, first. Fortunately, whenever I dropped her off in St Philip after classes on some evenings during the working week - as I had been doing for most of that First Term of 1981-82 academic year - Joyce would be very civil to me. She often even invited me to stop for a cup of coffee, which I usually accepted, and I very much got the impression that she liked me as a person and as the father-to-be of her future grandchild. However, she never brought up the subject about the baby's imminence - and nor did I, whenever I accepted her home-based hospitality.

At my own residence in Christ Church also, during that immediate period after the pregnancy announcement, I was letting sleeping dogs lie. I just did not know how I was going to tell my wife about the unexpected development in my – and, therefore, our joint – life. She seemed so happy during that period. It was probably after the First Term at Cave Hill Campus had already ended and, in line with the general Festive Season atmosphere in the air at the time, we both attended a Christmas party together. That had been at the home of a couple whom we had got to know well from meeting them often, usually at weekends, on our beach at Maxwell. Like us, they had two small children – a little girl about Noel's age, and a son of about Kim's – and they were also expats from England (though neither was connected with UWI). Philomena and myself duly went to the couple's party in the Atlantic Shores district of our southern parish and had enjoyed a good time there. When we had returned home, and I saw how happy she seemed to be about her life in Barbados at that time, that was when I made my momentous decision to tell her!

That was not because I had wanted to kill her happiness stone dead. Rather, it was because I just could not go on seeing my wife being so ignorant of a situation that was eating me up inside. I wanted to be open with her - and to let her know that her then current happy state of mind was built on sand. We were then both in the large kitchen of our Hygeia home - just after returning from our friends' party, via our back door. I looked at Philomena directly and asked her to kindly sit down. When we had both done so, I continued by telling her that I had something to reveal and that it would be the hardest thing that I would ever have had to divulge to her in my entire life. I saw, from her eyes looking at me, that she just could not imagine what it was that I had to let her know. Or what topic was so serious that its revelation could not even wait until the next morning. After all, she must have been thinking, we had just returned from a really great festivity, we were both extremely tired, and, surely, the matter could wait.

I then took my wife's hands, looked her in the eyes and told her good self two earth-shattering things. First, that I had been having an affair! She looked at me uncomprehendingly at that revelation. It was as if that had been the very last thing she might have imagined - given our happy life at home since our return from England in the summer and, even, in the light of the happy celebration which we had just shared together with our friends at their home that evening. I felt obliged, however, to continue with the second bombshell: namely, to disclose that the person involved with me had fallen pregnant! At that further revelation, Philomena burst into tears and I instantly held her in my arms and told her how very sorry I was for spoiling everything that we had built up in our marriage, and in our family life, thus far.

My wife, however, is, mentally, a very strong woman. She did not further react by hollering and screaming at me. Rather, still holding tightly to me, she quietly asked me to tell her who the person in question was. When I revealed that it was one of my students, she cried all the more. Then, still holding tightly to me, she invited me to go upstairs to our bedroom. In that episode of clinging to each other for physical and psychological survival, and in our trying to make sense of our then seemingly unravelling (formerly secure) marital life, we were once again truly man and wife!

Somehow, Philomena and I managed to get through the following morning, and then the Christmas period ahead, at home. Naturally, the two of us said nothing to our children and we tried to make the best of that current Festive Season for their sake. Thus, I remained in Hygeia during that period more than I was out of the house seeing Vere. On New Year's Eve, however - or 'Old Year's Night', as they call it in Barbados - in order to compensate Vere for my absence in her life of late, she and I agreed to go out together in order to 'see in' 1982. That was because it would be a dramatic, life-giving and life-changing, year ahead for the two of us (as well as for my matrimonial family, naturally). Perhaps, it had been at her insistence that she had come to pick me up in her mother's car at my home. I had, reluctantly, gone along with the idea. At any rate, however, that last night of 1981 was the historical date when Philomena and Vere met for the first time. Philomena did not invite 'the other woman' into the house. Nevertheless, they were civil to each other, at least, when I had introduced Vere to my wife and our three children. I then said goodnight to Philomena and our offspring and told them that I would see them all again in the morning. Speedily, I made my way out of my family's home and into Vere's borrowed car.

That episode was, perhaps, the first time I had felt the tug of love in two competing directions and it made me feel absolutely terrible. I consoled myself, however, with the viewpoint that if I was truly going to be a father to Vere's baby also, then that scenario would likely work most smoothly if Philomena got to know Vere as well. And the sooner rather than the later that happened, seemed to be the better way forward. As I tried to dance with Vere at the particular New Year's Eve party - which was held at the Sam Lord's Castle Hotel in St Philip parish - I could not help thinking about Philomena being alone at home with our children. Nor could I avoid being very worried about what 1982 held for them - as well as for Vere, our new baby and myself.

*Chapter 22*

# The Earlier Part of the Second Term of my Third Academic Year at UWI – Spring 1982

The New Year came along soon enough and before I knew it I was back teaching again at Cave Hill Campus – with Vere attending classes in two of my subjects as usual. At some stage, she and I must have agreed that, as her pregnancy was just starting to show, she would have to share the news with her fellow-mature-student, and very close friend, Angela. It was at Angela's home, near Bridgetown, that the two of us had been intimate for the very first time - immediately prior to my family's trip to Europe the previous summer. I was rather worried about the fallout, for me, that such a disclosure would cause – as well as for my job at the University. I agreed with Vere, however, that Angela should be told – especially, as Vere trusted her so well. Her friend's reaction, however, was one that was completely unanticipated by either of us!

Angela, who seemed to me to be of East Indian extraction - who normally possessed dark, shoulder-length, hair - cut it all off, immediately after hearing the news from Vere! Accordingly, Vere's long-term friend then looked somewhat like a male 'skinhead' – the type of youth who used to cause trouble at English football matches back in the 1960s when I had been at school. Such was the shock which Angela evidently took from Vere's news that not only did the former destroy her previously attractive hairstyle, but she also promptly stopped inviting Vere to her home - or even talking to Vere, as regularly as before. Perhaps, the tipping point for Angela was not so much that Vere was pregnant and that I was the father-to-be. It was, seemingly, more to do with the fact that I had decided to stand by Vere in her decision not to abort the baby.

Despite, Angela's dramatic reaction to Vere's revelations, however, Vere and I agreed that we could both trust her old friend not to spread the news around the Law Faculty or wider afield. Nevertheless, though shaken somewhat by Angela's apparent 'protest', I was also slowly getting used to my decision that I would stand by Vere – whatever the fallout. So much so that, when it came to my next overseas trip on behalf of the Faculty to the UWI campus in Mona, Jamaica, I invited Vere to come with me. That happened towards the end of January 1982, and I did not tell Philomena that I had done so - for fear of further upsetting her unnecessarily. Moreover, since that overseas visit would be the very first that I would ever be making with Vere, I went to some trouble to arrange for an adventurous itinerary. That was helped by the fact that UWI would be paying for my ticket, whilst I would, naturally, have to fund Vere's.

After leaving Barbados on a 'British West Indian Airways' ('BWIA') flight bound, ultimately, for Jamaica, Vere and I disembarked, before the final destination - in 'San Juan' on the island of 'Puerto Rico'. I had certainly been there once or twice before, but it would be Vere's first visit. The island was a 'Territory' of the United States - though not one of the 50 'States' of that country. From the many American films which I had seen over the years, the huge cars and wide streets of San Juan, really made me imagine that I was in mainland America – though, in fact, I had never been to 'the States', thus far, in my life. Vere and I, however, did not stay in that busy capital of the island for long during our visit. Rather, we made for the 'Rio Pedras' district a few miles outside, by air-conditioned bus, in order to look around the 'University of Puerto Rico'. That educational institution I had visited at least once previously. Moreover, it was in that outlying district that we were able to find an inexpensive hotel for ourselves - as well as eat well, and economically, in one or other of the several restaurants or cafés to be found in the lovely old campus of the university. There was also a shopping centre nearby, where Vere was able to try on, and buy, some suitable dresses for her growing pregnant condition.

We only stayed one night and part of two days in Puerto Rico. For the two of us, it was a nice change from our own island home in Barbados - and far away from the pressures which we had both, suddenly, been forced to get used to during the previous academic term and the earliest part of the then current one. I was then on a UWI 'duty visit', however and, so, I had to get that out of the way - before the two of us would be able to properly enjoy some more 'down time' in the greater Caribbean region. Accordingly, the day after our arrival in Puerto Rico – in the later afternoon – the two of us caught our onward BWIA flight to Kingston, the capital of Jamaica. Again, it was Vere's very first visit to that large Caribbean island, and the two of us decided to look for somewhere to stay in the centre of the metropolis itself. That was because, I, in particular, and with Vere in tow, did not want to run into some of my other UWI colleagues from Barbados who were attending the same meeting as myself. Somehow, we managed to find somewhere on the east side of Kingston - just off the main road from the airport to the city and, perhaps, only one mile or so from its very centre. It was of a lower standard than the place we had stayed at in Puerto Rico - but we planned to 'rough it', as necessary, for the short time only that we would be in the Jamaican capital.

The next morning, despite my better judgment, I invited Vere to travel with me, by bus, to the Mona Campus of UWI – as she agreed that she would be happy to amuse herself exploring that campus (which was very much larger than its counterpart at Cave Hill in Barbados) whilst I would be attending my meetings inside one or other of the offices there. By the early afternoon of that day, however, with all my appointments behind me, the two of us were free to explore the Mona area (including visit the zoo located there) - before returning to our lodgings, near downtown Kingston, to have dinner. The following day would see us begin a stimulating adventure - away from the capital - which I really wanted Vere to experience.

My initiative was to take Vere on a type of journey which, perhaps, she had never had the pleasure of in her life before – and which, though I had plenty of personal knowledge of the same in Europe, I had only ever enjoyed once before in Jamaica itself. That was to take an overland train trip! Such an excursion was possible because, in those early 1980s days, the island in which the two of us then found ourselves still had a working railway line between its two largest cities – namely, Kingston in the south-east and 'Montego Bay' on the north-west coast. And I had previously enjoyed myself so very much in making that earlier trip to 'MoBay' - as Jamaicans called their second city - that I wished to replicate it with Vere on that particular latest sojourn of mine. Naturally, that was in the hope that she would enjoy such an experience also. Thus, early on our second morning in Kingston, the two of us got ourselves to the station - situated on the southern side of the city centre and within view of the Caribbean Sea - in order to catch the (perhaps, once-a-day only) train to MoBay. Certainly, our train left at about 9am and, if there would have been another one to the second city that day, it would only have been in the afternoon, most probably, and would, thus, have arrived too late for us to see anything of MoBay by daylight.

In fact, Jamaicans had a special name for their train – namely, 'the Diesel'. And it was indeed a special, and unusual, mode of transport for the islanders – for it took a long time to travel from the capital to the second city, and it did so extremely slowly. Most local folks trying to get from one of those cities to the other would, most probably, opt to go by private car, or even use a public bus - as that journey of, perhaps, 100 miles or so could then be done in about three hours. With the Diesel, however, it was going to take Vere and myself some four hours or more! Time was on our side that day, however. Moreover, owing to the price of tickets to travel on that railway being so extremely low, the two of us were able to purchase 'First Class' ones – to enable us to travel in somewhat more comfort than the ordinary fare would have afforded us.

Our journey began, more or less on time, out of Kingston's station - very slowly. Eventually, we made some short stops at exotic-sounding places such as 'Spanish Town' and 'May Pen'. As it trundled westwards, the Diesel began to turn in a northerly direction also - and into the mountains which we could see on our right. In doing so, we eventually reached stops such as 'Porus' - where we could look out and see the orange-coloured soil of the land surrounding us. Someone - perhaps our ticket-collector who came by at intervals during our journey - was to tell us that the vivid colour of the landscape had to do with the fact that it contained bauxite, which ingredient was used to manufacture aluminium. Indeed, factories where the silvery metal was produced, we could see, from time to time, outside our windows. Travelling on still further north-westwards - and ever upwards, it seemed to me - we stopped at more quaintly-named stations such as 'Balaclava' and 'Appleton'. The latter, I told Vere, was the place where the famous white rum of Jamaica was produced.

It was somewhere around that possible alcohol-producing area that, suddenly, we discovered that our train had been boarded by a group of ladies each selling various products. Competitively, they invited Vere and myself to buy some of their respective wares to help us further enjoy the remainder of our journey. I seem to recall that the local name for such traders was 'higglers'. Each of them carried a tray on her head and sang out a list of their merchandise, in the very same order: 'Popcorn, mint-balls, cigarettes…'. The entirety of their list now evades my memory, but Vere and I found the vending process quite entertaining. That was especially because of the way the items in question were pronounced. Thus, in such a way that the first word came out something like 'paap-carn', for example. At any rate, the two of us did indeed buy some of the offered goods for sale. In my case, I chose some exotic fruits which I would not have been able to find in Barbados, such as a 'carambola' (or 'star fruit') and some 'sapodillas' (or 'naseberries').

The higglers in question were not travelling with us all the way to MoBay, however. Just two or three stations after they had boarded our Diesel with their products, Vere and I witnessed them disembarking again. That was probably for them to await the MoBay to Kingston train - which would soon after be coming along to take them back to their home station. And it was at the station of their exiting our train, that our railway journey began to descend. We were surely then well on the way back to the sea and, soon, stopping at more unusually-named stations such as 'Catadupa'. Much more familiar, to me, was the stop or two following - which carried the name 'Cambridge'! That had been a huge surprise for me the first time that I had stopped there on my earlier journey. For, I had never expected that the English university city, of my younger student days, would have had a namesake up in the mountains of a far-away Caribbean island. At any rate, it was all downhill from Cambridge, Jamaica after that. And some four hours or more after we had left downtown Kingston, our Diesel had also passed 'Montpellier' and 'Anchovy' and had arrived at the terminus of the journey in MoBay.

And then, Vere and I had to decide what we would do with our time in Jamaica's second city. We had both already agreed that we did not want to just take the return train back to Kingston – even assuming that there had been a last one available that afternoon which had not already departed. Rather, we had decided that we preferred to see something of MoBay first. That meant that we would have to find a place to stay the night, prior to returning to the capital the next day. We ended up going to quite a nice hotel – which I seem to recollect actually called itself a 'motel'. It was situated not far from the roundabout leading to Jamaica's second biggest airport – 'Sangster International', located just a few miles outside the centre of MoBay. Once installed in our room there, we left our belongings inside it and then made the journey back downtown, in order to have a look around and then find somewhere to have our dinner. I can remember our eating in a café-like place in the city centre – which had the kind of hub-bub somewhat like one often experiences in a Barbados rum shop. Nevertheless, the food which was served up to us I cannot remember being less than satisfactory. Indeed, it well have been something like the famous Jamaican dish of 'jerk chicken', complemented with rice and peas.

MoBay was then famous for being the major touristic destination in Jamaica – perhaps, mainly for Americans and Canadians during that particular era. And although Vere and myself had brought our respective swimming gear with us on our trip, we did not seek to venture into the sea on the evening of our arrival on Jamaica's northwest coast. Rather, we were content to merely take an after dinner stroll around the downtown area of the city – as well as out to one or two of the larger tourist hotels – in order to get our bearings of that famous fleshpot in world tourism, for future reference. We both agreed that MoBay made a pleasant change from busy Kingston and that it was a place that we would like to return to, for longer, at some future time.

The next morning did not find us swimming in the sea either. For one thing, our motel was at least a couple of miles from the touristic strip of MoBay – which was on the other side of the city from where we were located. Moreover, our particular location seemed to be dominated by the major international airport on the other side of the roundabout from our accommodation. And although the sea was perfectly visible to us beyond that airport, there seemed to be no easy access to it without our having to walk, for a few miles perhaps, to get beyond its perimeters.

Accordingly, after enjoying our leisurely breakfast, Vere and I had to make a decision which very much involved staying on dry land and leaving the ocean for a future time. That was to agree upon just how we were going to return to Kingston. Was that to be by a return trip on the Diesel - or otherwise? Without too much ado, we soon concurred that to merely do the reverse of the journey which we had enjoyed the previous day would likely dilute that first happy experience for Vere. That left the possibility of our, instead, taking a cross-country bus back from downtown MoBay. Teasingly, however, I suggested to Vere that we could try doing something that I had been quite good at in Europe – especially during my former student days. That was for us to engage in doing some hitchhiking! To my delight, Vere was keen to try it – notwithstanding her pregnancy.

As a result, with our relatively small amount of belongings, the two of us made the short walk down the hill from our accommodation and as far as the roundabout leading to MoBay's airport. On another of the exits from that circular traffic island, however, was the road which led – eventually – back to Kingston. At a spot that was several yards from the commencement of that main thoroughfare to the Jamaican capital, I showed Vere how to hitchhike using one's thumb's in a waving motion. The two of us thus began to go through the relevant actions whilst, perhaps, getting odd stares from passing motorists. That was because hitchhiking was not something seen very often in Jamaica - or perhaps anywhere else in the Caribbean, for that matter. Before long, however, a saloon car screeched to a halt on our side of the road. I quickly ran up to the driver and told him that my friend and I were trying to get back to Kingston – after coming up to MoBay by the Diesel the previous day. To my delight, the young man – whom I shall call 'Peter' for these purposes - told me that he too was driving all the way back to his home in Kingston and that he would be happy to give my 'lady friend' and myself a lift to the capital. When I went back to inform Vere of Peter's kind offer, her smile of approval told me everything that I needed to know.

Thus, after us two hitchhikers had quickly placed our belongings in the boot of Peter's car, the three of us were soon motoring along on that main, non-motorway, road back to Kingston. At the start of that journey, Vere and myself told Peter more about ourselves – including the facts that we were merely visiting Jamaica for a few days and what our respective connections with UWI were. The road in question was both hilly and windy in places, but the scenery outside the car made a nice contrast from that which we had observed (on the, mainly, orange-coloured landscape) from our train windows the previous day. I, for one, was very happy that Vere and myself had decided to return to Kingston by our very unorthodox – for Jamaica - hitchhiking method.

Relatively early into our journey, however, there came a point when we found ourselves in traffic and driving behind a truck. That vehicle had a flat-bed containing some timber - which was sticking out beyond its rear end. Suddenly, whilst Peter had been fully engaged in conversation with Vere and myself, the truck stopped suddenly and Peter, alas, did not realise it had done so for a for a few more seconds. As a result, Peter's car almost went into the back of the truck! Worse still, however, one of the pieces of timber, protruding beyond the rear of the truck, seem to be coming straight at my face, with speed, as Peter jammed on the brakes of his car to avoid what seemed like an inevitable collision. Without even time to say a prayer, I realised, for an instant, that the timber was going to hit my head. Miraculously, however, I saw the wooden plank pass above my face and scrape the top of Peter's car - just before the latter came to a sudden stop, inches from the bumper of the truck.

I had just, therefore, had a close encounter with death! That is because: if the plank had been located just few inches lower in the bed of the truck, it would have taken my head off, as Peter's car nearly crashed into the back of it. Vere saw what had happened and quickly grabbed and hugged me. She then asked me whether I was all right. I was still somewhat in shock, as I answered her in the affirmative. Peter and the truck driver also realised what had happened and had both got out of their respective vehicles in order to inspect the resulting damage. Fortunately, though the paintwork was slightly scraped on the front part of the roof of Peter's car, neither that vehicle nor the timber in the truck had been significantly damaged. Moreover, neither had there been a collision between the two vehicles.

After a few minutes, therefore, both drivers were able to continue on their way without having to involve the police or their respective insurance companies. Inside, Peter's car, however, the three of us continued to discuss the 'near-death incident' for some time thereafter into our onward journey to Kingston – with Peter profusely apologising for driving quite so close to the truck and not being able to see its brake lights when its driver had performed some kind of emergency stop. For my part, I kept trying to reassure Peter that I did not blame him for the near-miss, and that Vere and I were extremely grateful to him for giving us the lift in the first place.

It was probably as a result of Peter feeling some sort of responsibility, for the shock that I had been caused, that a surprisingly nice offer came from him as we later approached Kingston and the end of our journey. I had been telling him that we still had another night in Jamaica but had not yet arranged an hotel in the capital for us to spend it in. That prompted Peter to tell us that - although he did not own his own home but shared one in the capital with his mother and siblings - he would be willing to ask his lone parent whether Vere and myself could spend the night with his family. At once, I looked at Vere - for her silent confirmation - and then told Peter that his two passengers would be delighted to stay overnight with his family, if that became possible.

And so it was that Peter and his two hitchhikers came to spend the night in the same family home in one of Kingston's suburbs that evening – after Peter had sought, and had obtained, the necessary consent of his mother for a couple of surprise guests from Barbados to stay with them. After the relative anonymity of our nights in hotels or motels in Puerto Rico, or Kingston and MoBay in Jamaica, it had felt good to me to be part of, or near to, a family's life once again. That was also because Peter's mother and siblings turned out to be just as kind and God-fearing as Peter himself – and I, for one, fully enjoyed our time in their home that evening and night as well as the next morning. As I went to bed on the night of our stay, however, I once more reflected upon how lucky I then was to be still alive - after what had happened on the road from MoBay to Kingston earlier that day. Had the Almighty, perhaps, been giving me a warning about the life that I was then leading?

At any rate, the next day Peter kindly gave us a lift once more. On that occasion it had merely been across the capital and along the scenic strip of land, with the sea on both sides, which leads to an area called 'the Palisadoes'. It was on that area that Kingston's airport – the 'Norman Manley International' – was located. Vere and I gave our fervent thanks to Peter for all he, and his family, had done for us since our meeting with him in MoBay the previous day. We then exchanged addresses - with promises to keep in touch with each other - and then said our farewell.

Peter did not wait to see whether Vere and myself managed to safely check in for our BWIA flight to our next destination. That should have been to the neighbouring island of 'Hispaniola' – or, rather, the western part thereof, which was the French speaking 'Republic of Haiti' (as opposed to the eastern part comprising the 'Dominican Republic'). Specifically, the two of us were scheduled to fly to the Haitian capital, 'Port-au-Prince'. We were in for a huge surprise, however. For, when we arrived at the check-in desk, we were told that there was no flight for us! I cannot recall whether it had simply been cancelled for that particular day or whether, perhaps, it had been overbooked and there was simply no longer any space for us. Be that as it may, we were told to come back 'on Monday' for the next scheduled flight - it being a Saturday that day. And, being relatively naïve about the rights of flying passengers in those early days of mine living in the Caribbean, I did not insist on the airline putting us up for the two days that we would then have had to 'lay-over'. Instead, I simply began worrying about where Vere and I would be able to stay for the two delayed nights in question.

It may be that there were already, at the BWIA counter, a few taxi drivers tipped-off by the airline and waiting to assist stranded passengers such as Vere and myself. At any rate, the two of us were soon approached by such a person - who asked us whether we needed a taxi ride somewhere. Vere and I quickly agreed with each other that we just could not put ourselves back on Peter and his family's kindness once more. Accordingly, we readily admitted to the taxi driver in question that, although we would have liked a ride back to Kingston, we had nowhere to stay. That is when he made a proposal to us which came out of the blue. He offered to put us up at his own home in the capital, if we were to pay him the taxi fare to get there, as well as that for the return journey on the Monday morning! More than that, he said that he would only charge us a very small amount of 'rent' for our staying with him the two nights. Vere and I looked at each other and immediately agreed to the 'deal' put forward by our 'Good Samaritan'.

The taxi driver in question was relatively young – perhaps, only in his 30s. He was also tall. The most distinctive thing about his appearance, however, was that he wore long and unkempt dreadlocks on his head – *à la* 'Bob Marley', the famous 'reggae' musician and native of the island on which we then were. On our way to his taxi, he told us that his name was 'Jah-One' and that he lived by the tenets of the 'Rastafarian' religion. He also revealed that he owned his own house and lived there with his female partner.

When we arrived outside Jah-One's home, on the airport side of Kingston, I noted that it possessed a strange number. It was something like '8 and ¾'. That was the first time, therefore, that I would ever be staying in a dwelling, anywhere in the world, with an address which possessed a number that included a fraction! The house was situated in 'Camperdown Road' and, looking around me, I could see that some of the neighbouring ones also possessed a fraction as part of their own respective numbers.

That was not the only thing that I found unusual about the situation in which Vere and myself found ourselves. That was because, once inside Jah-One's home, I could smell the heavy scent of marijuana which pervaded the residence. That particular drug I knew, from having previously read about Bob Marley and other Rastafarians, was part of the lifestyle of members of the sect and, in Jamaica, was usually referred to as 'ganja'. I asked Vere in a whisper - when Jah-One had left us alone for a moment - whether she thought she would be able to tolerate such a ganja-filled atmosphere for the two days of our stay. I was pleased, therefore, when she gave me an affirmative answer with a subtle nod. I further murmured to her that we would just have to go out of the house - for walks in central Kingston and the like - as often as possible during our stay. Soon, after our agreeing that the two of us would indeed remain in the Camperdown Road house for the whole weekend, Jah-One came back into the living room where we were talking with his partner. She was a young woman, who wore a turban which completely covered her head and who seemed to be just as friendly as her male partner. She kindly asked whether Vere and myself would like to join her, and Jah-One, in the meal which she had started cooking in her kitchen next door. The two of us visitors readily agreed to do so - not least to keep up the bonhomie which had already been established between the four of us inside the home.

One thing that was immediately clear to me about the meal which we all subsequently shared. It was a wholly vegetarian one. No meat had been included and it may well have comprised the famous Jamaican ingredients of 'ackee and saltfish'. Ackee, when cooked, was yellow in colour and looked like scrambled eggs. It came from a tree, however, and, thus, was not an animal product at all. Saltfish was salted cod - which had to be soaked well before cooking and tended to be rather flaky when served in a meal.

In the end, Vere and I managed to spend our unexpected extra weekend in Kingston in the home of Jah-One and his partner. Very often, however, we were out and about exploring the capital as much as we could. One of those excursions included our taking the ferry across 'Kingston Bay' to a small town called 'Port Royal'. There, we visited the military station which had once been under the charge of the famous English seaman, 'Horatio Nelson'. We also took the opportunity to swim in the Caribbean Sea from one of Port Royal's several beaches.

And before we knew it, the Monday morning, which the two of us awaited, had arrived and Jah-One was taking us back to Norman Manley International Airport. That was after we had thanked his partner for all her kindness to us in the couples' Camperdown Road home. Having paid Jah-One for both our fare as well as the 'small rent' which he had requested for our stay with him, we effusively thanked him also for rescuing us a few days before and for looking after us in his home over the following days. He then kindly escorted us, with our luggage, to the BWIA check-in. On that later occasion, the staff manning the counter seemed pleased to see Vere and myself and were soon confirming that we definitely had seats on that morning's flight to Haiti. With that positive news, we were able to take our final leave of Jah-One and then follow all the necessary steps to enable us to finally board our plane to Port-au-Prince.

The flight took about one hour before we reached that destination. Once again, Vere and I were going to be in for an adventure. It would also be my first trip to Haiti – so, even I did not know what to expect. And it was something of a culture shock, to me, once we had landed. If San Juan, Puerto Rico had seemed like a rich mini-America, upon our arrival there the previous week, Port-au-Prince's airport, and what we found immediately outside it, was at the other end of the scale. Haiti was clearly a very poor country and there was no disguising that. If, however, I did not know my geography of the Port-au-Prince area, from prior research I had learned that the place to stay was in a suburb, just north of the capital, named 'Petionville'. Accordingly, that is where Vere and myself started to head for - upon our exiting the airport.

We might have originally wanted to go there by means of a taxi. Immediately outside the airport, however, we saw lots of brightly-painted vehicles full of passengers. They were like small mini-buses, but with their two sides removed and replaced by two or three bars, on each - presumably, to prevent the passengers from falling out as their conveyance progressed along. Vere and I soon learned that each such vehicle was called, in the local French patios, a *'tap-tap'*. At the front, the destination of each such vehicle was stated and when Vere and I saw some with 'Port-au-Prince' stated thereon, we agreed that we would take one - in order to get to Petionville, via the capital. We were soon on board one, heading to our first destination. It had enough room for the two of us and our luggage – along with other passengers transporting similar impedimenta or otherwise. It was quite a squeeze and one of the lasting memories from that experience was my thinking that many of the people on board did not worry, too much, about using deodorant. Given the poverty - which I could see as I looked out of both sides of our *tap-tap* from time to time - I thought to myself that the 'need' for a body deodoriser was just a first-world issue. For the evidence being then picked up by my nose told me that the average person, in that new country in which I then found myself, had many more important matters of life and death to worry about than non-essential 'extras' - such as applications to help their bodies to remain odour-free.

In any case, within about 30 minutes of boarding our colourful conveyance, we found ourselves stopping in the middle of downtown Port-au-Prince – near a covered market. I suggested to Vere that, perhaps, we should get out at that point to ask for directions to enable us to go on to Petionville - and also to seek a recommendation for a reasonably-priced hotel in that district. In so doing, we entered the market in question, and I soon spied a young, Black woman who was selling wooden figures which, perhaps, she had sculpted herself. She seemed to be a likeable person from the start and I approached her with the question: 'Do you speak English?' To my delight, she answered fluently, in the same language, to confirm that she did, and then asked me how she could help. I explained that my friend and I had just flown in from Jamaica (although our homes were in the different Caribbean island of Barbados) and that we had previously learned that there were some good hotels in Petionville. I added that we wanted to know whether she might have a specific one to recommend to us and whether she could tell us how to get to that place - by *tap-tap*, if at all possible. The woman promptly introduced herself, and though I have long since forgotten her name, I will call her 'Marie' for these purposes. Having revealed my own name and that of Vere's to Marie, she was soon able to help the two of us with all the matters I had asked her about. As a kind of repayment, I suggested to Marie that Vere and I would return to visit her, on another day, in order to purchase one or two items from her stock of sculptures to take back to Barbados as souvenirs. Marie seemed pleased with our offer and willing to trust that we would really return on a later occasion to buy some mementoes from her.

At all events, Vere and I were soon following Marie's advice and finding ourselves travelling uphill in a *tap-tap* - from the stiflingly hot and crowded streets of downtown Port-au-Prince, to the more salubrious and cooler suburb of Petionville. As our transport climbed ever higher, the dwellings really did look like houses that Vere and I were used to seeing back in Barbados, or even in Camperdown Road, Jamaica. That is because they were constructed of concrete, instead of being merely shacks made of wood, and galvanised corrugated sheets for roofs, such as we had seen so often on the road from the airport.

Soon, the two of us found ourselves outside the hotel in Petionville which Marie had recommended - and, there, we disembarked from our *tap-tap*. One of the first things that I remember seeing, on our going to the reception, was a photo of 'Baby Doc' and his wife. The former was 'Jean-Claude Duvalier' - the then 'President of Haiti'. He was the son of 'Papa Doc' – the President before him, who had been notorious for remaining in power by killing-off thousands of his political opponents when he had felt it necessary. I whispered to Vere, that during our stay in that hotel, as its management seemed to be political in outlook, we had to be very careful. More specifically, I suggested that we should avoid expressing opinions about matters relating to Caribbean, or more local, politics - either to each other in public, or to any other guest or staff at the establishment.

Be that as it may, the hotel looked clean and the price of our two-nights' stay – with meals - was very reasonable. Above all, there was a swimming pool available for us to use and that was something that the two of us wished to do after the heat we had just sustained in downtown Port-au-Prince. Accordingly, we swiftly decided to accept the offer of the room, which the receptionist had told us was available for us, if we wanted it.

And so, for the first time perhaps since we had left Barbados, Vere and I could truly relax. We had no appointments for the following few days, all our meals were included in the fee we were paying, and there was a swimming pool available for us whenever we needed to cool off. Consequently, for the rest of that first day and much of the next, we did not go far from the hotel but simply took things easy and tried to recharge our batteries. Eventually, however, I, for one, wanted to see something of the 'real' Port-au-Prince. Thus, by the early evening of our second day - when the heat of the afternoon had subsided - Vere and I took a *tap-tap* to return to the downtown area of the capital, first of all, seek out Marie once more. When we did so, we thanked her again for helping us out the previous day, and then set about looking at her sculptures. We were both seeking items which were affordable, and easily portable, for us to take back to Barbados as keepsakes. One of the objects which I can still remember choosing for my home – though Vere selected different gifts for her mother's – was a wooden sculpture of an old man smoking a pipe. It was, perhaps, carved from the trunk of a small tree, and only about one-foot high. The handiwork was exquisite - and yet, Marie only asked me for a very modest price for it. To her stipulated charge, I added something more - as a kind of 'tip' for all the help that she had previously given to Vere and myself.

By the time that the two of us 'souvenir hunters' had finished with Marie, it was later in the evening. We, thus, decided to walk the length of the long, main road on which the market was located. It did not seem properly paved to me, and yet it was full of traffic – especially with the ubiquitous *tap-taps*, going in both directions. It was the people we passed, however, whom I noticed even more at that time. Most were poorly dressed and barefoot – as I had once been even when going to school in my native Montserrat in the 1950s and early 60s.[63] But even I, and my then little brother John, had surely never been so very poor. The proof of that was evidenced by the fact that, when we were going back to catch our *tap-tap* in order to return to Petionville, evening had fully fallen and some of the folk in downtown Port-au-Prince were already settling down in doorways of buildings such as the main post office. They seemed homeless, therefore, and forced to sleep outdoors and exposed to the elements. At least, my younger brother, John, and myself had never been homeless whilst growing up in our native island some thirty years or so before. Witnessing such a situation was hard for me to stomach – especially knowing that, soon afterwards, Vere and I would be returning to our hotel in Petionville, where we would have a comfortable bed, food, drink and plenty of water to keep ourselves clean with.

After, perhaps, another uneasy night for me in our hotel above the Haitian capital – largely no doubt owing to my conscience making me lose sleep in the light of what I had seen that day in the centre of the capital – our final morning came in that French-speaking republic. Vere and I had a good breakfast at the hotel before taking the necessary two *tap-taps* – one to return to the main road downtown, and the other to take us on to the airport. Once more, I was looking forward to the next adventure on our trip. On the one hand, that was because the poverty I had been witnessing in the Haitian capital was beginning to get me down. That was especially because I had realised that, even if I did give some money to the one or two persons who accosted us to do so (near Marie's market and elsewhere), there were thousands more behind them whom I could not help and, thus, my charity would have been just a tiny drop in the ocean. In addition, in getting away from Haiti I would be flying on an airline that I had wanted to travel with for many a year but never had, thus far. That was 'Air France'. Moreover, that new experience ahead included my taking Vere and myself to a territory, in the Eastern Caribbean, which neither of us had yet visited – namely, the French island of Martinique.

In due course, therefore, the two of us had checked in with Air France and had boarded one of its planes for our flight. What a contrast, I found on so doing, from the world which Vere and I had just left behind in downtown Port-au-Prince. Suddenly, I felt that the 'third world' was behind me and that I was a back in Europe. Certainly, the Caucasian air hostesses on board, with their make-up and, no doubt, liberal use of deodorant, made me feel that I was 'returning to civilisation'. At any rate, our plane was soon taking off - on time - and flying over the Caribbean Sea in an eastern, and then southerly, direction. It was heading towards the 'Lesser Antilles' island chain of the Eastern Caribbean. In so doing, it would have to pass over, or very near, my native island of Montserrat. We were, however, much too high, or it was too cloudy, to enable me to make it out during our journey. After some time - perhaps up to two or more hours after we had taken off from Haiti - our plane started to descend. It was going to make one stop before Martinique (which fact I had not appreciated when Vere and I had first boarded). That was at the other '*département d'outre-mer*' of France situated in the Eastern Caribbean – namely, the island of Guadeloupe.

In fact, Gaudeloupe is the next large island south (and a little east) of Montserrat. Like

Martinique, France regards that island as 'part of the Republic of France' - and, indeed, one of its 'departments' (which are somewhat like larger versions of the 'counties' found in England), such as 'Aveyron' or 'Herault' on its mainland. A true department, therefore - which just happens to be '*outre-mer*', or overseas. Alas, although all passengers on board our plane were asked to disembark at Gaudeloupe, perhaps so that it could be cleaned, Vere and I were not allowed to leave the airport itself, to have a look around that new island for both of us. There would not have been enough time for us to do so adequately in any case - for, within 30 minutes or so, the two of us were back on board and our flight was taking off again for our intended destination of Martinique.

Before very long after retaking to the air, we seemed to be descending again. That was because - for there is only a relatively small distance between the two French islands - with only the English-speaking island of Dominica between them (excluding small islets such as 'Marie-Galante', for example). Accordingly, at that stage in our journey, our Air France plane was acting somewhat like the island-hopper airline which Vere and I knew well from living in Barbados and which went by the name of LIAT (or Leeward Islands Air Transport, to give it its full name). During that era, one would usually take LIAT flights from our home island to neighbouring English-speaking ones such St Lucia and St Vincent - or even wider afield to Dominica, Antigua and Montserrat, for example. But, in island-hopping during our journey, Air France must have been acting exceptionally - for its high international reputation, at that time, was based upon its being a long-distance airline. Perhaps, therefore, the next stop for our own Air France plane - after Vere and myself had disembarked - in Martinique, would have been the French capital of Paris itself.

At any rate, disembark in Martinique the two of us finally did. And in doing so, once more we had the challenge of finding somewhere to stay for our two nights there. On that occasion, unlike in Haiti for example, we were able to find a tourist board office open at the airport itself. And, with the help of one of its personnel there who made the necessary phone call, we managed to secure a provisional booking at a guest house in the capital, 'Fort-de-France'. Moreover, owing to our being informed that the distance to our accommodation was only a few miles away, for once we used a taxi to reach it.

Once safely within our temporary base, I told Vere that one of things that I very much wanted to do, whilst in Fort-de-France, was to visit the university there. As so often in my Caribbean visits outside the English-speaking islands, my motive on that occasion was to try to establish a relationship with a counterpart lecturer in Comparative Law at that educational establishment. I had in mind discussing with him, or her, the possibility of a student exchange between my students in that subject and their opposite numbers at the Martinique university. In other words, something similar to the relationship which I had already started, and executed, with the Universidad Central de Venezuela, or UCV, in Caracas during the previous academic year. Vere was fully in support of my idea and, thus - after a good breakfast at our accommodation the following morning - the two of us made our way to the relevant campus on the outskirts of Martinique's capital.

The university in question was called the 'Université des Antilles' - the latter French word being the equivalent of the English words 'West Indies' – and we found its base located at 'Campus de Schoelcher' (the equivalent of my own 'Cave Hill' back in Barbados). With Vere, going off on her own to have a wander around the campus in question, I took it on myself to visit the *'Faculté de droit'*, or Law Faculty, situated within its grounds. Alas, my good experience at UCV, Caracas - of finding a relevant teacher of Comparative Law who was enthusiastic about my student exchange idea - was not to be repeated in Martinique. I failed to find any lecturer there who taught *'Droit comparé'*. The best that I was able to achieve that day, was to make an exchange of visiting cards with the administrative secretary of Faculty- with a view to following up my initiative at some time in the future.

Feeling somewhat deflated by my experience, I suggested to Vere that we should spend the rest of the day having some fun by the sea. For, that day would be the last full day of our time away from Barbados. We had asked the management at our guest house where the best beach in the neighbourhood of the island's capital was situated. The answer came back that it was located in a place called 'Trois Islet'. Naturally, therefore, Vere and I decided to go there that afternoon. To do so, however, we had to take a small ferry which started from a jetty near our accommodation. (The latter was situated in downtown Fort-de-France, near a statue of 'Josephine' - the local-born wife of the 'Emperor Napoléon' of France). Our shuttle boat took us across a bay to enable us to reach the resort in question. When we got there, the two of us were not to be disappointed. It was like being back on the golden sands of Barbados – but with some French flare added into the mix. We, thus, made the most of it by having our first swims, in the sea, since we had visited Port Royal in Jamaica. Moreover, in relaxing with our drinks in one of the nearby beach bars afterwards, we even made an acquaintanceship with a local couple. They were each of mixed race and, thus, *café-au-lait* in colour. A little older than Vere and myself, perhaps, they were able to speak to us visitors in very good English and help us to pass our day in pleasant conversation - with lots of laughter included. Moreover, they clearly wanted to keep in touch for the future and, shortly before Vere and I left them to take the little ferry back to the capital, we were to exchange addresses and promises to keep in touch.

And then it was back to our guest house for one last night there. Even if I was able to enjoy that final evening in Martinique, the following morning would have been a huge wake-up call for me. For, I had been able to suspend my family cares - as well as my teaching ones - for the week or so that Vere and I had been away travelling around the Caribbean. From then onwards, it would be back home, and 'back to school', for me. I am pretty sure, also, that I would have been one of the most reluctant passengers boarding the LIAT plane that was to take us back to Barbados from Martinique. So distracted would I have been that I doubt whether I even noticed whether our plane flew directly between the two islands or, perhaps, made an intermediate stop in St Lucia. At any rate, I can no longer recall any eventful details from that last sector of our round-

Caribbean tour in that early part of 1982.

Upon Vere and myself arriving in Barbados, I collected my car (which I had left at Grantley Adams International Airport) and drove her to the home which she shared with her mother, Joyce, in St Philip parish. No doubt, I exchanged a few pleasantries with Joyce, but I would not have stayed long. That was because I wanted to get to my own home, as soon as possible, in order to see Philomena and our children. I had missed them greatly whilst away and had felt extremely guilty about their being alone at home whilst I had been having fun in Jamaica and other places in the Caribbean. Moreover, I had brought some presents home for each of them – including a nice outfit which I had purchased for Philomena in Puerto Rico, as well as some wooden toys for the children which I had bought from Marie in Port-au-Prince, Haiti.

Philomena and children all looked really happy to see me and received their respective presents with glee. Of course, in my wife's case, she had no idea that Vere had been with me on my UWI 'duty trip'. Accordingly, she did not treat me any differently from how she would have done after my return home from any other overseas university visits which I had made in the past. More than that, she seemed eager to tell me something or other, but waited until after the children had all gone to bed later that evening. That was when she took me by the hand and sat me down in our kitchen. Then she revealed the words which she seemed to have been dying to tell me ever since I had entered our Hygeia home earlier that day:

'I have been to our doctor and he has confirmed that I am pregnant! The baby will be due sometime in September!'.

With that stunning news, what more could I do but take my wife in my arms and hold her tightly. After asking her whether she and her doctor had been 'sure' about her pregnancy, I was quick to reassure her that I fully understood that it was the Almighty's plan that our little family of three children should have an additional sibling. I was also swift in trying to convince her that I was already accepting of the Almighty's gift to us - even if it was something that we had not exactly jointly prayed for from Him. Certainly, it was perfectly clear to me that my wife was very happy to be having a new baby and that the thought of not proceeding with her pregnancy would never have occurred to her.

It was only later, perhaps - when the two of us were in bed together - that the enormity of the situation hit me. The two women in my life were now pregnant at the same time! How on earth was I going to even tell Vere about Philomena's news? And what was her reaction going to be? How was the full realisation of my future additional responsibilities going to affect my state of mind, and my ability to continue effectively with my teaching duties (as well as function properly) at UWI? One of the things which I would then have most wanted to do, therefore, was to attend Mass over the weekend in question in order to pray about my situation and to ask the Almighty to help me, Philomena and Vere through what seemed to be a most difficult, if not impossible, situation.

And then the Monday eventually arrived – perhaps the first one of February 1982 – and it was back to my teaching duties at UWI. That would have included my having to give a lecture in Comparative Law during the morning as well as tutor for three hours on the Law of Tort in the afternoon. When those latter classes were over, I would have arranged to drive Vere to her home in St Philip. Perhaps, I had even given her a hint, after my morning lecture, that I had something very important to discuss with her that evening. During our cross-country drive, therefore, I stopped my car *en route* to her home – perhaps at 'Gun Hill' in the parish of St George - with a view to breaking the news to her.

There was simply no easy way to do it. I just had to come right out and tell her. Consequently, I blurted out: 'Philomena is pregnant! She gave me the news after you and I returned from Martinique'. Vere was stunned - as much, perhaps, as I had been upon first hearing my wife's news a few days before. Moreover, she most likely would have immediately started to work out the implications that Philomena's pregnancy would mean for my relationship with her - and our own baby, expected earlier that year. Vere reacted by saying something like: 'I bet she got pregnant on purpose – in order to get you back!'. I felt obliged to tell her that, despite the unexpected developments, I had no intention of going back on my statement made in front of our mutual friend, John, to stand by her and our own baby. Despite my words, however, Vere seemed still in shock, and upset, by the tidings which I had just given her. I soon realised that I would just have to prove to her that I had meant what I had said, as witnessed by John, about supporting her - by my future actions, and not merely by my words.

Meanwhile, back at home, Philomena was, naturally, asking me what I intended to do about giving Vere up - now that I had my own prospective new, and 'legitimate', baby to think about. I would have told her, by then, that I was in the habit of driving Vere home from UWI regularly - after preparing my classes in the evening - and that I had no intention of ceasing to do so. As delicately as I could have done, given Philomena's newly-confirmed health situation, and that of our own unborn baby, I made it clear to her that, although I would be remaining living at home with my family and supporting her through the pregnancy which had just begun, I also felt obliged to support Vere through her own also (short of leaving my home to go and live with her in St Philip).

*Chapter 23*

# The Later Part of the Second Term, and the Third Term, of my Third Academic Year at UWI – Spring and Summer 1982

Even before I knew that Vere had become pregnant in the First Term of the 1981-82 academic year, I had been thinking about asking for a sabbatical period away from UWI - of perhaps one-year's duration. That would have been in order for me to become even more experienced in Comparative Law. By the coming summer of 1982, I would have been at Cave Hill Campus for some three academic years and, thus, I was in a good position to ask for a 'break'. Moreover, my group's visit to the UCV in Caracas, Venezuela, the previous teaching year, had taught me that I needed to become more fluent in at least one of the foreign languages, of one of the countries whose Laws and legal system I was looking at for the purpose of my course in Barbados. Owing to that course being largely comprised of French Law - especially in the second part of it, commencing in the January of each academic year - a Masters course in Comparative Law, in France, would have seemed to be the ideal programme to try to get into for my proposed year out. Upon my perusing publications such as the '*International Encyclopedia of Comparative Law*', however, I had been unable to find what I was looking for.

In due course, however, something else jumped out at me during such researches – which was being provided in a neighbouring country of my primary target. That adjacent state was Belgium. I discovered that one of the universities in its capital city, Brussels, offered a Masters degree course in Comparative Law which ran over the period of one academic year. The plus point was that it was taught in English. The down side, however, seemed to be that the university in question was the Dutch-speaking (or, more precisely, Flemish-speaking) 'Vrije Universiteit Brussel' (known, in short, as the 'VUB'). That was a negative factor for me since I would really have preferred to be taught at a French-speaking institution. That was because I wanted to improve my French, for the purpose of being able to tackle French legal materials, in their original language - and so as to be all the more fluent in that foreign tongue when I returned to UWI to teach my course, after my sabbatical year.

Be that as it may, through Professor Ralph Carnegie - who was either the Dean or Head of the Teaching Department in the UWI Law Faculty during that 1981-82 academic year - I applied for the one-year sabbatical period as well as for the Belgian course in question. Fortunately for me, he supported both applications – with enthusiasm, it seemed to me.

Such was the position, therefore, as the Second Term of the 1981-82 academic year was coming to a close towards Easter of 1982. Both Philomena and Vere were pregnant. Both expected me to be (and I very much wanted to be) available to support each of them. In addition, I had an outstanding application to spend the following academic year outside Barbados in order to go and study in Belgium. It was, thus, a fraught time for each of the three persons in question. For, although I continued to live at home with Philomena and was there with her and our three existing children throughout most weekends, during the week it was otherwise. For, from Monday to Friday – and my special 'Family Only Wednesdays' began to fall in abeyance by this time - I would arrive home really late in the evenings - after spending them with Vere, in my attempts to be as supportive to her as possible. Accordingly, I would always miss seeing the children when I reached Hygeia – since they had all gone to bed long beforehand. Moreover, as I also left quite early in the mornings during the working week, it meant that I also only saw them fleetingly before leaving for my UWI duties at Cave Hill on weekdays.

In such a scenario, something had to give. And it did! That was by Philomena taking the initiative to do something about the overall situation. For, one weeknight, I came home late from work as had become usual - after first dropping Vere off in St Philip at the residence of her mother and herself. Hygeia was empty! There was, however, a letter left for me on the table in the living room. It was from Philomena and it started off by saying: 'Yes, David, we have gone!'.

My heart sank! And it went even deeper still, as I read the letter further. Philomena wrote that she just could not bear to be in Barbados at the time of the birth of Vere's baby, in the near future, and to witness me being a father to it – whilst at the same time knowing that a brother or sister for our existing three children was also going to be born a few months afterwards. As, the letter went on, Philomena revealed that she had shared her anguish with some of our friends in our Marriage Encounter group - including the leader in Barbados, Father Pat. They had all advised her to get in touch with her mother, back in Swindon, to ask whether she, and the children, could all come back to live with her - at least until the new baby had been born. Philomena revealed that such a step was exactly what she had taken - and that her mother had said 'Yes' to the idea. In addition, my wife's letter revealed that, by the time that I had read the missive in my hand, she and our children would already be on a flight back to England that evening – using air tickets paid for by the Catholic Church in Barbados, through the intervention of Father Pat. Philomena assured me, in the letter, that she had not told her mother the real reason why she could not bear to stay in Barbados any longer at that time. Rather, that she had merely suggested that it was all to do with her not wanting to have another bad Barbadian birthing experience - after the one that she had suffered when she had delivered Claire-Louise at Queen Elizabeth Hospital, Bridgetown the previous year.

I was devastated! My wife and children had left me. My life seemed to me to be at a crossroads, immediately after I had read Philomena's letter. All that I had studied and worked for, during most of the 1970s as a Law student – namely, to bring my wife and our small family to 'Paradise', and to work and live there 'happily ever after' - had, as of that day, been shattered. What was I going to do? No doubt I cried somewhat, as I repaired to bed shortly afterwards – in order to allow the reality of my situation to hit me in my prone position. Somehow, I had really thought that I would have been able to go on 'supporting' both of the two women in my life - simultaneously, and throughout both of the pregnancies involved. Somehow, I had imagined that my back was broad enough to carry the burden of doing that and that somehow, and in some way, we would all be able to live together happily, in due course – in some kind of *ménage à trois* operating between the adults, and with, by then, the four children of Philomena and myself, as well as the single newborn of Vere and my own self.

My 'dream', quite clearly was just that. It was an abstract idea that reckoned without the deep feelings of my wife – and, no doubt, Vere's also. Next morning, however, I had already begun to become philosophical. The first thing that I decided to do was to write to Philomena and let her know how sorry I was about her decision to return to England with our children. I was at pains to reassure her that such a step would never have been suggested by me and that I had been confident that our 'situation' could have eventually resolved itself, satisfactorily - if we had only stuck it out together in Barbados. Nevertheless, I promised to send her a part of my salary on a regular basis, so that she would have an income to support herself and our children until the new baby arrived. Also, that I would do my best to be in England, with her, when that event occurred. I was careful not to write anything about Vere in my letter, however. That was because I already suspected that Philomena's mother would want to read whatever I wrote to my wife - if possible - in an effort to glean the 'real' reason why her daughter had decided, so suddenly, to return to England, with her existing children, prior to having her new baby.

Meanwhile, back in Barbados, I had to tell Vere the news of the unexpected development in my - and our - lives. I seem to recall that I waited until we were on our way home, in my car after classes the following day, before I made the revelation. She too was taken aback by the turn of events and may even, like me, have felt a sadness for Philomena as well as huge guilt that 'but for our affair, the life-disruptive step that Philomena had just taken would never have occurred'. Nevertheless, we both saw at once that I had been experiencing a physical and mental 'pull' - in two opposing directions - since Philomena had told me of her pregnancy – regarding with which of them I should physically be with, when I was not teaching, in the run up to the expected births in question. And that, finally, such tug-of-war had been resolved in favour of Vere.

And yet, neither Vere nor myself thought that it would be a good idea for her to come to live with me at Hygeia immediately after Philomena had left. We both seem to decide that she should continue to live at her mother's house in St Philip – at least until her exams were over that June. By her so doing, I would be able to get on with giving my normal revision classes at UWI - and she, with her own preparation for her five 'Finals', without any distractions from me (or accusations of 'favouritism' from any of her fellow students, owing to two of those five subjects being ones which I lectured her and/or tutored her in).

Eventually, however - when I was already involved in marking the Comparative Law and Conflict of Laws written exam papers, or scripts, from my Final Year students, as well as the Law of Torts from my Second Year tutees - Vere and I decided that she should indeed move into Hygeia with me. Philomena and the children had already safely returned to England, and settled in with her mother, from about two months before and Vere was in the last month of her pregnancy. She told me that, though her own mother, Joyce, was then a practising midwife and very much wanted to be involved with the birth of the due baby, such a scenario was the 'last thing' that she (Vere) wanted to happen. Accordingly, just like with the birth of Claire-Louise, the baby was planned to be also born at the Queen Elizabeth Hospital (QEH) in Barbados' capital. And, once more, that was to happen through the organisation of her general practitioner - a male doctor - who would arrange a hospital midwife for Vere, as necessary.

After Vere had taken up residence with me in Hygeia, I continued on my daily routine of going to the Law Faculty each day, in order to mark my exam scripts as usual. Fortunately, I did not always have to leave her alone during that period, as she had a good friend from her schooldays – one 'Patricia', or 'Pat', who was herself already a single-mum with a young daughter. Pat was able to visit Vere at Hygeia for companionship and, no doubt, discussions from time to time of what the birthing-process ahead for Vere could be expected to be like.

I cannot imagine what my (formerly very close) neighbour, Mrs Payne, downstairs thought about the whole situation – with Philomena and the children having returned to England, and a heavily-pregnant Vere having moved into Hygeia to 'fill the vacuum'. I coped by trying not to think, too much, about how disappointed the old lady might have been with me. And, fortunately for me, when we did see each other – fleetingly, from time to time, in the garden of the house - she was only ever civil to me, as I was to her.

Perhaps, it was on the very day that I had completed all my marking of the examination papers, in my office at Cave Hill Campus, that I received a phone call there from Vere. She told me that her waters had broken but that, thankfully, Pat was then with her. She added that Pat had offered to drive her to the hospital in Bridgetown. In something of a panic, I replied that they should go ahead with that plan and that I would come and meet her at the hospital just as soon as I could. When I reached the QEH, however, I had to ask at reception which ward Vere had been taken to and I quickly followed up on the information given in reply – as well as the directions received on how to get to the much sought-after location. Nonetheless, upon arriving at the ward, though I was able to see Vere, fleetingly - and discover that the birth was very imminent - just as with the arrival the previous year of the daughter of Philomena and myself, Claire-Louise, I was asked to remain outside the birthing room. That was because, exactly as in Claire-Louise's case, Vere's doctor was not present on the scene to give the necessary permission for the baby's father to be present at the birth. Accordingly, the midwife was wholly in charge of the proceedings, and she also happened not to agree about the presence of the baby's other parent during the birth process.

Be that as it may, within about 30 minutes of my arrival outside Vere's room at the QEH from UWI, I heard a cry. The midwife soon appeared and told me that I could then go inside the space which was formerly forbidden to me – in order to meet my 'new baby daughter' and her mother! I quickly did as I had been bidden and saw a tired-looking, but delighted, Vere - holding our curly-haired little girl in her arms. I hugged them both and said 'Well done!' to Vere. At that moment, all was forgiven - as far as the midwife having excluded me from the birth was concerned.

I stayed with Vere and the baby as long as the hospital would allow me to do so that evening. We two new parents discussed matters long into the evening - such as where new mum and baby would go immediately after being discharged from the QEH. Vere told me that, of course, her mother, Joyce – as both a midwife and now a new grandmother – very much wanted her and the baby to come to Joyce's home in St Philip, in order for Joyce to look after them. Vere and I agreed, however, that she and the baby would come to live with me at my Hygeia home in Christ Church parish, where, she assured me, she would feel much happier.

Much sooner than it had taken Philomena to be discharged from the QEH after having Claire-Louise – possibly, after only two days since the birth, instead of the four as in Philomena's case - Vere and the baby were being driven to Hygeia by me. By then, I had already registered the baby's name at the main registry next to the then Supreme Court buildings in central Bridgetown. For, that is something else that Vere and I had agreed upon, during her time recuperating in the hospital after the birth. We agreed that our daughter would definitely have my surname - but that it should also have hers as well. We were also like-minded on the baby being given two French Christian names, which we both happened to like. And so, I had registered her as 'Mikaëlle Eloise Brathwaite Bradshaw'. Giving our baby my own surname, was, it seemed to me, the strongest evidence that I could provide to Vere that I meant to keep my promise to stand by both her and Mikaëlle for the future - whatever tribulation for her parents lay ahead as a result.

And much trouble did indeed begin very soon after I brought Vere and Mikaëlle – whom we began to call 'Mikki', almost from the first – to live in Hygeia. For, although Vere's mother, Joyce, had met her granddaughter, at least once or twice during visiting times at the QEH whilst they had still been there, she (Joyce) was not at all happy that her daughter had chosen me, over her own mother, as the person with whom Vere and Mikki would live in those earliest days. Joyce showed her probable ire in relation to that situation by vowing not to come to Hygeia to visit the baby. Worse still for me (and unbeknown to myself until much later), she let one or two of her contacts at UWI know that I was Mikki's father.

Nothing official ever came to my notice from UWI, however – concerning the lecturer-student relationship, and its aftermath - during that period. Nevertheless, I will always remember an incident that occurred a week or so after Mikki's birth. That was when Pat had been visiting with Vere and Mikki at Hygeia and I was at a Law Faculty examiners' meeting. When the gathering came to discuss what class of degree to award Vere (from her exam results, which were then in front of the examiners) and that body eventually decided to give her an 'Upper Second Class', one of my colleagues immediately looked me in the eye and whispered to me: 'Mission accomplished!'. Accordingly, that remark made me wonder whether word was out - at least among one or two of my colleagues - that Vere had given birth to her baby and that I was the father. For myself, however, despite the said barbed comment, I still felt able to stand up to my paternal responsibilities in Barbados and to take on, fully, the consequences of standing by both Vere and Mikki.

As luck would have it, I had to make another UWI duty visit to Jamaica - soon after Vere came out of hospital with Mikki to live with me at Hygeia. That gave me the opportunity, therefore, to try to patch things up with her mum - by my agreeing, with Vere, to drive her and Mikki to Joyce's home for them to stay there during my absence in Jamaica. And Joyce seemed so happy about such an arrangement that it left me thinking that all would be fine between Mikki's parents and her grandmother, for the future - once I had returned from my overseas UWI trip. Alas, that was not to be. For, having had her daughter and granddaughter at such close quarters during my absence in Jamaica, it seemed to me that Joyce wanted to keep them, permanently, with her at her St Philip home. My coming there to drive them back to mine at Hygeia – and thereby 'taking Vere and Mikki away' - immediately after returning to Barbados, was the final straw for Joyce. Thereafter, a rift was to form between herself and me which would, perhaps, be a very long-term one.

At about the same time as the examinations processes were moving forward at UWI - and in the few months prior to Mikki's birth - I had been exchanging regular letters with Philomena in England. In mine to her, as well as sending money, I was continually asking after herself and the children. Moreover, I had reassured her that I would be there for her in England when our new baby was about to be born. She, in turn, had given me news that Noel had started his formal education at her dad's old primary of 'St Mary's RC School' in Swindon – the one of which he had been the founding headmaster, and which Philomena herself had attended prior to going on to St Joseph's, in the same town, where she and I had first met. The burning question for me, however, was: How on earth was I going to be able to keep my promise to be there for my wife, when our new baby was about to be born?

The answer came to me via the post – with the acceptance of my application to study for the Masters degree in Comparative Law at the VUB in Belgium. That was coupled with the wonderful news, given to me by Professor Carnegie, that my application for a sabbatical year away from UWI - to study for my postgraduate Law degree at the Brussels university - had been accepted. Accordingly, as the new baby of Philomena and myself was due that coming September and I was not due to begin my Brussels

*Fig. 47: Philomena (pregnant with our fourth child) - with Kim, Claire-Louise and Noel, on a visit to Bath, England in the summer of 1982 – after leaving Barbados to live with her mother, Mrs Maureen Harrison, in Swindon during her pregnancy*

*Fig. 48: Noel, standing in front of the sign for 'St Mary's RC Junior and Infants School', Swindon, England – the school of which his maternal grandfather, Mr Thomas Basil Harrison, was the first headmaster, and which Noel attended as a pupil from the summer term of 1982*

course until the following month, it meant that I could spend some time in England with Philomena, our existing children and the new baby until I would have to leave to begin my course. Moreover, in Belgium I would be near enough to England to be able to come over to visit Philomena, and our children, on a regular basis during that coming academic year.

What, however, would happen to Vere and Mikki during my sabbatical year? Once I had heard the good news of the acceptance of my place on the course in Belgium - as well as having received the go-ahead from UWI for my sabbatical year - it did not take long for Vere and myself to decide that she and our baby would come to live with me in Brussels during the year in question! What, however, would they do whilst I was with Philomena and our children, during the period I was with them in Swindon awaiting the birth of the new baby? I asked Vere to really think hard about whether she had any friends in England with whom she and Mikki might be able to spend time, whilst I was with Philomena and the children in Wiltshire. Fortunately, she was able to come up with the name of a former school friend. That person was 'Rosie' - with whom she had been at 'Queen's College' in Barbados, years before, and who was then working as a nurse in the Birmingham area of the English Midlands. Vere wrote to ask Rosie whether she and Mikki would be able to stay with her in her Birmingham home for a few weeks – and, if so, to kindly send a separate letter inviting Vere and Mikki to come to England for a holiday with her. The latter was needed because, in those early 1980s days, Vere only had a Barbados passport (upon which she had added Mikki soon after Mikki's birth) and they would need a sort of visa in order to gain entry into England and stay for a while. As it turned out, Rosie was keen to help out her old schoolfriend and promptly sent back the letter of invitation for Vere and Mikki – with which they were able to secure the necessary visa-like stamp in Vere's passport, to enable her and Mikki to visit, and stay, in the United Kingdom for some time.

There were other practical matters to also sort out at that time, however. Those included the question of the air tickets for Vere, Mikki and myself to England. For some reason, I could not buy tickets that would be valid for a London-Barbados return flight at the end of the following academic year in, say, July 1983. Or, rather, I could not afford to buy such tickets. There was less of a problem, however, buying return tickets for the three of us that were valid for six months exactly. Accordingly, the latter were the ones which I purchased - with a view to paying something extra, in due course, with the airline in question in order to extend their duration. The essential thing was that Vere and Mikki had valid return tickets back to Barbados - in addition to the visa-like stamp in Vere's passport - to allow them to gain entry to England when the three of us flew there together in the near future.

If, however, the three of us had all the necessary paperwork and tickets sorted out for our flight to Europe, there was nevertheless going to be an unexpected practical problem in our making that flight – namely, Vere's mother, Joyce! That was because Vere made it very clear to me that if Joyce ever got wind of her daughter and granddaughter 'emigrating' to Europe - for even as short a period as one academic year – she (Joyce) would do everything in her power to scupper such a plan. And, no doubt, she would have been able to that by complaining to my UWI employers - which institution knew nothing of the plan for Vere and Mikki to accompany me during my forthcoming sabbatical year.

Vere, Mikki and myself, therefore, needed help to keep our 'doing a midnight flit' from Barbados well away from Joyce's knowledge and potential interference. That assistance was to be provided by a much older female friend of Vere's - a woman whom Vere had known for several years previously and who owned a large home in Atlantic Shores, Christ Church parish. Part of that residence was used by her to run an old people's home. Vere always called that older lady 'Aunt Ruby' - for the sake of politeness - and that 'courtesy relative' seemed to be like me too, and be totally behind the plan of Vere and myself to take Mikki away from Barbados to live with the two of us in Brussels during my sabbatical year ahead. Aunt Ruby also had a senior lady 'girlfriend', to whom Vere also gave the honorary title of 'Aunt' - whose Christian name was 'Daphne', but whom Vere usually called 'Aunt Daph'. Whilst Aunt Daph did not seem to warm to me as much as Aunt Ruby, I perceived her to be happy enough to go along with helping Aunt Ruby to assist Vere, Mikki and myself in our joint enterprise to set up a temporary home in Belgium.

One of the flaws in the plan to keep things from Joyce was that she had, for a long time, been trying to befriend Aunt Ruby. During that period, she was in the habit of phoning, or even visiting unannounced, Aunt Ruby's place – often to complain about me, it seemed, and to try to obtain up-to-date information about what her daughter and I were planning, especially in relation to Mikki. Aunt Ruby, therefore, was somewhat stuck in the middle between mother and daughter. She always reassured Vere and myself, however, that - without being outwardly rude to Joyce - she always tried to get rid of Joyce's calls, and visits, as soon as possible and, certainly, gave nothing away to her regarding our plans for our going to live in Europe.

Shortly before the 'secret flight' to England, however, I needed to pack up all the household belongings at Hygeia and move out of that former family home of Philomena, myself and our three children. In doing so, I found it a sad proceeding! And the memories of happier days spent there with my wife and our offspring - as well as of wonderful visits from friends from Europe such as Berndt, Moni and Miriam for Miriam's first birthday celebration - would flash though my mind as I prepared to move out. I also had to take my leave of Mrs Payne, my neighbour downstairs. Although she may have had good cause for being antagonistic to me by then, bless her soul, she showed me no anger and was ever the polite old lady that I had always known her to be. She even told me that she fully understood my wanting to take my sabbatical year in Europe and was happy that I would soon be reunited with Philomena and our children in England. We parted on good terms, therefore, and I even, finally, gave away (to her niece) the bicycle, with the basket on the front, which I had brought from Leeds University when my family had first moved into Hygeia in August 1979.

With the help of Aunt Ruby, and some workman she knew, my belongings (and some of Vere's) were transported on the workman's truck from Hygeia to Atlantic Shores, and then stored in a disused garage at the front of Aunt Ruby's home. She assured me that she would ensure that those belongings would remain safe, during the time away of Vere, Mikki and myself, and that we could collect them again when we returned from Europe in due course.

For the last day or so of our time in Barbados, prior to leaving for England, Vere, Mikki and I stayed at Aunt Ruby's home. A panic set in, however, when Joyce phoned Aunt Ruby to say that she was intending to visit to discuss a 'rumour' which she had heard about my leaving for England shortly - and taking Vere and Mikki with me! Perhaps, Joyce had been passing Hygeia in her car, at the time I had been packing up my belongings in the recent days just past, and had put two and two together. More than likely, however, Joyce had a contact at UWI and, by that time, it would have been official news that the University had granted me a sabbatical year to study at a university in Europe – and, again, she had drawn the logical inference.

At any rate, if Joyce was on her way to visit Aunt Ruby uninvited, Vere, Mikki and myself had to make alternative arrangements - regarding where to spend our last evening. That is when Vere's other courtesy aunt stepped into the picture to save the day. For, Aunt Daph – who usually lived at Aunt Ruby's but who also owned her own home in a different part of Christ Church parish – quickly invited the three of us to come and spend our last hours in Barbados that day with her at that other residence of hers. She also offered to drive us there, in order to treat us to a final meal with her, as well to the airport afterwards to enable the three of us would-be fugitives to make our 'escape' that coming evening.

As a result, a premature *'au revoir'*, and 'thank you for everything', had to be said to Aunt Ruby at her Atlantic Shores home that day. And, some hours later, Vere and I found ourselves repeating the experience with Aunt Daph at Grantley Adams International Airport. Even as I was doing the last, I was wary that Joyce would suddenly appear from nowhere - to make a scene and to do her best to prevent me from taking her daughter and granddaughter away from the native land of all three.

Thankfully, my imagined scenario never came to pass. And as our BWIA plane took off, I breathed a heavy sigh of relief that a major challenge concerning Joyce had been overcome. No doubt, I thought to myself, she would create merry hell when she discovered that Vere and Mikki were with me in Europe – without even having said goodbye to her. Undoubtedly, also, UWI would hear about the matter, via her! For the time being, however, I was only looking forward – for I still had some major challenges ahead. Not the least of these was my need to take Vere and Mikki to a safe place in England - and then get to Philomena, as fast as possible, in order to keep my promise to be with her before our new baby was born.

*Chapter 24*

# The First Arrival of Vere and Mikki in England; and the Birth of the Fourth Child of Philomena and myself – September 1982

After an uneventful flight, the plane carrying Vere, Mikki and myself duly landed at Heathrow Airport in London. There was no one to meet us there - when we eventually cleared immigration and exited the terminal. Fortunately, all the paperwork we had put in place for Vere and Mikki was in order - and they experienced no problem in getting permission to land and stay in England (at least, for the six months' validity of their return tickets to Barbados). I had guessed that there would be a 'National Express' coach available from the airport to Birmingham. That speculation was proved correct when the three of us, with Mikki in her pram-buggy, reached the coach station near the terminal from which we had exited. Vere made a quick phone call to Rosie in Birmingham - to let her know that the three of us had just arrived safely. Then we three 'new arrivals' were soon on our way to Rosie's current home city, by coach - after Vere had told her of the estimated time of our arrival there. Rosie had also suggested that we simply take a taxi from Birmingham Coach Station to her home address - which Vere possessed from the several letters which had passed between them in recent weeks. Our would-be hostess had also told Vere, in their telephone conversation, that the two places were relatively near each other and that she would wait indoors for us to arrive with her.

From the commencement of that first step of our journey in England, my heart was sad. That was owing to my then being once again in the same country again as Philomena and our children but, nevertheless, being unable to call her to let her know that (not least because her mother still had no telephone at her home). Because of that lack of a quick and direct way of contacting my marital family, therefore, I was determined to call my own mother as soon as I could. That was to ask her for permission to stay with her from the following day - and to urge her to please get a message to Philomena and our children for them to meet me at my mother's home, that next day, if at all possible. I made that the requisite call as soon as we had arrived at Birmingham's coach station - some hours later. *En route*, however, I quite enjoyed telling Vere about some of the places which we were stopping at during our journey. Not the least of these would have been the world famous university city of Oxford.

Vere, Mikki and myself did, eventually, reach Rosie at her home and she turned out to be most welcoming – even to me, whom she had never met before. She also seemed delighted to be meeting Mikki for the first time. Moreover, it was clear to me that the old schoolmates were absolutely overjoyed to be back in each other's company - after the several years since Rosie had first emigrated to England. The enthusiastic and happy way they were chatting to each other, thus, helped to reassure me that Vere and Mikki would spend a welcoming and delightful time in Birmingham - whilst I would be away in Wiltshire looking out for Philomena and my original family. And even though Rosie's place was only an apartment, or 'flat' - rather than a house – nevertheless it contained two bedrooms. Accordingly, there was more than adequate accommodation and space for two old girlfriends and one small baby. I was, thus, able to leave Vere and Mikki, the following morning, with peace of mind and knowing that Rosie would be taking good care of my 'other family' and that I could focus, fully, on Philomena and our children whilst in Swindon.

Accordingly, after spending a pleasant night in Rosie's flat, with the two old Bajan schoolmates and Mikki, I took my leave of the three of them and walked the mile or so back to Birmingham's coach station with my luggage. A new - and very uncertain - set of challenges were awaiting me, a few counties away in Wiltshire, and my emotions were churning up. What would it be like seeing Philomena and my children again - after so many months of being apart from them? Whatever the worst case scenario might turn out to be, I was nevertheless very much looking forward to seeing them all again – as well as my own mother. That was the case, as my coach for Swindon left Birmingham - for the two to three hours' drive to the south which lay ahead.

It was an easy five-minute walk from Swindon's Coach Station to my mother's home situated at 16 Alexandra Road. That was the house in which I had grown up during most of my schooldays in Wiltshire during the 1960s and early 1970s.[64] It was wonderful to be 'home' again and to see Mum for the first time since the summer holidays of Philomena, myself and our children the previous year. It was also delightful to see my only sister – Sylvia – again, who was still living with Mum at that time and who it was who, most likely, got my message to Philomena, at Mrs Harrison's home, that I would be back 'home' in Swindon that afternoon.

Within a short time of my arrival at Alexandra Road, however, I heard the doorbell ring to announce the arrival of the members of my family that I most wanted to see – my wife and our children, Noel, Kim and Claire-Louise! Philomena gave me her wonderful smile, and we were embraced warmly and lovingly at the door. Her tummy had grown much more than when I had last seen her in Barbados, some five or six months before. That did not stop the two of us from hugging each other as tight as we reasonably could without causing any danger, or damage, to our baby inside her. Eventually, I had to let her go - in order to be able to look at, and then hug in turn, each of my lovely children. They had all grown taller since I had last seen them, and our daughter had become a good walker (and talker) - which she had not been able to do, quite so well, when I had last seen her. All three were beautiful children. How, I asked myself, could I have put their, and my wife's, happiness in jeopardy because of my selfishness in Barbados?

Whatever had constituted the straw that had broken the camel's back in Barbados - and which had caused Philomena to decide to return to England with the children some half a year before - it was immediately clear to me, from our embracing, that she had forgiven me and wanted me back in her life again. And whilst my sister played with Noel, Kim and Claire-Louise outside in my mother's back garden, my wife and myself became close again – closer, perhaps, than we had been since around the time that our expected new baby had been conceived in December the year before.

I too wanted to be back with Philomena and the children, and the least that I could do in that regard - for the time being - was to walk with them back to her mother's home in Southbrook Street. For, as stated, that is where they had been staying in Swindon since their return to England earlier in the year. When we had arrived at Mrs Harrison's back gate, however, it was Philomena's suggestion that I should not come inside. For, as she told me, it was a little too early - to announce the fact - to my mother-in-law - that I was back in my matrimonial family's life. With a heavy heart, therefore, I kissed my wife and children, outside their then current home, as we made an agreement to all meet up again at my own mother's home the following morning.

No sooner than I had arrived back at Alexandra Road than Philomena was calling my Mum's phone there, from a public call box, to speak to me. Her mother, she told me in an alarmed voice, had asked her and the children to leave - as a result of their coming to see me that day and spending time with me! 'My God', I said to her - and then asked myself what on earth were we going to do. I knew, deep down, however, that my own mother would not deny me if I asked her to let my wife and her grandchildren stay with her for the time being. I, therefore, told Philomena to please get her own, and the children's, belongings ready and that I would come for them, in a taxi, within the next 30 minutes or so.

As soon as I had put the phone down, however, a better idea came to me. I was the eldest of the three Bradshaw brothers - and the youngest, George, still lived in the town. He was a single man at the time - after having been married and divorced - and he was then living in a flat in a district of Swindon called Toothill. I phoned him, explained the emergency and asked him whether I could bring Philomena and the children to his place – at least for the weekend - whilst my wife and I tried to arrange some more permanent accommodation for herself and our children. Bless his heart, my brother, said 'Yes' straight away – whatever misgivings he might have had at the back of his mind regarding my sudden request.

When the taxi, which I had hired from Swindon's railway station - a mere 200 yards or so away from Mum's home - arrived outside the back gate of Mrs Harrison's home, Philomena and the children were already there waiting for me. They had with them all their worldly possessions, so far as I could see. My wife was to tell me that her mother had carried out her determination to 'evict' them - and had even 'helped' in bringing their belongings to the back gate. There was no sign of my mother-in-law, however, so the potentiality for an altercation between her and myself dissipated by her non-appearance.

Somehow or another, we managed to get ourselves, and all the belongings, into the taxi and then get driven to George's home - about three miles away - without too much ado. It was a huge relief for me when I saw my younger sibling and perceived that he really did not mind having a 'house full' - at least on a temporary basis for the weekend in question. Living alone, as he was doing, it seemed to me as though he regarded it as being something of an adventure to be hosting his elder brother, sister-in-law, two nephews and one niece - for a few days at least. If my brother was happy about the temporary situation, however, my emotions were rather at the other end of the scale. I needed to call my mother and explain the unexpected developments to her, regarding Mrs Harrison. I then had to beg her to allow Philomena and the children to stay with her at Alexandra Road - at least until Philomena had given birth to the new baby. When I made the call to Mum, whilst she was understanding of my matrimonial family's then current plight, she nevertheless asked us to stay put with George for the weekend in question whilst she got her home in order, and ready for my family's coming to live with her and Sylvia there.

Having thus spoken to my mother, and then explained her decision to Philomena, the two of us could then begin to try to enjoy being with my brother. We took the children to the nearby public playground many times that weekend - as well as helped George to do some shopping and the cooking of meals to feed all of us during the period in question. We also watched, together, the television which my brother had in his living room. It was on the sofa in that space where Philomena and I slept at night, whilst the children shared his spare bedroom and bed inside it. One programme which I will always recall, from that never to be forgotten 'homeless weekend' of my matrimonial family, was a live broadcast from 'Monte Carlo, Monaco'. Most likely, it was transmitted on 'BBC Television' and it showed the funeral of the former 'Hollywood' film star, 'Grace Kelly' - who, as the then 'Princess Grace' of that principality, had recently died in a car accident in the hills above her royal palace. That day - Saturday, 18th September 1982 - also happened to be my 30th birthday!

When the weekend in question was over, I rang my mother on the Monday morning to ask her what time would be best for my family and I to come to move into her home. She answered me with some unexpected news! During the weekend, she recounted, she had met up with a member of Swindon's West Indian community - a man whom I shall call for these purposes, 'Mr Thomas'. She went on to tell me that she knew, before the meeting, that he owned two houses in the town - one for himself and his wife in 'County Road', and another in 'Volta Road' which he rented out to tenants. As it happened, when she had visited Mr Thomas, he had confirmed that he did have some vacancies at his Volta Road place - as there was only one tenant there at that time, who occupied only one of the three bedrooms in the house. Mr Thomas, had also confirmed to her that he would be willing to rent the two vacant bedrooms to my family and myself - as long as we were happy to share the kitchen and bathroom with the other tenant. Without hesitating - in order to consult with my wife about the unforeseen development - I requested Mum to kindly accept Mr Thomas's offer and told her that my family and I would first come to her home that morning. That latter step was in order to give me, whilst Philomena and the children stayed with my mother for an hour or so, a chance to go to visit Mr Thomas at his County Road home to effectuate all the necessary paperwork - and pay any advance deposit and rent – which he required, in order to allow my family to move into his Volta Road house. When I, afterwards, told Philomena what had been arranged, she seemed as relieved as myself that our growing family then had a 'place of our own' in Swindon – sort of!

After, thus, thanking my brother - profusely - for all his kind hospitality to us in our dire emergency, another taxi was soon taking my matrimonial family, and belongings, back to Alexandra Road. I left my wife and children at my mother's house in order for me to walk the half mile or so to County Road to see Mr Thomas in his own home there. I found him to be a friendly Jamaican man – whom I seemed to vaguely remember from my time of growing up in the town as a teenager. He was happy to help me and my family out of our difficult situation and, moreover, he did not try to exact a very high rent from me for doing so. In addition, he walked with me to his Volta Road house and showed me the place – including the two upstairs bedrooms which my family would occupy, whilst his other existing tenant had the single bedroom downstairs. Upon seeing the facilities, I knew Philomena and the children could be happy there and - after obtaining the necessary set of keys from Mr Thomas - I went to fetch my family and our belongings from my mother's home.

Once we were installed in the Volta Road house – which was number 14 – I breathed a major sigh of relief. For having upset the apple cart by my arriving out of the blue - in the sense of the placidity which Philomena had enjoyed at her mother's home in the run up to the birth of our new baby - I rather hoped that having a place of her own, from then on, would help her to regain that peacefulness. There was one potential obstacle to that happening, however – namely, the other tenant. How would he feel, when he came home that evening, to find the house filled with a family of five other people?

As luck would have it, that other tenant turned out to be a really nice man. He was Welsh, and had his home somewhere in South Wales – in the 'Swansea' area, as I recall. He told Philomena and myself that he merely commuted from there to work in the Swindon area during the week, and then went back home to his wife and family at the weekends. My wife, myself and our children would, thus, have the house to ourselves every weekend and would merely have to share the kitchen and bathroom with him from Monday evening to Friday morning during the week. Let us call that other tenant 'Mr Williams' for these purposes. If he had felt that his nose was somewhat put out of joint by the unexpected development of having a house full of people sharing its facilities – for, it seemed that our landlord, Mr Thomas, had not consulted him prior to my family moving into the rented house – he never once showed his displeasure at having us in the premises with him. Indeed, he rather tended to remain in his bedroom, once he was home during the week, and left us to watch the only television set located in the living room of the dwelling.

Having secured a home for my first family, therefore, I then needed to touch base with Vere and Mikki up in Birmingham. By that time, I had explained to Philomena that I had taken a sabbatical year off from my teaching duties at UWI for the coming 1982-83 academic year in order to study for my Masters qualification in Comparative Law at a university in Brussels. Without mentioning that Vere and Mikki were also going to be with me during my time in Belgium, I was able to assure my wife that Brussels was not so very far away and that I would be able to come to visit her in Swindon on a regular basis during my time on the Belgian degree course. What I told her seemed to keep her calm, as she would still have a solid base in Swindon – near my mother's home, if not also her mum's – immediately after the new baby was born. Moreover, Noel would be able to continue going to school at St Mary's (about one mile away from Volta Road) during the academic year.

I contacted Vere by telephone soon after Philomena, myself and the children had moved into Volta Road. She seemed to fully understand why I felt that I needed to remain in Swindon until the new baby was born – and seemed happy enough to be staying on at Rosie's Birmingham home. That was especially the case as, she assured me, Rosie was only too delighted to be sharing her flat with her two guests from her native Barbados.

In those earliest days at Volta Road, therefore, Philomena, the children and myself played ourselves in slowly, into the new home - as we awaited the arrival of our fourth child. Noel continued going to school at St Mary's during that period and, owing to the fact that I never once saw Mrs Harrison throughout the duration of my latest Swindon sojourn, it meant that Philomena would walk our eldest child to school, and bring him home in the evenings, whilst I looked after Kim and Claire-Louise at Volta Road (or took them to the nearby public playground at the 'County Ground', for them to get some exercise from time to time).

And then, one night during the last week of that September month - after the children were already in their bedroom asleep and she and I were repairing to bed ourselves in the neighbouring upstairs bedroom - Philomena, felt her waters breaking! As was usual in such a situation, I panicked at first and then slowly began to think more clearly. I soon realised that I would have to get my wife, by taxi, to the then local maternity unit at 'Princess Margaret Hospital', or 'PMH', in Swindon. For, that medical institution had already been earmarked for her through her then local Swindon general practitioner doctor. What was to be done, however, about our sleeping children in their bedroom? I urged Philomena to please 'hang on' - whilst I sprinted to my mother's Alexandra Road home, just about two minutes' run away. When I returned - about 10 minutes later - my sister, Sylvia, was with me and I had already called the necessary taxi, from Mum's home phone (as well as phoned ahead to the maternity unit at the PMH to say that Philomena was coming in, since our baby seemed to be on its way).

Not surprisingly, Philomena was delighted to see me again - with her sister-in-law in tow - and to know that a taxi was already on its way. Sylvia seemed happy to come to baby-sit the children - and may even have offered to do so, from some days before, if she was ever needed. When the cab arrived, my wife and I picked up her pre-packed suitcase - containing her nighties and other essential items for her hospital stay - and the two of us passengers and the driver were soon motoring through the then quiet streets of Swindon and up to its 'Old Town' district where the PMH was situated.

Our entry into the birthing room at the PMH could not have been more different from what Philomena and I had experienced on the night of Claire-Louise's birth in Barbados. There was only one female midwife to receive us - but she did so quietly and calmly. Moreover, she had absolutely no difficulty with me being with my wife in the birthing room, whilst she delivered our child. Perhaps, therefore, owing to that midwife's calmness and welcome, Philomena was able to deliver our fourth child relatively quickly and - it seemed to me - without any undue difficulties. Certainly, no doctor needed to be summoned for additional help - or any forceps used, as in the case of the birth of our firstborn offspring, Noel, in Cambridge almost exactly five years before (to the day). Within one hour to 90 minutes after our first arrival at the PMH that night, accordingly, our latest baby had been safely delivered and duly made its first healthy cries. A little boy – born in the wee hours of the morning! Another beautiful being – given life by the Almighty to enable him to join his equally beautiful siblings in the world! The date was 29th September 1982 – and, for the first time, my wife had given birth to a child of ours who was not born on a Friday. It was in fact a Wednesday – but he seemed just as healthy, and full of life, as his older siblings had been on the day of their own respective births.

Naturally, I had been delighted that Philomena had seemed to have had an easier time of giving birth on that latest occasion – when compared to her 'bad experience' with the arrival of our daughter, in Barbados, some 21 months before. I hugged her and congratulated her on doing so magnificently well - considering all the adverse circumstances she had faced during her pregnancy in general, and during the last few weeks of it (since my arrival from Barbados) in particular. In those initial minutes after our baby's arrival, I would have given anything to have been able to stay on with my wife and latest son as long as I could – and, certainly, until it became time for them to leave the hospital and come home to our rented accommodation in Volta Road. As it was, however, I was also mindful that my sister was babysitting our other three children in my family's temporary home, and that I would have to relieve her of her duties before too long - so that she could go on to her work as a secretary in a company situated somewhere in the town. Consequently, I only stayed with Philomena and the baby for a few hours and, at about 5am that early morning, I reluctantly took my leave of them both – after first promising to return to see them again, later that day, in order to bring Noel, Kim and Claire-Louise with me to meet their new little brother. I then walked the two miles or so, including down 'Victoria Hill' from Swindon's Old Town, and was back at Volta Road by about 6am.

Despite the early hour - and after giving Sylvia the happy news that her new nephew had been safely delivered by Philomena and that both mum and baby were doing well - I asked my sister whether she would mind waiting just a couple of minutes more whilst I went to the nearby telephone box to make a call. Upon her agreement, I ran the 100 yards or so to the public kiosk and phoned. Notwithstanding the fact that it was still before daylight, my call was answered – by Jane, the partner (or fiancée by then, perhaps) of Philomena's brother, John. I gave her the good news about our fourth baby's safe arrival and took the trouble to tell her which ward to tell John that Philomena and the newborn were to be found at the PMH. I did so knowing that John would soon be also passing on the glad tidings to his (and Philomena's) mother, Mrs Harrison. Indirectly, therefore, I was enabling my mother-in-law to get news of the birth of her latest grandchild and to enable her to go to visit her daughter and that latest descendant of hers, that very morning. That step I very much suspected that my mother-in-law would be wanting to do, as soon as possible - despite the 'eviction' which had taken place from her home not many days before.

And so it proved! For when I returned to the Maternity Unit of the PMH that afternoon - with the new baby's two elder brothers and sister in tow - Philomena was to tell me the news that her mother had already come to the hospital to visit her, and her latest grandchild, earlier that day. I, for one, was happy to receive those tidings - for it meant that mother and daughter were already on their way to effecting a reconciliation in their relationship - which had only been ruptured by my sudden reappearance on the scene a week or two before. My visit with the children was, accordingly, a happy one, and Philomena and myself had much fun trying to assure our elder three that the new baby was 'their' baby – 'their' new brother – and not so much a child of their mummy and daddy. When the, then, six of us were altogether there in that ward - full of other new mums, their babies and visiting relatives and friends - it made me fully realise just what a rupture I had caused to my matrimonial family's life by what I had done in Barbados outside my marriage. In all honesty, on that day and in the days which immediately followed, I very much wanted to stay with my wife and our then four children. And yet, I knew, at the same time, that I had other responsibilities to also think about – relating to another family located somewhere in the Midlands of England.

Philomena and our new baby came home to Volta Road a few days after the birth, in the earliest days of October. I remember that I hired a taxi for the purpose and was with them during the drive down the hill from the hospital. My mother had kindly offered to babysit the other three children whilst I had gone up to the PMH to collect mum and baby. Nanny Bradshaw would have been delighted to have been able to pick up and cuddle the newborn, once it was home - as perhaps she had been unable to do when she had visited him and his mum in the hospital's maternity ward. Moreover, it was a lucky thing that my mother's home was only about five minutes' walk away from Volta Road, as I knew that Philomena would very much need her help in the days ahead - in the light of what I felt I had to do regarding the next stage of my life.

By the time that Philomena had come home to Volta Road with our newborn, we had already been able to discuss and reflect upon the name which we were going to give him. Somehow, we jointly decided that we liked the name of 'Carl', but I argued for the German spelling of 'Karl'. Without dispute, however, we happily agreed on a second Christian name of 'Stefan' – simply because we both liked it. And, as with his two elder brothers, my wife and I decided that our new baby should also have at least one other Christian name – which we eventually agreed should be 'Joseph', after my paternal grandfather, 'Joseph Leacock Bradshaw' of my native island of Montserrat. I regret to say, however, that despite the agreement of our new baby's names, I did not make time to go to the Register Office in Swindon to make the necessary registration, and obtain a birth certificate, prior to what I did next.

Having waited until the first visit of the district nurse to Volta Road to check on Philomena and 'Karl' - and to declare that all was well with them both - I then told Philomena that I had reluctantly decided to leave for Brussels to commence my Masters studies at the university there. I promised her, however, that - because the Belgian capital was not really that far away from Swindon and, perhaps, even nearer than, say, Edinburgh in Scotland - I would be able to come back to Volta Road to visit her and the children fairly regularly during my academic year ahead. Naturally, I still had not told her that Vere and Mikki had arrived with me in England, and that they were waiting in Birmingham for me to come to collect them in order for them to continue their life with me in the new country of my proposed studies. Even so, Philomena was, predictably, very upset by my news but, stoically, told me that she understood that my going to the Brussels university was for the betterment of my future teaching career. She told me that she took solace from the fact that I had offered to come back to see her and the children in Swindon on a regular basis. Nevertheless, it might well be imagined how utterly disgusted with myself I felt in taking my leave of her and our then four young children – one of whom was a newborn. I also had to say 'so long' to my mother and sister at Alexandra Road. I guess, as I write this more than 40 years later, that I must have blotted out what I had imagined that each of them might have been thinking of me, in a moral sense - as I left my wife and children in Swindon in order to merely pursue studies in a foreign country.

*Chapter 25*

# My First Term on Sabbatical Leave at a Belgian University – Autumn 1982

Guilt, and shame, is all that I must have felt - as my coach had left Swindon for Birmingham, after the tearful farewells had been made at Volta Road. I gave Philomena the address of the Vrije Universiteit in Brussels - the VUB - in case she needed to contact me urgently. That was because I had no accommodation, pre-arranged, in that city for the coming academic year and, thus, had no forwarding home address to give her in advance. As my coach got closer to Birmingham, however, I had to start looking forward in time to what lay ahead in the immediate future for Vere, Mikki and myself regarding our onwards travel to Belgium together.

The first stage of that time ahead was relatively straightforward. It consisted of the rapprochement with that other small family of mine at Rosie's Birmingham flat. I had experienced a highly emotional time in Swindon surrounding the arrival of 'Karl', moving into Volta Road with my matrimonial family beforehand, and making sure that the new baby, his mum, brothers and sister had a relatively comfortable shelter for the foreseeable future. Thereafter, I had abruptly left them all again. It was, thus, something of a jolt to be back with Vere and Mikki once more. Nevertheless, I soon realised that I cared for both of them too – and wanted to make sure that they were happy and secure with me for the immediate future. Accordingly, after spending a happy evening and night at Rosie's place - during which Vere and I did not speak about the arrival of my latest baby (which I had phoned her about from Swindon a day or two after his birth) - we said goodbye to Rosie. We also gave our hostess our profoundest thanks for all that she had done for us during the past three weeks or so – particularly in accommodating Vere and Mikki for every single day of them. Eventually, we took our leave of Rosie by setting off, by taxi, for Birmingham's coach station. There, we bought tickets to take us to the counterpart terminus at 'London Victoria'.

I had expected to be able to buy tickets at the Transalpino office in the nearby railway station - which I had last used for getting Noel and myself to West Germany the previous year - to enable the three of us to get a night train to Dover, and then a ferry to the Continent, that very evening. As it happened, however, the tickets which we could purchase cheaply were only for travel the following day, during daylight hours. It meant, therefore, our having to overnight in an hotel in the Victoria area of London that evening – after my using an agency on Victoria Station to find us something suitable, with all the additional expense which that process entailed for us. The rate which we paid included breakfast at the upmarket place, however - so we started off our train trip to Dover the following morning having eaten well.

And then it was on to the ferry to take us to the Belgian port of Ostend – just as I had done with Noel in the summer of the previous year on our way to the Schuhmacher family in West Germany. Upon arrival in Ostend our tickets then allowed us to travel to the capital of Belgium. Vere and I had agreed, however, that we would only be staying in Brussels long enough for me to register myself at the VUB, and to get details from the VUB of how, and where, I could start looking for accommodation for the three of us for the coming academic year. That is what we did, therefore, during our afternoon in Brussels. We spent about a three-hour visit there all together - for the purpose of achieving the two purposes in question. After that, it was back to one of the three main stations in the Belgian capital in order to continue our journey by train further east.

In fact, the three of us were heading for West Germany! Just over the border from Belgium, surprisingly enough - to the city of Aachen. For, in that frontier municipality lived the elder of my two younger brothers – that is to say, the middle brother of us three Bradshaw boys - who was named John. It was John who had been born immediately after me in the Caribbean, and who is also the subject of my first book *Growing up BAREFOOT under Montserrat's sleeping Volcano*.[65] I had last seen John during the previous year's summer holidays to England of Philomena, myself and our then three children, when he had still been living with his partner, Marion, their son Lee and John's two sons from his (by then dissolved) marriage to Janet. In the intervening period, however, and similar to my own case, John's personal life had gone somewhat awry – owing to the presence of 'another woman' in that life. To cut a long story short, John and Marion, by the October 1982 period in question, were no longer together. Marion had taken Lee away from their Swindon home, for him to live with her somewhere else. And John's two older sons, Mark and Wayne, had been placed into foster care – with the same foster parent. At all events, John, during that early October period in question, was working and living in Aachen. Accordingly, I had written to him to ask whether Vere, Mikki and myself could come and stay with him in West Germany for a short time - until I could find somewhere for the three of us to live in Brussels itself. Naturally, I had been obliged to explain to him about my 'second family' in my letter of request - written from Swindon whilst I had still been with Philomena and the children there.

Once more, a brother of mine rescued me that autumn of 1982 by immediately answering 'Yes' to my surprise request from out of the blue. And, thus, it was that Vere, Mikki and myself turned up at John's Aachen flat – the address of which I had first obtained from my mother in Swindon, before writing to him with my plea for temporary shelter. My brother proved to be most welcoming to his three temporary visitors and seemed to really like Vere and Mikki - from his first introduction to them. I only stayed in Aachen for one night, however, and immediately set off back to Brussels, the following day, in order to try to sort out the much needed accommodation in that city for Vere, Mikki and myself.

Through the guidance of the VUB's accommodation office, I managed to find something on the top floor of a very large house – perhaps, some three to four miles from the centre of Brussels, but only two or so from the university which I would be attending from that very week. Alas, I was in a precarious financial state, as I was still not sure when, and how, I would be obtaining my salary from UWI during the sabbatical year in question. Moreover, given the urgency with which I had to acquire the needed accommodation, the place that I found was very far from being ideal. Indeed, it consisted of two rooms only – a bedroom and a living room cum kitchen. The toilet and bathroom were outside the flat, and had to be shared with the tenant in the other flat on the same floor. I took the place, however, since, at least, it was 'a room (or two) of our own' and the rent for it was, seemingly, affordable at the time. In addition, my future landlady – whose surname (unforgettably for me) was 'Kassenellenbogen' - seemed very friendly, and she lived with her family in the much larger accommodations in the two floors below. Having paid the requested advance rent and deposit to the seemingly affable landlady, in addition to signing a lease for the whole of the period of my academic year at the VUB - I immediately caught a train, from the nearby main station of 'Brussels Midi', and headed back to Aachen to fetch Vere and Mikki.

I spent a second night at my brother's flat in the West German border city. During that time, I got the impression that John had really got on well with both Vere and Mikki and, thus, was not sorry that they had become a *de facto* part of our Bradshaw family clan. Early the next day, however, I wished my brother a fervent good luck with his own new life on the European Continent, and a temporary goodbye (since I did not know when I would be seeing him again). Certainly, he gave me the impression that he did not see his long term future in West Germany - but also that he had no real idea of what he wanted to do with his life ahead, in the medium-term. With a final and sincere 'thank you', Vere and myself took a taxi back to Aachen railway station with Mikki, and soon the three of us were on our way back to Belgium, and its capital city, to begin our new life there.

*En route* to Brussels, I was at pains to let Vere know, in advance, that our 'flat', in our new home city, was going to be underwhelming - since it was so very small. Vere, however, convinced me that she would not mind what she found on our arrival - as long as it meant that the three of us would be able to live and be together. Thus, when we eventually reached our top floor place in the Kassenellenbogen house – after taking another taxi from Brussels Midi station on that last occasion – Vere had already been primed about what to expect. Fortunately, for me, she seemed to be not at all disappointed - and also ready to make the best of our situation - once we had first crossed over our new threshold together.

The three of us would be sharing the only bedroom. Accordingly, we would have to act and speak quietly in it - whenever Mikki was asleep in her carrycot there. The other room was somewhat larger however – and, among other things, contained a table and at least two chairs. Such furniture would enable us to have our meals in a seated position – which would be important for Vere and myself. That was because we both realised, from the first, that we would largely be eating them at home - as cooked on the portable stove situated in one part of the room (which space also contained a sink, with hot and cold running water).

As soon as the very next morning, I was forced to leave Vere and Mikki in our new flat in order to go off to my first classes at the VUB. That university was located in a district of Brussels which is called 'Etterbeek'. In order to allow Vere to begin to get to know the neighbourhood of our new home whilst I was at my classes, however, I gave her enough money to do some shopping for the essential items which we would need for our new place - as well as for some of our very first meals there. I also promised to help her to do a larger shop at the coming weekend - when I would be free from having to attend the VUB.

In order to save money for our little household, I walked the four 'kilometres' or so (in Belgian distance terms) to my first classes. It was a somewhat strange, but exciting, experience for me to be a student once again – for the first time since my Bar Finals course in London in 1977-78, some five academic years or so before. As usual, however, I was determined to get the best out of my course and to try to come as close to the top of the cohort in my class as possible. That first morning, I discovered that I was the only one in it from the Caribbean. There were, however, a few other Law graduates from English universities – perhaps as many as four or five. There were also others from English-speaking countries, including the USA, Canada and even Bangladesh, as I recall. Several, however, were Dutch, or Flemish, speakers who had obtained their first degrees in Law from the VUB itself. The course, as stated earlier, would be taught in the English language so I had nothing but great respect for all those who were registered on the course and whose first language was other than my own mother tongue. In all, perhaps, there were about 30, or so, of us on the course.

After deciding that I already had an advantage because the course was being taught in my native language, I was rather alarmed to see that there were perhaps seven to 10 different subjects comprising it. Those included classes in 'European Economic Community (or EEC) Law' (which I had studied before at Cambridge University) and 'World Trade Law' – but, even so, the number of required courses much exceeded the usual four or five, which I had been used to as a Law student or teacher at Kingston, Cambridge, Leeds or UWI. Moreover, of all the subjects which were on the curriculum, there seemed to be only one in which I was really interested for my future teaching, and for ameliorating my own Comparative Law course, when I returned to UWI the following summer. That course was named the 'Law of Obligations'. It was the one which dealt with the Belgian Law of Contract and Tort. And, as I already knew that such legal areas were based on the Belgian civil code of Law, or *Code Civil* - which itself was based on Napoleon's *Code Civil* in force in France - I was delighted. That was because, in my own Comparative Law course at UWI, I taught some aspects of the French Law of Contract and Tort, from Napoleon's French *Code Civil*, and I was most interested to see how similarly (or otherwise) cases were decided in Belgian Law under its local equivalent Code.

I was thrilled also - from my first day at the VUB - to discover that our teacher in that most interesting course for me was a then current government minister who only taught at the university on a part-time basis. He was a middle-aged, bearded man - with glasses - whose name was 'Mr De Croo'. It was thus wonderful for me – when waiting for him to turn up for our first class – to have him appear about ten minutes late, to apologise for the delay 'because [his] meeting with the King had overran'! It was also something special to realise that one of our teachers at the VUB, at least, was then connected with the very highest echelons of Belgian society – in his regular job outside of our university.

If I was less interested in some of the other courses on my Masters programme, I was nevertheless determined to, at least, gain some knowledge from the lecturers in those other subjects regarding 'how to teach'. I, thus, watched carefully our teachers in each of my courses and saw that, on the whole, nothing surpassed what I had already experienced at, say, Cambridge in relation to how to put legal points over to students. It is, perhaps, true to say that most of the teachers at the VUB had their prepared set of notes, for their own respective class in question - and were happy to simply read from those notes as we, the students, made our own from what we heard and considered worthy of recording.

And, thus, my new life as a Law student in Brussels began. I assiduously attended every lecture scheduled for me that first week - in my determination to be among the best in the class as usual. I never stayed behind after classes ended, however - to enable me to socialise with my fellow students. That was because I had Vere and Mikki back at our flat to rush back to. Nevertheless, during classes or the breaks surrounding them, I started to make acquaintances - if not actually friends - from among my fellow students. One of those was an American – the type of go-getter young man that I had come across whilst doing my postgraduate Law degree at Cambridge University during the previous decade. He had an unusual first name – something like 'Rivers', which moniker I shall give him here for these purposes. After class one day during our first week - or certainly very early into the new academic year - Rivers and I began exchanging experiences about where we were each living in Brussels and the problems we, respectively, had to overcome in finding somewhere to live in the city for ourselves and our dependents. It turned out that not only was he also in Brussels with his wife and baby daughter, but he also lived in the same district of the city as me – a mere quarter of a mile, or so, from the flat of Vere, Mikki and myself. It was soon after that discovery that Rivers decided to invite me to come to dinner with my partner and child - whom I had also told him about during our conversations.

Accordingly, a day or two after Rivers' surprise invitation, Vere, Mikki and myself found ourselves in a very nice upper floor flat in our Brussels quarter, being introduced to Rivers' wife and baby. Unlike our own place, Rivers and family had everything self-contained within their flat – including their bathroom and toilet – and, generally, had far more space than we did in our own place. Vere and I bought a bottle of wine for our hosts and gave it to them on our arrival. I knew straight away, however, that we would never be able to return the invitation - given the lack of facilities which we possessed in our own Brussels home. That turned out to be just as well, since Rivers continually complained, throughout the meal, about how expensive he was finding life in Belgium. That outlook, perhaps, accounted for what Vere and myself agreed – on our way home afterwards - were the meagre rations which the two of us had been provided with during the dinner in question, though neither of us was ungrateful for having received the invitation in the first place.

Life in our new city, however, was not all about university classes, nor about 'dinner parties' with one or other of my classmates. Rather, it was as much more about my being able to show Vere something of a Continental European metropolis – given that it was her first time in Europe in general, and on the Continent in particular. In those earliest days after our arrival, accordingly, we went for lots of walks in our neighbourhood and, sometimes, even as far as the centre of Brussels several miles away - whilst pushing Mikki in her carrycot as we went along. At the latter, we would have visited famous tourist spots like the '*Grand Place*' and the nearby statue of the little boy urinating and known as the '*Manneken Pis*'. The two of us, however, soon discovered that a particular tram route – that of the number 99, in those days – went past the end of our road and then continued all the way to the royal palace, or '*Palais Royal*' in the city centre, a few hundred yards from the *Grand Place*. Moreover, we also found out that drivers of trams in Brussels, at that time, were not interested in giving out tickets to ride on their vehicles - or in checking whether passengers had bought them in advance. In other words, if you simply board one of the doors at the back of a tram, the driver (without more ado) would soon close it, as well as all the other doors of his vehicle, and continue with his journey. Of course, I knew that there was a risk that an inspector could always join the tram somewhere along its journey and ask to see tickets. That was a gamble which Vere and I discussed in advance - before we both decided to take the risk. As a result, Brussels became our oyster – by tram – and we often took Mikki in her carrycot on the number 99 to visit the *Palais Royal* area, where there was a children's play park, as well as the *Grand Place* and surroundings (if we felt like interacting with tourists, or simply experiencing the medieval heart of the city for a new time).

Vere and I also soon discovered that the number 99 actually went beyond the Brussels city centre also. Indeed, that it travelled beyond the *Palais Royal* for a good few miles further - to the far northern side of the capital from where we lived, and terminated at another tourist spot known as the '*Atomium*'. That was a place with an attraction which looked like an enlarged model of an atom – so 'blown up' in scale that visitors could actually go inside it during an outing there. Consequently, we often took Mikki for a longer tram ride to that more distant part of the city – not only to see the *Atomium*, but also to enjoy the green countryside that lay in abundance around the landmark.

By about the end of October to the middle of November 1982, therefore, Vere and I had established a new life for ourselves and our daughter in Belgium and we were making a go of things. But what of my other family back in Volta Road, Swindon, England? I am most ashamed to admit that I just could not handle having to properly deal with establishing a successful new life as a Masters Law student in Brussels - as one of a family of three persons - with actively thinking about doing the 'right thing' by my other family back in Swindon and, also, actually discharging my obligations to that other, first, family of mine. Worse still, I let slip my promise to Philomena, to take steps to, regularly, come back to visit her and the children at Volta Road during my Brussels course.

If, however, I had felt that I could only actively think about one of my two families during my earliest weeks in Brussels at the time, the matriarch of my other, deserted, family had not forgotten to actively think about me! She wrote to me, via the VUB. Receiving her letter brought me to my senses – very quickly! It made me realise that I had to go back to England to see her and our children! But when - and how? Philomena's letter told me lots of news. The most important, perhaps, was that our youngest child had, by then, had his birth registered. His name was officially 'Carl'! She stated that she had decided to go back on what we had agreed about the German version of that name. I immediately accepted what my wife had done in that regard - on the basis that, since she was the person who had borne the pain of giving birth to our youngest son, I was not really in any position to gainsay her. She also told me that her mum, Mrs Harrison, was again actively in her life. That my mother-in-law would come to Volta Road, every weekday about 8am, to take Noel and Kim (who had also started in the infants' section at St Mary's in Swindon, by then) to school – and then bring them home again in the afternoon when classes were over. Moreover, my own mother and sister were regular visitors to the home of my matrimonial family - and would often bring nappies and other

*Fig. 49: Philomena, holding the recently-born, Carl – and with his elder sister, Claire-Louise – at the Volta Road, Swindon home which the family had rented from September 1982*

things which she needed for baby Carl in particular, or for all the children in general. Very importantly, she also told me that the tenant from Wales, Mr Williams - who had been the sole occupant of the Volta Road house when we had first moved into it in September - had, by then, found alternative accommodation and, so, she and the children then had the whole house to themselves. Finally, she wrote that though - as a result of all those developments, she and the children were coping they were all missing me!

Receiving my wife's letter was to have an immense, and profound, effect on me. No longer could I keep her and the children out of my mind. I felt the pull for my having to return to see, and be with, them again. I told Vere about the letter and my feelings that I needed to go back to England to be with my other family. I wanted to write to Philomena to tell her so. Before I did so, however, Vere told me that she suddenly remembered that she had another good friend, from her Barbados youth, who then lived in 'Stockholm, Sweden' and whom she would have loved to visit and see again, whilst also living in Continental Europe. That old friend was Swedish and might have first met Vere whilst living in Barbados, previously, because, perhaps, she (the friend) had worked for the Swedish Embassy or government there. Before long, therefore, Vere and I agreed that

*Fig. 50: Baby Carl, being held by Kim, in a formal portrait including Noel and Claire-Louise taken at 'Debenhams' department store in Swindon in December 1982 – as arranged by Philomena during the Author's absence in Belgium whilst living there with Vere and Mikki*

she would write to her friend in Stockholm and ask whether she, and Mikki, could come to stay with her and her family over the forthcoming Christmas period. In that way, I could reply to Philomena's letter to promise her that I would be home to spend my VUB Christmas and New Year holidays with her and the children in Swindon. Without waiting for the reply to Vere's letter, therefore, I finally wrote back to Philomena to tell her that I was coming home to stay with her and the children in just a few weeks' time. After taking that step, I felt a lot better about myself. For, I was once again focussed not only on one of my two families at any given moment. Rather, I was trying to think of them both of them at the same time – if only inadequately regarding each of them!

Unsurprisingly, Philomena wrote back almost immediately to say how much she welcomed my letter and was looking forward to having me back in Swindon for the Christmas and New Year period ahead. I was, thus, on tenterhooks for the next week or so - as Vere awaited a reply from her friend in Stockholm to say whether our plan for her, to go to spend the Festive Period ahead, was 'on' or not. The two of us were greatly relieved, therefore, when a letter arrived for her - covered with exotic stamps and which included the word 'Sverige' on each of them. It was from her friend in the Swedish capital, whom I shall call 'Anni' for these purposes. When Vere opened it, the news was positive. Indeed, that reply made it clear that she and her husband could not wait to welcome Vere and Mikki to their home in Scandinavia. It also set out, in detail, the name of the main station in Stockholm which her prospective Barbadian visitors should come to - and how she would come to collect them from that terminus (once Vere let her know the date and time of arrival, after buying the tickets for herself and Mikki).

My next challenge, therefore, was to try to obtain the necessary train tickets to get Vere and Mikki to Stockholm for the forthcoming December to January period in question. In fact, we soon found out, on a visit to the Brussels Midi ticket office that Mikki was still too young to require a ticket and that we would only need to buy one for Vere. Once I had re-checked when I would need to restart at the VUB after the Christmas break, we decided that Vere and Mikki would only need to return to Brussels a day or two before the Monday in question. Moreover, that they could leave for Sweden as soon as my classes at the university ended before the holiday - perhaps, during the third week of December. Accordingly, we duly bought Vere's ticket and got details of the time of the train which she would travel on to 'Copenhagen' from Brussels Midi - and then, that of the connecting train from the Danish capital, as well as the time of its arrival in Stockholm. Once we had the necessary ticket and train times information, I breathed a sigh of relief as Vere could then write to Anni to let her have the necessary information for collecting her Bajan guests for the coming Festive Season. I was, then, confident that Vere and Mikki would be well looked after, and that, therefore, I could next concentrate on getting back to Swindon as my classes at the VUB drew to their end during that December of 1982.

I well remember seeing Vere and Mikki off at Brussels Midi station - as they began the first part of their journey to Copenhagen. I quickly helped Vere to find a good seat.

We successfully did so - at the end of a carriage where Mikki's carrycot could be placed nearby and out of the central passageway, and thereby enable Mikki to be close to her mum when sleeping in it. Whilst Mikki was awake, Vere would have been able to hold her in order to entertain her - as their train passed through new places for the two of them, such as 'Hamburg' in West Germany, before continuing over the border into Scandinavia. I told Vere that she was in for a wonderful adventure in travelling all the way to Denmark and then Sweden for the first time, and that I was sorry as I was not going along on the trip also. Vere answered that she knew that she was in for a good time, in the days and weeks ahead - and, that whilst she and Mikki would miss me, she well understood my position in deciding that I had to go back to England, in the meantime, to see Philomena and the children there.

*Chapter 26*

# Christmas with Philomena and Our Children in Swindon; and my Second Term on Sabbatical Leave in Belgium – December 1982 to Spring 1983

And set off for England is exactly what I did next. After seeing Vere and Mikki off in their Scandinavia-bound train - and without even waiting to spend another night at the flat in Brussels - I took a small suitcase containing some of my belongings from that dwelling and then caught the number 99 tram to the northern suburbs of the Belgian capital. I alighted somewhere south of the final stop at the *Atomium* – and which intermediate halt was close to the motorway going westwards to cities and other places such as 'Ghent', 'Bruges' and Ostend. From that major highway, I started to hitchhike – for the first time since I had last done so with Vere in Jamaica earlier that year. One of my lifts – if not the very first – was from a man driving an English registered car who happened to be returning to England too. However, he was going to do so via the French seaport of Calais. And, even though I had envisaged travelling back to the UK via the Belgium port of Ostend, I naturally accepted the lift to its French counterpart. I then bought a single ticket for a ferry crossing, during the coming night, to Dover. Once in England, I continued my hitchhiking initiative back to Wiltshire early next morning and, even though I had to travel via London and obtain another lift from the English capital, I was successfully back in Swindon by the afternoon of the December day in question.

Thus, my long-overdue rapprochement with my matrimonial family finally took place! I found it wonderful to be back with Philomena and our children once again. Noel and Kim were already on their school holidays and I noticed immediately how they, and their siblings, had all further grown since I had seen them last at the beginning of October. That was particularly the case in relation to our youngest - Carl. He had developed into a chubby babe in arms, with fairish hair and great big eyes. I was, thus, amazed as to how well Philomena had, single-handedly, done in keeping each of our sons - and our lovely curly-haired and also chubby, Claire-Louise - looking so hale and hearty. That realisation made me feel ashamed, once more, that I was putting my first family through such a relatively difficult time in Swindon - without my personal presence and day to day help - simply because I was pursuing an initiative in Belgium to get myself better educated. Whatever were my faults and actions deserving of condemnation, however, my wife gave me a wonderful welcome 'home'. The three elder children, though a little wary of me at first, also gave me lots of hugs and a warm reception . They also made me feel that, somehow, they had missed me. Certainly, it was clear to me that Philomena was determined that our reunited family of six would have the best Christmas ever, and that my first return to the Swindon household was not the time for any condemnation of my past actions, or quizzing about my time away in Belgium.

One nagging worry of mine, however, was what I would say to my mother-in-law when she next came to visit the family – as I fully expected her to do, perhaps as soon as the very next day. For, as stated earlier, she had played a major role in getting Noel and Kim to school every week day whilst I had been away, and, thus, I fully expected her to continue that regular contact with our two eldest children (if not with Philomena and all four of our offspring in general). Bless her soul, however, Mrs Harrison must have decided that it was better for her (and my nuclear family) to 'stay out of the way' during my time back with my family - and she never once came to interrupt our togetherness. Perhaps, Mrs Harrison had already, secretly, given Philomena the children's Christmas presents from herself, to hide away for them until the big day. If so, that should have told me that my mother-in-law really did not intend to show up and 'spoil' my matrimonial family's reunion. But, as stated, I was reluctant to completely believe that.

The six of us, therefore, had a very cosy time together during the two weeks or so that I was home with them for that December 1982 Festive Season - and I really got the chance to get to know my youngest son, Carl, properly for the first time. We tended to stay inside the Volta Road home for most of the time – when we were not all going to the children's play area at the County Ground in order for our older offspring to have turns on the swings, slides or other equipment there. Certainly, we all watched an awful lot of television – children's programmes as much as possible in the mornings, but also family films at other periods which could be enjoyed by most of us at the same time, if not also by baby Carl. One note of sadness, however, did pervade that special period for me. That was the fact that I was too ashamed to show my face for Midnight Mass on Christmas Eve - either at the nearby 'Holy Rood RC Church', where Kim had been Christened in 1979, or at 'St Mary's RC Church' nearer Mrs Harrison's home, where Philomena and myself had been married in 1976 and Noel Christened in 1977. The latter place was ruled out for me because I thought that my mother-in-law was bound to be attending that very Mass. The former was also a 'no-no' because many of Philomena's and my own former school friends were likely to be in attendance at such Mass. And I certainly did not want to run into any of them and have to explain what had happened to our growing family's 'Barbados idyll' - or why we were then living apart for most of the time (with most of the family back in Swindon and me in Belgium).

Be that as it may, for that Yuletide, I (and the rest of my matrimonial family, so far as I could perceive it) had a fine time together. We were warm in a house that we then had all to ourselves. Moreover, my mother and sister still lived not very far away and would either visit us with Christmas goodies for the children and ourselves, or they would invite us over to visit them, for the same or similar, at their Alexandra Road home. In that regard, it was relatively easy for me to enjoy being back 'home'. That was owing to the fact that my mother never once quizzed me – as she would have been justified in doing – about what I thought I was doing by living away, in a foreign country, and leaving my wife to cope with bringing up our four children single-handedly. Somehow, it seemed to me that my dear mum appreciated that, during that period, I had some difficulties in my life but that I would, somehow, make things right for the future. Accordingly, I was able to pass the period in question in a cocoon of happiness – neither thinking too much about my studies in Brussels, nor, it must be admitted, worrying about Vere and Mikki in Stockholm (whom I had telephoned, at least once, on the home number for Anni which Vere had given me and, therefore, knew that they had safely arrived at, and with, their hosts in Sweden and were being well looked after there).

All too soon, however, the idyll was over. The New Year duly arrived and - by the start of the first week of January - it was time for me to return to my Belgian life. Taking my leave of Philomena and the children was, naturally, a major wrench. Somehow, however, I did not feel as guilty as when I had left them the previous October - when Carl was only a few days old. By that New Year of 1983 he was already a bonny baby and there seemed little chance that he would not continue to thrive - even in the context of my matrimonial family's relatively straightened circumstances. Moreover, on that later occasion, I really felt that, for the future, I could keep my promise to come back to visit and stay with the family in Swindon more regularly. That was as a result of the relatively easy way in which I had managed to hitchhike back to that Wiltshire town - over only one night and two half days. Tears were nevertheless shed, as I left my family at the Volta Road home - in order to get a bus from the nearby Swindon terminus to take me to the M4 motorway, in order to begin my hitchhike back to the Belgian capital.

The return to Brussels turned out to be equally straightforward and I reached the city with just a few lifts. The one memorable hiccup in the process, however, had been in relation to my last. That turned out to be from a lorry driver who was ultimately driving somewhere east of the Belgian capital - perhaps to Liège, or even to Aachen in West Germany. Although, he was going near Brussels, therefore, he did not want to go into the centre of the city. Rather, he preferred to take the ring-road motorway around it, in order to do a by-pass. I accepted the lift nevertheless, thinking that I might still be able to hitch a further lift into the centre. Alas, that turned out not to be a successful step for me – and, indeed, might have got me arrested, since one is not supposed to hitchhike, or even walk, on the motorway in Belgium. Accordingly, I ended up trekking, perhaps, up to five miles or more - from where the lorry driver had dropped me on the motorway - during the night and early hours of the following morning. It was a lonely undertaking, during which I had felt at my lowest ebb for the first time in quite a while. That was mainly because of the memory of Philomena and the children whom I had left behind. It was also partly because, during my long walk to the Brussels flat, I saw lots of empty champagne bottles (and other party detritus) in front of homes of local families who had evidently recently celebrated the coming of the New Year together. Such family leftovers brought home to me that I was then separated from mine. That is to say, both from my first one back in Swindon and also, at that very time, from my second one whose members had gone to Sweden for their own Christmas holidays.

Get home to my Brussels flat I eventually did, however - by walking, with my luggage, all the way from my drop-off point on the by-pass motorway. Naturally, I was exhausted by the time I had done so but there was just enough time for me to recover before I had another appointment to keep. That was to go to Brussels Midi railway station in order to meet two people off a train which would be arriving there that evening. I did so at the appointed hour and - more or less on time - a very long train came into the platform announced for its reception. Because of its length, however, I just did not know from which end of the train to start looking. I started to worry, after a minute or two, that the reason I was there was going to prove futile. Moreover, I began to panic a little as to what I was going to do next – if my expected passengers were not, in fact, on the train. And then, from one of the middle carriages of the international express in question, I saw them. Vere was holding Mikki - as she struggled to get the carrycot and pushchair off the train, as well as her suitcase. I ran to help her achieve the exit, from the railway carriage, of herself, our daughter and their belongings. They were back - after their Scandinavian adventures - and seemed very pleased to see me! I was very happy to see the two of them also - back in Brussels, safe and sound.

For the life of me, I cannot now recall whether it was just before, or just after, I had returned to the VUB for my Second Term there that Vere and I decided to embark upon one of our craziest adventures yet – together with Mikki! I rather think, however, that it was about the middle to end of January 1983 and, thus, it had probably occurred after my recommencing classes again. Certainly, the initiative was commenced, and took place over one weekend and entailed Vere, myself and our daughter trying to make a trip to Paris! That escapade arose because, since first starting to live in Brussels, I had many times compared, to Vere, the Belgian capital to that of its French counterpart – unfavourably. In doing so, I had sung the praises of Paris many times to her - and especially the fact that, like London and the 'Thames', the French capital had a river, the 'Seine', running right through the middle of it. I also argued to her that the latter river added to the beauty of Paris, whereas Brussels had no such natural feature. In addition, after her very recent adventures of travelling to the Danish and Swedish capitals of Copenhagen and Stockholm respectively, Vere very much wanted to see the French equivalent - especially as it was so much nearer to Brussels than those two Scandinavian metropolitan cities.

There were at least two misgivings, however, which I had about embarking on the adventure to Paris. First of all, it was the middle of winter and, thus, not exactly the ideal time of year to be making international trips with our daughter, then about seven months of age. Moreover, our finances were such that Vere and I could not really afford to pay the train fares to the French capital and back - if we also wanted to have some spending money for a hotel and other expenses whilst in France. Despite those drawbacks, however, Vere and I somehow persuaded each other that we would, nevertheless, set out on our adventure – by hitchhiking, once more! That was something that we had not done, together, since about one year earlier whilst together in Jamaica. The weather conditions in the Caribbean island were, naturally, very different from what we were then experiencing in Europe in that earliest month of the New Year. Indeed, as there was snow all around the Belgian countryside, there was every chance that we would find much the same wintry situation on the other side of the Belgo-Franco border.

Despite those inauspicious circumstances, however, we wrapped Mikki up in as many woolly layers as we thought advisable, put on her coat, gloves and shoes, did much the same for ourselves (including clothing the two of us in the heavy coats which we had brought with us from England), and set off one Friday early afternoon. Our first goal was to get to the most southerly point that we could on the Brussels tram network, after changing from the nearby number 99, somewhere in the city centre, to a different numbered one going further south. I took the trouble to make a cardboard sign, with the word 'Paris' written in bold letters upon its face, and soon Vere and I found ourselves standing on the slip road to the motorway heading southwards to the French border and Paris. Naturally, Mikki was with us - safely tucked up inside her carrycot - and we also had her buggy, and our small suitcase (containing the few essentials which we would need for our daughter and ourselves during the trip). Try as I might, I can no longer recall the exact details of our journey south which suggests that it must have been straightforward and uneventful. Somewhat to my surprise, perhaps, the fact that we had quite a lot of bulk with us, including Mikki's vehicle of carriage and sleeping, did not appear to put off some of the drivers heading in our direction. Accordingly, in, perhaps, just two or three lifts, we ended up in one of the northern suburbs of the French capital near 'Montmartre' that Friday evening. Moreover, without having any real idea of where we would stay in the city prior to our getting there, we soon found ourselves accepted by a landlady for our staying two nights - in one of the 'pensións', which we first saw near our disembarkation point from our last lift that day.

I was relieved, but happy, to have arrived safely with Vere and Mikki in the French capital - after 'talking it up' to Vere for so long - and to have been able to keep my promise to Mikki's mum to show her something of that world-renowned city one day. That state of contentedness, at how relatively easy fulfilling my word had been, caused me to suggest something which I now look back upon with amazement - and shame, if the truth be known. For, after feeding Mikki and putting her to sleep in our room in the pensión, I proposed to Vere that we leave Mikki sleeping, and just the two of us venture out to give her a first look around one or two places that I knew in that part of Paris. Without any pressure from me, Vere agreed to my idea. As we went out of the front door of the pensión, the landlady saw us. I half anticipated that she would call us back to admonish us for leaving a baby on its own in our room. When she did not, however, Vere and I continued with our exit. And so it was that I was able to show her the outside of the famous '*Sacre Coeur*' cathedral, in Montmartre itself, that first evening - as well as the '*Moulin Rouge*' theatre nearby. Vere already knew that the latter establishment was world-famous for being most associated with the 'can-can' dance and I was happy to see her appreciating her visit - even though we neither had money, nor time, to go inside the theatre to see one of its shows. After about two hours of local sightseeing, however, the two of us thought that we had better return to our accommodation to check on Mikki - in case she had woken up in the interim and was then crying. To my relief, when we did so we, thankfully, found our daughter still fast asleep. It had been taking a huge risk in leaving her alone, however, and only afterwards, when in bed, did I consider some of the scenarios of our having left Mikki alone – not least, someone 'kidnapping' her in that huge city where Vere and myself had no relatives or friends to help us locate her again.

The next day, with Mikki safely with us in her carrycot, the three of us made our way by an underground train, or '*metro*', to '*Bir Hakeim*' station on the 'Left Bank' of the River Seine. I knew from several previous visits to Paris - mainly during my days as a Law student in England - that the particular stop in question, on the French capital's underground system, was perhaps the nearest to one of the world's most famous landmarks. That latter tourist attraction was mainly what I most wanted Vere to see for herself at the earliest opportunity that day. The 'Eiffel Tower', or '*tour Eiffel*', was the goal in question - and when the three of us had emerged from the nearby metro, Vere could already see it, and seemed excited at the sight. And although we ourselves could not afford to actually take the lift to the top of the edifice - as most of our fellow tourists seemed to be wanting to do, were actually doing, or had done whilst we were in its vicinity that morning - Vere seemed happy enough to be able to see it for herself, touch one to two of its bases, and then walk around the green space of the '*Champs de Mars*' in which it was located.

Having shown Vere the main 'World Heritage Site' which I wanted her to actually visit in Paris for her very first time, the rest of the day was then ours to look around the centre of that city at our leisure. In so doing, I took her from the Eiffel Tower - and over a bridge across the Seine - to the building, a few hundred yards on the other side, which is called the '*Trocadero*'. There, the two of us and Mikki should really have taken some photos together, with the Tower in the background - though I can no longer recall whether we had a camera with us that day. At any rate, just the sight of that world-famous monument in question - from our wonderful vantage point on the 'East Bank' side of the river - should have imprinted a lasting impression onto Vere's memory which I hoped that she would remember for the rest of her life. After that, she and I pushed Mikki in her carrycot onwards to the '*Arc de Triomphe*', and then along the '*Champs-Élysées*'. Walking down the latter famous avenue together - back towards the river - and subsequently turning left at what I regard as one of the most chaotic traffic roundabouts in the world, the '*Place de la Concorde*', I was soon able to show Vere the celebrated

'*Louvre*' museum. Or, rather, the outside and grounds of that particular establishment. For although I reminded Vere that, perhaps, the most well-known painting by 'Leonardo da Vinci' was housed inside the building in question - namely, the 'Mona Lisa' - we both knew that we could not afford the entrance money required to enable us to actually go and see it.

After the *Louvre*, the three of us continued walking along the Right Bank of the river to the next bridge, and then we crossed it to take us on to the island in the Seine known as the '*Île de la Cité*'. There, I was able to introduce Vere to a famous religious building - of which she had heard, even from since her schooldays in Barbados – namely, '*Notre Dame Cathedral*'. From those earlier times, she would also have heard the story of the 'Hunchback' which belonged to that church. We were to spend quite some time exploring its interior - as well as walking around its grounds. Afterwards, we did some further sightseeing on the other side of the Seine – thus, on its on its Left Bank once more. By the time we had bought some '*baguette*' bread from a '*Boulangerie*', some meat from a *charcuterie*, cheese from a *fromagerie*, and other items to accompany the first three from a small shop - which we had come across on that 'more bohemian' side of the capital - we were able to have an 'authentic' Parisian meal. I was, thus, satisfied that I had given Vere as good an introduction to the French 'City of Love' as I reasonably could - given our parlous financial situation at that time. Certainly, I was confident that, thanks to my efforts, her first impression of the capital was a very favourable one and that she would want to revisit it in the future and, preferably, sooner rather than later.

By the time we returned to our *pension* that Saturday night, Vere and myself were very tired. So also was Mikki - even though she had been able to have one or two short sleeps in her carrycot during our tour of downtown Paris. Accordingly, there was to be no nocturnal outing, without Mikki, for us parents that evening. We both needed to slumber soundly, so as to be full of energy for the challenge ahead – namely, of safely getting ourselves back to Brussels the following morning. When Sunday arrived and we had fed Mikki and had eaten our own breakfast at the *pension*, we took the *metro* to a station as far northwest on the Paris system as we could get. That was to enable us to reach the motorway which was going back to the Belgian border. At the relevant slip-road to join that express road, I remember that the three of us had to wait for some time – and, perhaps, up to one hour or more – in order to get lucky with our first lift. I still had the cardboard sign which we had used to help us successfully arrive in Paris. On that later occasion, however, I held up the other side on which I had written the word 'Bruxelles' in bold capitals. Though I began to worry, and start again to wonder about the wisdom of the overall initiative which had commenced two days before (when no one stopped for us during those 60 minutes or so), I was eventually to experience some relief when a white van finally pulled up. It contained only one person – namely, a young, male driver. The van carried the red number plates of a Belgian vehicle! And although the driver was to tell us that he was not in fact going all the way to our destination, he added that he was certainly going to cross the border into his native Belgium and could drop us south of the capital - in the French-speaking city of 'Charleroi'.

Vere and myself jumped at the offer and, accordingly, found ourselves, with Mikki in her carrycot, in the company of a very friendly Belgian man. He took his time during the drive northwards. We also made one or two stops at service stations along the way - where Vere and I bought him cups of coffee and something to eat, as our 'thank you' for his kindness in taking us with him. It was the driver's view, during these stops, that Vere and I should consider taking the train from Charleroi - back to the Belgian capital. That, he added, was because he thought that we would only be arriving in the former city when it would already be getting dark and it was somewhat dangerous, perhaps, to be out with our baby hitchhiking, as evening and night were falling. He also kindly offered to actually drop us at Charleroi railway station - so that we could catch a train to Brussels immediately and without the need for any further use of our thumbs. Vere and I accepted the friendly advice, thanked our driver profusely when he eventually delivered us to the station in question, and were soon paying passengers on board a Brussels-bound train - along with Mikki, her carrycot, buggy and our suitcase. Fortunately, it was only about 40 miles between the two cities. Consequently, the unbudgeted train fares which we had to pay, did not cause Vere and I too much difficulty regarding the limited funds we had taken with us for the weekend in question. We made sure that we got off our train at 'Brussels Centraal' station, however - so that we could catch the nearby number 99 tram, to get us to our flat nearby one of its stops. We thereby avoided the cost of a taxi from Brussels Midi (which was even nearer to our residence, but not accessible to it by tram from there). At any rate, the three of us reached our Brussels home, safely, that night. And what was one of the highlights of our time in Europe - namely, a trip to Paris - had successfully been accomplished over the course of one January 1983 weekend.

On the Monday morning, after our return from Paris, it was back to school for me at the VUB. I was still trying to make a go of being one of the best students on my programme at that stage in the academic year. It was slowly becoming clear to me, however, that - owing to my difficult personal situation with having to balance the subsistence of the two families in my life, it would be too much for me to do really well on my course. Moreover, I began to feel really guilty about just having had a lot of fun in the French capital with Vere and Mikki, whilst Philomena was stuck at home in Volta Road, Swindon having to struggle to take care of our four children in my absence. Indeed, I was haunted by the thought that the possibilities of even a weekend's international 'fun' trip to Paris for Philomena, during that era of hers in Swindon, would surely be the very last thing on her mind – whilst I had recently done exactly that! As the term progressed, therefore, I found myself becoming ever more depressed about my 'conflict of familial obligations' situation. Vere noticed this and asked me what was wrong. One day, at our dinner table - one of the only bits of furniture in our little flat - I blurted out to her: 'Vere, I am not happy! I cannot live with myself, knowing that Philomena and our children need me, whilst I am having "fun" living with you and Mikki here in

Brussels'. At long last, I had dared to tell her what had been on my mind for some time.

Day by day, after my announcement, Vere and I discussed what we were going to do about my mental affliction. She quickly accepted, it seemed to me, that I was in turmoil because I had been trying to balance, in my mind for quite some period, my obligations to my two families. Also, that such had been especially the case since I had returned from my Christmas trip to Swindon – and that my conscience was telling me that I had come down on the wrong side of the scale in trying to resolve my dilemma. Little by little, therefore, we both came to the same conclusion – namely, that I would only feel I was 'doing the right thing' by returning to Philomena and the children. But then the question we both had to answer was: 'What was to become of Vere and Mikki' – if I did so return?

Fortunately, all three of us in Brussels still had the return halves of our air tickets which had brought us to London from Barbados. It was probably Vere herself, therefore, who suggested that she and Mikki could use their return portions to go back to their native Caribbean island – but with a major twist, which even I had not thought of. She said that she could write to Aunt Ruby - our mutual friend who had helped us 'escape' from Barbados with Mikki, without being prevented by Vere's mother, during the previous September. In her letter, she could ask Aunt Ruby whether she would be willing to look after Mikki for the future. That is to say, bring Mikki up as her (Aunt Ruby's) foster child – whilst Vere returned to England, for the academic year ahead, in order to study to qualify as a Barrister and get Called to the English Bar in London. Vere's idea was a wonderful one to me, and immediately made me feel a lot better. That was because I then felt able to write to Philomena to tell her that I was 'coming home' - on a long-term basis to her and our children. Accordingly, whilst Vere played her part by writing to Aunt Ruby to put the idea of the latter fostering Mikki from about the following September of that year, I also took steps to, firstly, go to the Administration in the VUB's Law Faculty. The latter happened because part of the joint overall plan of Vere and myself for our respective futures including my asking the VUB Faculty whether I might be allowed to discontinue from my Masters course in question, and re-apply to return to the programme for the following academic year, 1983-84. I also informed the VUB that I would, at the same time, be requesting my employers at UWI to extend the sabbatical period, that I was then currently on, by one further academic year. Vere and I then had until about the middle of March 1983 to put all the foregoing steps of our joint plan into place. That was because the return parts of the air tickets to Barbados, of Mikki and herself, expired exactly six months after we had left the island the previous September.

The Almighty seemed to have been on the side of both Vere and myself – at that particular time. For, first of all, she soon received a reply from Aunt Ruby stating that the latter would be delighted to foster Mikki whilst Vere pursued her legal studies in England for the future. Aunt Ruby was an unmarried, middle-aged, woman who had never had a child herself. It was perhaps unsurprising, therefore, that she might have been keen on Vere's fostering idea - since that might have meant that she could regard Mikki as the child she had always wanted to have, but could not in the natural order of things. At about the same time as Vere received the good news from Barbados, however, I also obtained the permission from the VUB to return to 'start over' from the coming academic year. I can no longer recall the reasons which I gave in my application to do so, but it probably had to do with my having stated that my personal family situation did not enable me to continue the course for the then-current academic year - and, fortunately for me, no searching questions had been forthcoming, in reply, from the university in that regard. Finally, I obtained written permission from UWI to take a further sabbatical year 'to complete my studies' at the VUB – subject to one condition. That was that I returned to Barbados, for at least two weeks in June of that year, to help with the marking of some of UWI's Law Faculty's exam scripts – including those in Comparative Law. That course had been given in my absence by an American lawyer - one Bruce Zagaris - who had been recruited to take over the course from me temporarily at Cave Hill Campus. Owing to my wanting to obtain the additional sabbatical year in question so much - in order to help me to repair my family life with Philomena and the children - I naturally accepted UWI's condition of my returning to do the stipulated marking of exam papers. It was not a difficult decision - since returning to Barbados, even for a short time during the month of June ahead, would allow me to see Vere and Mikki again. It would also enable me to witness, for myself, just how well our daughter was getting on with Aunt Ruby and, thus, judge how the prospective fostering relationship, in Vere's absence as a Bar student back in England, might work out in the longer term.

There was one last major obstacle to overcome before Vere and myself could put everything in place. I had to go downstairs one day, perhaps by the middle of February, to ask our landlady, Ms Kassenellenbogen, to kindly release me from part of the period of the lease of our top floor flat. It may be remembered that I had rented our dwelling for the whole of the academic year ending about June 1983. I was, thus, asking for a big favour - namely, to be excused from having to pay rent for about three months - from the date we wanted to quit our flat during the following month. Though she was far from happy about the unexpected development, our landlady seemed to accept that for 'personal reasons' Vere and I had to take our baby back to England in the near future and, thus, needed to quit Brussels at short notice. Reluctantly or not, however, she gave her permission for Vere and myself to leave our flat with Mikki – without any financial penalty.

And so it came to be that, sometime in about the second week of March 1983, Vere, Mikki and myself travelled on the train from Brussels Midi to catch our night ferry at Ostend port. Unexpectedly, whilst boarding our ferry and then queuing up to try to obtain a cabin for the three of us, I ran into one of my, now former, fellow students on the course at the VUB. She was one of the small number of Law graduates from England on the programme. She told me that VUB had just ended its Second Term and that she was going home for the coming Easter vacation. That made me feel awful - as it reminded me that I had failed to accomplish what I had originally come to Belgium to achieve – namely, to be a success on the VUB course, and an outstanding one at that. Nevertheless, I was able to tell my ex-VUB-classmate that I was only taking a temporary absence from our joint programme for 'family reasons' and that I would be back to complete it, from the beginning of the coming academic year.

Vere, Mikki and myself managed to obtain one of the few remaining cabins, not yet booked, for the English Channel crossing to Dover that night. As we had all our belongings from our former Brussels flat, there was no question of our hitchhiking during that particular journey. Accordingly, we had bought train tickets all the way back to London Victoria – with the night cabin for the crossing being an additional extra which I had paid for. I had made that additional outlay on the basis that our English Channel crossing, in our private compartment, might have been the last time that the three of us would sleep in the same space whilst on an international journey. At any rate, the second train part of our journey eventually came to an end in London and then the three of us switched to a coach to take us to Birmingham from Victoria Coach Station. We were then on our way to stay with Vere's friend, Rosie - for a last day or two - before the date of Vere and Mikki's flight back to Barbados. Vere had written to her Midlands-based old school friend, for the second time in a calendar year, to ask permission for the three of us to come and stay with her - pending her return to the Caribbean with Mikki - and Rosie had instantly agreed to the request. In the meantime, however, she had moved from the flat relatively near to Birmingham's coach station - which we had all stayed at the previous September - to a small house in the relatively-nearby town of 'Dudley', which she was then buying. Accordingly, once the three of us arrived at the coach station of England's second largest city, we had to transfer to the nearby New Street Station railway station - in order to catch a train to Dudley, which was about a 30 minutes' ride away.

Eventually, after our long journey from Brussels, the three of us made it to Rosie's new place - safe and sound. Fortunately, the house turned out to be within sight of Dudley's station, and just a few minutes' walk away. Rosie, true to form, seemed really happy to see her old school friend again - as well as Mikki. If she was disappointed in me, regarding my breaking up my little household of three - in order to return to my larger, and first, family in Swindon - she never let that show. Rather, she again welcomed me into her home - as much as she did Vere and Mikki - and the three of us visitors (as far as I could see) had an enjoyable stay during the time we were with her. During that short sojourn, Vere would have told her about her adventures with Mikki in Sweden at Christmastime, as well as about our joint adventures in Paris soon after the New Year - among other things.

The day of Vere and Mikki's flight (and indeed my own, which I was *not* going to take) back to Barbados soon arrived, however. Accordingly, the three of us had to make the reverse journeys - by train from Dudley and then coach from Birmingham back to London Victoria - before a further onward journey to Heathrow Airport. I can no longer recall how we chose to get from Victoria to the airport – whether by a further coach or via the 'London Underground'. What I will never forget, however, is that the three of us were running late when we finally arrived at the check-in desk of the BWIA airline taking Vere and Mikki back to Barbados. So late in fact that the two of them only just made it before the flight was 'closed'! One of the last things they were told - before I had to say a fervent goodbye and give them hurried hugs and kisses prior to their disappearing *en route* to their departure gate - was some alarming news. That was the fact that, although they were then safely on the flight in question, their bags would probably not be so – and, moreover, such luggage might only arrive on the following day's flight to Barbados. Nevertheless, as I left the airport, I breathed a huge sigh of relief that Vere and Mikki had made their flight and were, thus, able to use their respective air tickets – the validity of which would have expired that very day!

*Chapter 27*

# Spring and Summer 1983 in Swindon with Philomena and Our Children (and a Side Trip to Barbados)

With Vere and Mikki safely on their way back to the Caribbean and the sunshine – and to Aunt Ruby's lovely and spacious home by the Caribbean Sea in Atlantic Shores, Barbados where I knew she would look after them royally – I suddenly realised that I was on my own again. Moreover, that, in a sense, I had got my old life back. As I travelled back to Swindon (with my own belongings from Brussels) – and I can no longer recall whether I did so by train or coach, though I suspect it was by means of the latter in order to save money – I was thinking about the future ahead. I knew that I was doing the 'right thing', however, in returning to my wife and our four children. In addition, I was determined to make a success of that new beginning – including taking my matrimonial family back to Belgium with me, to enable me to complete my course at the VUB from the coming academic year (starting in October) and, thus, make a success of that educational initiative also. On the other hand, I told myself that I also still had, at least, moral obligations of support to Vere and Mikki and that I would do my best to discharge those properly - but always with my greater, and more weighty, obligations to my wife and our children being put as the first priority.

Needless to say, when I walked with my suitcase across from the nearby Swindon Bus Station to the Volta Road house, Philomena was delighted to see me and gave me the biggest hug that she seemed able to muster. With tears in my eyes, I continued to hold her for some moments at the door and then told her: 'I am home! For good this time'. I then took turns in hugging and kissing each of our four little ones – Noel, Kim, Claire-Louise and baby Carl. Once more, I noticed how each of them had grown, even more, since I had last seen them at the beginning of January – especially Carl, who was almost six months old by then. And, once more, I marvelled at my wife - regarding how she could have sustained the children so very well, in addition to herself, in both a physical and mental sense since I had last been with them all. In accounting for that positive state of affairs, she told me that her mother had continued to help out on a daily basis regarding getting Noel and Kim to school - despite my having returned to the family for Christmas and New Year. Naturally, my wife's explanation caused me to wonder how things would pan out between myself and Mrs Harrison - once she discovered that I was then back with my matrimonial family on a permanent basis.

Be that as it may, once Philomena had welcomed me back with a meal for all of us around the table (except for Carl who was able to breastfeed, as Philomena held him with one hand) I told her about my idea for us all to move to Belgium for the coming academic year - so that we could all be together whilst I completed my studies at the VUB. Philomena seemed somewhat surprised by the idea, though she quickly became agreeable to it, since it would mean that our whole family would continue to be together after we departed from Swindon. Like me, therefore, Philomena seemed to regard what we would do for the future - and where we would be to do that - as being secondary to the primary matter of us all being together in the months, and years, ahead. With that positive reception of my idea, about our all living in Belgium, from my wife, I then told her of my determination to get a job whilst I was in Swindon - for the six months or so ahead, until it was time to recommence the programme, which I had taken my sabbatical for, at the VUB in Brussels. I suggested that such employment would keep me busy during such forthcoming half-year period - and, perhaps, even enable us to buy a car so that our family could more easily move around the town, and the wider Wiltshire county area, together as one unit.

The very next morning, therefore, I walked up to the reference section of the public library, situated below Swindon's Victorian 'Town Hall', and asked for that day's edition of the local newspaper – *'The Evening Advertiser'*, or *'Adver'*. To my amazement, inside its pages I discovered that there was a local 'Law Centre' established in the town. That, therefore, meant that there existed a place where people of modest or no means could go to get legal help and advice on matters such a social security issues, landlord and tenant disputes and, perhaps, even minor Criminal Law infractions. I had worked at such a centre, for one year, during my days as an undergraduate at Kingston Law School, Surrey during the 1970s. I was most interested, therefore, to see that the concept of such a legal establishment had, by then, also been realised outside London – and, indeed, right there in my former Wiltshire home town. I was, however, even more amazed to see that the Swindon Law Centre was looking for a researcher, for about a period of six months. That person's job would be to look into the problems of juveniles getting into trouble with the Criminal Law in the town, and then write a report about what legal provision should be made for them, by the Law Centre and others, into the future. It seemed astounding to me - God-given almost - that there I was looking for a job, for about half a year, and that, at the very same time, an employment opportunity had arisen in a legal field (in which I had some experience), for much the same sort of period as I was then available. If I ever needed a sign from the Almighty that I was embarking on the 'right course', in coming back to Philomena and the children at that time, then, I concluded, that was it.

Still in a state of mild astonishment and excitement, I left the library to go to the nearest newsagents. There, I bought my own copy of the *Adver* to take home, in order to show the job advertisement to Philomena. When I had soon done so, she, too, could hardly believe the opportunity that had arisen for me. Nevertheless, pulling myself together, and with her help, I immediately set about making my application for the vacancy in question. I recall that a CV was asked for, plus a letter of application, in which two referees had to be given. That latter point could have been a major problem for me. I remembered, however, my former lecturer at Kingston Law School - who had once given me a part-time teaching job on one of his courses whilst I had been a Bar Finals student during 1977-78. I speculated, and hoped, that he might be willing to help me out again with my latest project. That person was 'Mr Peter Sills'. I called him, and told him that I was then on sabbatical leave from UWI. I also filled him in about the advertised, six months', job in Swindon and of my wish to apply for it. Finally, I asked him to help me secure it, by being my referee. Thankfully, he readily agreed to do so.

My second referee, for the purposes in question, was the person who was in charge of the Law Centre in the Old Kent Road, South East London, where I had worked whilst a student at Kingston during 1974-75. That person was one 'Mr Dennis Gordon' - a partner in the firm of solicitors which had run the Centre. And, thus, though handwritten, I was able to duly make my application to the Swindon Law Centre. Thereafter, I just had to await my fate in order to see whether my 'new beginning' with my first family would get off with a flying start – with me being in employment until it was time to return to Belgium.

The Law Centre in Swindon was located about a quarter of a mile from the public library in which I had found the advert for the job in question - and, so, near the centre of town and almost next door to the public swimming baths in 'Milton Road' where I had first learnt to swim, properly, whilst a schoolboy in Swindon. Within the week of my sending in my application, I received a reply inviting me to attend for an interview. The letter also told me that I was one of two candidates shortlisted for the research post in question. In due course, I was to discover that the other person in the frame was a lady lawyer from New Zealand, who just happened to be sojourning in the town for a number of months also. Accordingly, I knew that I had some serious competition when I went to the offices to face a panel of three interviewers. Two of them were male and lawyers - and I was to discover, later, that the younger was actually a product of the famous English public school at 'Eton'. I shall call that younger man 'Michael' for these purposes, and the older male 'Robert'. The third person was a middle-aged woman who was not legally qualified but who, I was told, was the Centre's specialist in Social Security matters. I shall call her 'Mary' for these purposes. My three evaluators gave me a good grilling regarding why I was then in Swindon. They seemed satisfied, however, that I had grown up in the town, had a mother, siblings, mother-in-law and brothers-in-law who all lived there at the time, and that I was on sabbatical leave and was choosing to spend time with my family in the town. I must also have revealed that I was in fact on my way to study for a Masters Law degree at a university in Belgium, but had time on my hands for six months or so before I had to leave Swindon for Brussels – hence my ability to take up the medium-term research post in question. I certainly did not mention that I had already spent time at the VUB, and had interrupted my studies there to return to my first family whom I had left behind in Swindon since the previous September. At any rate, the panel appeared content with my answers. That perception was confirmed when, a day a two later, I received a letter at Volta Road telling me that I had got the job for which I had applied at the Law Centre.

Naturally, I was delighted. I guessed that one or other of my three interviewers had merely telephoned Peter Sills, and Dennis Gordon, and had received good reports from them about myself – positive references, hopefully, based on their knowledge of me before my time in Barbados and at UWI, and before the personal scrapes that I got myself into since meeting Vere at that Caribbean university. My spirits were, thus, raised to the highest level that they had reached for many months - if not for over the whole of the past year or more since, I had first told Philomena of my infidelity with Vere and the fact that a child had been conceived as a result. So delighted indeed was I, that I immediately discussed with Philomena the idea of our getting a car as soon as possible – to help me in my new job, but also to enable the six members in our family to move around as a single unit. That is when my wife told me – for the first time - that most of the money that I had been sending for her and the children, from Barbados, had been put into a savings account in her mother's name and that Mrs Harrison had custody of the book from which that account was accessible. In other words, that whilst Philomena and the children had resided with my mother-in-law, the latter had, in effect, 'kept them' without using the money I had been sending for my family from the Caribbean. Philomena, therefore, told me that she would promptly go to her mum's house and ask her for enough of the funds, from the savings account in question, to enable us to buy a second-hand car.

After my return from Brussels to live at Volta Road, Philomena's mother stopped coming every weekday morning - as she had previously done, in order to take Noel and Kim to school. Instead, whilst I stayed home with Claire-Louise and Carl, Philomena would do the needful regarding getting our eldest two children to school at St Mary's (which was located quite near her mum's home). It was, therefore, easy enough for Philomena to pay a brief visit to her mother's residence to let her know how the six of us were getting on at Volta Road. My wife could also give my mother-in-law the 'breaking news' about my new job at the Law Centre and then ask her about letting Philomena have about £500 or so, from the savings account in question, to enable our family to buy a used car. Bless her heart, Mrs Harrison cooperated fully with her only daughter's request about the money and, soon after, Philomena and myself were poring over the pages of the *Adver* to see what vehicles were available for sale therein, and whether we could afford any that we liked the details of.

Once more, we were in luck! That is because we discovered a 'Renault 4' for sale – the same model of car as the first one which Philomena and myself had ever bought, whilst I had been a student at Cambridge University and which we had christened '*Noddy*'.[66] When the two of us visited the vendor's family home in the Toothill district of the town, after leaving the children with my mother at her home whilst we did so, we discovered a red-coloured counterpart of our former (green-hued) Noddy. Moreover, our test drive in it seemed to tell us that it really was a 'good runner'. Accordingly, my wife and I bought our latest Renault 4 for a little less than the price advertised in the Swindon newspaper – which itself was less than the amount of money which Mrs Harrison had kindly given us from the savings account in question. The extra amount from my mother-in-law's largesse could, therefore, be used for insuring the car for me to be able to drive it legally. Thus, on the day of purchase, the six members of my family were able to drive around the town in it together – with Philomena in the front passenger seat, Noel, Kim and Claire-Louise immediately behind, and Carl in his carrycot in the compartment further behind (which was accessible from the fifth door of the vehicle at the back).

From the day of the acquisition of our latest car, my family's standard of living seemed to improve in a major way. For one thing, instead of Philomena having to walk with Noel and Kim to school, I could now drive them there – as well as collect them at the end of their day. In between, I could then proceed, in the car, to the Law Centre to work on my research project. And, by so doing on a daily basis, my confidence increased in relation to meeting and greeting at least a few of the mums who also were taking or collecting their children to or from the school. That was especially the case in relation to those with offspring in Noel's or Kim's respective classes. During that first period of my doing the 'school run', I can remember one of those mum's saying boldly to me: 'So, she has got you back then!'. To that well-meaning comment, I simply smiled and said 'Yes'.

And what about the job at the Law Centre itself? That was largely left up to me as to how I went about my work on the project. One of the things it seemed useful for me to do in that regard was to find out about the boys' (and girls') clubs in Swindon – which, to my mind at least, would have provided positive things, at that time, for teenagers in the town to do and, thus, distract them from being tempted to go in any criminal direction. I also thought it useful for me to attend the session of the 'Juvenile Court', in the town's 'Magistrates' Court', at least once a week - in order to observe the sort of crimes which teenagers in the locality were in the habit of committing. For that latter process, I remember that I had to obtain the special permission of the 'Chief Clerk' of the town's Court - since Juvenile Court sessions were not open to public (unlike the case with the hearings in the ordinary adult Court). I still recall that his name was 'David Brewer' - a fellow qualified Barrister - and that, when we had met in his office in the Court and he learned of my legal background and of the project in question, he readily agreed to my request to attend the Juvenile Court sessions every Wednesday morning during the period of my research.

For the first time in ages, therefore, I began to feel 'normal' in my mind once again. I was going to work every weekday – and taking two of my children to school on the way – like many other young fathers in the town. I was earning money for my family - which we could spend, largely on food and other household provisions, by going to the supermarket in our car together at the weekends. We, thereby, avoided the necessity of Philomena having to carry heavy loads of shopping home, on foot (as had been the case whilst I had been absent from Swindon, and during which period she had been there alone with the children). In addition, my wife and children could all go for rides with me in our car, as one family, at weekends to places like 'Coate Water' (which was a country park, with a huge lake, on the edge of the town), or even wider afield around the county of Wiltshire such as 'Avebury' and 'Silbury Hill' – and, once only, even as far as Cambridge in the East of England.

*Fig. 51: Philomena, the Author, Noel, Kim, Claire-Louise and baby Carl, visiting 'David and Ellen Fleming' (and their daughter, 'Alice') in Cambridge, England in the summer of 1983 – one of the longest trips the newly-reunited six members of the Bradshaw family had made in their recently-acquired Renault 4 car, from their then home in Volta Road, Swindon. David Fleming was then a 'Fellow' at Trinity Hall – the Cambridge University college where the Author had studied Law during the 1970s*

As the summer months arrived, therefore, I was feeling that my life was settling down into a 'proper' family one, once more - and Philomena and myself were even able to start planning for the future academic year ahead in Belgium. We realised, early on, that we would have to think about getting Noel and Kim into school when we moved together across the English Channel. That is when I came up with the idea of our trying to get them into the 'English School of Brussels' – a private, fee-paying, institution – on the basis that Philomena could offer to teach at the school, in return for a reduction of the fees that our boys would have to pay to attend. Ideally, my wife did not really feel ready to go back to school teaching again. She had interrupted her career in that profession once our first child, Noel, had arrived whilst we had still lived in Cambridge in the 1970s. Nevertheless, she was willing to go along with my initiative - if it meant keeping our family together. We, therefore, started looking, every week during that period, in the '*Times Educational Supplement*' to see whether there were any vacancies - at the Brussels school in question - for a subject which Philomena could teach. Alas, we found none that was suitable.

What we did discover, however, was an opening at the 'Antwerp English Primary School' - situated in what is Belgium's second-largest city. That latter metropolis is located some thirty miles to the north of Brussels on the 'River Scheldt'. The Antwerp school simply wanted a general primary school teacher – something which Philomena had been during her very first year of teaching (after qualifying) - in Hendon, North London - just before we had married in 1976. It came to me, therefore, that if Philomena and I decided to base our family in Antwerp, then she could apply for the job in question and, if successful, I would take the burden on myself of commuting, daily during the week, to Brussels and back – in order to attend my course at the VUB.

Philomena's application to the Antwerp School, was duly sent off, therefore – after I had helped her to complete it. The two of us kept our fingers crossed and, fortunately - within a short time - she received a reply from the headmistress of the institution. She had written to Philomena that she herself – a woman named 'Janet' – was an Englishwoman, who came back to England regularly at weekends to visit her ailing mother living somewhere in the 'Home Counties'. Janet, accordingly, invited my wife to attend for an informal interview with her at the 'Cumberland Hotel' near 'Marble Arch' in Central London – to which Philomena, with my urging, happily accepted. The six members of our family, therefore, drove down to London on the day of the interview in our Renault 4, and, whilst their mother was having 'Tea' and an exchange of views with Janet in one of London's premier hotels, I played with the children in nearby 'Hyde Park'.

Philomena came out of her interview and back to us in the park with a huge smile on her face. She told us that Janet turned out to be a young woman of about the same age as herself. That the headmistress of the Antwerp school in question was a most sympathetic person. Best of all, that she had offered Philomena the job for the coming academic year – if my wife really wanted it! My wife added that she had discussed with Janet the issue of our family's need for accommodation for the year ahead and that the latter had come up with an offer in that regard also. That was that she (Janet), and her then current flatmate in Antwerp, were wanting to give up their then rented flat and move on to separate accommodations. Moreover, Janet had added that she would be willing to ask her current landlady whether our Bradshaw family could take over the lease in question, for the coming academic year. In addition, Janet had told Philomena that the landlady was not anticipated to give any problems regarding such a prospective transfer. Finally, Janet had suggested that, even though my wife had already accepted the offer of the post in question verbally, she (Philomena) should nevertheless come to visit the Antwerp school, with Noel and Kim, in order to make sure that they would all be happy to be attending it from the following September – to which idea Philomena had also readily agreed.

It was, therefore, a happy family unit that made the return journey to Wiltshire from London that particular afternoon. Philomena had landed herself a new job in an Antwerp primary school, and our two eldest boys had obtained a place in the institution. Moreover, it looked like she had also managed to organise accommodation for our family – via the good offices of the headmistress of the school. Philomena and myself just had to work out how we were going to get her and our two eldest sons to Antwerp – in order to visit the school, Janet and her colleagues, and, perhaps, have a look around our future accommodation in the Belgian city. We quickly came to the conclusion that the easiest thing to do was not for all our family to make a car and ferry journey to Belgium, but, rather, for only Philomena, Noel and Kim to travel to Antwerp and back – by train. Accordingly, we booked tickets for the three travelling members of our family to start from Swindon, go on to 'London Liverpool Street Station' - by underground, once they reached that of the 'Great Western Railway' terminus at London Paddington - and then on to 'Harwich' for the night ferry to the 'Hook of Holland'. We also booked a cabin for them for the crossing. From the Hook there was a train connection to 'Antwerpen Centraal' station with, perhaps, just one change at 'Rotterdam'. The return journey, one day after their arrival and stay with Janet in her Antwerp flat (which she had successfully arranged, with her landlady, to vacate for our family to move into) was the reverse of the outward journey – including Philomena and out two eldest taking a cabin on the night ferry once more. In staying behind in Swindon to babysit Claire-Louise and Carl on my own, for the few days which the excursion to Antwerp and back entailed, I was delighted. That is because it meant that my wife was able to have some 'fun' by engaging in some international travel – something which she had not experienced since coming to England from Barbados over one year before. Moreover, it also meant that our sons, Noel and Kim, were also having one of the greatest adventures of their lives, thus far – by travelling to two Continental countries, with just each other and their mum, for the very first time.

Clearly, having returned from Brussels to live, on a full-time basis, with Philomena and our children once more, my main focus in my everyday life was on them. I had not forgotten about Vere and Mikki, however, and - on the day after my arrival in Swindon after our decamping from Brussels - I had telephoned Aunt Ruby's number in Barbados to check that the two of them had arrived back in that Caribbean island safely and were, then, securely under the shelter and protection of Vere's honorary relative. To my relief, Vere was able to confirm that they were so, and that all was well with both herself and Mikki. Thereafter, Vere and myself exchanged letters about once a week - to keep each other abreast of how we were each getting on, whilst being apart from the other, and in the aftermath of our failed experiment of living together, with Mikki in Belgium. On her side, she was mainly making plans to return to England for her studies (which, she hoped, would lead to her becoming a lawyer by being called to the English Bar) - and also allowing Aunt Ruby (and her good friend, Aunt Daph, who had helped us when we had 'escaped' from Barbados, with Mikki, the previous September) to slowly take over the 'mothering' of Mikki. The latter step was so that it would not be too much of a wrench when it became time for Vere to eventually leave our daughter alone with the two aunts in order to depart for England. On my side, I was able to tell Vere about how I had been able to acquire a temporary job with the Law Centre, and even buy an old car. More importantly, I was able to inform her of the exact dates that I would have to return to Barbados in order to do my two-week stint of marking exams at UWI. Through her, I sought permission from Aunt Ruby for me to stay with her, Mikki and the two aunts at Ruby's Atlantic Shores home during my sojourn in Barbados – and was given it, with pleasure, it had seemed to me. Our mutual friend, and prospective foster carer of our daughter, was quick to let me know, through Vere, that I was welcome to stay at her home and that Aunt Daph would even pick me up from the airport when I first got back to the island.

One of the joys of being back in Swindon again, from the spring 1983 period in question, was that it enabled me to re-establish my contact with a few former school friends in the town with – with whom I had lost touch over years of my living away since 1971. One of those persons was my old 'best friend' at school - as I have called him in my second book, *Swimming without mangoes*[67] -'Philip Boguszewicz'. My rapprochement with him had been almost miraculous - as it turned out that he and his wife, 'Cindy', as well as their children, were then living just one street away from Volta Road! Indeed, their address was at 'number 141 Broad Street' – the very house where a former girlfriend of mine, 'Eileen Gordon' (or 'Katy'), and her family, used to live at, after moving there from a few doors away from my own family's home in Alexandra Road. Another long-standing friend was my fellow 'Leeds United Football Club' supporting mate - whom I also wrote about in the same second book,[68] and who had once accompanied me (in the late 1960s) to many a football match in London, and elsewhere, to see our favourite team play against other sides based in England's capital city and other places. That other friend was 'Roger Higgs', who by then was married to 'Sheila' and living in 'Courtney Road', in the Walcot district of Swindon, with their three children. Again, I was happy to re-establish my old friendship with him in 1983, even though, by then, he was no longer a Leeds supporter but a 'Queen's Park Rangers' one - owing, he told me, to his having been born not far from that latter club's home base in West London.

At any rate, it was owing to my renewed friendship with Roger that I was able to get a very reasonable air fare to take me back to Barbados in June 1983. For, he had a friend who worked in Swindon's town centre at a firm of travel agents called 'Thomas Cook'. And, through that friend, I was able to get the 10% discount on the return ticket price in question (which the friend was entitled to himself, and which he also gave to his mates such as Roger, for their holiday flights). Accordingly, even though I was only obtaining a relatively small fee for my research job at the Law Centre, payable in monthly instalments on my request, I was able to afford the London-Barbados return fare in question - with the aid of the discount gifted to me by Roger's friend. Moreover, the management of the Law Centre seemingly had little difficulty in granting my request to be allowed to take two weeks away from my research work with the Centre, in order to carry out my UWI duties (and which were a condition of my continued sabbatical period away from my main employer). Naturally, Philomena was none too pleased about my travelling back to Barbados without her and the children. She had actually seen my return ticket, however, and knew that, on that particular trip, I would come back to her and the family in Swindon very much sooner than when I had left them to return to Brussels in the January of that year.

And so, sometime near the middle of June 1983, I flew from London Heathrow back to Barbados. Vere and Mikki were at Grantley Adams International Airport to meet and greet me - fondly. Aunt Daph was there with her car also - and whilst her welcome might not have been as effusive as that of Vere's, she seemed pretty happy to see me too. After all, I had consented, through my recent letters with Vere, to her and Aunt Ruby becoming the *de facto* foster mothers of Mikki - from not many weeks ahead, when Vere herself returned to England to study. Aunt Ruby, too, seemed very happy to see me when we all reached her Atlantic Shores home. I had always found her warm, as well as most likeable - and that latest encounter of mine with her was no different. I soon discovered

*Fig. 52: The Author with Mikki, about a year after his temporary return to Barbados in the summer of 1983. Although this photo is taken later than during that short visit of his (to mark UWI examination papers), the venue in it was the 'Atlantic Shores' home of 'Aunt Ruby' where the Author stayed with Mikki and her mother, Vere, during the 1983 sojourn*

that she had set aside a room in her house for myself, Vere and Mikki – a downstairs *en suite* room, with the Caribbean Sea just outside our door. I could not have wished for a better reception, and accommodation, had I been forced to stay at one of the island's better hotels.

I was not, however, in Barbados for a holiday. Perhaps, therefore, as soon as the very next day, after the delights of the rapprochement with Vere and Mikki the previous evening, I had to drive myself to Cave Hill Campus to start my examiner's duties. In doing so, I used my old Skoda car. I had leased it to a man from Guyana the previous September - just before Vere, Mikki and myself had left Barbados for England, *en route* to Brussels. The man in question had failed to make all the agreed payments under the lease arrangement during my time in Belgium. Accordingly, I had agreed with Vere, for her to repossess the car, once she and Mikki had returned to the island in March, and to use the car for herself. I was, thus, also able to use it myself, during my temporary stay - in order to drive the eight miles or so from Atlantic Shores to Cave Hill to do the necessary marking in my old Room 4 at the Campus. Bruce Zagaris, who had taken my place as the lecturer for my Comparative Law course during the 1982-83 academic year and had already 'first- marked' the papers of his students in question. As a consequence, I merely had to second-mark them. He had also returned to his native USA by the time I had turned up at the Campus - as his temporary contract with the UWI Law Faculty had ended. I, thus, had my old room there to myself - and I shut the door to it and beavered away at my agreed task, as I always did when marking scripts. After the first day of being 'back in the saddle', it was as if I had never been away from my UWI main employers for any length of time at all.

It was somewhat strange, however, being back at Cave Hill - with several of my colleagues asking me how I had got on during my sabbatical year in Belgium. It would have undoubtedly been quite embarrassing for me to tell those who asked that question that I still had unfinished studies in Brussels and that I would, in fact, be returning for a second sabbatical year. I neither mentioned the fact that I had interrupted those studies for family reasons, or that I was then working temporarily in Swindon, England (with a Law Centre there, whilst trying to re-establish my family life with my wife and our children). After a few days, however, I felt more comfortable in myself about being back at UWI. I was also pleased with the job that I was doing as an examiner – a process which, as stated, only took me a little while to get myself used to once more. As well as marking scripts for Comparative Law, I also had to second mark those for at least one other subject. I can no longer recall, however, whether that was just for The Conflict of Laws or whether the Law of Tort was included as well. Be that as it may, by working assiduously during each of my full days in Barbados, including the weekends, I was able to finish all my allotted marking on time. Moreover, I was able to play my part in the subsequent examiners' meetings – just as though I had never been away from UWI for almost one full academic year already.

Fortunately, I still had a few days free once my examining duties were over at Cave

Hill - and before I had to return to England. I was able to spend these, happily, with Vere and Mikki. The three of us were able to go to nearby Oistins Beach to try to teach Mikki how to swim – despite the fact that she was then not yet one-year-old and only just learning how to walk. We were also able to go wider afield together in the Skoda, and whilst doing so, I tried to enjoy my time with Mikki, especially, to the full. That was because I knew that, though I would be seeing Vere again pretty soon, such would not be the case with our daughter.

All too soon, however, the idyll in Barbados was over and I had to return to England. Once more, Aunt Daph took me back to the island's airport and I said a heartfelt goodbye to her, having already done the same to Aunt Ruby at Atlantic Shores. It was an even more fervent and tearful farewell which I gave to Mikki and Vere (who, naturally, had also come to see me off). For although I knew that, all being well, I should be seeing Vere again in Europe before too many more months had passed, it would be at least one full year before I would next finally return to Barbados and get the chance to see our daughter again.

An odd thing happened during my journey back to Swindon. Philomena and myself had agreed, before I had gone to Barbados, that we would both go to a reunion Mass. That was to be held at the Lower School of our *alma mater*, St Joseph's, in the town - on the very Sunday that I got back into the country. The plan was that I would just get back home to Swindon in time to allow my wife and myself to take our children to my mum's in Alexandra Road to ask her to babysit, whilst the two of us went on alone to the reunion Mass. As luck would have it, however, my BWIA flight back into Heathrow was delayed and arrived late - perhaps by up to two hours. Upon landing, therefore, I quickly phoned my mum to beg her to please go to Volta Road to babysit the children there, and to tell Philomena to go on alone to the school and that I would meet her there, directly from Swindon's railway station. To save time, I then tried to avoid having to go into Central London and Paddington Station to get a train to Swindon - by asking one of the black London taxi cabs to take me to 'Reading' railway station (where I would be able to pick up the London to Swindon train, about halfway along its route). To my consternation, none of the taxi drivers, whom I asked, was willing to take me to Reading. I was, thus, stymied in my plans and ended up having to travel to Paddington station after all – by London Underground. By the time that I had arrived at that London terminus, I was really running very late and, thus, reconciled myself to only arriving during the reunion Mass in question. I only hoped that I would get there before it had finished. Fortunately, I was able to get a taxi outside Swindon's station, driven by a Bradshaw family friend. He, at my urging, quickly drove me to Volta Road, where I was able to drop off my suitcase, and then on to St Joseph's School about a further mile away. The Mass had reached somewhere around its mid-point, but I was able to spot Philomena in the throng and then go and sit next to her in the open air and sunshine. I squeezed her hand at an opportune moment - to let her know that I was back safely, and full-time in her life once more. Moreover, afterwards we were able to mingle with one or two former classmates from our Swindon schooldays, as well as one or two of our ex-teachers - some of whom were to be somewhat incredulous when I told them that I had just come straight from Barbados to be at the Mass!

*Chapter 28*

# Vere's Return to England; and my Setting Up Home in Belgium with my Matrimonial Family – from Late Summer 1983

One of the initiatives which I dreamt up, as part of my work at the Law Centre, was to make a series of visits to some of the other such centres around England. That was to enable me to see what each of them was doing as far as providing advice and assistance for juveniles who had got into trouble with the Criminal Law in their respective geographical area. After obtaining the go-ahead for the mission from the management committee of the Swindon Centre, I was able to make a first trip to the 'Liverpool Law Centre', where I stayed with an old sixth form classmate, named 'Cathy'. She lived in nearby Manchester at the time – so, quite close to Philomena's native city. During the same trip, I also visited the 'Leeds Law Centre' and was, thus, able to stay with a former colleague from my days of teaching at Leeds University - a 'Ms Allison Wolfgarten'. And it was as part of the same initiative, perhaps about a month after those two North of England visits, that I subsequently made a journey to the West Country to visit the 'Exeter Law Centre'. During that latest research outing, I was able to meet, and stay with, my former classmate at Kingston Law School, 'Kim Economides' - who, by then, was a Law lecturer at 'Exeter University'.

The duty trip to Exeter, however, also had an ulterior motive. That was to allow me to meet up with Vere on her return to Europe - in order to start preparing for her Bar studies, commencing at about the end of August. A number of potential issues had to be overcome, however, for that get-together to take place effectively. First, I did not want to upset Philomena by telling her about it – hence the need for it to be part of one of my duty visits to different Law Centres around the country. Secondly, both Vere and I were wary that the UK immigration authorities might give her some problems if she tried to land at London Heathrow. That could happen, for example, by those 'gatekeepers' either not allowing her to enter the UK at all, or, perhaps, restricting her stay to perhaps six months, say - when she knew that she would need at least two academic years to qualify for Call to the English Bar. Accordingly, she was to agree with me that the better idea was for her to take the regular flight from Barbados to Brussels – our former home city – which was then being run by Caribbean Airways (on a move from Luxembourg, which country it had previously preferred as its Continental European base for its transatlantic service to Barbados). We chose the latter option because we figured that she should have little problem getting the Belgian immigration officials to let her into their country. And then she would only have to contend with the UK ones, once we had arrived in Dover from a cross-channel ferry (which we thought might have 'softer' vetting processes than those used on Caribbean visitors coming into England via one of the London airports). The challenge for me, however, was that I would have to travel to Belgium to meet her there!

My original plan, therefore, was to drive my family's latest Renault 4 all the way from Exeter - after the Law Centre visit and meet-up with Kim Economides there - to Dover along several south coast main roads. I would then get a return car ferry ticket from Dover to Ostend, drive to Brussels from that Belgian port in order to collect Vere at 'Zaventem International Airport', and then the two of us drive back to England together via the Ostend-Dover car ferry.

The first part of my plan went swimmingly and I passed seaside places like Bournemouth and Brighton *en route* to Dover, before I sustained a puncture. I put on the spare wheel and continued on with my mission to make sure that I was at Brussels Airport in good time to meet Vere when she arrived there from her Barbados flight. Amazingly, however, within 50 miles, or so, further on – in the town of 'Hastings' - I sustained yet another puncture! As stated, I had already used the spare wheel. Moreover, it was evening by then and all the garages, which I could see in the part of the town where I found myself, were closed for business and I could not, therefore, get a repair to one or other of the stricken tyres. Mindful of my promise to Vere to meet her at Zaventem Airport, however, I decided that I would just have to go on to Brussels by train – and leave the Renault 4 behind, for repairs to be made to the tyres when I returned for it later. Going to Hastings railway station, I discovered that I could, indeed, get a train – but only to 'Folkestone', instead of Dover, and from which port there would be a night ferry to Ostend later that evening. I, therefore, bought myself a return ticket to Brussels, via the Folkestone-Ostend ferry, and that is how I managed to get to Zaventem Airport, in the Belgian capital, with a little bit of time to spare the next day and, so, able to meet Vere off her flight from Barbados. When she eventually emerged from the 'Arrivals' exit of the terminus, she was smiling happily – quite unaware of the drama which I had sustained with my car and its two punctures the day before. I was also happy to see her and to know that the first part of her journey, to get back into life in England, had succeeded. I would have plenty of time to tell her about my car problems and the fact that we would not, as planned, be going on to the UK generally, or London specifically, by my latest motor - but would, rather, be doing so by train.

Soon afterwards, and subsequent to Vere telling me about the ease with which she had been able to pass through the Belgian immigration authorities at the airport, the two of us found ourselves on a train bound for the west of our former host country where we had lived with Mikki until earlier that year. *En route*, I asked Vere whether she would like to have a lunch stop and a look around either Bruges or Ghent. That was because, when we had lived in Brussels, we had never been able to afford to go to visit either of those two 'medieval' cities. In the end, Vere and I agreed on Ghent since I had never myself visited it - although I had 'Brugge', as the former is known by its local Flemish name. We thus alighted at Ghent, or 'Gand' in Flemish, checked in Vere's suitcase at the left luggage office in the station, and then had a most pleasant day in the sunshine strolling along the banks of the canals that we found there. As much as myself, Vere seemed to enjoy the medieval architecture of the waterside buildings as well as the churches which we passed along the way. They were a huge contrast, I well knew, from the scenery of Barbados - which she would have left behind just a matter of 10 hours or so beforehand. And, when we needed a rest, we bought some sandwiches and drinks at one of the small supermarkets which we passed during our wanderings and tarried a while to consume them by a lake located in a large park nearby. We then returned to Ghent's main railway station, recovered Vere's luggage and then set off on the next train bound for Ostend.

As with our last ferry journey from that Belgian port to England the previous March, we were fortunate in being able to obtain a cabin for our latest night crossing of the English Channel. Instead of Dover, however, the next morning we found ourselves arriving at the smaller ferry terminal, situated to the west of the primary Kent port – namely, that of Folkestone. It was then that I became most anxious. That was because my whole plan of Vere arriving at Brussels Airport, instead of London Heathrow, depended on her encountering little or no problem as she showed her Barbados passport to the immigration official, to whom she had to report, in order to pass further into England. I went to him first and, after having no problem with him myself, watched from a distance (on the 'free to go' side of the immigration booth) as Vere followed me. To my relief, she was reunited with me again within about two minutes. My plan had succeeded! Perhaps, she had been treated as just a tourist to England who was then living in Belgium. Or, perhaps, she had told the official that she was coming to England to inquire about doing postgraduate legal studies there and had been allowed an initial entry of six months to sort things out – with the possibility of elongating her initial permission to stay, during that original time period. Whatever the case, Vere was officially, and legally, in England - and the two of us found ourselves free to go on together into the interior of the country!

In fact, although we were headed for London – where Vere had another friend from her Barbados schooldays living in an eastern district of the capital called 'Ilford', who was named 'Yvette'. We, naturally, had first to head, by train, to Hastings in order for me to recover, and repair, my car. The first part we did, fairly smoothly, via a change of railway line at 'Ashford'. Upon arriving at Hastings station, we had quite a hill to walk up, with myself being encumbered by Vere's suitcase as we did so. Fortunately, however, my Renault 4 was only parked about a quarter of a mile up that promontory. Vere watched as I took off the punctured tyre from my car. Again, I was lucky - as there was a garage which repaired cars, and tyres, not too many yards away, on the very hill where I had left the vehicle. I was, thus, able to take the tyre, which I had just removed, to that service station for fixing. Given my bad luck on the journey trying to drive to Dover from Exeter - when I had sustained two punctures in one day - I was careful to also take along the first punctured tyre for repair also. With the holes in both tyres duly fixed, and those repairs paid for, I was able to return with Vere to the car with one of them, refit the wheel in question, and then drive the two of us to the garage to collect the other (which would be my spare wheel, in case of any further punctures *en route* to London). Finally, therefore, Vere and I could set off for London in the Renault 4.

We took the by-roads on the way northwards to England's capital, rather than the motorway. That is because, though having been with each other for about 24 hours already by then, Vere and myself still had a lot to talk about. Not only did I need to catch up with news from her about our daughter, Mikki, but I also needed to know exactly what her plans were to enable her to study to obtain the qualification for Call to the English Bar. For, that was her main goal in coming back to England – and which attainment would enable her to get admitted as a practising lawyer, or Attorney-at-Law, in her native Barbados in due course. From our conversation on that journey to London, as well as beforehand during our train and ferry trip from Brussels Airport, I learned several news things from Vere. Those included the fact that she would be living in Ilford - with Yvette and her Barbadian civil servant husband, in their home there, during the two years that she expected to be in England to complete her studies. Also, that during the first year she would have to attend a college in London to study for, and pass, some extra, peculiarly English Law, subjects. Those 'extra' courses, she told me, were ones which the English 'Bar Council' required to be passed in order to treat her Law degree from UWI – her 'LL.B' - as equivalent to that obtained by a graduate in Law from an English university. Only then, would she be allowed to go on to do the Bar Finals course and exams, during her second year in England – which exam passes she would need in order for her to be Called to the English Bar as a Barrister-at-Law. One of those 'peculiar' extra subjects – which she would have to study, and pass, in her first year - would be English 'Land Law', but others may have included English Constitutional and Administrative Law. I also learned, during our drive to London, that in her last six months or so in Barbados, Vere had applied for, and had obtained, a place at a college near Waterloo Station in the capital - where she would be able to study the necessary extra subjects during her first year in England.

By the time Vere and I arrived at Yvette's house in Ilford, therefore, I was fully abreast of Vere's plans for her immediate, and longer-term, future in England. I was also reassured that Mikki was thriving with the two 'aunts' back in Barbados - and that neither of us needed to worry that our daughter would not be well looked-after whilst Vere was in Europe. We both discussed the fact, however, that if Vere was not going to complete her studies in London until two years hence, I would be back in Barbados, to recommence my UWI teaching duties, some one year before her! I told Vere, however, that though I would be returning to her native land with Philomena and our children from the summer of that following year ahead, I would nevertheless go to see Mikki as much as I could – and, indeed, try to include her in my own Bradshaw family's life, as often as possible, during her (Vere's) absence after I had returned.

Yvette and her husband both turned out to be very pleasant people – of about the same age as Vere and myself. The two of them were kind enough to allow me to stay for one night with Vere in their home. That was not only to enable me to take a leisurely leave of the new arrival to England, but also to drive her, the next day, to visit her Waterloo-based college so that she could register as one of its new students for the year ahead. Those matters I managed to accomplish - before driving back up the motorway to Swindon, Philomena and our children that evening. Once more, the two women in my life were back in the same country. I felt much happier on that occasion, however. That was because I was satisfied that I had the 'balance of rightness' correct - and that living with my wife and children in the Wiltshire town, for the time being, was what the Almighty would have wanted me to do.

That is not to say, on the other hand, that I was not in regular touch with Vere during those latter days of mine as a researcher at the Law Centre in Swindon. For, she would often phone me at the Centre from Yvette's home phone. Invariably, one of my colleagues – Michael, Robert or Mary - would answer, and she would say something like: 'This is the Ilford Star calling for David Bradshaw. Is he there?'. No doubt, after a while my colleagues must have started to wonder why a newspaper from East London was so often trying to call me on the phone - and exactly what my connection was with that part of the English capital. To the best of my memory, however, none of them ever asked me such questions to my face. Moreover, through such calls, I learned that Vere was settling down well with her legal studies and that, from her phone conversations with Aunt Ruby, our daughter was also doing great in Barbados.

With Vere settled in London, I, with Philomena and our children, was able to enjoy our summer in Swindon - especially once the school holidays had arrived and before we had to take steps to further prepare for our move to Antwerp. Moreover, as well as making those Round-England trips to Law Centres in cities like Liverpool, Leeds and Exeter, I was fully immersed in my Swindon-area research by visiting places such as the boys' clubs and the Juvenile Court. I particularly enjoyed going to the last, once a week, on a Wednesday to witness cases for myself - and to note down names, addresses, offences charged as well as outcomes in the proceedings in question. Through that step, and with the agreement of the Chief Clerk at the Court, I came up with a novel idea which I wanted to recommend in my prospective report. That was to write to the parents of each juvenile defendant whose case I had witnessed – and such defendants were invariably boys – to suggest a meeting between each such defendant, his parents, and the respective victim against whom the crime in question had been committed. My idea was that if each such young defendant could but see the effects which his crime had caused to his respective victim, it might help him to never go down that criminal road again. In my view, that might especially be the case if each such proposed respective meeting, which included each young offender in question, was buttressed by diverting his energies, for the future, into sport or other activities available at one or other of the several boys' clubs in existence in or around the town.

So content was I with the progress that I was making in my work in Swindon, and with my matrimonial family's life in the town - during that summer - that when Philomena's French penfriend, 'Evelyne', wrote to us to ask whether she, her Spanish husband, 'Manuel', and their two daughters, 'Karine' and 'Mikaëlle' (from whose name I had got the idea for Mikki's 'proper' Christian name), could come to spend a short holiday with us at our home in Volta Road, I immediately told Philomena to reply in the affirmative. Accordingly, not too long before departing for Belgium, we had a house full – with not only our own six persons, but also Evelyne's four. Though small, our Volta Road rented home had three bedrooms and somehow – mainly with Philomena's strategic planning – we managed to squeeze all 10 persons of the two families into the dwelling, for up to one week or so.

*Fig. 53: Evelyne (left) - with Philomena – at her native village of 'Le Truel, Aveyron, France', near the city of 'Rodez'. This photo is taken by the banks of the 'River Tarn', which flows through the village, a few years after Evelyne, her husband Manuel, and their two daughters – Karine and Mikaëlle – came to visit Philomena, the Author and their children at Volta Road in Swindon, Wiltshire, England in the summer of 1983. Accordingly, the photo shows Evelyne much as she would have appeared in 1983 – as well as Philomena, of course*

Naturally, it being the summer, Philomena and myself tried to take our guests out of the house as much as possible. Thus, I recall that, for example, one day we all went, in the two families' cars, to 'Lydiard Park', on the western outskirts of Swindon, for a picnic lunch – during which Manuel made a 'sangria' for us all, according to a recipe which he had learned from his native 'Pamplona' region of Spain (and which included wine and oranges, to the delight of all the children except, perhaps, young Carl). On the one Sunday our guests were with us, we drove, again in the two cars, to the nearby town of 'Lechlade' on the Wiltshire and Gloucestershire border for a special outing. That was in order for us all to have a cruise on the River Thames - which has its source not many miles to the west of Lechlade, and which flowed through that little town on its way to London, some 70 miles away. The cruise would have been largely my idea of a special treat for our lovely Franco-Spanish family - since it included Sunday lunch on board, as well as travel on what is, perhaps, England's most famous river (from our visitors' point of view, at least). Even wider afield, Philomena and myself decided that we also had to take our guests even wider afield - again using their own car as well as ours, but with the children mixed up in the vehicles *en route* - to the relatively nearby famous university city of Oxford. There, we had a wonderful day out together, visiting one or two of the more famous colleges of the seat of learning - including 'Magdalen College', in order to let the children see, and get close to, the deer living in its grounds, as well as to enable our party to have another lengthy picnic (without sangria on that occasion), by the riverside there. For once, Evelyne might have perceived Philomena and myself to be in relatively straitened circumstances - compared to the times when she had visited Swindon as Philomena's teenage penfriend, and had stayed with the Harrison family in Southbrook Street. Nevertheless, she gave Philomena and myself every indication that she, her husband, and their children had enjoyed a delightful time with us in our little Volta Road home - during their week or so in Swindon.

Before I knew it, however, Evelyne and family had returned to France and the school summer holidays were rapidly drawing to their end. It was, thus, time for me to seriously think about how I was going to effectuate the move of my family to our new home, and life, in Antwerp – a city which I myself had never yet visited (but which, as seen, Philomena, Noel and Kim had done, very briefly, just a few months before). Philomena had told me that although her new headmistress, Janet - into whose flat in the Belgian city we were moving - did have a washing machine installed in the dwelling, she (Janet), was going to take it with her when she moved out. Accordingly - given the number of our children and the amount of washing they and ourselves produced - Philomena and myself decided that we would just have to take our own washing machine, and separate tumble dryer, with us to Belgium when we made our move. Through my old Swindon friend, Philip, I had been introduced to the Saturday auctions which took place at a venue in Swindon's Old Town called 'The Planks', and I had accompanied him there on one occasion. During that unusual visit (for me), I had managed to successfully bid for both of the requisite machines in question. Accordingly, as we would very much be in need of them in Belgium also, there seemed nothing for it but to export them with us. That decision meant that our family would need to hire a small truck to transport our household goods - including the two machines (which were very heavy), to Antwerp when the time came for our transition there.

*Fig. 54: Evelyne's Spanish husband – Manuel – holding Claire-Louise, during the visit of the Franco-Spanish couple, and their two daughters, to the Volta Road, Swindon, Wiltshire then home of Philomena, the Author and their children in the summer of 1983. From left to right: Mikaëlle, Claire-Louise, Manuel, Kim, Noel, Philomena, Karine, Carl, and the Author*

*Fig.55: Philomena and the Author looking after their four children AND the daughters of Evelyne and her Spanish husband – Manuel – on the banks of the River Thames at Lechlade on the Wiltshire-Gloucestershire border during the Franco-Spanish family's visit to the Volta Road, Swindon, Wiltshire then home of Philomena, the Author and their children in the summer of 1983. From left to right: Philomena, Noel, Claire-Louise, Mikaëlle, the Author, Kim, Carl and Karine*

As a result, when the day of our international move finally came, Philomena and I spurned the idea of our merely trying to use our Renault 4 car for that purpose. Rather, that vehicle would have to stay to behind whilst we hired a not-too-large truck for all our possessions - including our washing machine, dryer, television, the clothing of all the family, some bedding that did not belong to our landlord and so forth. Prior to the hire, Philomena would either have taken the children to Mrs Harrison's home, or invited her to come to visit them and herself at our Volta Road home whilst I was at work at Law Centre. Once more, it would have been a wrench for my mother-in-law to have had to say goodbye - not only to her sole daughter but also to the only grandchildren she then had. It would, therefore, have been a leave-taking that was akin to what she had once 'suffered' in August 1979, when only Noel and Kim had been in existence - just before Philomena, myself, and the first two of our eventual four children, had emigrated to Barbados to enable me to take up my job at UWI. Up to that more recent time in late August 1983, I had still not crossed paths with my mother-in-law since leaving Belgium for Swindon the previous March. Nevertheless, I had still been able to appreciate the sadness which she would have felt in saying goodbye on that second occasion - more than I had done on our emigration to Barbados some four years before. Silently, I vowed to myself that, once Philomena, the children and myself returned to the Caribbean in the summer of 1984, in order for me to recommence my career at UWI, I would do my best to make sure that we all came back to visit Mrs Harrison and my own mum in Swindon on an annual basis, if at all possible.

In the case of my own mother living at nearby Alexandra Road, once more I had little doubt or misgivings that my family and myself would be back to see her again in the not-too-distant future. Nor, indeed, that she might even come out to visit us in Barbados, once we all eventually got back there. Consequently, there would not have been so many tears shed when Philomena and myself took our children round to 'Nanny Bradshaw's house' in Alexandra Road to engage in that send-off from my mother. In any case, I myself would see her again soon – when I returned to Swindon with the truck from Antwerp, in order to give it back to the hire company, as well as pick up my family's Renault 4 to drive myself back to Belgium.

With Philomena's help, I managed to get the two heaviest items of our personal possessions into the truck, via its back door – namely, our washing machine and tumble dryer. And then, with our children all in the front cab with me (and Philomena holding Carl in her arms), I drove off from Volta Road to make my way to junction 15 of the M4 motorway - situated on the outskirts of Swindon - to start the journey to London and beyond. I can no longer recall how we all arrived on the south side of England's capital – whether through its centre, or around it using the 'North Circular Road' and then its southern counterpart perhaps – but we must have managed to do that, in an uneventful way. The journey further south to Dover, and then the day ferry crossing with the loaded truck to Ostend, was also completed without any misadventure. After that, there was a drive along the familiar motorway, which I had hitchhiked on the previous January, eastwards towards Brussels. I did not have to proceed as far as the Belgian capital on that occasion, however. That is because there was a motorway intersection when we reached the suburbs of Ghent, and I took the northern option towards Antwerp. Thereafter, the route we were taking that day was entirely new for me - but we, nevertheless, made the outskirts of our new home city uneventfully within the hour of our turning off the highway to Brussels. Then, it only remained for me to face the challenge of finding my way to our new home address.

Fortunately, Philomena remembered that the flat we were going to live in - situated in 'Lamorinierestraat' - was quite near to the Antwerp English Primary School on the south side of the city. And, as we left the motorway slip road and drove towards the city centre, Philomena spotted the road in which her future school (as well as that of Noel and Kim) was situated. Thereafter, she was able to direct me to our new home street - since she had previously walked the route with Janet, her new headmistress, when she had visited the school, and Janet's then flat, with our eldest two boys not so many weeks before. After that, it was just a case of my parking - illegally - outside the flat whilst Philomena quickly went to our new landlady's home nearby - the address of which Janet had given her in advance – to obtain the keys to allow us to gain entry.

When Philomena came back, a short time later, with the vital metallic devices, she and I were able to use one of them to enter the block of flats in question. Whilst my wife took the children up to the flat – which she pointed out to me was some two floors up from the road in which we were parked - to look after them there, I tried to unload the truck as quickly as possible. That was because I was worried about the police stopping by, owing to my illegal parking. With Philomena and our children looking down on me from the height of our new dwelling, I worked quickly and emptied the truck by merely putting everything inside the entrance of our new block. The moving upstairs would have to wait until I had driven the truck onwards, to a legal position nearby. There were two items left inside the truck, however, which I just could not manage by myself. Accordingly, I had to shout to Philomena to leave the children for a few minutes and come downstairs again to help me. Those possessions were our much-needed washing machine and dryer - and between the two of us, my wife and myself managed to also get them inside the block's entrance hall. Then, it was just a case of my quickly driving the truck around the corner to a legal parking space, on a neighbouring road, and returning to my family - full of expectation!

When I eventually got inside our flat - via a lift which was available on the ground floor - I was not to be disappointed. Indeed, I was to be most impressed with what Philomena had managed to find us for our new home – via the excellent contact, and wonderful assistance of, her new headmistress. Compared with the place in which Vere and myself had rented in Brussels, 'Flat 4 at number 198 Lamorinierestraat, Antwerp' (which was the full the address of our new home) was a luxury apartment. For one thing, it had three bedrooms, a living room, a toilet room as well as a separate bathroom, a kitchen and an adjoining dining room. The feature which I loved the most, however, was the high ceiling of each of those rooms - which gave the dwelling an air of great space. And the icing on the cake, for me, was the fact that the flat also had a little balcony which adjoined the smallest of the bedrooms, and which overlooked Lamorinierestraat below, as well as some of our neighbours' flats on the other side of the street. I could see, at once - and after that first viewing of mine - that our new home was a place in which I could be happy and, equally importantly, my wife and our children could be so, as well.

To avoid blocking the entrance hall of our new apartment building, I promptly set about bringing up to our flat everything – little by little, over several trips and via the lift – which we had unloaded from the truck. I did that all by myself - except for the washing machine and dryer, which Philomena needed to help me load into the lift and then unload prior to our bringing them inside our residence. As we were doing so, the door across the landing from our front door opened. A senior couple - who were, perhaps, in their late 50s or early 60s - came out to introduce themselves to us. They spoke in English, and told us that their names were 'Mr and Mrs Huybrechts'. Philomena and myself, in turn, introduced ourselves with our own names - and then my wife went to bring the children from inside our flat, in order to present them to our new neighbours also. It was only after that friendly, but unexpected, set of exchanges that Mr Huybrechts suggested that he help me with the transfer of our washing machine and dryer - still just outside the lift at that stage - to the place inside our flat where Philomena and myself wanted them. I jumped at my new neighbour's offer and we both set about lifting the two heavy items in question, one by one, and then walking them – instead of sliding them as Philomena and I had previously done – to the bathroom inside our new abode. Meeting Mr and Mrs Huybrechts, so early on in my family's arrival in Antwerp, proved not only useful but also seemed like a wonderful omen to a future happy sojourn in our new home. For that unexpected encounter was an intimation, it seemed to me, to a domestic life ahead for us that was *à la* the happy periods which Philomena and myself had spent, years before, in Coton, Cambridgeshire and then Leeds, Yorkshire thanks, in part, to the friendship which we had enjoyed with our nearest neighbours during both eras.

After one night's stay in our new flat, perforce I had to leave Philomena and our children, once more - in order to take back the rented truck to Swindon. I made sure, however, that my wife had enough funds to see her through the immediate days ahead until I returned with our family's Renault 4. I would have to be back no later than just before Philomena and our two eldest sons were due to start their respective new 'working lives' at their new school in Antwerp. That was because I could then babysit Claire-Louise and young Carl, as well as also try to find them a nursery school (where they could spend their weekdays whilst I commuted to Brussels and back, in order to attend my re-commenced course at the VUB in the Belgian capital). I, thus, had about a week or so to return to Swindon, finally clean up my family's former Volta Road home, and make suitable arrangements with members of the Law Centre for my writing and submitting the report - from Belgium - of my researches for them over the previous months.

My return journey to Swindon from Antwerp was as uneventful as the outward journey with my family had been. That was so except for one unforgettable incident. For, on board the ferry from Ostend, I had bought a duty-free bottle of whisky for my landlord at Volta Road. That was intended to be as a token of the appreciation from Philomena and myself for what he had done for us, and our children, in giving us somewhere decent to live for the past year or so. That was especially the case in relation to the time that we had been expecting our last child, Carl, and given that he had already rented out part of the house to someone else. For some reason, I decided to secrete the bottle in the back of the truck - even though, most likely, I was within my duty-free allowance, in only having one bottle of alcohol with me. As luck would have it, however, in driving the truck through the 'Nothing to declare' exit on arrival from the ferry at Dover, a Customs official stopped me. He asked me to confirm that I really had nothing to declare and, after my doing so, he proceeded to search the truck. He started with the cab at the front at first, and then proceeded to the rear. Alas, at the latter place, he found the hidden bottle of whisky! And whatever my allowances might well have been, the proposed present for my landlord was 'confiscated' - owing to my 'non-declaration'. Accordingly, one of the first things I had to do in Swindon, therefore - after returning the truck - was to go to a regular off-licence to buy a replacement for the confiscated alcohol. That was to ensure that I could give our Swindon landlord the present from my family, after all - but at a much greater cost to our household budget.

Before finally returning to my matrimonial family in Belgium, I had to liaise with my management committee at the Law Centre for permission to complete, and then submit, my report for the Centre only after I had already moved to Antwerp and commenced my course at the VUB. Indeed, I also needed to be allowed to delay that submission deadline until as far away as up to the Christmas period ahead. Moreover, I also had the nerve to ask my ex-Etonian colleague, Michael, whether I could lodge with him for a few days after I had finally moved out of the Volta Road house, and prior to returning to Philomena and our children in Antwerp. I knew that he was a bachelor, lived alone in a three-bedroom house in the 'Eastcott Hill' district of Swindon just above the Town Hall, and thought that he might well appreciate my company for a few days. Michael said 'yes' to my suggestion – and so it was that I was his house guest, for the last few days of my time in Swindon as a consultant to the Law Centre.

What happened in those last days, however, is something which, with hindsight, I might well have avoided doing. I invited Vere to come to come up from London to visit me in Swindon. The idea was that, as the mother of our daughter Mikki, she should see something of where Mikki's father had grown up, from a pre-teen, and had gone to school – as well as something of the surrounding county that was part of his life during those bygone years. Naturally, the 'Ilford Star' jumped to the idea – but I then had to ask Michael whether a 'friend of mine' from London could also stay at his house during my last day or two with him. My Law Centre colleague again gave me an affirmative answer at once, and even went to the trouble of making up his second spare room for the surprise visitor – who I eventually told him was a female, when the time seemed appropriate.

I cannot recall now whether Vere came up to Swindon by train or coach, but she duly arrived in the town and I met her and took her to Michael's house in my Renault 4. It might well have been a Thursday evening - after she had finished all her classes for the week in question at her Waterloo-based college. I would thus have been able to use the light of a late summer's evening to show her my own school at St Joseph's (the then 'Lower' part in 'Queen's Drive'). I also showed her 'The Lawns' - in the part of Swindon's Old Town where I had attended the last two years or so of my primary school education in the town, and which I had so much enjoyed, as revealed in *Swimming without mangoes*.[69] Most certainly, also, I took her to see my former home in Alexandra Road - so very near Swindon's railway station and where I had grown up from the age of nine years old. Given that my mother was still living in that home, I had to be careful to merely drive Vere past the house without stopping – although, with hindsight and given that Vere was the mother of my mum's Bajan grandchild, it might have been the better - or 'more right' thing to have done if I had stopped and had taken the trouble of introducing the two ladies to each other.

The day after Vere's first arrival in the town was a working one. That is because, as part of my last piece of research work for the Law Centre, I set out to do some investigations into the records of some of the recent cases heard by the Juvenile Court in the more-prosperous-than Swindon municipality of 'Salisbury'. That city is situated in the southern part of my later childhood's county of Wiltshire – and I took Vere with me in the Renault 4. *En route* to Salisbury, accordingly, I was able to show her (without stopping to explore) the stones of Avebury as well as Silbury Hill nearby. With Vere at my side, I then spent some hours inside the Magistrates' Court building looking at, and noting down, the type of cases which came before the Juvenile Court there, their outcomes, and the 'affluence' or otherwise of the districts from which the young defendants in the cases in question came. Such research covered the period of over a year or two, ending with the date in question. I undertook the examination in question in order for it to provide me with some data with which to compare my findings from the Juvenile Court of Swindon (which is located in the more northern, and poorer, part of the county). After our 'day in court', Vere and I were free to explore Salisbury a bit - including our venturing inside the famous cathedral there (which, reputedly, then possessed 'the tallest spire in England'). We even had time to visit the archives of the local newspaper, in order to look for a photo printed in one of its editions from the 1970-71 academic year when I had played for the Wiltshire Schoolboys football team in Salisbury - and a photographer from the local paper had taken the team's photo, as part of the reporting on the match in question. Perhaps, even in those 1983 days, I was thinking of writing memoirs of my life at some unforeseeable time in the future - such as this present volume - and realised that I would need illustrative photos to go with any such text that I might produce. Alas, we never did find the sought-after photo. We had little problem, however, in finding our way back to Swindon via 'Stonehenge' - so that I could show Vere one of the more-famous landmarks situated within my adopted county.

Logistically, it would have made sense if I had finally taken my leave of Swindon, and Michael, the following day - by setting out for Antwerp, with Vere as my passenger, so that I could drop her off in Ilford *en route*. Alas, I do not recall doing that. What I positively remember doing, however, was making one last visit to Alexandra Road, without Vere, in order to say goodbye to my mum and sister in their home at number 16. In so doing, it would not have been a sad occasion, since we would all have expected to be seeing each other again in the not-too-distant future – whether back in Swindon, or even in Barbados. And, no doubt, my mother would have mainly wanted me to greet Philomena and the children for herself, and also given me some presents to treat them with, once I was back in Antwerp.

By the first weekend of September 1983, accordingly, I found myself driving in my Renault 4, south of London and on the M2 heading towards Dover once more – with Vere having returned to the capital city, and my closest blood relatives in Swindon all behind me. I was heading for the European Continent once more – and I had no plans to be back in England for a long time. Ominously, perhaps, the fog descended as I drove further south along the motorway towards the Kent ferry port. So much so, in fact, that I really thought at times that I might run into the vehicle ahead - or that the one behind might collide with me. Eventually, however, the road ahead became clear – perhaps signalling to me that I, and my family waiting for me in Antwerp, had a new start in front of us and that our future pathway would be a clearer one for us all over there.

*Chapter 29*

# Starting a New Family Life, and New Academic Year, in Belgium – Autumn and Early Winter 1983

My journey on the other side of the English Channel in Belgium was uneventful – and fog-free! I duly arrived in Antwerp, parked our family's Renault 4 - legally - in a side road near Lamorinierestraat and was, very soon after, safely reunited with Philomena and our children. Once more, we six were together again and I could not foresee any change to that situation between that early September time of 1983 and our return to Barbados - at the end of my coming VUB academic year - in June or July 1984.

One of the things that I immediately set about doing - the following morning after my return to Antwerp - was to try to get the television (which we had brought from Volta Road) up and running in my family's new country. That was so that the children could have something to watch, and entertain themselves with, whilst they were at home in our new flat. I soon discovered, however, that the set would not pick up any programmes by my merely switching it on. Accordingly, I went to one of the television repair shops - situated in one of the nearby thoroughfares, leading to the city centre, named 'Belgielei' - and took some advice from one of the workers there. A local internal aerial was suggested by one of the employees and I duly bought the suggested item. Alas, to my disappointment, the purchased item also did not solve the non-reception problem at all. Instead, all that my children and myself managed to see was a white screen, whenever we turned the set on with the new aerial in place. During that process, however, I spotted a socket outlet in our new living room, which suggested that Janet, or one of the previous tenants in the flat, had once invested in receiving programmes by cable television. I, thus, connected our English TV's cabling to the outlet in question and, to my delight, found that a picture appeared on the screen – with audio for a local Flemish programme! Moreover, when I tried to change the channel, such a switchover worked and I was able to pick up a French-speaking channel, perhaps broadcasting from Brussels. Further experimentation allowed me to also receive a programme in Dutch from nearby Holland - as well as one in German from the country of my penfriend Berndt Schuhmacher, which was located further to the north and east of Antwerp. The most delightful discovery, however, was when I continued searching and managed to locate a station that was most familiar to myself and our family – namely,

BBC Television from the United Kingdom! I was thrilled by what my 'trial and error' had thrown up. Perhaps, however, my offspring were even more so - since, henceforth, they would be able to watch children's programmes, such as '*Sesame Street*', not only in Flemish but also in the languages of some of the other countries surrounding Belgium!

Even more important for our family, than my sorting out the TV situation in our flat, was our finding a suitable nursery school, in our neighbourhood, where Claire-Louise and Carl could be placed during each coming weekday of the then-current academic year. In other words, a place where our two youngest children could be looked after whilst Philomena, Noel and Kim went to their school and I commuted, by train, down to the VUB in Brussels. Perhaps I had got the tip-off from our kind neighbours, the Huybrechts - but, from whence it had come, it would lead to a major boon in our family's life. For, quite soon after receiving the helpful guidance, Philomena and myself found ourselves attending a Catholic, church-run, nursery school - situated about two miles away, on the other side of the nearby 'Berchem' railway station. We were there with our two youngest children for interview and with the fervent hope of them both being accepted into the school. It was also crucial, in relation to the budget of my wife and myself, that the fees which the institution would charge would be minimal or none at all. The two of us were most relieved, therefore, when the nursery not only accepted both of our children without hesitation but also told us that the fees in question would be very small - perhaps, just enough to cover our children's meals and snacks during the day.

With Claire-Louise and Carl duly sorted out regarding their care whilst the rest of our family were out of the flat each weekday, it was only left for me to organise my own situation out in relation to my weekdays commuting to the Belgian capital. Owing to the fact that, in my First Term at the VUB, I would largely be repeating much of what I had already done the previous academic year, I thought that I would be able to both attend my classes at the university as well as do some part-time work whilst in Brussels during my day-time hours there. What work could possibly fit the bill for me, however? Whilst at Cambridge University in the 1970s, I had heard about something called a '*stage*', or work placement, which the 'European Economic Community', or 'EEC' - as the future 'European Union', or 'EU', was called in those 1980s days - offered to certain students from that English university and other such leading academic institutions in Europe. It was paid work, as I had understood things, but such a placement also gave a successful applicant a taste of the real workings of the EEC. The venue of such work experience was at the 'Berlaymont Building' near the centre of Brussels - and very close to the 'Schumann' railway station which was just a few stops away from that of 'Etterbeek' (the closest stop to the VUB). Accordingly, it seemed a feasible proposition for me to attend my lectures at the VUB in the morning and then travel by train to Schumann and the Berlaymont Building to work as a *stagiare* at the EEC in the afternoon. Those two parts of my days in Brussels would, thus, have to be completed before my third - which involved my taking a commuter express train back to Antwerp, from 'Brussels Nord' station also nearby, in the early evening and in time to collect Claire-Louise and Carl from their nursery, prior to its closing for the night. That was the plan which I tried to put into operation by my making an application for a *stage* to the EEC during the weeks that I was at home with my toddler son and his older sister - once Philomena and our two eldest offspring had already started their new lives as teacher and pupils, respectively, at the Antwerp English Primary School.

Alas, owing perhaps to the lateness on my application to the EEC for the year in question, that institution did not offer me a paid *stage*. It did, however, accept me to come and work at the Berlaymont on a voluntary basis - more or less whenever I wanted during my year at the VUB. In accepting the less-than-optimum offer, and I was assigned to a certain department in the building and under a certain director there. I had taken up the offered opportunity, since I considered that the experience might be useful for the future and that it would look good on my CV - if I ever gave up my post at UWI to return to work in England or Continental Europe, whether in an academic capacity or otherwise. Moreover, the lack of payment to me for my gaining such experience was not an insuperable obstacle since I had managed to obtain some income from elsewhere in Belgium. For, through the Belgian Embassy in London, I had applied for a bursary to help me take up the place on the course at the VUB for the 1983-84 academic year. In making that application, I had not mentioned the fact that I had already started the course in question at the Brussels university and was actually returning for a second bite of the cherry. To my delight, however, the Embassy granted my application and I was awarded a welcome bursary, in Belgian francs - payable monthly by a cheque which came to our Antwerp flat, for me to be able to cash at one of the banks near our home.

The money from the bursary, of course, came in really useful for my family's budget - since I was not going to be obtaining my salary from UWI during that second sabbatical year which I was then taking away from that Caribbean-based institution. Indeed, without it, I might not have been able to afford the season ticket which I had to purchase on Belgian Railways in order to get me from Berchem station - which was much nearer to my family's flat than that of the main 'Antwerpen Centraal', some two miles further away - to Brussels and back each working day, once I had restarted my student life at the VUB. The cost of such season ticket was, to me, surprisingly cheap - for the one hour or so commute in question, and two-hour round-trip. It involved about the same distance and time as, say, Cambridge to London - but the cost of such a season ticket in England would have been unaffordable for me at that time.

Accordingly, come the end of September, or early October 1983, I was a commuter from Berchem to Brussels and back. I had put in place a regular process - which I enjoyed and got used to quite quickly. As early as about 7am, Carl (in his pushchair), Claire-Louise and myself would leave our flat to go to our Renault 4. I would then drive them to their nursery school a couple of miles away – which, surprisingly to English eyes perhaps, was always open at that early hour. There, I would find the staff happy to welcome my children for the day (and to integrate them with several other children who were already there before us). By 7.30am, I would be parking my car on the bridge over the motorway between Antwerp, proper, and the Berchem district thereof. And at about 7.45am, I would be on the express to Brussels. With a change at Brussels Nord, for a slower train which went to Etterbeek (via Schumann and other intermediate stops), I could be at the VUB for my first lecture at 9am.

There was at least one interruption - to that tried and tested process - during the First Term of my return to the VUB for the 1983-84 academic year. That occurred during one of the first weeks of that recommencement - in the October of that primary teaching period. Some of our lecturers at the VUB had arranged a trip - for all of the students on the Masters course in question - to visit the neighbouring country of Luxembourg, and then Strasbourg in France. Its purpose was for us to see, first-hand, some of the EEC institutions 'at work'. The mini-tour was a free one for us students - paid for by the EEC - and I cheekily asked whether my eldest son (who was learning French at his school in Antwerp) could also come with the group, if I agreed to accept the invitation to participate in it. To my surprise, the VUB said 'yes' to my 'no-chance' request. Accordingly, Philomena had to seek permission from her headmistress, Janet, for Noel to be away from her school for the week or so in question. Moreover, in order for me to be away for the stated period meant that Philomena would have to get up, much earlier than usual, so as to be able to take Carl and Claire-Louise to their Berchem nursery before her school. That was because she still did not have a driving licence at the time, to enable her to take them in our family's Renault 4. There was, however, a tram which went from our part of Antwerp over the motorway to Berchem. Accordingly, that is what she used in order to get our two youngest to their pre-school – prior to returning to her starting point (with Kim accompanying her all the while) for her usual walk to the Antwerp English Primary School. Such a rigmarole – which had to be repeated in the evening, after school, in order for Philomena to collect our two youngest and bring them home – must have added at least an extra hour to her usual travelling time, in each direction. I am sure, therefore, that my wife would have been delighted when I finally returned with Noel from our travels in Luxembourg and France and, so, able to take that added logistical burden off her shoulders.

And what of that trip south to Luxembourg and Strasbourg? The outstanding memory is that my son was a great hit during its progress - and that, indeed, several of the female students on the expedition seemed to want to 'adopt' him. We visited the 'European Court of Justice', located just outside Luxembourg City, on the first day and I recall that Noel had a lot of fun playing with the device in the great hall of the court which allowed you to twiddle a knob to get instant translations of the proceedings going on in front of the judges therein. I also recollect that the case, which our group actually sat in on to listen to for a while, was being argued by lawyers in the Danish language, and which, therefore, was of very little interest to a small boy of just over six years of age.

I also recall our group moving on to France, and staying in a very comfortable hotel in the middle of Strasbourg. We were there to visit the 'European Parliament' (during the part of the month in question when it transferred itself from its usual seat in Brussels) as well as the 'European Court of Human Rights'. If the proceedings at those major Continental institutions, which our group also actually witnessed, no longer stay in my memory, the lovely breakfasts at our hotel each morning remain easily recallable. That is especially regarding the way the young lady students in question competed among themselves to sit next to Noel, in order to 'look after' him during each such meal. Nor can I ever forget taking Noel for a walk around the centre of Strasbourg, by myself and during that special father-son bonding time - and then proceeding with him into one of the bookshops in order for me to try to buy him a suitable souvenir from the trip. I ended up purchasing for him his very first French book – '*Pierre et le Loup*', or the fairy tale of 'Peter and the Wolf'. I thought it most fitting for my son, since it was written in simple French – a subject which Noel was already learning at his Antwerp school - and I, therefore, hoped that it might help him with that subject, when he returned home to Belgium. I am happy to say that Noel has kept that little volume all his life since then and that - as I write this some 40 years later - it sits in the bookshelf of his old room in the house which Philomena and myself now live near Cambridge and in which Noel was also to live in for many years.

*Fig. 56: Noel with the Author in Strasbourg, France - as part of the 'Vrije Universiteit Brussel', or 'VUB', field trip visit of students and lecturers to some of the institutions of the 'European Economic Community', or 'EEC', located in that city – during the autumn of 1983. It can be seen how popular Noel, as the son of one of those VUB students, proved to be with at least one of the female members of that visiting party*

Once Noel and myself had returned to Belgium with the VUB group, we left our coach in Brussels and went home to Antwerp to be reunited with Philomena and our other three children. It was good to be back in the bosom of my family once more, and thereafter I put my head down to do my daily weekday commute to my morning classes at my Brussels university (after first dropping Claire-Louise and Carl off at their nursery), and then my afternoon unpaid *stage* work at the Berlaymont Building in that city. In truth, the latter was not really any real work at all and, basically, I found myself with a number of other (largely also unpaid) *stagiaires* - from all over Europe - in a relatively small room with our female director, in which there was hardly enough chairs for everyone to sit if we all happen to be there at the same time. Though I personally had no special project given to me by that director to work on, I still liked to mix with the up-and-coming, young 'Eurocrats' from across the EEC and enjoyed the 'international vibe' which I perceived as existing inside the Berlaymont Building - as well as the fact that I had been given a pass to go and come from it whenever I wished. I, thus, persisted in attending, and staying within the crowded office inside its precincts, after my VUB classes - even if most of the time I was mainly trying to work on preparing an article there regarding a piece of EEC legislation relating to The Conflict of Laws (which, as seen before, was one of the subjects which I had previously taught at UWI – and which I would be teaching again in Barbados the following academic year).

And what of my family's home life, in general, during that First Term of 1983-84? Basically, we were only all together, for any length of time, at the weekends. On Friday evenings, however, Philomena would usually give our children (and their parents) a special treat. That would require her, on the way home from school with Noel and Kim, calling into the equivalent of an English fish and chip shop - which was situated just around the corner from Lamorinierestraat. At first, I had thought that the name of the emporium was actually '*Kip an der spit*' - as that was sign which was prominently lit up in the evenings in its windows. Only later did I learn that those Flemish words actually translated as 'Chicken on the spit', or 'Barbecued Chicken' perhaps. At any rate, whenever Philomena and our eldest boys went there, it was not to seek roasted poultry at all. Rather, they were after some large sausages called '*frikadellen*' – as well as chips. All our family liked the slightly sweet taste of those large 'bangers', and they were a treat for us all – especially as it meant that the children's tired mother had an evening off from having to cook dinner for the six of us. Usually, I would arrive home only after first picking Claire-Louise and Carl up from their nursery - which meant that the other three members of my family would be eagerly awaiting us before all six of us could begin our special Friday evening dinner together.

Saturday was usually a leisurely day in which Philomena and myself did not go very far with the children. She, perhaps, would use up most of the morning, after our family breakfast together, to engage with the washing machine and dryer - which we had so painstakingly brought over from our former Swindon home – in order to do the family's laundry which had accumulated during that current week. Meanwhile, I would help our offspring find children's programmes which captured their interest - from amongst the many multi-lingual channels available on our television set. I would often watch such programmes with them – making any necessary translation for them as I was able to. *Sesame Street*, in Dutch and German, was perhaps their favourite at that time, and that educational (and amusing) programme enabled Noel and Kim, at least, to learn their numbers, in both of those languages, really well. On a Saturday afternoon, we would often, after lunch, walk to a nearby park - which not only had a wonderful open green space for running about in, and a grandstand, but it also possessed a children's play area which included some swings and a slide for our children to exhaust themselves using.

Sundays, however, was the day when we would all go out for a drive in our Renault 4. If I did not feel like going too far afield, we would simply travel as far as the wide river on which Antwerp was built – the Scheldt, in the Flemish language. We would follow that watercourse, by using the road next to it on the other side of the city centre, in order to get close to the commercial docks which ran for miles in that part of our new home metropolis. There, the children would become animated when they saw, up close, ships large and small – some often loading or unloading different types of cargo, as we drove slowly along. Philomena and myself would always try to spot the overseas country in which each such vessel was registered, and then tell our findings to our children. That was so that they might get an idea of how far away each ship in question had come, in order to reach Belgium.

We drove to Antwerp's port, perhaps, about one Sunday in every month. On the other three available, we would usually go farther afield. Indeed, we would make an international journey – by driving over the border into Holland. For Antwerp was really not very far away from the southern frontier of that neighbouring country and we could reach the small Dutch town of 'Bergen op Zoom' within 30 to 45 minutes from leaving our home. As well as letting the children feel that they were already seasoned travellers in Continental Europe, the small town in question had a major attraction for them. That was a wonderful children's play park with lots of play equipment not to be found in its counterpart, a short distance from our flat back in Antwerp. Moreover, being a Sunday morning whenever we arrived there, we often found that the facilities in the Dutch park were very much underused – perhaps because local children preferred to have quiet mornings at home on that 'day of rest'. At any rate, our children always seemed happy whenever we told them, on a Sunday, that we were going to drive to Holland that day – surely, not so much because of the international nature of the trip but, rather, for the fun that lay in wait for them at their favourite Continental play park which our family had so far discovered.

One of the things that I especially remember, from our domestic life during that pre-Christmas 1983 period in Antwerp, was how well Claire-Louise was doing at her nursery. Her good progress had to do with the fact that the personnel at the pre-school centre, which she and Carl attended in Berchem, spoke Flemish to all the children in their care and did so in interesting and comprehensible ways. Accordingly, our daughter used to come home in the evenings being able to sing some of the songs, in that language, which she had learned from her carers during the day. To this day, I can still recall the opening words (and accompanying tune) of one of those - which she would willingly sing to the rest of her family around our dinner table at home. Those were: '*Klein, klein kleutertje...*

*wat doe je in mijn hof*. I was able to discover, perhaps from one of my colleagues on the Masters course with me at the VUB who was Flemish, that the words translated into English as something along the lines of: 'Little nursery child (or toddler), what are you doing in my garden?'. Whether strictly correct or not, I for one felt proud that our daughter, of only two going on three years at the time, was already starting to be 'fluent' in a second language.

If, however, my home situation and commuter's life to and from Brussels were both proceeding well in the lead up to Christmas 1983, there was one major obligation that was still outstanding - which I needed to put right, since it was very much exercising my conscience during that period. That worrisome issue was the overdue report of the research work which I had done for the Swindon Law Centre between about March and September 1983. After finally returning to Antwerp with the family's Renault 4 in the latter month, and during those few weeks before my restart at the VUB, when I had babysat Claire-Louise and Carl whilst Philomena and our two eldest sons went to their new school, I had been able to focus, somewhat, on drafting the requisite report – and had begun trying to write its opening chapter, at least, from all the raw material and data which I had brought with me from Swindon. Alas, I had not got very far by the time that I had restarted my course at the VUB. Moreover, my taking up the unpaid *stage* at the EEC only added to the lack of time which I had for the project. Sad to say, therefore, that as the autumn of 1983 progressed towards the winter months, I simply put my report-writing obligation on the backburner, with a vow that I would return to it during the coming Christmas holidays. Unfortunately, however, I failed to communicate that unilateral decision of mine to the management committee, or to anyone else at the Law Centre – even though I had thought that the best communication would be to actually send in the completed report early in the New Year, together with a covering letter apologising for its lateness.

And, thus, the Antwerp English Primary School's Christmas holidays – as well as those which I had from the VUB and my EEC activity – duly came along. It would be the first time in our lives that Philomena and myself would be spending the Festive Season in Continental Europe, and, thus, it would also be the same for our children. That was because my wife and I had decided that our finances simply did not allow us to travel back to our relatives in England for the Yuletide break. Moreover, to me at any rate, it seemed that it would be a more 'peaceful' time for my family if I did not have to worry about crossing paths with Philomena's mother in Swindon, had we indeed decided to go back to Wiltshire for Christmas and the New Year. In truth, the decision not to go back to Swindon for the holidays was mainly mine, even though that particular mindset meant depriving the two grandmothers, living in our most recent former hometown back in Wiltshire, of their grandchildren - during a Yuletide season which was meant to be one 'for children', and 'being with' them.

Philomena and myself, therefore, made the best of that winter holiday time as much as we could - for our four offspring - and we tried to indulge them in the peculiarities of our first Belgian Christmas. Those matters included the fact that present-giving, for that Festive Period in that country, seemed to be on the 8th rather than the 25th December. Moreover, there were two main figures that children expected to get those presents from. To my mind, they looked nothing like the traditional 'Father Christmas' to be found in England, Barbados and many other countries of the world - with his red suit and snowy-coloured beard. Instead, the Belgian counterparts were '*Sint Niklaas*' (more popularly known, in our Flemish-speaking Antwerp, as '*Sinterklaas*') and '*Zwarte Piet*'. The first, 'St Nicholas', was an old man with a white beard alright - but he was dressed in the robes of a bishop and carried a mitre. The latter was his helper - whose name translated into English as 'Black Peter', and who looked more like a juvenile Black-African boy.

Philomena was to take all four of our children to meet *St Niklaas* and *Zwarte Piet* in one of the stores in Berchem which they were visiting during December. Perhaps that had happened on the 8th itself, whilst I had been away on my daily Brussels commute. I can recall that a few photos were taken of my family's visit and that one of them shows that our Carl was none too happy with his encounter with the present-givers - which, fittingly for the season, took place in '*Drie Konigenstraat*' (Three Kings' Street) – and that he found at least one of them frightful enough to make him cry.

The only other outstanding memory for me from the Belgian Festive Season in question was when Philomena and myself, after putting our children to bed – or at least the two youngest ones – had stayed up on 31st December to 'see in' the New Year. At midnight, we were able to hear the hooters on many of the vessels on the River Scheldt blaring away for, perhaps, five minutes or more. The racket made it seem as though the river was just around the corner from our flat - when in fact, its nearest point was perhaps up to two to three miles away.

Sadly, I have to reveal that, given the respite from my daily weekday commute to Brussels and back, I took full advantage of the 'down-time' which the Festive Season brought and did little or no course work during my end of year period at home with my family. Instead, I managed to convince myself that my first priority was with Philomena and our children and I put what energies that I still had into them – hardly leaving home for the period. I also persuaded myself that I was merely recharging my batteries for the New Year ahead, in order to complete all the outstanding matters which I then still had on my plate – both in Brussels and at home.

*Fig. 57: Carl, being held by Philomena as he meets 'Sinterklaas' and 'Zwarte Piet' to receive a Christmas present from them in Antwerp, Belgium during December 1983. As can be seen, despite what should have been a happy occasion, he is non-too-happy with the encounter*

*Fig. 58: Claire-Louise with 'Sinterklaas' and 'Zwarte Piet' in order to receive a Christmas present from them in Antwerp, Belgium during December 1983. The fact that she is sticking her tongue out, during the meeting, shows that she, like her younger brother (Carl) before her, is non-too-comfortable with the encounter*

*Chapter 30*

# What should have been my Second Term at the VUB 1983-84 – Spring 1984

In early January 1984, in the week before I was due to go back to the VUB, there was an unexpected ring on the doorbell of our flat. That was something that had hardly ever happened, since we had moved into it the previous September. Moreover, normally such a ring would be via the button for our bell - which was situated outside the entrance to our block of flats in Lamorinierestraat. On that occasion, however, the person ringing was already inside the building and, thus, directly outside our door. When I opened it to see who was calling us, I got the shock of my life. It was Michael – my former colleague at the Law Centre, and the person with whom I had last stayed in Swindon before finally leaving that town to drive my Renault 4 to Antwerp, a few months before! He would have been one of the last persons whom I would have expected to have seen that evening.

When I had recovered from my 'jolt from the blue', I invited my former colleague into the flat. One of his first words were: 'This is a nice apartment!'. My opening utterances to him, however, were firstly to introduce him to my wife, and then our four children in turn - and, thereafter, to ask him my burning question: 'How did you know where I lived in Antwerp?'. Michael then explained that, as I had previously told the Law Centre people that I was leaving Swindon to study at the VUB in Brussels, the Centre had contacted that university and, through the Secretariat at the Faculty of Law there, had managed to successfully obtain the home address of one of its students – namely, myself. Michael, with Philomena and the children out of the way in one of the bedrooms, then asked me, nicely, whether I had the completed report to give him to take back to Swindon. I immediately confessed that, though I had started it, it was nowhere near being completed. I then asked him whether he would allow me a few more weeks in which to finalise everything and send the finished report to Swindon – perhaps, by the end of January. My former colleague then told me that his mandate, from the Law Centre's management committee, was to collect from me as much of the report that I had already done - plus all the raw material and other data which I had amassed during my time working on the project - for him to take back to the committee. Clearly, Michael did not want to return home from his detective assignment empty-handed and I, thus, resolved at once to help him as much as I could. After all, he was my friend who had let me stay in his home in my final Swindon days the previous September – even if he was a disappointed one at that moment (as far as his findings about my behaviour were concerned).

Whilst Michael waited in the living room, therefore, I set about collecting (from inside the bedroom of Philomena and myself in the flat) the draft report thus far - as well as all the raw material and data relating to it, that I could find. I was extremely embarrassed to show him how very little of the former I had actually done, but he seemed happy enough that what I had been able to give him, in total, would satisfy the members of his management committee that he had discharged their commission to him to the full. Within the hour of Michael's arrival outside our flat, therefore, Philomena and myself were saying goodbye to him there - and then I was accompanying him inside the lift with his collected material and, eventually, seeing him off into Lamorinierestraat. As I watched him go off into the night with his 'booty', I knew that the particular day in question would mark a new turning point in my life!

That evening was the beginning of a very slippery slope for me towards one of my deepest ever depressions. For one thing, I felt that I had let down Michael - and all my friendly colleagues at the Law Centre - in not producing for them the report, which had been the reason for my being given the research job in Swindon in the first place, during the previous March. I had continually apologised to Michael for that failure whilst he had been with me in the flat earlier. It was clear to me, however - from his decision not to allow me further time to complete the report - that he (and, presumably, my former Law Centre colleagues) had already lost faith in my ever producing the requisite document in question in a finalised state. The other thing that had knocked the wind out of my sails - as I had watched Michael go off into that early January night - was the thought that: from that day on, the Administration at the VUB also knew about my work at the Swindon Law Centre the previous spring and summer, and that I had failed in my obligations to that Centre. Moreover, it also knew that I was a 'wanted man' by the Wiltshire legal institution. In other words, that as far as the VUB was concerned, I was in someone else's bad books – in addition to having already blotted my copybook with the VUB itself for having failed to complete its legal Masters programme the previous academic year.

To myself, I thought: how on earth will I ever be able to face again, the staff in the Administration at the VUB, as well as my lecturers - who were all bound, eventually, to hear of my failings regarding the Swindon institution? In the depression which overcame me in the hours and days after Michael's visit to my family's flat, the answer slowly came to me as follows: 'Take the line of least resistance'. By trying to follow that course, I decided that I did not need to 'face' the VUB people again. Rather, I would simply become a full-time carer for the two youngest children of Philomena and myself and say goodbye to ever getting my Masters in Brussels - after all. Indeed, I concluded that I need never do the commute to Brussels again – and that it really did not matter that, in so doing, I would also be giving up my connection and regular visits to the EEC Commission at the Berlaymont Building in that city. Slowly, I justified my decision to myself by telling Philomena about how much the family would save by my not having to buy a season ticket to the Belgian capital in the months ahead - or pay the (admittedly modest) fees to the Berchem nursery for its looking after Claire-Louise and Carl during the coming months of 1984. Moreover, I argued to my wife, my spending time with our two youngest children would enable me to bond with them in a greater way than I had done in the past - and, thereby, make up for the first six months or so of Carl's young life, when I had been living apart from the family during my first attempt at the VUB Masters programme by living (without her and our four children) in Brussels.

Philomena, was not at all happy about my decision at first. She was, however, willing to go along with it. That was as long as it did not affect her commitment to continuing to teach at the Antwerp English Primary School for the remainder of the 1983-84 academic year - or the attendance of our two eldest sons, as pupils there, during that period. I reassured her about those matters, as well as the fact that my job was still open at UWI - which meant that we would only need to leave Belgium during the coming summer, in order to enable our family to return together to Barbados in time for me to start teaching at Cave Hill Campus again at the beginning of the forthcoming 1984-85 academic year.

And so it was that I came to be a full-time, stay-at-home, father to Carl and Claire-Louise - during the first months of the New Year of 1984 and into the spring of that year. Naturally, at first, I felt a complete failure for not having delivered what I had promised to do for the Swindon Law Centre - and, even more so, for not completing, for the second year in succession, the Masters degree in Brussels (which, after all, was the primary reason for my family being, and living, with me in Belgium). As the weeks and months slowly went by, however, the more I managed to convince myself that, having been responsible for bringing the two youngest children of Philomena and myself into the world, I had a greater priority in life to look after them - as opposed to seeking more (and unnecessary) qualifications in the Belgian capital. Every school day, therefore, I could help prepare breakfast for Philomena, Noel and Kim. And only when our two youngest had woken up, naturally – as opposed to the untimely risings which I had been forced to subject them to when I had been a commuter to Brussels up the New Year – did I make and give breakfast to them, as well as have some myself. Afterwards, at about mid-morning – and provided that it was not raining - the three of us would usually then take a leisurely walk to the nearby park containing the bandstand and swings, to enable the children to play for an hour or so, until it was time to return to our flat for lunch (the ingredients for which Philomena would usually have left for us before going out to school in the morning). After lunch, the two children would then have their siesta nap - before waking up in time to catch a children's programme or two on the television, whilst we all waited for Philomena and their two elder brothers to return home from school. A variation on that theme could be my putting Carl in his pushchair in order to take him, with Claire-Louise, wider afield - to a larger park nearer the city centre, which contained a lake and, thus, water fowl for the children to engage with. Or, on those days, when it rained in the morning, we three would stay at home whilst I entertained the children by reading to them - from one or other of the many children's books which Philomena had managed to amass since returning to England from Barbados in the spring of 1982.

So well did the 'therapy' of being a full-time dad to our youngest two offspring agree with me that, by about March 1984, I soon began to feel capable of 'facing the world', outside our home situation, once more. Some evidence of that was my affirmative answer to a question which Philomena put to me about that time, which had emanated from one of her young female colleagues at her Antwerp school. That fellow teacher – let us call her 'Mandy' – was in charge of taking a group of children from the school to play squash at some outside centre. For some reason, the coach which Mandy had been using up to the period in question was no longer available and she somehow found out - possibly, through general chit chat with Philomena in the staff room at the school - that I played the racquet sport in question (or, at least, used to do so whilst our family had lived in Cambridge in the 1970s). One day, therefore, Philomena came home from work and asked me whether I would like to be her school's squash coach for the remainder of the academic year. That, she had added, would be on a once a week basis - for which services Mandy, on the school's behalf, would pay me a cash sum on each occasion. As stated, I gave a positive answer.

I did not want Mandy to know - or the school's headmistress, Janet - that I had given up my course at the VUB. That was because I would have been most embarrassed if ever I had to meet with either of them in the near future, and either one might have been speculating about the mental cloud that I would probably have been under at the time. Accordingly, I suggested to Philomena that she let Mandy develop the impression that the forthcoming Wednesdays, when I said I would be available to do the coaching in question, was the one day per week when I did not have to commute to Brussels for my course. Thus, when I eventually met Mandy for the first time, I was able to look her in the eyes without any excessive self-consciousness on my part.

That introductory meeting, and then the subsequent ones, took place at the 'Antwerp Squash Club' - situated not far from the centre of the city and its main railway station. In order to get to the venue, I had to drive our family's car there - and also bring Claire-Louise along with me. Sad to write now, however, that I always felt obliged to leave Carl behind, in his cot in his room – always hoping that he would be already asleep after his lunch, before I exited our flat with his sister in order to make it to my teaching appointment on time. Mandy turned out to be about the same age as Philomena, or perhaps even a bit younger, and she wore very fashionable clothes – including an eye-catchingly 'hip' leather jacket. At our initial encounter, however, she had brought about 20 children from the school - so there was no way that I could let them all play a conventional game of squash on the club's two courts - which had been reserved for the school there, for the hour or so in question. Fortunately, the venue had plenty of smaller-sized racquets to enable each child to loan one each, and also enough spare balls for every child. I was, thus, able to start teaching about five pupils, in each court, how to practise hitting their respective ball against one or other of the side walls of the court, on a regular basis. Thus, little by little, each of my charges learnt from me how to strike their individual ball with the middle of their racquet - before repeating the exercise as many times as possible in their allotted time. After about 10 minutes, the other five pupils, waiting outside the first court, would have their turn – again for another 10 minutes or so, before the first lot returned for another go. Similarly, I would do the same with the 10 or so pupils who had the second court to themselves, after first dividing it into two halves – those actively playing, and those awaiting their turn.

By taking on that extra activity outside my home, therefore, and doing so week by week up to Easter, I slowly began to feel that I was playing myself back into normal life in society. That I was rehabilitating myself, so to speak. Indeed, my having to meet Mandy each week with her pupils from the Antwerp school, and then having to instruct the latter face to face, seemed to do my mental condition a power of good. In addition, my earning some extra income for our family's budget from my coaching duties at the squash club - instead of having to rely mainly on Philomena's salary from her school teaching duties - also helped to improve my state of mind greatly.

Whilst matters were starting to 'normalise' for me in Antwerp, however, I had also been keeping in touch with Vere in England, by letter – and, through her, discovering that Mikki was going from strength to strength with the two 'aunts' in Barbados. I can no longer recall which of the two of us first suggested it but, by the coming Easter time of 1984, she and I had already agreed that we two really had to meet up again. That was mainly because we had not seen each other since I had left England the previous September. The venue, however, I am pretty sure was my idea – namely, 'Holland', a country which Vere had not yet visited, so far as I knew. In order to be able to make the meeting with Vere possible, however, I had to be straight with Philomena and tell her about Vere being then a resident in England and studying to become a Barrister at a college in London – as well as about the arrangements which the two of us had made for Mikki to be fostered in Barbados, during Vere's absence from the island. I argued with my wife that I needed to meet up with Vere in order to discuss Mikki's future. No doubt, however, Philomena was not at all happy - to put it mildly - about my leaving the family again to be with Vere (even temporarily). My wife seemed to believe me, however, when I promised to be back home with the family in Antwerp after only one weekend away in Holland.

And so it was that on the Saturday before Easter 1984, I found myself waiting for Vere, in the early morning, at the ferry terminal at the Dutch port of Hook of Holland. She had, in our exchanges of letters leading up to the meeting, agreed to take the overnight ferry journey from Harwich in Essex and would, presumably, have got to that English Cross-Channel seaport by train from London Liverpool Street railway station. Just like my meeting with her at Zaventem Airport, Brussels, the previous year after her disembarkation from the plane she had boarded in Barbados - after a delay which had made me worry that she had missed the vessel meant to bring her on her international voyage in question – Vere, on that later occasion (after, perhaps, one hour after her ferry had docked), eventually came walking out from the 'Arrivals' area of the Dutch port. She was full of smiles at seeing me again and gave me the impression that such cross border journeys were something which she did on a very regular basis. For my part, I was delighted to see her again too – and also looking forward to showing her some of the better things which I knew that Holland had to offer the first-time visitor there.

I remember that, for budgetary reasons - far from seeking accommodation in a pricey hotel for Vere's visit - I had somehow managed to rent a caravan, of all things, situated within a park full of static varieties of the same. The 'dwelling' had at least two bedrooms, a toilet, shower and kitchen. It also possessed heating - which was a blessing, since it was still a relatively cool time of the year – especially at night-time. Vere seemed to find the accommodation perfectly acceptable - and also convinced by my argument that luxury, or even major comfort, was not the main thing she should be looking for. That, I had also successfully argued – it seemed to me – was because we would be 'touring' Holland so much, that we would only need somewhere, basic, to sleep at nights. Certainly, that first afternoon, after checking in and leaving our suitcases in our caravan at the site, we drove off to the seaside resort of 'Scheveningen' – which makes me think now that the caravan site in question was somewhere near 'Den Haag' (or 'The Hague'), which major European city is within 10 miles or so of the coastal fleshpot, first named. There, we spent a leisurely afternoon lying on the beach near some dunes – as we respectively gave each other news we had not had space, nor time, to write to the other about in our recent letters. It might only have been during that first period of relaxation together that I broke the tidings to Vere that, once again, I had discontinued my course at the VUB in Brussels. Certainly, I would not have wanted to earlier give her an example, or precedent, for abandoning her own then-current course, which she herself had travelled to a new country to attend and pass. I was, accordingly, much relieved when she gave me her own news that her pre-Bar-Finals course - at her college near London Waterloo station - was still proceeding well.

For me, however, the highlight of Vere's visit to Holland had to wait until the following day – which was Easter Sunday. That was the occasion on which I introduced her to the Dutch capital city of 'Amsterdam'. Alas, I cannot remember my taking her to church that day to attend a Mass or otherwise – even though we were both Christians (she being an Anglican to my following the Catholic faith). I can, however, recall showing her - after driving in the Renault 4 to the Dutch capital - walking with her along the route which I had followed on previous visits to the metropolis. That would have included progressing from the 'Centraal Station' to the 'Damrak', over several canals, and on past 'Anne Frank's House' before arriving at the 'Rijksmuseum' – and then our spending time inside that venue, looking at famous paintings such as Rembrandt's 'The Night Watch'. I also took her on to the nearby 'Vondelpark', to show her the place where my old friend from Swindon - Raffaele Finelli - and myself had spent his birthday on my first major trip to Northern Europe, by 'Inter Rail', in the summer of 1973. The *pièce de résistance*, however, would have been when I, eventually, took Vere to an Indonesian restaurant - which I had previously visited in the 'Red Light District' near Centraal Station - for her to have her first ever '*Rijsttafel*' (or 'rice table') meal (that is to say, one consisting of many little dishes, all (or most) of which include rice).

All in all, therefore, when we drove back to our caravan park that Eastertide evening, I was satisfied that I had given Vere as good an introduction to Amsterdam as I had of Paris - when she, Mikki and myself had visited the French capital together the previous year. She still had one more full day remaining of her stay in Holland, however, and I went to sleep that night pondering where I could take her before she would have to catch her ferry back to England on the coming Tuesday. In what seems amazing to me now, not only did I come up with the idea of taking her over the border into Belgium - and on to my Antwerp flat to meet Philomena and the children - but, astonishingly, Vere also agreed to the suggestion!

With the vision of over 40 years' hindsight, my idea of taking Vere to my home in Antwerp now seems like an absolutely crazy one. Moreover, it is almost unbelievable to me, now, that she would ever have concurred with the initiative. Equally so, that I would ever think of imposing Vere on Philomena - without my wife's prior knowledge of the idea, and her advance approval. But drive Vere across the border to Belgium, from our Den Haag area base, I did. Perhaps, I had been thinking ahead, regarding my family's return to Barbados - and about Mikki's possible position in that unit, once we were back on that island. It might well have been my fervent hope that, if Vere and Philomena were to become friends in advance of that return, it could make it much easier for Mikki to play a meaningful part in the Bradshaw family unit, on a regular basis, once we were back in Barbados. And that such could be the case - short of my actually taking Mikki out of the custody of the two aunts in Atlantic Shores.

There was one other, much more simplistic, explanation for my notion of the two women in my life meeting up and spending time together under the same roof. That had to do with my hair! I had asked Vere to bring me, from England, a kit with which to perm my Afro barnet into what was then called a 'curly-perm' or 'jerry-curl' style - which many Black men wore in those days. I had not been able to find a local hairdresser in Antwerp to give me that particular style - nor, possibly, would I have been able to afford one even if I had done so. The way forward, therefore, seemed to be to have a home-made version of the requisite process carried out - and who better to perform that than the Black woman in my life at that time, working on me in my own home.

At all events, Vere did, indeed, accompany me back to my matrimonial family's flat in Lamorinierestraat. We had no telephone there and, thus, our unannounced arrival must have caught Philomena out in a major way - since she would not have been expecting me back home until the following evening (the day of Vere's return to England from Holland). My wife was naturally very pleased, at first, to see me - one day earlier than expected. That was until I introduced my unexpected guest! As might well be expected, from the outset however, and even though Philomena did not resist Vere's entry into the flat, the atmosphere was frosty between the two women. Moreover, I very soon discovered, from Vere's whispers to me, that she could not believe how comfortable my matrimonial family's dwelling seemed to be - compared to the little space which she, Mikki and myself had occupied in Brussels the previous year. When Philomena tried to warm up the ambience in the flat by making a meal for everyone, Vere, it seemed to me, went out of her way to show that she did not find the pasta dish, which my wife quickly cooked, at all palatable. That was despite the fact that the four children around her, and my wife and self, were clearly enjoying it. I was then able to pass part of the remainder of the post-dinner hour with Vere alone, in the bathroom, whilst she worked on my hair to give me the curly-perm which I wanted – and much amusement was provided to the children, when I emerged and went into the living room to show them the voluminous, 'bouffant' result of our visitor's handiwork.

Thereafter, we all made it through the evening by first reading some children's book together – with Vere joining in and seemingly genuinely trying to get to know each child in turn. We also watched some television together, before the children each said their respective 'good night' and went off to their beds. Noel and Kim would be sleeping in the bedroom of Philomena and myself (which we always shared with Claire-Louise, in any case), whilst their own room was given over to our visitor for the night. Carl slept in his own small bedroom, with the balcony overlooking the street below, as usual. There came the hour, however, when it was time for the three adults to also retire for the night. And what happened next is something which I was soon to reproach myself about. I asked Philomena if she would mind if I slept in the bedroom which we had temporarily given to Vere - on the argument that Vere would only have the possibility for that one last night with me, whereas Philomena would be able to sleep with me forever after that!

Naturally, my wife was not at all happy about that latest unexpected development in her day. Nor was I, as I lay in bed in Noel and Kim's room with Vere, thinking about how my wife must be really hurting by the decision which I had made an hour or two earlier. By midnight, therefore, and totally unable to sleep, I turned to Vere and told her that I had to leave her and go next door to share Philomena's bed instead – since, of the two women in the flat that night, I really felt, deep down, that my wife needed my presence more. That small step of going from one room to the other, perhaps, marked the blueprint for how my life into the future, and my relationship with each of the two women, respectively, would pan out thereafter.

Next morning came, eventually, and Vere, it seemed to me, was calm about what had happened the night before. We needed to have our breakfast early - since I had to take her back over the border for her ferry leaving from Hook of Holland later that day. Hopefully, the two of us would have waited for all four children in the flat to join us for that first meal of the day - and, certainly, Philomena would have helped me to make it. By about 9am, therefore, Vere and myself were on the nearby motorway driving northwards from Antwerp - and proceeding over the border, as well as, thereafter, passing cities such as 'Breda', *en route* to the leading Dutch seaport that we needed to get to. Philomena, as usual, had been gracious in saying goodbye to Vere - before we left her and the children in the flat - and may even have wished Vere good luck in her forthcoming legal exams. No doubt, however, my wife had breathed a huge sigh of relief when our visitor had left her present matrimonial home for good - and I guessed that I would be in for a major earbashing, when I next returned from Holland, for having the nerve to bring Vere there in the first place!

Once back in Holland, there was just no time for any more sightseeing of that country - prior to taking Vere to the port of Hook. I took my leave of the other woman in my life, sadly - for neither of us knew when we would see each other again. That would most likely take place in Barbados in more than one year's time – after Vere had actually written her Bar Final exams – since she had no plans to return to her homeland anytime during the rest of that year of 1984. I was also downhearted about what had happened during the night at the flat in Antwerp. Surely, it had underlined, to Vere, the fact that I saw my future with my wife and our children - steadfastly. True, Vere and myself still had Mikki in Barbados to support for the future - but, going forward, would that mutual obligation owed to our daughter be enough to keep the two of us closely connected?

At any rate, I returned to Antwerp from Hook somewhat lighter of heart. As a result of the meet-up in Holland, I then knew that Vere was getting on well with her life and studies in England and, through her and the news she had regularly received from the aunts in Barbados, that Mikki was also doing fine back in the Caribbean. Those assurances thus gave me peace of mind to go on with my own future plans – namely, to return (with Philomena and our children) to UWI in order to continue with my career and our family life in Barbados. Vere was ploughing her own furrow for the future and would, no doubt, be able to survive - well - without me being constantly in her life henceforth. Certainly, that is what I would have told Philomena was the importance of my meeting with Vere in Holland - even though I would no doubt have also apologised, over and over, for bringing Vere back to our home, unannounced, the previous day.

Within a day or two afterwards, therefore, our family's life in Antwerp was more or less back to normal – or as normal as it had been before the interruption caused by Vere's recent visit to the Continent. Indeed, from that time on, it seemed to me that Philomena started flourishing in her spirits once more - and I genuinely believed that what had happened in our flat, during the night of Vere's stay, was the underlying cause of such upliftment. Moreover, I began to notice, at that time, that Philomena often came home full of stories of episodes that had occurred during her day at school – both in her classroom and from exchanges which she may have had with her headmistress, Janet, Mandy or any of the other teachers during school time. In short, I found that she was finding her life, as a teacher, a vibrant one once more – when compared to being the stay-at-home mum which she had been since the birth of our first child, Noel, in Cambridge back in 1977. I suggested, therefore, that - when we returned to Barbados that coming summer - she should try to continue with her teaching. That idea was to try to ensure that the wonderful outgoing spirit, which she was then displaying, might continue after our family's relocation back to that favourite Caribbean island of ours.

*Chapter 31*

# The post-Easter period to Summer in Antwerp, 1984 – and Preparing to 'Start Over', Yet Again!

And so it was that from the Easter holidays in question - just as I was writing to the Administration at UWI to ask for its help in finding my family some suitable accommodation for when we returned that coming summer - Philomena was also writing to one of our friends, from our former Marriage Encounter group on the island, about a teaching job. That person was Mrs Margaret Wilson, the wife of the David who was a Bridgetown businessman. Margaret worked not at a school proper, but, rather, at a pre-school kindergarten. Indeed, she was the proprietor of that nursery establishment - which was situated in the upmarket district of Bridgetown called Belleville. Our eldest, Noel, had actually started his first days in the classroom in 'Mrs Wilson's School' during the academic year 1980-81 and had loved it. Alas, his career there had been interrupted when Philomena, whilst pregnant with Carl, had returned to England with our first three eldest children in early 1982. But, it seemed to me - and Philomena agreed - our Barbados friend's pre-school in question would be the ideal solution for getting Philomena into the teaching regime in Barbados.

Alas, at the same time as I was receiving less than helpful replies to my letter requests to UWI to help me find suitable family accommodation for our return to Barbados, Margaret was writing back to Philomena to state that she had no vacancy for a teacher at her pre-school. Moreover, even when I urged Philomena to send a reply, to say that she would be prepared to work for Margaret - on a non-payment basis until a paid-position became available - Margaret subsequently replied to also rule that idea out. Accordingly, as the Final Term of 1983-84 was progressing into the early summer months of that academic year, prospects for our smooth return to Barbados were looking far from rosy. I tried to reassure myself that things would work out alright in the end; that what mattered was that I had a post at UWI to go back to, with a decent salary attached; and that once we were back on the island our domestic situation would sort itself out. And before very much more time had elapsed, sunny days had arrived in Belgium and the half-term holidays for the Whitsun period were upon us.

Given that first proper blast of summery weather, I told Philomena that I wanted to make a final holiday trip with her and our children - in our Renault 4 - to one of the neighbouring countries. Ideally, I would have really liked to have gone quite far afield - to somewhere 'exotic', like Denmark, for example. Not having been able to afford to have our car serviced during all the time we had been in Antwerp, however, I was worried that we might have a breakdown somewhere far from home - if I were to risk driving it across too many international borders. Accordingly, Philomena and myself decided that we would only go as far as the neighbouring state of Luxembourg – a place which, of our four children, only Noel had previously visited. Since Antwerp was at the north-western end of Belgium, we would have to traverse the country to its south-eastern region in order to reach the Luxembourg border - so a good number of miles would still be involved even to accomplish our proposed, relatively modest, road-trip.

One sunny morning, therefore, we all set off in our Renault 4 for our family's first holiday since we had all initially arrived in Belgium the previous autumn - to enjoy a half-term break in which we would have to overnight somewhere. Philomena and myself sat in the front of the car - with our three eldest children behind us, and Carl propped up in his carrycot at the very back. I found myself in surprisingly good spirits as we got going.

We drove along the most northern motorway in Belgium, close to its border with Holland as we progressed eastwards. Eventually, we left the Flemish-speaking area of Flanders, where our home city of Antwerp was situated, and entered 'Wallonia' – the French-speaking region of the country. There, we came upon the largest city in that region, and Philomena and I decided to make it our main *en route* stop. It was called Liège in French, but 'Luik' in Flemish. Not even Philomena or myself had ever visited that Belgian metropolis before and, thus, we certainly wanted to have a good look around it, in order to get a feel of the place. Not before taking our children to the nearest park that we could find, however - to enable them to play, and expend some of their pent up energies from the hours in the car which it had taken us to reach that part of our journey. The 'pit stop' also enabled us to feed ourselves with the picnic which Philomena had prepared in advance for our lunch. Alas, I have only managed to retain a limited memory of the places of interest that we encountered with our children after the meal break - apart from the wide river which flowed through the city, an island in the middle of it, and one of its cathedrals in its central district. When we eventually continued with our journey, however, I was content that we had made an important stop, which most of our family could one day look back on as having been worthwhile.

After Liège, we continued driving south-eastwards, towards the Luxembourg border. *En route*, we entered a region known as the 'Ardennes' – a forested area mainly full of pine trees, it seemed to me. It was here that - to my surprise - we passed the small town of *'Spa Francorchamps'*. As we did so, the name suddenly triggered a memory in my mind. I had heard of it before – in relation to the 'Belgian Grand Prix' in 'Formula 1 motor car racing'. I decided, therefore, that such a place would have to be our next stop. That was because I wanted my boys, at least - and even though I knew that their sister and mum would likely be less interested - to see one of the major car racing circuits in all the world. It would be great, I thought to myself, for Noel and Kim to be able to share, with their male peers at their Antwerp school, after the holidays, the fact that they had visited such a famous Formula 1 hotspot during their vacation. For about an hour or so, therefore, we took another break from our journey, and made a walkabout on part of the circuit nearest the small town - before going on to our main destination of the day.

Luxembourg City turned out to be a very busy place - when we eventually reached it in our car that evening. We had booked no accommodation in advance - but I very much wanted our family to stay in a hotel, at least for one night, during our road-trip. We found ourselves in the city centre when we stopped, and I asked Philomena and the children to stay in the car whilst I went and made enquiries about what it would cost us to stay in one of the many hotels – some of them looking, to me, rather grand – which we could see nearby. For some reason, I was drawn to the one called 'Hotel Bristol' – the same name as that which I had stayed in by Lake Geneva three years before. That latest one, however, was situated just a short walk from where I had parked our car in the city centre and had no lake, or any *Jet d'Eau*, near it. Chancing my arm, I went up to the reception, where a young man was in charge. I put my cards on the table straight away, and said that my wife and myself were in the city with our four 'very small children' and that we just needed one family-sized room for the night. I added that even a room with a large double bed would be enough for us. The young receptionist must have taken pity on me, for he said that he did have such a room available – and also told me the price. It was on the high side – but a lot less than two rooms would have cost our budget, and which I had feared he might have stipulated our having to take for a family of six persons. I accepted the room at the price offered – without even asking to see it first – and that is how Philomena and myself came to spend one of the best nights we had ever shared as a family, in a foreign country, and away from our home base. In fact, the room contained a number of beds and we had no trouble at all experiencing adequate sleeping spaces which were pleasant and comfortable to lay our respective heads on for that night. The 'continental breakfast' of croissants, toast, jam, and the like - which we were all able to partake of at the hotel the next morning - was like the icing on the cake for our children, as well as for their parents. Thereafter, we were ready to 'do' our own bespoke sightseeing tour of the Luxembourg capital, including visiting the huge river-valley below the city's cathedral – but which only contained a tiny watercourse, in addition to a children's playground (which our four offspring were able to make full use of).

*En route* back to Antwerp, we returned northwards by keeping to the west of Liège and, thereby, reaching one other memorable place in French-speaking Wallonia. That was another riverside city – one with the name of 'Dinant'. Philomena and myself both liked the vibe of the place – and, especially, its rocky outcrop on one side of the water and the craft, including several huge barges, which were going up and down as we walked alongside the riverbank. Our children enjoyed the place, however, mainly because we managed to find a wonderful play park for them there, just under part of the rocky outcrop which had caused me to want to stop in the city in the first place. After our pleasant sojourn in attractive Dinant, it was back northwards, via the Belgian motorway system, to Antwerp. My family had passed a pleasant, if short, holiday with the help of our car. The next time we would be making a major journey in it might well have been for our emigration purposes – which Philomena and myself still had yet to plan, as we re-entered our comfortable flat in Antwerp, with the realisation that we just had one last half-term of the school year left before we would have to say goodbye to it.

One of my biggest headaches, on our return to northern Belgium for that last half-term of Philomena, Noel and Kim at the Antwerp English Primary School, was wondering whether or not we, as a family, had enough funds to pay for our air-tickets back to Barbados. I can no longer recall precisely how the tariff worked in those mid-1984 days, but I seem to recall that even children over the age of two years had to pay the full adult fare for international flights. That would have meant, therefore, that my family had to find five full air fares from Europe back to Barbados – since only our youngest, Carl, would still be under the cut-off age when we were due to fly back to the Caribbean that summer. Moreover, even he would not be accompanying the rest of us scot-free, since under-twos still had to pay some 10% of the full adult fare!

Luckily, our family had amassed some small amount of savings during our time in Antwerp – which I kept in a bank situated in Brussels, in US dollars. Moreover, we still had Philomena's salary from her school coming to her until the end of the academic year – as well as my scholarship moneys from the Belgium Government provided for my attending the Masters degree course at the university in the Belgian capital (owing to the fact that I had failed to tell that Government that I was no longer participating in it!).

One day, therefore, I drove our Renault 4 to Brussels to visit my bank there. I went via the motorway system because I was on a serious mission, and, thus, I ruled out taking a more slow, leisurely journey along the ordinary roads. That pressing objective was to try to close my account in the capital city and withdraw all the funds in it – in cash – that is to say, in US dollars. There was method in my madness in doing so, since the Barbados currency – the 'Bajan dollar', in common parlance – was directly linked to its US counterpart, at an exchange rate of 2:1 in favour of the American 'greenback'. If, therefore, I had any US dollar notes left over, after paying for my family's air tickets, I would be able to use them, easily, on our return to Barbados – without even having to go into a bank on that island to change them into the local currency. That is because, the US dollar was treated almost as though it was 'legal tender' in the country that my family would be returning to, very shortly after my closing of the Brussels bank account.

How on earth, however, were Philomena, our children and myself going to return to Barbados? Would we really have to spend our meagre funds to all travel back to London in order to catch a flight from Heathrow or Gatwick Airport to do so? Such a prospect did not appeal to me – especially as I had already felt obliged to reluctantly decline the invitation to the wedding, in Swindon, of my only sister, Sylvia, and her fiancé, 'Herman Boston', on 30 June 1984. That 'turning down' had been on the basis that my family and myself in Antwerp just could not afford the cost of our returning to England for the great family event. I, thus, felt that it would have left me in very poor light in the eyes of my sister, mum, and other family in Wiltshire if - just one month or so after the family nuptials there (which we had avoided on the basis of our impecunity) - my matrimonial family and myself were to turn up in England again, merely in order to proceed to one or other of London's two biggest airports.

It might be recalled - at least from my book *Fledging and Learning to Fly*[70] - that Philomena and myself had spent our honeymoon in Barbados after our wedding in Swindon in July 1976. To get there, we had flown to the West Indian island via Luxembourg – on an airline founded by one 'Sir Freddie Laker' and named Caribbean Airways. In researching for the various ways, and means, by which my family might return to Barbados in those mid-1984 days, I happily discovered that Caribbean Airways was still in existence, and had continued to operate flights to Barbados from London. To my joy, I also found out that although such flights no longer went via 'Findel Airport' in Luxembourg City, they did however stop-over, briefly, to pick-up and set-down Continental-Europe-based passengers at Zaventem Airport, Brussels! That discovery really made me feel that the Almighty was on the side of my family and myself – not least because it meant that we would no longer have to go back to England in order to get our flight to Barbados.

It was one thing, however, to have an air-route back to the Caribbean - seemingly, divinely tailor-made for my family. It was quite another to be able to afford the fares charged by the relevant airliner to use that air route. In those pre-Internet days of 1984 - and the non-existence of the ability to search 'online', therefore - I decided that I needed to get the help of a local travel agent in order to book our tickets. Or, at least, find out about the availability of flights from Brussels to Barbados for all six members of my family - and how much it would cost us all. In doing so, I chose such an agency which was situated just around the corner from our Lamorinierestraat flat - in the very busy, dual carriageway, thoroughfare named Belgielei.

When I first went (with Claire-Louise and Carl in tow) into the travel agency in question – during the last days of June 1984 - we were met by a most friendly middle-aged man, whom I took to be the sole proprietor of the concern in question. To my delight, not only was he able to find seats for all six members of my family, sitting together on a suitable flight the following month (after term had ended at the Antwerp English Primary School) but the cost thereof was just about affordable. That was so, however, only if we used the US dollars which I had extracted from my closed Brussels bank account a few days or so before. I, therefore, immediately asked him to provisionally book the flight in question for my whole family – which he was willing to do on the basis that I paid a deposit to him for that purpose. When I told him that I only had the recently-acquired US currency on my person at the time, the travel agent told me that he would happily hold that currency as my deposit, until I brought in Belgian francs on another occasion, soon, to pay for the requisite tickets. He gave me an appropriate receipt for my deposit and I happily left his 'shop' with my elder daughter and youngest son to return home to await Philomena's return from school with Noel and Kim. Naturally, I eagerly wanted to tell her the good news, and to make sure that she was fully on-board with what I had provisionally reserved for us all - before I went back to the agent the following day to confirm the booking.

Philomena was delighted with what I had done at the agency, in relation to our family's return flight to Barbados. She agreed, however, with my more measured thinking – post my first encounter with the agent – that we should try to get him to accept payment of the fares due for our tickets, piecemeal in Belgian francs (as, and when, she received her last two monthly salaries for working at her Antwerp school). Also, therefore, that I then try to recover the US dollar deposit (which I had given him) for our immediate use in Barbados - when we first returned there the following month or so. As a consequence, that was the approach which I had in mind, when I returned to the Belgielei agency the following morning.

To paraphrase the Scottish poet, 'Robert ("Rabbie") Burns', however: The best laid schemes of mice and men often go awry! And such 'awryness' is what occurred when I requested the travel agent to not only make a firm booking for my family's air tickets, but also to return my US dollars deposit in so doing - in exchange for piecemeal payments, in Belgian francs, that I offered to make to him (the larger proportion of which I had brought along with me to pay him with that day). 'I am sorry, Sir, but I have already used your US dollars in my business - yesterday!'. That, indeed, was the response which I received from the agent. His witnessing my disappointment at that response, however, may have led him to immediately accept my suggestion that my family pay for our tickets in a 'bit by bit' fashion – and only pick up the tickets in question, from him, when we had paid the full amount due.

Despite the unexpected turn of events, I nevertheless left the agency still reasonably happy. That was because the agent had established to me that my family - from that day - had confirmed bookings to fly back to Barbados from Brussels, on a certain date towards the end of July that year. That meant, therefore, that Philomena and myself could really start preparing hard for our return to the Caribbean. Naturally, that also meant our having to begin 'downsizing', in relation to the possessions we had acquired - over more than a year of living together as a family again in, first of all, the house in Volta Road, Swindon and, then, in our present flat in Lamorinierestraat, Antwerp.

Philomena and myself discussed how best to accomplish that process of ridding ourselves of most of our household 'effects'. We came to the conclusion that we would have a kind of small-scale 'garage sale' – but one located in our flat itself, as we neither owned nor rented a lock-up in which to keep our Renault 4 whilst in Antwerp. How and where, however, were we going to advertise such an event? The thought came to one or other of us that, maybe, we could have a birthday party for Kim - who would be five years old on the coming 6th July – and either hold the sell-off to parents of his invited friends that same day; or merely tell them (during the party) about when the future day and time of the proposed sale would be (which we would set for a week or so after the festivity for Kim).

The latter approach is what came to pass – with our choice of garage sale being set for the Saturday morning following that on which the party had taken place. Philomena and myself, accordingly, found ourselves organising a full-blown birthday party – with lots of non-family invitees – for any one of our four children, for the very first time in our lives. By a twist of fate, however, we had also held a small celebration for Kim on his fourth birthday, the previous year, whilst we had still been living at Volta Road in Swindon. At that earlier celebration, however, only my old friend Philip Boguszewicz, his wife, Cindy, and their four young offspring ('Pip', 'Donna', 'Samantha' and 'Simon') – of, roughly, our own children's ages, had been invited and had attended. In contrast to that earlier celebration, most, if not all, of Kim's invitees to his 1984 party were his friends from his class at the Antwerp English Primary School – and they came accompanied by one, if not both, of their respective parents. If memory serves, most of those children and their minders turned out to be of Indian origin – or, at least, persons who emanated from the sub-continent – who worked in the diamond industry, for which Antwerp is famous. Luckily for myself, I had not known, in advance, of the 'posh' milieu of such parents - or else, I might well have developed cold feet regarding ever holding a birthday party at our relatively humble home. That is because, upon seeing and hearing the parents in question, I rather assumed that many, if not most, of them lived in large houses - if not mansions - in the greater Antwerp region. Nevertheless, my wife and I made the most of the occasion, and we gave our second-born the best party that we could afford at the time. Moreover, we were able to announce the forthcoming garage sale to the parents who were there with Kim's invitees – as well as show them some of the effects which we were wishing to sell. Not least of those included the washing machine and dryer - which Philomena and myself had experienced so many problems with, when transferring them from Swindon to Antwerp, and into our flat, the previous August or early September.

It was those two 'white goods' items which had really determined when we would have the subsequent garage sale – since they were such a vital part of my family's domestic life that we needed to use them 'up to the last'. We thus had to put off the sale until just before our Barbados-bound flight – as I certainly did not wish Philomena to have to go to an outside laundrette in order to keep our family's clothes clean, up to the time that we were emigrating from Belgium. The sale went off well, however, shortly before we finally had to set off for Zaventem Airport – and Philomena and myself were able to get shot of most of our effects, which would have proved impossible for us to pack to accompany us on our Barbados-bound flight. Perhaps, the only set of major items that we did not manage to sell, and which would, perforce, have to remain in the flat when we decamped from it, was the comfortable three-piece suite (which the 'posh' diamond industry worker-parents of Kim's classmates, seemingly, had no need of). Even our dining table, however – at which Vere had once sat to have a meal with Philomena, the children and myself – and its accompanying chairs, were sold!

There was one major item, kept outside the flat, which also belonged to my family and which, logically, should have been one of the effects in the garage sale. That was our family's car – our red Renault 4. It had been a 'loyal servant' to us since we had acquired it the previous year in Swindon and had never broken down on us – not even once – despite the long drive emigrating it from Swindon, the many weekend trips we had made in it to Bergen op Zoom in Holland, and even the recently-made Whitsun 'tour' to Luxembourg and back! To my shame, however, I decided that we needed to have that trusty car for one last journey – even more than the reasonable amount of proceeds it, perhaps, might have fetched in the garage sale. That final drive that I had planned was for it to convey us to Zaventem Airport on our last morning in Belgium.

Before that final day in our adopted European country, however, there was one more – to me, vital – thing which I had felt obliged to do before my 'legitimate' family would quit the Continent for Barbados. That was to take my leave of one part of what might be termed my 'illegitimate' family. That part - or the person whom I regarded as constituting the 'majority' of that part - was, of course, Vere. I had last seen her a few months before at Eastertime, when she had come over from England by boat to meet up with me in Holland – and when she had even made a, one-night only, side trip with me to my matrimonial family in our Antwerp apartment. Being based at her Bajan friend's family home in Ilford near London, that trek of Vere's - by ferry across the North Sea (from Harwich in Essex, to Hook of Holland) - had been quite a feat of endurance. I could not, therefore, easily ask her to repeat that experience - quite apart from the cost which she would have incurred in coming to the Continent to visit me again for a second time in just a few months. Accordingly, by exchanges of letters, Vere and I agreed that our next meeting – our last in Europe for, perhaps, many years to come – should take place in England, a week or two before my legitimate family decamped from our Antwerp home to fly back to Barbados.

There were several reasons why I had felt guilty in making that July 1984 trip to Dover from one of the Continental Channel ports (which I now rather think was most likely that of Calais in France, since I had hitchhiked and that would, perhaps, have been the most popular destination for any car, or lorry, driver picking me up in Antwerp). For a start, I had turned down the invitation to my sister's wedding in Swindon, which had happened just the previous month, on the excuse that I (and my family) could not possibly afford to travel to England (as we were facing the high costs of our re-emigrating to Barbados). Here I was, however, doing just that (albeit with the use of my thumbs!). Secondly, whenever the name of Vere was raised in my home in Antwerp, the hackles of Philomena quite naturally rose up. Nevertheless, I felt that I had to try to get my wife's reluctant 'permission' for my travels to England to meet with my mistress - the mother of my daughter, Mikki, in Barbados. In fact, if Philomena never ever gave me her 'blessing' for my proposed 'last meeting in Europe with Vere', she also did not stand in my way of it taking place. That was, perhaps, because she slowly took on board my arguments that Vere and myself had to meet again - if only to discuss my future relationship with our daughter, Mikki, once I landed back in Barbados, in just a few weeks hence. Be that as it may, my being responsible for bringing the rupture into my matrimonial family's life, and my having to ask Philomena's acceptance of yet another temporary disruption to that family's domestic happiness, was always prone to make me feel both ashamed of myself and burdened with guilt.

Where, however, was the venue of that final European rapprochement with Vere to be? The answer was simple: Nowhere other than the port town of Dover itself. The agreed plan between the two of us was that she would travel down from London – by coach – to the 'Eastern Docks' side of the town, just as if she was a regular passenger about to catch a ferry to go off to Calais, Ostend or some other Continental port served from that English counterpart situated in the county of Kent. I would then know where to look for her when I disembarked from my real Cross-Channel ferry journey. Meeting up with Vere again – in Dover – was not as fraught an enterprise as Vere travelling to meet me in Hook of Holland on the night ferry from Harwich a few months before. My heart was in my mouth, nevertheless, as I went towards the waiting room for foot passengers bound for the Continent - who were awaiting the call to join the ship they had booked tickets for. As I opened the door to the holding area, however, there she was – wearing a white and blue stripey top, just like a French matelot about to go to sea! As we hugged, I told her that her choice of outfit was most apposite – despite her not really having any intention to sail away that particular day. We then we set off to search for a bed and breakfast (or 'B&B') establishment - from among the many located on the main road immediately outside the Eastern Docks.

The two of us had very little trouble in quickly finding somewhere suitable for us to stay. It was in a family home - just a stone's throw from the port - run by a conservative-looking, middle-aged, couple. I rather thought that neither of them was particularly happy about Vere and myself – after correctly perceiving us, perhaps, as being an unmarried couple (since Vere wore no wedding ring, even if I did mine) who was wanting one of the rooms in their B&B which contained a double bed. They took our booking for two nights, nevertheless – after first exacting our payment in advance!

The weather was fine, and suitably summery, on that first day of our stay in Dover – which was a Saturday. After leaving our luggage in our room, I was soon taking Vere up to the 'top of the town'. That was to introduce her to the impressive, and extensive, 'Dover Castle', which dominated the countryside for miles around - and which can also be seen from a long way out at sea, surmounting the 'White Cliffs' for which the town is also famous. Whilst surveying the English Channel from the vantage point of the castle - and perhaps being able to see the coast of northern France some 22 miles away - I probably told Vere about the time that I ran away from home, whilst still a schoolboy in Swindon. That had been with my schoolmate, and best friend, Philip Boguszewicz, during the 1960s - in our attempt to stow away ourselves on one of the Cross-Channel ferries and 'start a new life' somewhere on the Continent.[71] Vere, knowing me as well as she did by then, would not (even for one moment) have been surprised at my audacity – even at that much earlier, and adolescent, age of mine – or at my stupidity in not having thought ahead about how Philip and myself were going to survive, had we been successful in making it to the other side of the Channel.

Again, our landlord and lady's misgivings about having obvious lovers, and not spouses, staying together at their 'respectable' establishment was palpable - to me, at least – as they served Vere and myself breakfast at the table the next morning. Or, perhaps, it was simply that our hosts had never had a Black couple stay with them before – though, for a port town in 1980s England, that would have been hard to believe. As I remember things, we were the only guests staying in the B&B that particular weekend and, thus, I felt comfortable enough, despite any perceived disdain from our hosts. Accordingly, I ate well - in preparation for the initiative which I next wanted to embark upon with Vere.

That adventure was to take her to the nicest municipality which I personally knew of, anywhere in that particular English county in which we then found ourselves. As it happened - and I do not think that I had planned such an outing in advance of meeting with Vere that weekend - the place in question was only about 20 miles away from Dover. I considered it to be one of the glories in the whole of England, however. It was the seat of the top Anglican churchman in the country and, thus, known worldwide, perhaps, mainly because of that person. The place is the City of Canterbury and the person, at that time, was one 'Robert Runcie' - the primate of the said city (who happened to be a fellow graduate of my old college at Cambridge, Trinity Hall, and the person who had married Prince Charles and Lady Diana Spencer at St Paul's Cathedral, London just three years before).

I had not been to Canterbury myself since my trip to West Germany with my eldest son, Noel - just after that royal wedding - and Vere had never visited it herself either (although her coach from London may well have passed through it *en route* to Dover the previous day). Owing to its relative nearness to Dover, the weather being fine, and our lack of spare funds on both sides, it was very easy for me to persuade Vere that the two of us should try to hitchhike the 20 miles or less to Canterbury – a pursuit which we had not engaged in, together, since we had travelled back from Paris to our flat in Brussels, with our daughter, Mikki, in the snow in January the year before. On that later, much warmer occasion, we quickly obtained a lift to our intended destination – merely by standing just outside the Eastern Docks with a piece of paper, containing only the 'C' word on its face. A quick car ride up the very steep hill from the town, and then along the A2 high road from the top, enabled us to disembark in the centre of the cathedral city within an hour or so of our leaving our Dover B&B. I, thus, had plenty of time to show Vere not only the interior of that number one Anglican church in England – including the spot where 'Thomas à Becket', a former Archbishop of Canterbury, had been murdered in 1170 – but also the walls surrounding the city, upon which we could both walk (and where I had played a kind of game of hide and seek with my son, Noel, on our way to West Germany in 1981).

As I recall, it proved somewhat more difficult for Vere and myself to hitchhike out of the city and back to Dover after we had seen enough of the cathedral and its environs. That was because not all vehicles leaving Canterbury were bound for the Kentish port - whereas those leaving the latter's docks there were nearly all travelling at least as far north-west as the world famous city in question (and many going beyond to London, or even further afield). Make it back to our B&B before nightfall we managed to do, however - in time to buy some fish and chips for supper in our room, before retiring to bed for our final night together that summer - and, perhaps, for a year or two ahead (if not beyond even that!).

Back to Antwerp, and my matrimonial family, it was for me the following morning - after first seeing Vere off, and onto the coach taking her back to London. I travelled back to the Continent on another Cross-Channel ferry (to Ostend on that occasion, more than likely, since I always found it easier to hitchhike in Belgium than in France). Then it was full-speed ahead - to enable me to help Philomena, and our children, pack those carefully selected belongings which we would be taking back to Barbados with us very soon afterwards. We would have to be quite unsentimental with ourselves - or, rather, I would have to be so with myself (and the rest of the family, perhaps) - as to what we would bring with us. That was because we were very constrained - by at least two considerations. First, we had to restrict ourselves to the baggage allowance that Caribbean Airways limited us to - and for Carl, as a 10% fare-paying passenger under the age of two years, he had rather less than the normal full allowance (if memory serves). Moreover, we would be travelling to Zaventem Airport, Brussels in our relatively compact Renault 4 - and, with six passengers squeezed into it, that did not leave much space for a lot of luggage at the best of times!

As well as packing up our effects, however, the other major thing on my mind - upon my return from my latest assignation with Vere - was the question: Where on earth was my family and myself going to live - once we had arrived in Barbados from our flight from Belgium? As previously indicated, I had been in correspondence with Mrs Velma Abrahams - at the Cave Hill Campus of UWI on the island - about that crucial domestic matter, for several months prior to our departure date. She was the employee at the University who was in charge of arranging accommodation for its lecturers recruited from outside Barbados. Moreover, she had been wonderful to my family and myself back in 1979 when we had first arrived on the island after leaving our home in Leeds, England - following the ending of my employment at the oldest university in that Yorkshire city. Indeed, it had been owing to Mrs Abrahams that my family had ended up in our home, named Hygeia - situated on Maxwell Coast Road in Christ Church parish, and just a short walking distance from the Caribbean Sea. In writing to her, therefore - in the immediate weeks leading up to our departure from Antwerp - I was, thus, hoping that history might repeat itself and that my family would end up in an equally nice location. If not in Hygeia and/or the same island parish again (which I did not really believe would happen), then, at least, in a parish that was bounded (on one side) by the Caribbean once more - and especially one on the leeward side of the island and, thus, abutting that wonderfully blue, and usually calm, sea.

Alas, my experiences with Mrs Abrahams - that second time around - proved to be very different. I got the impression that she (and, thus, the 'powers that be' above her in the Administration of the University) had heard something of 'the Vere Affair' (most likely, via Vere's mother) and that, accordingly, neither she (Mrs Abrahams), in particular, nor the Administration, in general, was any longer sympathetic to my personal domestic situation. At any rate, she promised nothing to me and my family - accommodation-wise - in her letters back to me in Antwerp. In my frustration, therefore - during the last working week before we left our Lamorinierestraat home for the final time - I used some of my family's meagre funds to phone Mrs Abrahams at UWI's Cave Hill Campus. That was to ask her what she had done, or was doing, for me and my family - regarding where UWI was putting us up, when we first arrived back on the island, off the Caribbean Airlines flight from Brussels, that coming Saturday afternoon. During the call she gave me some solace by telling me that not only was she actively working on the matter but also that she had arranged for my colleague, Andrew Burgess – the then 'Deputy Dean' of UWI's Law Faculty at Cave Hill Campus – to meet us off our flight from Belgium (the details of which I had previously vouchsafed to her in one of my recent letters) and drive us to the accommodation, which she would have finalised for us by the Saturday in question.

With the major ducks, in our immediate future relocation plans, seemingly all lined up, I was fairly relaxed during the last day or so prior to the final drive in our car to the airport at Brussels. Philomena, Noel and Kim merely had to say their respective goodbyes to their colleagues, pupils or classmates at the Antwerp English Primary School and then we were more or less ready for our international decamping. There was to be no leaving party for them at the school, as far as I remember. Touchingly, however, when they came home from their last day, Philomena announced to me that Janet, her wonderful headmistress - as well as a few others of their colleagues - had told her that they were going to come to Zaventem Airport to see her, Noel and Kim, and the rest of our family, safely off!

Closer to home, however, we had to say goodbye to our near-neighbours, Mr and Mrs Huybrechts. Although we had not had a great deal to do with them during our time in our Lamorinierestraat flat – and, most certainly, we were never in and out of each other's homes – I somehow felt, and they caused me to feel, that if ever we encountered any emergency whilst living in our Antwerp residence, they would have been there to willingly help us. Indeed, I was to ask one last favour of them before we finally left for Zaventem. That was to put one of the unsold items, from our recent garage sale, into their storage space situated in the basement of our shared apartment block. That was the TV set, which we had brought over with us from our former Volta Road home in Swindon and which had served us well – through my (illegally, perhaps) connecting it to the cable network socket which I had discovered in our flat many months before. Remote as the possibility seemed, however, I somehow felt that - perhaps, one day in the distant future - my family and myself might return to live in Europe and that we would, once more, have the need of the audio-visual device in question. Thus, my thinking was very much one of: 'Waste not, want not'!

At all events, the Saturday morning duly came for us to leave our apartment at Lamorinierestraat for the final time. I guess that I must have left the keys to it with Mr and Mrs Huybrechts - for them to pass on to our shared landlords who lived a few streets away. What I certainly remember doing, however, during our exiting process, was parking our Renault 4 - illegally - outside the front door of the apartment block and packing our luggage into it as best as I could. I figured that, somehow, Philomena and the children would be able to squeeze themselves into whatever space was then left - after the effects, which we were flying to Barbados with, had been securely crammed into the car. Fortunately, my idea worked out. Perhaps, however, the most comfortable of the children - as we set off for the airport - would have been Carl, who was placed at the very back section of the vehicle, sitting up in his carrycot, and underpropped by a suitcase or two!

As I drove on the Belgium motorway system - southwards from Antwerp to Brussels Airport - the journey felt somewhat surreal to me. There I was on the cusp of a new life again – or, *en route* to a fresh start in that existence. I had miserably failed in what I had left Barbados to do – namely, to acquire a Masters degree in a Continental European university in my specialist subject of Comparative Law. Moreover, I had also failed to accomplish one of the seeming benefits of living in Belgium – namely, to greatly improve my French for the purpose of my teaching in that specialist subject. That was owing to the fact that I had attended a Flemish-, or Dutch-, speaking university and had - for the majority of the past year - lived in the Flemish-speaking city of Antwerp. So, although my Dutch had improved immeasurably from that experience - and I could even recite a nursery rhyme in that language (namely, *Klein, klein kleutertje*) – it would hardly be of much use to me back in Barbados when I recommenced my Comparative Law classes there. Above all, during that early morning drive - on a relatively empty motorway - I was wondering not only where my family and myself would end up living in Barbados, but also whether I would still remember how, and have the ability and confidence, to stand up in front of a class of students and teach Law. After all, it would have been two academic years since I had last done so!

Hard as it was for me to do, I made one positive decision about my family's immediate future as soon as we had arrived at Zaventem Airport. For I drove our Renault 4 into the 'long stay' car park. We were going to abandon our trusty carriage there – and, thus, be a car-free family for the immediate future. In doing so, I felt extremely guilty. That was not only because I had grown to love our car – a vehicle which had never broken down on us, and which therefore had given Philomena and myself the exact opposite experience from that which we had endured with our, frequently overheating, very first car (of the exact same make, which we had christened 'Noddy' and had bought in Cambridge in 1977 whilst I had been a student at the university there[72]). It was also because such mere abandonment had seemed to be a waste of a wonderful 'going concern' - and I hated to be party to such squandering of my family's very limited assets. Surely, I thought to myself, as we left our Renault 4 for the final time, one of our acquaintances in Antwerp could have made good use of it – even though there was a very slight chance that, like the TV set we had semi-discarded into the care of the Huybrechts couple in Antwerp, we would return to Belgium one day in the distant future to find that it was still functioning. On that somewhat unrealistic possibility, I would also have had to have hoped - beyond hope - that, upon such return, our vehicle would not yet have been confiscated from the long-term car park, but perhaps only subject to a huge parking bill to pay in order for my family to recover it into our possession. In, thus, acting in that, arguably, irrational way, I even rejected the idea that, perhaps, one of Philomena's former colleagues at the Antwerp English Primary School might have been glad to have taken it off our hands. In such a reasonably foreseeable scenario, all I needed to have done was to have been more organised in those final days of our sojourn in Antwerp – and have sold, or even given away, the vehicle before the Saturday morning in question, subject to reserving the right to use it to get my family and myself to the airport and it being later collected by the purchaser, or donee, from an agreed car park at the airport after our flight to Barbados had departed. I put such thoughts, and feelings of guilt, quickly out of my head and heart, however. That was because I had a more pressing matter preoccupying me – namely, that my family and myself had a flight to catch to take us to our new life - and I needed to put behind me worries from our 'old existence', including those concerning our much-loved motor car!

Also somewhat worrisome to me, in the immediate aftermath of leaving our Renault 4 behind in the airport's car park - as my family and myself struggled with our several suitcases and Carl's carrycot to the check-in counter of Caribbean Airlines - was how on earth would I be able to face Janet, and Philomena's other former colleagues from the Antwerp school, who had promised to turn up to see our family off. As it happened, although I had not seen much of my wife's headmistress during our time living in the largest city in Flanders – to whom my family owed everything for giving Philomena her job and our apartment in that metropolis, in the first place – she turned out to be as lovely as ever during that final meeting of our family with her. Moreover, I found myself to be somewhat tearful at the thought of my taking away from her an excellent teacher in Philomena, which she (Janet) would then have had the headache of trying to replace at her school for the immediate future. Other colleagues from the school were also there - including Mandy, the young, snappy dresser, who used to bring the school's pupils for their lessons with me at the Antwerp Squash Club and who would pay me, in cash, for doing so each week. Their presence, alongside Janet, only served to make me feel even more shameful for being the underlying cause of bringing to an end the budding relationships between my wife and two eldest sons, on the one hand, and members of staff at their former Antwerp school on the other.

Once my family and myself had checked in ourselves and our luggage, waved our final goodbyes to Janet, Mandy and their other Antwerp English Primary School colleagues present, and had passed out of their sight into the 'Departures' entrance of Brussels Zaventem Airport, there was just one determination in my mind: 'Onwards and upwards!'. For, it seemed to me, I had just one last chance left to me to be able to give Philomena, our four children (Noel, Kim, Claire-Louise and Carl) – and, if at all realisable as well, Mikki, back in her native island in the care of her two 'aunts' – a stable, long-term and happy life starting from when the Caribbean Airways flight, which we were about to board, landed in Barbados much later that day. Surely, I could not afford to 'blow' that final opportunity?

## NOTES

1 Lyric sung by Beyoncé, on the track 'LoveHappy' which is included on the LP by herself and her husband, Jay-Z, entitled 'Everything Is Love' – as reported in the Metro newspaper of the UK for Monday, 18 June 2018 at page 12

2 Lyric sung by Billie Eilish on the theme song to the 25th James Bond film 'No Time to Die', which was 'announced by Billie Eilish on January 14, 2020', according to https://genius.com/Billie-eilish-no-time-to-die-lyrics

3 In fact, the song was simply entitled 'Barbados' and, according to Wikipedia: 'was a UK Number 1 single released in May 1975 by Typically Tropical. "Barbados" entered the UK singles chart at number 37 in late June 1975, and five weeks later was a Number 1 for a week'. See: https://en.wikipedia.org/wiki/Barbados_(Typically_Tropical_song)

4 That earlier book was published in 2017 by Kingston University Press, UK. Its subtitle is: '*A Memoir of a Young Afro-Caribbean Man's Kingston, Cambridge and Barrister Student Days, as well as his early working and (inter-racial) married life, at Leeds University and elsewhere in 1970s England*'

5 That still earlier book was published in 2013 by Hobnob Press, UK. Its subtitle is: '*Memories of a West Indian lad's boyhood in the English railway town of Swindon during the 1960s and early '70s*'

6 That earliest book by the Author was published in 2010 by Montserratian (in Cambridgeshire) Publishing, UK. Its subtitle is: '*Memories from a Colonial Childhood in a British Caribbean Island, 1952-61*'

7 See note 4, at pp 41-44, re the Author studying the General Principles of English Law, at night school, as one of his subjects which he needed to study, and pass an examination in, to obtain Part 1 of the Associateship of the Institute of Bankers ('AIB')

8 See note 6 above

9 See Wikipedia at: https://en.wikipedia.org/wiki/Les_Dawson

10 See note 4 above

11 Indeed, my future colleague, and arguably, 'Best Friend' at the UWI Law Faculty at Cave Hill Campus – the future 'Professor Albert Fiadjoe' - was to publish a biography of Professor Georges, the details of which are: Telford Georges: A Legal Odyssey – published by 'Ian Randle Publishers' on 1st January 2008

12 See note 4, at pp 722-726

13 See note 4, at pp 629-633

14 See note 4 – at pp 433-434, and p 456, for details of the Author's, and his new wife's, meeting with the said newspaper Editor, in August 1976, and the article about them which the Editor published in the Montserrat Mirror dated Friday, 26th August 1976

15 See note 4 – at pp 506-509, regarding 'Noddy'. It was the Author's and Philomena's first ever car – a 'Renault 4', bought sometime between late 1976 and early 1977

16 See note 4 – at pp 409-411, regarding the Author's and Philomena's acquisition and use of their hired motor bike during the Barbados phase of their honeymoon trip in August 1976

17 See note 4 – at pp 406-414 – for details of the Author's and Philomena's time in Barbados during their honeymoon trip in August 1976

18 See note 6 – for details of the Author's first book about that earliest childhood of his, namely: *Growing up BAREFOOT under Montserrat's sleeping Volcano* (2010)

19 In fact, although Hurricane David does not seem to have caused any deaths at all in Barbados itself, it did kill 56 in the nearby island of 'Dominica' – and a massive 2068 deaths in the 'Dominican Republic' part of the island of 'Hispaniola', further north: see https://en.wikipedia.org/wiki/Hurricane_David

20 See note 4 above – at pp 264-269, for an account of the 'idyll' of the Author's summer vacation on the Greek island of Corfu in August 1974, with his then fiancée, Philomena

21 See note 5 above – at pp 260-264

22 https://en.wikipedia.org/wiki/Dutch_Guiana

23 https://www.squire.law.cam.ac.uk/eminent-scholars-archive/professor-ja-jolowicz

24 See note 5 above – at pp 90-91

25 See note 4 above

26 See note 6 above – especially from pp 18-45

27 See note 4 above – at pp 414-421

28 *Ibid* - at pp 592-595

29 See note 6 above – at pp 115-116

30 *Ibid* – at pp 150-152

31 *Ibid* – at pp 137-138

32 *Ibid* – at p 137

33 *Ibid* – at p 76

34 See note 4 above – at pp 415-417

35 See note 6 above – at p 145

36 See note 4 – at pp 216-220

37 See note 5 above – at pp 167-173

38 See note 6 above – at pp 115-117

39 See note 6 above – at p 38

40 See the Constitutional Reform Act 2005 in England; and the Ministry of Justice website in that country: www.justice.gov.uk

41 Which authority, or precedent, can be found in the 1964 volume of reported 'Appeal Cases' in England, starting at page 465 – or, as lawyers and others would more normally cite this case: '[1964] AC 465'.

42 'Civil Appeal No 70 of 1977'. In fact, that Trinidad case subsequently went on final appeal to the 'Judicial Committee of the Privy Council' in London, and the ultimate decision, and reasoning therefor, is reported in volume 1 of the 1987 'Lloyd's Reports', starting at page 218 – more usually cited as: '[1987] 1 Lloyd's Rep. 218'

43 Alas, things often move only very slowly in the Caribbean. My article did, indeed, eventually 'get published' in the *WILJ*, under the title: 'Enter Hedley Byrne – "Trini Style": A Critique of Pampellone and Another v The Royal Bank Trust (Trinidad) Ltd' – in the 1983 edition thereof, starting at page 87, more usually cited as: '[1983] *WILJ* 87'

44 See note 4 above – at pp 415-418

45 See: en.wikepedia.org/wiki/Mutiny_on_the_Bounty

46 See note 6 above – at pp 44-45

47 See note 4 above – at pp 722-727

48 See note 4 above – at pp 549-553

49 See note 5 above – at pp 244-247

50 See note 4 above – at pp 378-390

51 See note 5 above – at pp 220-223

52 See note 4 above – at pp 409-411

53 See that history recounted in the Author's book *Swimming without mangoes* (2013) – at note 5 above

54 See note 5 above

55 See note 4 above

56 See note 4 above – at pp 147-177
57 See, for example, note 4 above – at pp 471-474, regarding the first Christmas during the marriage of Philomena and the Author, spent with Mrs Harrison at her home in Swindon in 1976 whilst he was still a student at Cambridge University
58 See note 4 above – at p 126
59 See note 4 above – at pp 700-715
60 See note 5 above
61 See note 4 above
62 See note 5 above – at pp 271-285
63 See my book *a* – at note 6 above
64 See Swimming without mangoes (2013) – at note 5 above
65 See note 6 above
67 See note 4 above – pp 506-509
68 See note 5 above – at pp 100-102; and 132-139
69 Ibid – at pp 152-160
70 See note 4 above
71 See Swimming without mangoes, note 5 above - at pp 134-139
72 See *Fledging and Learning to Fly*, note 4 above - at pp 506-509, for example, for more details of 'Noddy'

*This book has been written for
ALL my Children – namely:
Noel, Kristian Kim,
Claire-Louise, Mikaëlle, and Carl*